Fairy Tales of London

Fairy Tales of London

British Urban Fantasy, 1840 to the Present

Hadas Elber-Aviram

BLOOMSBURY ACADEMIC
LONDON • NEW YORK • OXFORD • NEW DELHI • SYDNEY

BLOOMSBURY ACADEMIC
Bloomsbury Publishing Plc
50 Bedford Square, London, WC1B 3DP, UK
1385 Broadway, New York, NY 10018, USA
29 Earlsfort Terrace, Dublin 2, Ireland

BLOOMSBURY, BLOOMSBURY ACADEMIC and the Diana logo are trademarks of Bloomsbury Publishing Plc

First published in Great Britain 2021

Paperback edition published 2022

Copyright © Hadas Elber-Aviram, 2021

Hadas Elber-Aviram has asserted her right under the Copyright, Designs and Patents Act, 1988, to be identified as Author of this work.

For legal purposes the Acknowledgements on p. ix constitute an extension of this copyright page.

Cover design: Eleanor Rose
Cover image: Photograph 'Trafalgar Square at Night' by George Davison Reid, courtesy of Museum of London

All rights reserved. No part of this publication may be reproduced or transmitted in any form or by any means, electronic or mechanical, including photocopying, recording, or any information storage or retrieval system, without prior permission in writing from the publishers.

Bloomsbury Publishing Plc does not have any control over, or responsibility for, any third-party websites referred to or in this book. All internet addresses given in this book were correct at the time of going to press. The author and publisher regret any inconvenience caused if addresses have changed or sites have ceased to exist, but can accept no responsibility for any such changes.

A catalogue record for this book is available from the British Library.

A catalog record for this book is available from the Library of Congress.

ISBN: HB: 978-1-3501-1067-0
PB: 978-1-3502-0282-5
ePDF: 978-1-3501-1068-7
eBook: 978-1-3501-1069-4

Typeset by Deanta Global Publishing Services, Chennai, India

To find out more about our authors and books visit www.bloomsbury.com and sign up for our newsletters.

To Eran, the love of my life.

Contents

List of figures	viii
Acknowledgements	ix
Credits and permissions	xi
Note on texts	xii
List of abbreviations	xiii
Introduction: A tale of two fantasies	1
1 The phantom out of Oxford Street: Dickens's fairyland	27
2 The Martian on Primrose Hill: Wells's scientific romances	61
3 The bells of lost London: Orwell's and Peake's anti-fantasies	95
4 A pyramid of flesh on Villiers Street: *New Worlds* magazine and the Jerry Cornelius myth	131
5 'My home, the city': Secondary-World London	165
Notes	199
Bibliography	267
Index	291

Figures

I.1	'Jo the Crossing-Sweeper'	12
I.2	'A Boy in the Street'	13
1.1	'St. Dunstan in the West, Fleet Street'	41
1.2	'St. Dunstan's in the West. Fleet Street'	42
2.1	'The Door in the Wall', MSS	85
2.2	*Tales of Space and Time*, MSS	90
2.3	*When the Sleeper Wakes: A Story of the Years to Come*, MSS	92
2.4	'A Dream of Armageddon', MSS	93
3.1	*Titus Groan* chapters 60–61, MSS	99
3.2	'Mr Chadband'	102
3.3	'Swelter with Kitchen Urchin'	103
3.4	*Titus Alone* chapters 51–63(a), MSS	109
3.5	*Titus Alone* chapters 51–63(b), MSS	112
4.1	'London Fun Machine'	139

Acknowledgements

This monograph would not exist without the supervision and mentorship of Gregory Dart, my primary supervisor, who read and reread its early drafts with consistent freshness, sharpness, enthusiasm, intellectual rigour and good humour. It might never have been published without the unwavering support of Adam Roberts, who was as generous in his endorsements as he was penetrating in his comments. I profited greatly from the support of Simon J. James, who helped me hone my thoughts on Wells and shared his expertise in all matters from the scholarly to the practical.

I am deeply and gratefully indebted to Simon Bacon, who read the manuscript in its entirety twice and provided rich, erudite and invaluable input. Tom Dillon read its fourth chapter with great care and provided superb feedback. Ben Winyard provided in-depth commentary on an early draft of the first chapter to its considerable improvement. Tom Ue read a draft of the book proposal and provided astute and insightful commentary. Hugh Stevens co-examined the PhD thesis on which this monograph is based with kindness and acumen. My thanks too to the anonymous readers of the proposal and the MS for their input.

I owe a great debt to the faculty and staff of the University of Notre Dame's London Global Gateway, particularly Tony Keen, who shared his knowledge and expertise on the Jerry Cornelius books and the various editions of *Neverwhere* over many scintillating conversations. Warm thanks too to Alice Tyrell, JoAnn DellaNeva, Charlotte Parkyn and Joanna Byrne at ND for their unwavering support and encouragement, and to my ND students for their engaging insights and for keeping the topic fresh over the years.

I would also like to thank the team at Bloomsbury Literary Studies for their tireless work and unwavering patience and support, and for believing in my project. Particularly Lucy Brown, Ben Doyle, David Avital and Clara Herberg.

In addition to the thanks given earlier, this study also profited from the expertise of G. Peter Winnington, Nick Hubble, Rob Latham, Erin Horáková, John Davey, Luke Seabar, Michael Shallcross and Andrew M. Butler.

Dennis Sears, the imaging specialist at the Rare Book and Manuscript Library, University of Illinois Urbana–Champaign, invested untold hours scanning hundreds of Wells manuscripts on my behalf, with good spirit and abundant generosity. This monograph owes a great debt to Dennis in particular and to the entire staff at RBML, UIUC, more widely. I am also indebted to the staff of the Rare Books and Music Room at the British Library as well as the staff of Senate House Library, the University of Liverpool Science Fiction Collection, the Weston Library (Bodleian Libraries), UCL Special Collections, Guildhall Library, Marylebone Library, the Dickens Museum, Bishopsgate Library and the Barbican Library.

This study was generously funded by University College London's Overseas Research Scholarship and the University of Notre Dame's London Faculty Small Research Support Grants.

This monograph is dedicated to my husband, Eran Aviram. I could not have written it without the pillar of his unfaltering love. There are some debts too great for words, but he knows he is my everything.

Credits and permissions

The cover image, 'Trafalgar Square at night' (*c.* 1920–33) by George Davison Reid is reproduced with permission from © Museum of London.

The image 'St Dunstan in the West, Fleet Street' (1829), drawn by Thomas Hosmer Shepherd and engraved by James Baylis Allen, is reproduced with permission from © the Trustees of the British Museum.

The image 'St Dunstan's in the West. Fleet Street' (1838), drawn by Robert William Billings and engraved by J. Le Keux, is reproduced with the permission of Senate House Library, University of London, Classmark [B.L.] Godwin Vol. 1.

High-resolution images of Wells MSS are reproduced from, and courtesy of, the *H. G. Wells papers, 1845–1946, The Rare Book & Manuscript Library, University of Illinois at Urbana-Champaign*. Wells's writings are out of copyright, but non-exclusive permission to reproduce unpublished Wells MSS has been granted courtesy of United Agents.

High-resolution images of Peake MSS are reproduced from the Mervyn Peake Archive at the British Library, with the permission of © the British Library Board.

High-resolution images of Peake's drawings were provided by Alison Eldred, Artists' Agent.

Extracts and images from unpublished drafts of *Titus Alone* by Mervyn Peake and *Titus Groan* by Mervyn Peake reprinted by permission of Peters Fraser & Dunlop (www.petersfraserdunlop.com) on behalf of the Estate of Mervyn Peake.

Images 'Mr Chadband'; 'Swelter with Kitchen Urchin'; 'Jo the Crossing-Sweeper' and 'A Boy in the Street' by Mervyn Peake reprinted by permission of Peters Fraser & Dunlop (www.petersfraserdunlop.com) on behalf of the Estate of Mervyn Peake.

The illustration 'London Fun Machine' by Mal Dean (1969) is reproduced from the University of Liverpool Library, class mark PR6063.O59.F49 1976, with the permission of © Libby Houston.

Note on texts

Dickens's Christmas Books, novels and sketches are taken from the most recent editions of the Oxford University Press (1997–2009), variously edited, wherever such editions exist. Where an Oxford University Press edition does not exist, I used *The Nonesuch Dickens* (1937–8), edited by Arthur Waugh, Hugh Walpole, Walter Dexter and Thomas Hatton. *Household Words* and *All the Year Round* articles are quoted from the respective periodicals in which they appear.

Wells's scientific romances and short stories are taken from the most recent Penguin editions (2005 or 2007), edited by Patrick Parrinder or Simon J. James, unless a different edition was required to highlight textual variants. Where a Penguin edition does not exist, I normally used *The Works of H. G. Wells, Atlantic Edition* (28 vols, London: Unwin, 1924–7). For Wells's *When the Sleeper Wakes*, I used the most recent Broadview edition (2019), edited by John Sutherland. Wells's reviews in the *Saturday Review* are taken from the original magazine publication.

Orwell sources are taken from *The Complete Works of George Orwell* (1997–8), edited by Peter Davison. The extant manuscript of *Nineteen Eighty-Four* is taken from George Orwell, *Nineteen Eighty-Four: The Facsimile of the Extant Manuscript* (1984), likewise edited by Davison. This study follows the 1970 fuller edition of Peake's *Titus Alone*, compiled by Langdon Jones, which added material from Peake's manuscripts to create a more detailed picture of his intentions at the time of writing. Peake's *Gormenghast Trilogy* is quoted from the recent one-volume edition, *The Illustrated Gormenghast Trilogy* (2011).

New Worlds and *New Worlds Quarterly* editorials and articles are taken from the respective journals in which they first appeared. Jerry Cornelius stories and serializations are likewise taken from their earliest published versions, typically in *New Worlds* magazine.

This study follows Gaiman's *Neverwhere: Author's Preferred Text* (2005) in accordance with his wishes. Miéville's fantasy novels and short-story collections are taken from the UK Pan Books editions (2000–10).

Abbreviations

AYR	*All the Year Round*
CUP	Cambridge University Press
EUP	Edinburgh University Press
HW	*Household Words*
LUP	Liverpool University Press
MPA, BL	The Mervyn Peake Archive at the British Library
MPR	*Mervyn Peake Review*
MS\S	Manuscript\s
MUP	Manchester University Press
NW	*New Worlds*
NWQ	*New Worlds Quarterly*
OUP	Oxford University Press (including Clarendon)
PS	*Peake Studies*
RBML, UIUC	H. G. Wells papers, 1845–1946, The Rare Book & Manuscript Library, University of Illinois at Urbana-Champaign
SF	*Science Fantasy*
SFS	*Science Fiction Studies*
SR	*Saturday Review*
UP	University Press
YUP	Yale University Press

Introduction
A tale of two fantasies

What trick of topography is this?

The river twists and turns to face the city. It looms suddenly, massive, stamped on the landscape. Its light wells up around the surrounds, the rock hills, like bruise-blood. . . . I am debased. I am compelled to worship this extraordinary presence that had stilted into existence at the conjunction of two rivers. . . . Fat chimneys retch into the sky even now in the deep night. . . . Railways trace urban anatomy like protruding veins. . . .
. . . What trick of topography is this, that lets the sprawling monster hide behind corners to leap out at the traveller?[1]

This description of a character's first encounter with a fantastical city – 'a chaos-fucked Victorian London',[2] as China Miéville described it – focuses the opening of Miéville's *Perdido Street Station* (2000). The sprawling narrative that follows it inspired Sherryl Vint to consider Miéville as 'the centre of the renaissance of British science fiction and fantasy literature, often referred to as the British Boom'.[3] Miéville's innovations notwithstanding, to posit a renaissance is to invite an enquiry into the nature of the paradigm that is supposedly being reborn. The key definition of this paradigm, according to Vint, is that its 'fantastic fiction [is] set in an urban rather than rural setting',[4] forming a distinctly urban brand of fantasy that gives London pride of place. 'London is one of the cities that refracts literature with a peculiarly intense hallucinatory power',[5] Miéville has reflected, singling out 'Charles Dickens's London',[6] 'Michael Moorcock's London' and 'Neil Gaiman's London' as significant instances of this fantastical refraction.[7]

This book argues that the London-based fantasies of Charles Dickens, H. G. Wells, George Orwell, Mervyn Peake, Michael Moorcock, M. John Harrison, Neil Gaiman and China Miéville form a coherent tradition that champions fantasy literature as a politically and socially engaged genre deeply immersed in the forms and fashions of urban life. It argues that these authors cleaved to their belief in progress, liberalism and the ineluctability of urban life, together with their commitment to prose fantasy as an idiom for the social transformation of the city, even when such beliefs were challenged by historical upheavals, rival literary traditions and transformations in London itself. The study is framed by a reading of British fantasy literature from the mid-nineteenth century to the present day as a dialectical opposition between two distinct and often self-consciously opposed traditions: a tradition of 'Rural Fantasy', typified by writers such as John Ruskin, George MacDonald, J. R. R. Tolkien and C. S. Lewis, and one of 'Urban Fantasy', typified by the authors who form the subject of this study.[8]

This monograph thereby approaches fantastical British fiction from an angle that is somewhat lateral to recent Anglophone histories of genre, which have tended to reassert the distinction between fantasy and science fiction as a defining parameter of their studies. Roger Luckhurst, for instance, argues that 'SF is a literature of technologically saturated societies',[9] which 'imagine futures or parallel worlds premised on the perpetual change associated with modernity'.[10] Adam Roberts shifts the focus from technology and modernity to religion and world view, contending that 'SF expresses a particular dialectic that was originally determined by the separation of Protestant and Catholic world views'.[11] On the fantasy side, Lucie Armitt postulates that 'fantasy sets up worlds that genuinely exist *beyond* the horizon',[12] and Farah Mendlesohn asserts that 'the fantastic is an area of literature that is heavily dependent on the dialectic between author and reader for the construction of a sense of wonder'.[13]

This book owes a debt to these monographs and to other studies of science fiction and fantasy, but it differs from them in its interests and scope. Rather than defining the corpus and outer limits of science fiction or fantasy, this study cuts across these divisions in order to chart a tradition of socially and politically engaged London-based fictions that harness the tropes of the fantastic to affect the defamiliarization and re-envisioning of London. In so doing, it does not discount the differences between fantasy and science fiction, nor does it claim that its corpus of texts do not *also* belong to these genres. But this study is less concerned with the classification of literary works according to fixed genre conventions – assigning ghosts to the fantasy genre and time machines to the science fiction genre, for instance – as it is with affiliations of influence and historical development. Nevertheless, it engages with the developing definitions of science fiction and fantasy in order to refine its positioning of the narrative texts that form its subject matter.

The limitations of this study should be acknowledged from its outset. I am acutely aware that this book is devoted to a male canon of authors, all of whom are white, British and hail from a roughly lower-middle-class background. This focus on an exclusively male tradition is by no means to discount an equally important tradition of women writers that deserves a book of its own, one that would potentially bring together authors such as Mary Shelley, Edith Nesbit, Doris Lessing, Emma Tennant, Angela Carter, Maggie Gee, Mary Gentle and J. K. Rowling. I have no wish to do these authors a disservice by shoehorning them into this study. A companion monograph on this parallel tradition is currently in the works.

Another area not covered by this study is London-based psycho-geographical fiction, which includes the novels of Iain Sinclair, Peter Ackroyd, Will Self and Martin Amis, among others. While such fiction is often borderline-fantastical if not fully fledged fantasy, this study is concerned with London-based fantasies that focus on the social aspect of urban life, refracted through the prisms of the fantastic, rather than the psychological impact of urban space. Granted, those two aspects of London-based fantasy are not so easily distinguished as that statement implies, but one may tease out their differences by brief reference to the respective proponents of psycho-geography and socially engaged urban fantasy. Guy Debord, one of the leading proponents of psycho-geography, asserted that the movement was interested in 'specific effects of the geographical environment, . . . on the emotions and behavior of individuals'.[14] Miéville, by way of contrast, argues that 'we need fantasy to think the world, and to change it'.[15] These claims are substantively different – the first is about the vicissitudes of the individual, the second about changes to the fabric of society. Juliet John has made a similar claim for Dickens: 'Dickens was instinctively opposed to the privileging of the individualized psyche',[16] because his 'belief in the principles of communality and cultural inclusivity made the notion of a psyche-centred approach to people and society seem individualistic, divisive, and potentially elitist'.[17]

There are innumerable authors who do not fit in the earlier categories, and yet are still excluded from this study. Some have been purposely excluded, such as J. G. Ballard, whose fantastical fiction shares some general characteristics with the tradition charted in this study, but whose attitudes towards its authors and towards London have ultimately disqualified him. Rushdie's *Satanic Verses* (1988) was excluded because much of it takes place outside of London. William Gibson and Tim Powers have been deemed tangential because neither are British, and Robert Louis Stevenson because he lived much of his life outside of London (I take Michael Moorcock and Neil Gaiman to be borderline cases in this regard). William Morris, Arthur Machen and G. K. Chesterton are deemed outliers due to the reactionary world views that underpin their London-based fantasies, and Charles Williams's fantastical fictions similarly promulgate a Christian vision that distinguishes them from the largely secular fantasies of the authors discussed herein. Other authors and London-based fantasy novels have been omitted due to limitations of space, as for example John Wyndham's *The Day of the Triffids* (1951), and others still due to my ignorance of them. For the last, my apologies. In the final analysis, one book cannot cover everything. This study examines a single strand within the ever-expanding field of London-based fantasy, a tradition that was unusually vocal in its self-conscious acknowledgement of its practices and its predecessors. There are certainly other traditions, which can and should be mapped out in the future.

Some scholars have attempted to chart the history of urban fantasy and its roots in the life and literature of London,[18] but never in a full-length study. These scholars almost invariably single out Dickens as the 'patron saint' of the genre.[19] A closer look at the epigraph to this introduction, taken from the prologue of *Perdido Street Station*, provides a fair indication of why Dickens's London is so often hailed as the ur-city of urban fantasy. The passage's extravagant and lush use of language, together with the vivid accentuation of material filth and vertiginous points of view, powerfully recalls Dickens's London. The sleight of hand that creates this *'trick of topography'* bears broad similarities to Dickens's cityscapes, which are sharpened by the evocation of specific tableaux. *'The river twists and turns to face the city. . . . Its light wells up around the surrounds, the rock hills, like bruise-blood'* – behind these lines one may glimpse the fiery sunrise over the Thames in *Our Mutual Friend* (1864–5):

> the sun, blood-red on the eastern marshes behind dark masts and yards, seemed filled with the ruins of a forest it had set on fire.[20]

The narrator's confession that '*I am compelled to worship this extraordinary presence*' evokes the streets that 'steeped the souls of the people who were condemned to look at them' in the London of *Little Dorrit* (1855–7).[21] The city's '*fat chimneys* [that] *retch into the sky*' conjure up the chimneys of London in *Bleak House* (1852–3), where 'smoke [is] lowering down from chimney-pots, making a soft black drizzle'.[22] The '*Railways* [that] *trace urban anatomy like protruding veins*' evoke the new railway of *Dombey and Son* (1846–8), across which 'throbbing currents rushed and returned incessantly like its life's blood'.[23] In these and other instances, this '*sprawling monster*' of a metropolis echoes 'the monster, roaring in the distance' of Dickens's multiple,[24] overlapping visions of Victorian London.

One might argue that any post-Dickensian novel set in London must negotiate Dickens's influential rendering of the cityscape. George Gissing held that 'London as a place of squalid mystery and terror, of the grimly grotesque, of labyrinthine obscurity and lurid fascination, is Dickens's own'.[25] V. S. Naipaul recalled that before his immigration to Britain,

> the London I knew or imaginatively possessed was the London I had got from Dickens. . . . [I] was able with him to enter the dark city . . . fitting my own fantasies to his.[26]

Salman Rushdie's 'Influence' (1999) gave account that 'in my earlier novels I tried to draw on the genius of Dickens',[27] arguing that '[Dickens's] real innovation' lay in 'his unique combination of naturalistic backgrounds and surreal foregrounds'.[28] Rushdie cited 'Dickensian London' in particular,[29] and his (in)famous *Satanic Verses* features a key scene set in a simulacrum of Dickens's London.[30] As attested by these examples and others, Dickens has earned pride of place in virtually all post-Dickensian London writing. Yet this study is concerned with a single strand within this widespread influence, namely Dickens's special role in the formation of urban fantasy.

'The manner of stating the truth': Dickens the romancer

To discuss Dickens as a fantasy writer, and Wells as an author of science fiction, is to deploy anachronistic nomenclature. The term 'fantasy novel' as a literary category would have been opaque to a nineteenth-century reader,[31] and the term 'science fiction' was not in wide usage until the 1920s.[32] Victorian debates about the nature and role of the fantastic in prose literature commonly revolved around the terms 'novel', 'in which the events are accommodated to the ordinary train of human events',[33] and 'romance', 'in which the interest of the narrative turns chiefly on marvellous and uncommon incidents'.[34] Dickens's oeuvre often provided a case study for such theorizations, not least on account of his phenomenal success as a novelist. Dickens's contemporaries struggled to classify his fiction, so much so that it was often placed in diametrically opposite categories. David Masson hailed Dickens as a versatile writer 'who, in his Christmas stories, and in stories interspersed through his larger fictions, has given us specimens of his skill in a kind of prose phantasy'.[35] G. H. Lewes praised Dickens for the opposite quality – for his fidelity to reality, his unrivalled skill in painting 'the life he knew, the life every one knew'.[36]

Present-day scholarship has long since abandoned such binary thinking for a more attentive analysis of the blending of fantastical flights of fancy and realist social concerns in the multivalent textures of Dickens's fiction. 'Enter a Dickens novel and you enter a highly charged, multitudinous world, in which realism and imagination are interfused as never before or since',[37] Donald Hawes observed by way of elucidating Dickens's timeless appeal. Juliet John has contended that 'Dickens's novels in fact present a self-consciously idealized and problematized version of reality'.[38] Harry Stone has examined Dickens's 'fairy tale method',[39] demonstrating that in *Dombey and Son* especially, 'he set out to write a realistic story on the most up-to-date subject matter, . . . and at the same time he set out to make that story a magical fable of contemporary life'.[40] Elaine Ostry has advanced a deeper reading of Dickens's fairy-tale tropes, arguing that 'The fairy tale was not removed from social realities and values for Dickens, but acted as an effective vehicle for their understanding'.[41]

Dickens's own writings explicitly and consistently eschewed hard-and-fast distinctions between the novel and the romance, contending that 'What is exaggeration to one class of minds and perceptions, is plain truth to another'.[42] When criticized for deviating from strict realism, as for example by Lewes,[43] Dickens asserted his right to romance: 'I have purposely dwelt upon the romantic side of familiar things'.[44] He thus staked a claim for a romance of the commonplace, for dwelling on the romantic side of the familiar. For Dickens, the onus of literature was to create a 'fusion of the graces of the imagination with the realities of life',[45] a potent combination 'vital to the welfare of any community'.[46] He was adamant that 'the exact truth must be there',[47] but 'the merit or art in the narrator, is the manner of stating the truth'.[48] Dickens was thus committed to a social vision that relied on what Theodor Adorno once described as 'the negative knowledge of the actual world',[49] which Adorno elaborated on elsewhere as knowledge that derives from 'art works [that] signal the possibility of the non-existent'.[50] Anticipating Adorno by a century, Dickens maintained that realism was best gained through fantasy. Art emerged in the interstice between realism and fantasy, in the 'fanciful treatment' of reality,[51] where the familiar could become strange and thus be viewed with a fresh eye.

An odd unlikeness of itself: 'moor eeffoc' London

In his 'Preliminary Word' (1850), Dickens declared his intention 'to show to all, that in all familiar things, even in those which are repellant [*sic*] on the surface, there is Romance [sic] enough'.[52] This vision of unlocking the romance concealed beneath the surface of everyday life was crucially focused on the city, 'the habitations and the ways of life of crowds',[53] as well as on industrial modernity: 'the towering chimneys . . . spirting [sic] out fire and smoke upon the prospect' were likened to fairy-tale figures.[54] The city that loomed at the heart of Dickens's imagination was, of course, Victorian London, into which he cast 'all the dreaminess and all the romance' of his febrile visions.[55] As jotted down in his book of memoranda, Dickens sought to cast 'London – or Paris, or any other great place',[56] but most especially London, 'in the new light of being actually unknown to all the people in the story',[57] and thus 'getting a new aspect, and being unlike itself. An *odd* unlikeness of itself'.[58] Dickens thus sought to defamiliarize Victorian London in order to disclose its oddness, to open up a fresh view that excavated the fantastical undertow of the city.

G. K. Chesterton hailed Dickens as the evoker of 'the unbearable realism of a dream',[59] where 'things seem more actual than things really are'.[60] The 'whole secret of that eerie realism',[61] according to Chesterton, could be found in the deepest trauma of Dickens's life: his agonizing year of labour at Warren's Blacking factory, at the age of twelve. Copious ink has been spilled on the impact of the Warren's Blacking episode on Dickens's fiction.[62] For the purposes of this study, its chief interest lies in Dickens's boyhood experiences in a London coffee shop on St Martin's Lane, near the church of St Martin-in-the-Fields, to which he went for refreshment during the long days of his labour. As suggested by Chesterton and further argued by this book, the young Dickens's visits to this coffee shop were nothing short of the originary cause of his 'romance of familiar things', to paraphrase Dickens's preface to *Bleak House* and his 'Preliminary Word'. These visits lit the spark that ignited his life-long aspiration to re-imagine London fantastically. For Chesterton, Dickens's experiences in this coffee shop were the key to his 'after-writings':

> [Dickens] mentions among the coffee-shops into which he crept in those wretched days one in St. Martin's Lane, 'of which I only recollect that it stood near the church, and that in the door there was an oval glass plate with "COFFEE ROOM" painted on it, addressed towards the street. If I ever find myself in a very different kind of coffee-room now, but where there is such an inscription on glass, and read it backwards on the wrong side, MOOR EEFFOC (as I often used to do then in a dismal reverie), a shock goes through my blood.'[63]

This transformation of coffee room into moor eeffoc, the sudden realization that London could be seen anew, and differently, from the inside of the café and through the glass darkly of an oval glass plate embedded in the coffee-shop door, the sign inverted and inscribed in mirror writing, was the formative experience that brought forth Dickens's defamiliarized vision of a London 'unlike itself'. It was this special vision of an odd London, a London unsettled from its own likeness, and its reversed typographical correlative, which was at the core of Dickens's legacy to the London fantastic. It would re-emerge starkly, though always with a difference, in the figure of 'Rottcodd' ('doctor' in reverse) in Peake's *Titus Groan* (1946), as the inspiration for Jerry Cornelius in *New Worlds* magazine, in key scenes in Harrison's 'A Young Man's Journey to Viriconium/London' (1985/2003) and *Climbers* (1989), and in Miéville's city of 'nodnoL' in *The Tain* (2002).

No less a fantasy writer than J. R. R. Tolkien recognized 'moor eeffoc fantasy' as a distinct tradition of London-based fantastical literature that originated with Dickens and was taken up by Chesterton and (implicitly) Wells:

> there is (especially for the humble) *Mooreeffoc*, or Chestertonian Fantasy. *Mooreeffoc* is a fantastic word, but it could be seen written up in every town in this land. It is Coffee-room, viewed from the inside through a glass door, as it was seen by Dickens on a dark London day; and it was used by Chesterton to denote the queerness of things that have become trite, when they are seen suddenly from a new angle. That kind of 'fantasy' most people would allow to be wholesome enough; and it can never lack for material. But it has, I think, only a limited power; for the reason that recovery of freshness of vision is its only virtue. The word *Mooreeffoc* may cause you suddenly to realize that England is an utterly alien land, lost either in some remote past age glimpsed by history, or in some strange dim future to be reached only by a time-machine.[64]

This key passage is worth quoting in full, because it establishes three crucial points. First, Tolkien identified Dickens as the progenitor of a strand of fantasy that was rooted in London and committed to a project of defamiliarization. Second, he adumbrated a line of influence between Dickens's fantasy and Chesterton's, and strongly implied another such line between Dickens and Wells – his example of 'some strange dim future to be reached only by a time-machine' reads as a thinly veiled allusion to Wells's *The Time Machine* (1895), reinforced by his explicit reference, earlier on in the same essay, to '*The Time-Machine* [sic]' and its 'Eloi and Morlocks [who] live far away in an abyss of time'.[65] Third, Tolkien was dismissive of Mooreeffoc fantasy, remarking with unmistakable disdain that its 'only virtue' was 'recovery of freshness of vision'. But for Dickens, 'recovery of freshness of vision' was the cardinal virtue. Throughout his fiction, non-fiction, social realism and fantasy alike, Dickens asserted his commitment to the recovery of freshness of vision; or, in his phrase, to 'the romantic side of familiar things'.

Wells, Orwell, Peake, Moorcock, Harrison, Gaiman and Miéville showed their debt to Dickens's London and its moor eeffoc fantasy in their fictional and non-fictional writings, at times expressly and at others indirectly, and often in the course of their wider recognition of a tradition of fantasies of which Dickens was the founding father and they formed a part. In an interview given shortly after the publication of *The Time Machine*, Wells placed his scientific romances in a Dickensian vein of fantasy:

> The world may have been often enough described. The intricacies of human conduct may even approach exhaustion. But the modern fanciful method takes the novelist to a new point of view. Stand aside but a little space from the ordinary line of observation, and the relative position of all things changes. There is a new proportion established. You have the world under a totally different aspect. There is profit as well as novelty in the change of view. That is, in some small way, what I aim at in my books.[66]

Wells's deployment of 'the modern fanciful method' to 'have the world under a totally different aspect' powerfully channels Dickens's desire to reveal the romance of familiar things and lend London 'a new aspect'. This aspiration fed directly into Wells's *The War of the Worlds* (1897), where the narrator's decision to leave the posturing Artilleryman and brave London alone is prompted by a vision of London strongly reminiscent of Wells's claims above:

> I perceived a strange light, a pale, violet-purple fluorescent glow, quivering under the night breeze. . . . I knew that it must be the red weed from which this faint irradiation proceeded. With that realization my dormant sense of wonder, my sense of the proportion of things, awoke again.[67]

A juxtaposition of these two passages discloses a correlation between the rhetoric Wells used to describe the purpose of his scientific romances and the style of the narrator's revelation as he gazes upon a London defamiliarized by the luminescent red weed from Mars. In the interview he spoke of 'a new proportion established'; in *War of the Worlds* the narrator reawakens to 'my sense of the proportion of things'. The interview posits the 'profit' and 'novelty' of 'the change of view'; *War of the Worlds* attributes the narrator's newfound sense of purpose to the stirrings of his 'dormant sense of wonder' at the 'strange light' emanating from London. Thus, the resemblances between these passages suggest that London was at the centre of Wells's endeavour to cast 'the world under a totally different aspect'. For Wells, as for Dickens, London was a synecdoche of the world, and it was on London above all that Wells cast his 'strange light'.

Dickens's heirs were not always explicit about their literary debts, but when Orwell asserted that 'Dickens is one of those writers who are well worth stealing',[68] and that 'thinking people who were born about the beginning of this century are in some sense Wells's own creation',[69] he was surely talking about himself rather than speaking in the abstract. His assertion that Dickens's 'modern analogue' was 'H. G. Wells' speaks to the extent to which he considered himself the third link in a chain.[70] For Orwell, Dickens was a fantasist with a penchant for the grotesque, whose nominal realism concealed 'monstrosities' that were 'completely fantastic and incredible',[71] a 'morbid love of corpses',[72] and a 'taste for the macabre and the lugubrious'.[73] He was equally fascinated by Wells's 'early romances',[74] which he compared favourably to Verne's *voyages extraordinaires* in terms that echoed Wells's own descriptors in *War of the Worlds*: 'there is far more feeling of *wonder* in them.'[75]

In the vein of Dickens's romance of familiar things, Orwell was fascinated with 'the romance of London',[76] praising a book that he regarded as otherwise unremarkable for its intention 'to make a pattern of beauty from the eventless, dismal lives which interlace in a city office'.[77] Orwell accordingly promulgated a Dickensian vision that aspired 'to convey beauty' beyond and in spite of political authoritarianism and the ugliness of post-war life,[78] to show that everyday Londoners, in all their strivings and their failings, 'they too are human – they too are romantic'.[79] Or as he put it in *Keep the Aspidistra Flying* (1936): 'in the lives of common men the greed and fear are mysteriously transmuted into something nobler'.[80] *Nineteen Eighty-Four* (1949) features a London scene in which Winston is swept up by a wave of 'mystical reverence' for a corpulent prole woman who is hanging washed diapers while heedlessly singing a sentimental ditty fabricated by the Party.[81] True to the insight of *Keep the Aspidistra Flying*, Winston realizes 'for the first time that she was beautiful'.[82]

Dickens was the only author whom Peake expressly named as a source for *Titus Groan*, acknowledging his debt to 'the genius of Charles Dickens'.[83] This acknowledgement tallies with Peake's commission to illustrate a new edition of *Bleak House*, issued simultaneously with the final stages of his work on *Titus Groan*. In his notes to a BBC talk on book illustration, Peake contended that the illustrator must possess 'the power to identify himself with . . . the author he is interpreting, and also with the mood of the book'.[84] According to Peake's close friend and biographer Gordon Smith, 'This was particularly true of Dickens and the drawings he did for *Bleak House*.'[85] Peake cited Dickens's 'dark and deathless rabble of long shadows' as an especial influence,[86] and *Bleak House* and *Titus Groan* assuredly share a penchant for crepuscular imagery.

Although Gormenghast Castle strikes an ahistorical note on a cursory reading, early drafts of *Titus Groan* were set in London.[87] When Peake was asked about the inspirations for Gormenghast Castle, he gestured 'at the vast medley of chimneys and roofs and strange shapes in the evening sky' that made up London's cityscape,[88] prompting his interlocutor to speculate that 'perhaps something like Dickens' London shaped the Castle'.[89] This medley of chimneys and roofs resonates in the unnamed city of *Titus Alone* (1959), with its prospect on 'rosy plumes from countless chimneys'.[90] Peake's wife recalled that Peake possessed a special way of looking at London, which she described in terms that chime audibly with Dickens's romance of familiar things: 'Battersea Bridge, the Embankment, have never been more beautiful.'[91]

With the notable exception of John Carey, who observes that Peake's 'chaotic buildings, the junk-festooned interiors, . . . look back to Dickens';[92] Dickens's influence on Peake has been noted primarily in his style, less in regard to their shared social and urban visions. This is an omission, as Peake's visual art and writings alike display a commitment to the representation of the urban underclass that is nothing if not Dickensian. Peake's 'London Fantasy' (1949) gives pride of place to 'the sandwich-men and the hucksters',[93] as well as to the 'grocer in Hounslow' who suffers from his 'aunt with dyspepsia'.[94] *Titus Alone* likewise valorizes a dazzling range of underclasses from 'the beggars, the harlots, the cheats',[95] to 'the outcasts, rag-pickers, the rascals, . . . the dreamers and the scum of the earth'.[96]

Peake expressed his commitment to a Dickensian social vision through his charcoal portrait of 'Jo the Crossing-Sweeper' (Figure I.1). This drawing brings forth Jo's fragility and humanity in careful gradations of black and grey, responding pictorially to Dickens's demand of 'men and women, born with Heavenly compassion in your hearts' to assume responsibility for the Jos of the world,[97] 'dying thus around us, every day'.[98]

Peake's portraits of the downtrodden Londoners of his own day owe something to Jo in their muted backgrounds and haunted gazes, but they often carry a touch of defiance more reminiscent of the Artful Dodger. Several of these figures appear in Peake's sketches in recognizable London locations such as an arcade on Tottenham Court Road, a restaurant or café in Soho, a street market or a street corner. Yet neither Peake's illustration of Jo nor his sketch of a young boy who could be considered Jo's counterpart (Figure I.2) is placed in a recognizable London milieu.

Figure I.1 Drawn by Mervyn Peake, 'Jo the Crossing-Sweeper', c. 1945, in Mervyn Peake, *Sketches from Bleak House*, eds Leon Garfield and Edward Blishen (London: Methuen, 1983), 37.

Jo stands out against strokes of black charcoal, the contemporary boy against strokes of green watercolour. The contemporary boy, whom G. Peter Winnington has captioned as 'A Boy in the Street',[99] is reminiscent of 'the trouser-pocket boys' of Peake's poem 'The Cocky Walkers' (1937),[100] but unlike them he is not placed 'in the sharp / Stern corners of the street'.[101] One may speculate that Peake decontextualized these boys from a concrete London milieu that would have otherwise defined them, be it a crossing in need of a sweeper or a corner fit for loitering, thereby lending a touch of mystery to each. Where Jo's illustration carries a mute appeal to human compassion, the contemporary boy glares back in contempt. Both boys, for Peake, are precious figures whose image has been preserved and uplifted from the crowds of 'weird creatures that make up this dark hive called London'.[102]

Moorcock and Harrison, respectively the editor and books editor of *New Worlds* magazine in the 1960s and 1970s, explicitly fashioned *New Worlds* as a platform

Figure I.2 Drawn by Mervyn Peake, 'A Boy in the Street', c. 1930s, in *Mervyn Peake: The Man and His Art*, ed. G. Peter Winnington (London: Peter Owen, 2006), 165.

for experimental fantasy and science fiction that took its cue from Dickens. Moorcock's article for the December 1967/January 1968 issue lamented the fact that 'escapist sf and fantasy flourishes in profusion',[103] but expressed the hope that 'a truly popular but uncompromising literature may come about – our new Dickens may soon emerge'.[104] Harrison collocated Dickens's *Great Expectations* (1860–1) and Peake's *Gormenghast Trilogy* (1946–59) as points of contrast with *The Lord of the Rings* (1954–5), to the unmistakable advantage of Dickens and Peake. Contrary to *The Lord of the Rings*, as Harrison contended, *Great Expectations* and the *Gormenghast Trilogy* built 'a bridge between the reader's experience and a set of suppositions of which he can have had no experience at all'.[105] Thus, in common with Orwell and Peake, Harrison read Dickens primarily as a fantasist and *Great Expectations* as 'a poor boy's pipe dream'.[106] For Harrison, *Great Expectations* was a forbearer of the *Gormenghast Trilogy* in the sense that they were both fantasies deeply embedded in the social dimension of real life. Moorcock made a similar comparison between Peake and Dickens on a broader canvas: 'No other writer since Dickens has had the energy, the invention, the powers of observation, the capacity for rich and brilliant metaphor or the skill to control the flood of original invention',[107] Moorcock declared, 'And it is with Dickens alone that Mervyn Peake can be compared.'[108] In these remarks as well as others, Moorcock and Harrison were among the first expressly to recognize that Dickens and Peake formed a coherent line of influence of which they too were a part.

Gaiman's *Neverwhere* (1996) harks back to Dickens in a line of influence that runs through Chesterton. Gaiman has asserted that Chesterton's *The Napoleon of Notting Hill* (1904) 'hugely informed my own novel *Neverwhere*',[109] singling out Chesterton's ability to make 'the names of London places magical'.[110] Yet Chesterton associated Dickens with the same narrative strategy that Gaiman attributed to him. In a characteristic example of the semiotic playfulness with London place-names that had inspired Gaiman, Chesterton described Dickens's indelible connection to London as the experience of being 'crucified at Charing Cross'.[111] He wrote about Dickens's moor eeffoc fantasy, particularly its powers of rendering London 'mortally romantic',[112] in lyrical prose strongly reminiscent of *Napoleon of Notting Hill*. Gaiman may have been gesturing towards this longer lineage when he asserted in an interview about the 1996 BBC series of *Neverwhere*, of which the book is a novelization, that the characters 'were less Tarantino, more Dickens'.[113] He recalled elsewhere that he 'was reading *Bleak House* for pleasure' as he was hard at work on *Neverwhere*.[114] *Neverwhere*'s murderous duo of villains, 'Mr Croup and Mr Vandemar',[115] were accordingly described by him in a different interview as 'a couple of Dickensian assassins'.[116]

Their menacingly soft-spoken demeanour may well owe something to *Bleak House*'s Mr Tulkinghorn.

Miéville has deflected comments about the Dickensian resonances in his writing by attributing them to Peake, insisting in one interview that his characters are 'probably more Peakeian than Dickensian, really'.[117] Yet he has noted Dickens's influence on Peake – 'what is merely camp in Dickens becomes grotesquerie in Peake, and splendid for it'[118] – a statement which, given Miéville's frequent testimonies to Peake's influence, amounts to a tacit acknowledgement of Dickens's influence as well, via Peake's mediation. More directly, Miéville has acknowledged the impact of the fictional Londons of 'Dickens, Gaiman, Machen, et many al' on his own London-based fantasies.[119] Furthermore, Miéville's *The Tain* features a reverse London that stages Dickens's moor eeffoc fantasy on a grand scale. The city is named 'nodnoL' in consummate 'moor eeffoc' fashion,[120] forming a perfect mirror image of London where 'right is left, . . . and left right'.[121]

This is not to suggest that Dickens, Wells, Orwell, Peake, Moorcock, Harrison, Gaiman and Miéville were all of the same mind. They each held distinctly different opinions on literature, culture, society and politics, and their fantasies varied according to each author's style, political inclinations, social vision and creative energy. More broadly, their fantastical fictions moulded to the pressures of London history, from its imperial heyday as the capital of the British Empire, through the more pessimistic spirit of the *fin de siècle*, the cataclysms of the world wars and the Blitz, the Swinging Sixties, the closure of the docklands, the political friction of the Thatcher years, the rise of global capitalism, and the fluorescence of London as a global cosmopolitan city. But Dickens's legacy remains recognizable enough to suggest a tradition with clearly discernible links and a shared imaginative ethos. Dickens's rejection of hard-and-fast distinctions between realism and fantasy, his determination to affect social change through fantasy, and his fascination with the forms and fashions of London in all their dazzling grotesquery were the major components of the literary legacy that he bequeathed to his heirs. Each of these authors built upon the work of his predecessors even as he departed from it, in a literary tradition that is perhaps distinctive in the degree to which its practitioners were aware of their forerunners and their rivals alike.

Cockney fairyland

John Ruskin remarked of Dickens that he 'was a pure modernist – a leader of the steam-whistle party *par excellence*'.[122] He singled out Dickens as the proponent of an urban 'art of fiction' expressing 'the thwarted habits of body and mind, which are the punishment of reckless crowding in cities'.[123] Indeed, Ruskin recognized Dickens's special facility for rendering London fantastical, 'calling the Crystal Palace "Fairyland"',[124] as he put it, which for Ruskin went hand in hand with Dickens's 'distrust both of nobility and clergy' and 'his liberalism',[125] all of which Ruskin believed to 'have on the whole done harm to the country'.[126] In opposition to what he saw as 'the group of authors headed by Charles Dickens',[127] Ruskin valorized 'the true grotesque' that revealed a 'deep insight into nature'.[128] He found the purest examples of the noble grotesque in the pre-industrial Middle Ages, which he declared as 'the only ages',[129] extolling their 'miracle-believing faith'.[130]

Dickens never responded to Ruskin's attacks, probably because most of them were launched after his death. But he certainly opposed the medievalist sentiments that these attacks disclosed, criticizing those who sought to turn back the clock and thereby 'ignoring all that has been done for the happiness and elevation of mankind during three or four centuries of slow and dearly-bought amelioration'.[131] Dickens's aversion to medievalism cuts across his overt fantasy and his nominally realistic novels, finding expression in satirical characters such as 'the noble Refrigerator, at no time less than a hundred years behind the period' in *Little Dorrit*,[132] the red-faced gentleman in *The Chimes* (1844), and Mrs Skewton in *Dombey and Son*, who mawkishly extols 'the Middle ages'.[133] In a similar vein, Dickens's novels, articles, reviews and speeches reinforce Jay Clayton's assessment of the author as 'a believer in the Victorian gospel of progress'.[134]

Wells's distaste for Ruskin is well documented. His sense that 'the socialist movement in England was under the aesthetic influence of Ruskin' was one of the major bones of contention that eventually led to his separation from 'the unscientific Socialism of the Fabian'.[135] As he reflected in *Joan and Peter* (1918), 'In the place of Rousseau and his demand for a return to the age of innocence, we English had Ruskin and Morris, who demanded a return to the Middle Ages.'[136] Wells had no patience for this type of 'thoughtful headshaker moping for a return to medievalism'.[137] Staunchly challenging this impulse to escape and disavow modernity, Wells argued that 'the process of mechanical invention and discovery' was a key step towards social equality,[138] because it had enabled 'a period of rapid advance in popular education throughout all the Westernized world'.[139]

Late-Victorian fantasy author George MacDonald, who was Ruskin's personal friend and disciple, mounted a defence of the fairy tale – and by extension his own book-length fantasy novels that were packaged as fairy tales – by aligning it with 'all the realm of Nature'.[140] 'Nature is mood-engendering, thought-provoking,'[141] he observed, 'such ought the sonata, such ought the fairytale to be'.[142] The city, in contrast, was inimical to Fairyland, as MacDonald illustrated with a resolutely London-based example:

> Suppose the gracious creatures of some childlike region of Fairyland talking either cockney or Gascon! Would not the tale, however lovelily begun, sink at once to the level of the Burlesque – of all forms of literature the least worthy?[143]

MacDonald's choice of Cockney as the most corrupted form of fairy speech casts a revealing light on his attitudes towards fantasy and towards London. This passage suggests that the rough speech of London's working classes would defile the purity of 'the gracious creatures' of fairyland. A suggestion reinforced in MacDonald's short story, 'A Journey Rejourneyed' (1865), where the narrator condescends to 'the cockneys ... even if they have been ill-bred and ill-taught in the fostering city'.[144] MacDonald disparaged so-called fanciful or riotous forms of fantasy with much the same phrases, as if they too were cockneys: 'It is only the ill-bred, that is, the uncultivated imagination that will amuse itself where it ought to worship and work.'[145]

MacDonald's emphasis on Cockney slang as a bugbear within his wider objections to the Londonization of fantasy points to an enduring contrast between the Dickensian and the Ruskinian traditions of British fantasy. Ruskin, who yearned for a return to rural England, was appalled to witness the 'pure English,'[146] of '[Sir Walter] Scott's Lowland Scottish dialect' replaced by what he regarded as the 'degradations of cockneyism' in the mouths of Dickens's working-class Londoners.[147] He regarded this shift from Scottish dialect to Cockney slang as a sure indicator that Victorian literature was deteriorating, its wholesomeness tainted by 'phrases developed in states of rude employment, and restricted intercourse'.[148] The protagonist of MacDonald's *The Marquis of Lossie* (1877) likewise resolves to limit the number of his English servants because 'he would not have the natural country speech [of Scotland] corrupted with cockneyisms'.[149] Wells, in contrast, maintained that Dickens's renditions of Cockney speech rejuvenated the language and offered new resources for writers of his generation. Responding to 'some elderly pedant' who complained of his 'use the word "alibi" as an equivalent for "excuse"',[150] Wells drew on the Cockney slang of Dickens's most Cockney character – Sam Weller. 'Sam Weller gave a new twist to "alibi"',[151] Wells asserted, thereby 'carrying exactly the sense I gave it'.[152]

Tolkien and Lewis developed MacDonald's objections to Cockney-speaking fairies into more comprehensive theories of fantasy. Tolkien distinguished between the London-based Dickensian fantasy of '*Mooreeffoc*' and his own model of fantasy that creates 'a Secondary World which your mind can enter'.[153] Tolkien insisted that this 'Sub-creative Art' depends on the achievement and strict preservation of an 'inner consistency of reality' within its Secondary World,[154] maintaining a level of immersion that allows the reader, while 'inside it',[155] to believe that this fantasy world 'is "true"'.[156] Tolkien's Secondary-World fantasy thus admits no glimpse into 'this mortal world',[157] nor any access to 'our own time and space',[158] however remote. Where Tolkien characterized '*Mooreeffoc*' fantasy as urban and specifically attuned to London, his own paradigm of Secondary-World fantasy championed 'the story-maker who allows himself to be "free with" Nature'.[159] The ideal Secondary World, for Tolkien, was 'Faërie',[160] a rural and pseudo-medieval realm featuring 'horses, castles, sailing-ships, bows and arrows ... knights and kings and priests'.[161] He accordingly launched a staunch defence of reactionary fantasy:

> I do not think that the reader or the maker of fairy-stories need even be ashamed of the 'escape' of archaism. . . . For it is after all possible for a rational man, . . . to arrive at the condemnation, . . . of progressive things like factories.[162]

Among those who had failed to arrive at this 'rational' condemnation, Tolkien indicted Wells in particular. Obliquely referring to Wells's *When the Sleeper Wakes* (1899), a futurist vision of London where the city is encased in a glass dome and features moving walkways as the central mode of transport, Tolkien disparaged 'these prophets [who] often foretell (and many seem to yearn for) a world like one big glass-roofed railway-station'.[163]

Lewis similarly contended that fantasy must be segregated from the 'commonplace',[164] at the touch of which 'all magic dies'.[165] He accordingly wrote to the author Jane Gaskell with advice to this effect:

> In a fantasy every precaution must be taken never to break the spell, to do nothing which will wake the reader and bring him back with a bump to the common earth. . . . (Notice, too, the disenchanting implication that the fairies can't make for themselves lingerie as good as they can get – not even in Paris, which wd. [*sic*] be bad enough – but, of all places, in London.)[166]

Lewis's theory of fantasy thus valorized the remoteness and loftiness of the supernatural, disavowing 'the common earth' in a sentiment antithetical to Dickens's romance of familiar things. Still more so, Lewis focused his ire on London, 'of all places', the focal point and wellspring of Dickens's imagination. London featured occasionally in Lewis's *The Chronicles of Narnia* (1950–6), but chiefly as 'a beastly Hole' with which to contrast the grassy valleys,[167] 'little hills' and 'distant mountains' of his pastoral Narnia.[168]

Where Lewis's fantasies were pitted against London, his science fiction novels were pitted against so-called Wellsianity: 'the Scientific Outlook, the picture of Mr Wells and the rest'.[169] 'I liked the whole interplanetary idea as a *mythology*,'[170] Lewis explained, 'and simply wished to conquer for my own (Christian) pt. of view what has always hitherto been used by the opposite side'.[171] The phrase 'opposite side' is telling – as the earlier discussion hoped to make clear, Ruskin, Tolkien and Lewis consciously regarded Dickens and Wells as their 'opposite side', as a progressive and urban tradition rivalling their own.

As for that opposite side, Orwell lambasted Lewis for his championship of a school of Christian apologists whose 'special targets . . . have been T. H. Huxley, H. G. Wells, Bertrand Russell, Professor Joad, and others who are associated in the popular mind with Science and Rationalism'.[172] He criticized Lewis's *That Hideous Strength* (1945), which features an antagonist who plainly caricaturizes Wells, for its premise that 'the scientists are actually in touch with evil spirits'.[173] Countervailing this demonization of scientific progress, Orwell credited the 'advance of physical science' with the fact that 'The British working class are now better off in almost all ways than they were thirty years ago.'[174] Even at the height of his agonized grappling with the failures of technological progress, Orwell harboured little sentimentality towards the Middle Ages, which he described as a time when life consisted of 'lice, scurvy, a yearly childbirth and a yearly child-death, and the priest terrifying you with tales of Hell'.[175]

Peake resented contemporary reviewers' penchant for comparing *The Gormenghast Trilogy* to *The Lord of the Rings*. 'I rather thought I was writing for grown-ups,'[176] he told Moorcock, 'I can't see that I have anything in common with Tolkien.'[177] There was more than just the age of his readership at stake in this gripe. Peake objected to Tolkien's sentimentality: 'Mervyn had a rather trenchant comment to make about *The Lord of the Rings*',[178] one of his art students recalled, 'he described it as "rather twee" and mildly mocked the character of Goldberry, Tom Bombadil's lady-friend, as "precious"'.[179] Unlike Tolkien, who valorized 'the consolation of fairy-stories',[180] Peake's own vision of fantastical world-building was abrasive, heterodox and violent. 'As the earth was thrown from the sun, so from the earth the artist must fling out into space,'[181] he contended, because to 'complete from pole to pole, his own world' was a revolt against society on par with 'the smashing of another window-pane' or the 'shout across the lethal stillness of good taste and moderation'.[182] Thus, as James Gifford observes, while Gormenghast Castle appears to be sequestered in a pseudo-medieval world, its 'seemingly reactionary trappings' are utilized in service of 'an antiauthoritarian paradigm'.[183] In the *Gormenghast Trilogy*, the only constant is flux, a recurring theme that may have prompted Moorcock's contention that Peake was 'Tolkien's antithesis'.[184]

Moorcock and Harrison launched methodical attacks against *The Lord of the Rings* and Tolkienian fantasy more broadly. Moorcock wondered at 'the appeal of juvenile novels like LORD OF THE RINGS',[185] attributing this appeal to a 'refusal to face or derive any pleasure from the realities of urban industrial life',[186] coupled with a 'longing to possess, again, the infant's eye view of the countryside'.[187] He was adamant that such fantasy was not merely infantile – it was pernicious. To accept the premise that 'the little hills and woods of that Surrey of the mind, the Shire, are "safe",[188] whereas 'the wild landscapes everywhere beyond the Shire are "dangerous"',[189] was to tacitly acquiesce to a world view whereby 'Experience of Life itself is dangerous.'[190] For Moorcock, this world view was underpinned by class bias – these 'rural romances' of 'Tolkein [*sic*] and that group of middle-class Christian fantasists' pitted the protagonists against 'villains [who] are thinly disguised working class [*sic*] agitators'.[191]

Harrison wrote a series of articles that criticized Tolkien's brand of fantasy for peddling 'stability and comfort and safe catharsis'.[192] To posit a 'hermetically sealed' fantasy world,[193] according to Harrison, was a betrayal of the very idea of fantasy literature, because it perpetuated a stasis that could only ever be maintained by the author's artificial interventions. The result was merely 'emotional abstracts',[194] 'heroisms [that] are void',[195] 'battle-songs hollow'.[196] Harrison defined the ethos of *New Worlds* magazine against this 'literature of comfort' that offered 'a body of warm, familiar assumptions, reiterated from book to book'.[197] *New Worlds* marked a renewed attempt at the composition of fantasy literature that '*will* disturb you',[198] which draws on and refracts 'elements to be found all around us, the architectures and cultures and life-styles of the twentieth century'.[199]

Miéville declared Tolkien to be 'the wen on the arse of fantasy literature'.[200] 'Tolkien's worldview was resolutely rural, petty bourgeois, conservative, anti-modernist, misanthropically Christian and anti-intellectual',[201] Miéville contended, and he accordingly conceptualized *Perdido Street Station* as 'a deliberately anti-Tolkienesque fantasy'.[202] As he later recalled:

> I then made a checklist of the kind of things Tolkien does and set out to invert them: so where his is a feudal world, mine is capitalist; his is rural, mine is urban; his is very Manichean in its morality, mine is all about shades of grey.[203]

In this spirit of challenging Tolkien's 'nostalgia for rural life',[204] Miéville asserted that his fantasy was underpinned by a 'progressive' Marxism,[205] and that 'city life is simply more interesting to me than rural life'.[206]

Gaiman is the odd one out. He has bucked the trend of Tolkien-bashing and announced that '*Lord of the Rings* was, most probably, the best book that ever could be written'.[207] He likewise recalled that 'Lewis was the first person to make me want to be a writer',[208] and that as a young boy he read and reread the *Narnia* books with a passion. Gaiman's exception to this seemingly neat opposition between two traditions of British fantasy serves as an important reminder of the fallacy of binary structures. Binaries are the scaffolding of literary scholarship, occasionally erected for the convenience of critics, but easily collapsible under scrutiny. No two traditions, however consciously antagonistic, run in strict parallel to each other, but rather co-exist in a constant dialectic, playing off one another even as they carve out contradistinctive literary spaces.

For heuristic convenience, the rural, reactionary strand of British fantasy that concatenates the fantasies of Ruskin, MacDonald, Tolkien and Lewis may be assigned the provisional name of 'Rural Fantasy', capitalized for ease of distinction. In the same vein, the urban, progressive strand of fantasy that concatenates the fantasies of Dickens, Wells, Orwell, Peake, Moorcock, Harrison, Gaiman and Miéville may be designated by the provisional term of 'Urban Fantasy', similarly capitalized.

This coinage might provoke scepticism regarding the need for refined terminology, given the already-existing formulation of the non-capitalized 'urban fantasy'. To this objection one may reply that the term 'urban fantasy' has recently lost much of its critical valence due to aggressive marketing strategies.[209] In the past few years, urban fantasy has become a popular marketing label that is often used to advertise formulaic literature produced in spades for young adults. As David Langford observed in his recent addendum to the entry on 'urban fantasy' in *The Encyclopedia of Fantasy* (addendum 2012), since the entry's time of writing in 1997,

> Urban Fantasy has come to denote the subgenre of stories set in an alternate version of our modern world where humans (often with special Talents) and supernatural beings . . . interact via adventure, melodrama, intrigue and Sex.[210]

Alexander C. Irvine similarly remarked that 'any particularity the term once had is now diffused in a fog of contradiction',[211] and Farah Mendlesohn and Edward James quipped that urban fantasy currently 'seems to require werewolves'.[212] Indeed, this loose usage of the term has recently percolated into scholarship.

Helen Young, for instance, posits that urban fantasy can be set in 'small towns' as well as in 'cities',[213] and proceeds to stake a claim for a subsection of 'Suburban Fantasy' that is specifically '*not* limited to works which have city settings'.[214] To admit such broad usage, one might argue, is to strip the term of any meaningful utility.

Thus, to avoid using a label that has become a catch-all for lewd supernatural fiction, it seems necessary to develop a more precise terminology. That being said, this delineation of rival traditions of Rural Fantasy and Urban Fantasy is strictly provisional and makes no claims for essentializing *a priori* divisions in literature, which would be a dubious claim at best. It is a heuristic deployed for the sake of clarity and convenience, *tout court*.

Whose fantasy? Recovering the history of Urban Fantasy

The fraught interplay between Rural Fantasy and Urban Fantasy, which was ongoing since the middle of the nineteenth century, was for a time effaced by the phenomenal success of *The Lord of the Rings*. As Edward James observed, *Lord of the Rings* 'looms over all the fantasy written in English . . . since its publication'.[215] Tolkien's unprecedented popularity has often spurred scholars to define fantasy synonymously with Rural Fantasy. Fredric Jameson probably had Middle Earth in mind when he wrote of the fantasy genre as a 'vision of an immense historical degradation'.[216] Brian Atterbery declared plainly that 'One way to characterize the genre of fantasy is the set of texts that in some way or other resemble *The Lord of the Rings*.'[217] Darko Suvin argued that 'the common denominator of Fantasy seems to me the resolute refusal of any technology, urbanization, and finances associated with the capitalism of Industrial Revolution and "paleotechnic" (Mumford) machinery'.[218] Thus defined, fantasy literature emerges as a deeply conservative, anti-metropolitan and reactionary mode of writing.

Notwithstanding, recent years have seen a renewed interest in narratives of Urban Fantasy, even if that is not the name by which its latest fictions have been labelled. Moorcock has observed 'a trend away from traditional rural Tolkienesque fables towards well-written stories with a strong urban focus'.[219] He regards this turn as newly emergent, a 'modern school of urban fantasy' that 'appeals to readers not merely seeking escape but looking for versions of their own experience'.[220] Dirk Vanderbeke similarly argues that whereas 'such counter-worlds' of fantasy are traditionally 'set in a pastoral or rural environment',[221] recent fantasies have located 'doorways into a world that is and isn't ours . . . in the modern city and metropolis'.[222] Scholars have linked this urban turn to the 'British Boom' in speculative fiction,[223] pioneered by urban writers such as China Miéville, Ken Macleod, M. John Harrison and Neil Gaiman.

What present scholarship lacks is a deeper exploration of this school's historical development. Critics have gestured towards precursors – Dickens, Wells and Peake prominent among them – but their studies proceed upon the assumption that the division between rural fantasy à la Tolkien and urban fantasy à la Miéville is an altogether new phenomenon. This study argues otherwise. The following chapters chart an Urban Fantasy tradition that stretches from the early nineteenth century to the present day.

Chapter 1 fleshes out the differences between Urban Fantasy and its Rural counterpart through a comparison between Dickens's *A Christmas Carol* and Ruskin's *The King of the Golden River*. It examines Dickens's dependence on the London nightscape as the wellspring of his fantastical imagination, focusing on *The Chimes* as its case study. Exploring the role of obsolete material objects in Dickens's London-based fiction, it analyses *The Haunted Man* as a textual node where these themes intersect and intertwine in the grotesque distortions that take hold of Dickens's London by night. The final sections consider Dickens's role as an editor of prose fantasy, leading to speculation on his contributions to the development of the scientific romance and gesturing to a chain of influence that runs from Dickens to Bulwer-Lytton to Wells.

Chapter 2 considers the development of the Urban Fantasy tradition in the final decades of the nineteenth century and the beginning of the twentieth. Contextualizing its analyses within the 'Battle of the Books' between the realist novel and 'stories of the impossible' that raged across the pages of the periodical press, the chapter argues that Wells carried on the Dickensian mode of liberal-progressive London-based fantasies but transposed it to the 'field of scientific romance with a philosophical element'. Drawing on a range of Wells's London-based scientific romances and fantastical short stories, together with unpublished manuscript material, the chapter examines Wells's Urban Fantasies as a multifaceted expression of his growing frustrations with the intransigence of the London elite and the common Londoner alike.

Chapter 3 explores the trials and tribulations of the Urban Fantasy tradition in the shadow of the World Wars. It argues that Orwell and Peake struggled to engage positively with the city and advance a liberal world view at a time when the core values of liberalism and progress, and the concomitant belief in the city as a space of hope and change, were cast into serious doubt. They thus devised new strategies for writing liberal-progressive, London-based fantasies, championing the British fantastic by defining it against an oversimplified image of American 'scientifiction' that glorified violence and fetishized technology. Their Urban Fantasies accordingly privileged Dickensian locality over Wellsian universalism, celebrating small-scale acts of 'common decency', which constituted the only viable form of resistance in the beleaguered city.

Chapter 4 centres on the renewal of the Urban Fantasy tradition in *New Worlds* magazine on the backdrop of Swinging London and the economic downturn of the 1970s. It analyses Moorcock's and Harrison's endeavours to fashion *New Worlds* as a platform for liberal-progressive, socially engaged London-based fantasies, which they explicitly framed as a return to the paradigms established by Dickens, Wells and Peake. Focusing on the myth of the assassin-cum-rock star 'Jerry Cornelius', the chapter traces the growth of this myth into a patchwork of short stories, extracts and serializations across multiple issues of *New Worlds* and beyond it into novels and off-shoots penned by a diverse coterie of authors.

Chapter 5 focuses on the relatively recent turn in Urban Fantasy towards fully fleshed alternative Londons, or recognizable variations thereof. It suggests that this new permutation encodes an escapism that runs counter to the political and social engagement at the heart of the genre. The chapter explores the strengths and limitations of metropolitan world-building in Gaiman's *Neverwhere* and in a range of Miéville's fantastical fictions. It concludes with a retrospect on the Urban Fantasy tradition, contextualized by T. S. Eliot's essay 'Tradition and the Individual Talent'.

Patrick Parrinder has compellingly argued that we live in 'the Age of Fantasy'.[224] If so, this begs the question – whose fantasy? The pseudo-medieval tradition of Rural Fantasy has by and large served a conservative, reactionary agenda. But from its inception, Rural Fantasy has been shadowed by its Urban 'opposite side', the liberal-progressive, future-oriented and socially committed strand of the fantastic. This side is too easily forgotten or maligned. In 1997, Germaine Greer casually elided the differences between *The Lord of the Rings* and *Nineteen Eighty-Four*, tarring them with the same brush as books in which 'flight from reality is their dominating characteristic'.[225] Twelve years later, an esteemed British academic made the sweeping generalization that science fiction 'is in a special room in book shops, bought by a special kind of person who has special weird things they go to and meet each other'.[226] As recently as 2015, a writer for *The Guardian* lamented the popularity of Terry Pratchett as a sure sign that 'our concept of literary greatness is being blurred beyond recognition'.[227] These remarks, and others of similar tenor, showcase the extent to which scholars of fantasy and science fiction still face an uphill battle. One may hope that recovering the history of the Urban Fantasy tradition can play a small part in the wider struggle for the recognition of science fiction and fantasy literature as serious fields of study, worthy of respect within academic circles and outside of them. Scholars need but reconsider the assumed equivalence of socially engaged literature with generic realism, and look for radical ideas in the transformed cityscapes of a reconfigured, haunted, invaded, futurist, neo-Victorian, grotesquely animate, post-apocalyptic, otherworldly London, which has been a constant in our fiction for nearly two centuries, endlessly transformed yet ever familiar in its fantastical material topographies.

1

The phantom out of Oxford Street
Dickens's fairyland

'A ghastly heap of fermenting brickwork': The rise of Urban Fantasy

This study argues that fantastical London literature began to coalesce in the 1840s, with the writings of Charles Dickens. Yet as ever with such sweeping statements, it demands immediate qualification. Fantastical fictions set in London, in part if not entirely, were published before Dickens arrived on the literary scene. John William Polidori's 'The Vampyre' (1816) and Mary Shelley's *The Last Man* (1826) are cases in point. William Blake, Percy Shelley, Leigh Hunt and Charles Lamb all wrote about London in ways that could be construed as fantastical. But Dickens pioneered a new kind of prose fantasy that consciously placed London at the front and centre, as will be argued further in this chapter.

The rise of London-based fantasy in the mid-nineteenth century is rooted in deeper historical currents. Raymond Williams has argued that the 'contrast between country and city, as fundamental ways of life',[1] which structures the opposition between Rural and Urban Fantasy, emerged with starkness in Britain, because the Industrial Revolution 'occurred there very early'.[2] From within Britain and outside of it people flocked to London, which was increasingly hailed as the sublime 'capital of the world'.[3] Between 1800 and 1851, the number of houses in London nearly tripled,[4] and its population grew from less than 1 million to over 2 million,[5] compared to 1.2 million in the rival Paris.[6] By 1851, the proportion of Britons living in cities had surpassed the proportion of those living in the country for the first time in British history,[7] and over 13 per cent were living in London.[8] 'London is as good an epitome of the world as anywhere exists',[9] Masson wrote in 1859, 'If any city could generate and sustain a species of Novel entirely out of its own resources, it might surely be London.'[10]

The dark side of these changes has been well documented by both the journalists and reformers of the time and later scholars. Edwin Chadwick's report cast light on the jarring discrepancies between the housing conditions of the affluent and the impoverished populations of London.[11] One consequence of this discrepancy being, as Chadwick had shown, that in the poorest districts of London the average morality rate was twice as high as that of the more well-to-do areas.[12] London's frantic expansion had devastating effects on the English countryside, as rural areas and towns were being recalibrated into London suburbs or annexed for railway development. Many agreed with William Cobbett's assessment that London had become a 'monstrous WEN [that] is now sucking up the vitals of the country'.[13]

This image of London as a monster was not new – Daniel Defoe had already proclaimed it a 'great and monstrous thing' in the eighteenth century[14] – but in the nineteenth century the monster became the predominant trope for the London imaginary. As Luckhurst has argued, with 'the huge expansion of the metropolis in the nineteenth century',[15] 'London becomes a sublime object that evokes awe and evades rational capture'.[16] Thus, Dickens wrote of London as 'the monster, roaring in the distance';[17] Ruskin imagined it as 'a ghastly heap of fermenting brickwork',[18] Wells gave London pride of place among 'the monster cities' that he anticipated in the near future,[19] and MacDonald painted a visceral, if allegorical, picture of 'the monster whose faintly gelatinous bulk' lay 'over all the vast of London'.[20] London's limitlessness, its shifting crowds and shocking juxtapositions, and its power to absorb and reshape Britain in its own image, seemed to compel writers of all genres and political persuasions to reimagine their capital city in the fantastical grammar of the monstrous sublime.

The difference between Ruskin and MacDonald on the one hand, and Dickens and Wells on the other hand, was in their attitude towards the London monster. Ruskin and MacDonald dreamed of turning back the clock to an idealized, pre-urban, pre-industrial medieval past. They thus set their fantasies at the bottom of secluded valleys, in the thick of ancient forests and at the peaks of towering mountains, their noble-hearted protagonists often threatened by the corruption of ugly cities, but inevitably preserving their purity and emerging triumphant. Dickens and Wells, in contrast, set their fantasies on London's streets, among the London markets and stalls, and in the heart of the London crowd, celebrating the city and revelling in its potentialities. This is not to say that their attitude towards London was Utopian, but that where Ruskin's and MacDonald's fantasies were conservative and reactionary, Dickens's and Wells's were progressive, broadly liberal and democratic in their sensibility, upholding their conviction that for good or ill, the future of humanity lay in the metropolis.

'The inventor of this sort of story': Dickens's London-based fantasies

In a letter to the Earl of Carlisle, dated 2 January 1849, Dickens provided a rare glimpse into his thoughts about London-based fantasy. The letter responded to the Earl's criticism of Dickens's fifth and final Christmas Book, *The Haunted Man and the Ghost's Bargain* (1848). In this letter, Dickens asserted that his Christmas Books had inaugurated a new genre, one that uniquely combined the urban and the fantastic:

> As the inventor of this sort of story, I may be allowed to plead that I think a little dreaminess and vagueness essential to its effect.
>
> . . . the heaping up of that quantity of shadows, I hold to be absolutely necessary, as a preparation to the appearance of the dark shadow of the Chemist. People will take anything for granted, in the Arabian Nights or the Persian Tales, but they won't walk out of Oxford Street, or the Market place of a county town, directly into the presence of a Phantom, albeit an allegorical one. And I believe it to be as essential that they come at that spectre through such a preparation of gathering gloom and darkness, as it would be for them to go through some such ordeal, in reality, before they could get up a private Ghost of their own.[21]

To the best of my knowledge, this letter comprises the only surviving evidence of Dickens's explicit acknowledgement that he was 'the inventor' of a new kind of fantasy, one that was resolutely urban and deeply and inextricably imbricated in the forms, fashions and codes of the city. His letter expressed the conviction that his London-based fantasies were quintessentially different from supernatural tales set in a distant land, such as 'the Arabian Nights or the Persian Tales', because they were set in London, and an urban setting demanded new strategies for the composition of supernatural fiction. To set one's phantom just off of Oxford Street, Dickens argued, necessitated 'a preparation of gathering gloom and darkness', 'the heaping up' of shadows. Dickens thus maintained that 'this sort of story' required a transitional phase from the natural to the supernatural, from the high street to the phantasmagoric apparition, a medium of shadowy obfuscation that modulated Oxford Street into a ghostly London.

This chapter explores Dickens's shadowy London and its fantastical permutations in three of his Christmas Books: *A Christmas Carol* (1843), *The Chimes* (1844) and *The Haunted Man*. It juxtaposes Dickens's *A Christmas Carol* with Ruskin's *The King of the Golden River* (1851), with a view to further tease out the differences between Rural and Urban Fantasy and their opposing attitudes towards London life and urban modernity. It discusses *The Chimes* as a site of tension between Dickens's liberal-progressive politics and his imaginative investment in a lost London demolished by urban renovation. *The Haunted Man* will be read as an allegory of Dickens's London-based fantasy and its attachment to material objects. The final sections trace the science fictionalization of Dickens's imagination, concluding with Dickens's role as midwife to the scientific romance and suggesting a line of influence between Dickens and H. G. Wells through Edward Bulwer-Lytton's *A Strange Story* and (in the next chapter) *The Coming Race*.

In his autobiography, Ruskin described *The King of the Golden River* as 'a fairly good imitation of Grimm and Dickens, mixed with a little true Alpine feeling of my own'.[22] But as Suzanne Rahn points out, Dickens's influence on the story is far less discernible than the Grimms',[23] set as it is 'in a secluded and mountainous part of Stiria [Austria]'.[24] Written two years before *A Christmas Carol* – though published eight years after it in Christmas 1851 – *The King of the Golden River* reads like a Victorian author's homage to the Grimm Brothers. Ruskin admired the Grimm fairy tales for fortifying children 'against the glacial cold of selfish science'.[25] His aversion to so-called selfish science, and longing for a more submissively religious outlook on life and death, finds ample expression in *The King of the Golden River*.

The story opens 'in old time',[26] in a pre-industrial world surreptitiously presided over by the eponymous 'King of the Golden River'.[27] It follows the fortunes of three brothers named Schwartz, Hans and Gluck, who live off 'a valley of the most surprising and luxuriant fertility' by the manual farm labour of Gluck and the family servants.[28] In traditional fairy-tale fashion, the two older brothers abuse the youngest brother Gluck and become rich off the people and the land. But they receive their comeuppance with the intervention of two supernatural figures: the personified 'South-West Wind, Esquire' who dries up their 'Treasure Valley' in retribution for their poor hospitality,[29] and the King of the Golden River, who transforms them into black stones after they refuse to learn their lesson. The kind-hearted Gluck, in turn, inherits the Treasure Valley, which is fully restored to its former glory after he shows compassion towards those in need.

The plot often seems to be a pretext for Ruskin to set forth his rich and vivid evocations of sublime nature. *The King of the Golden River* is rife with lyrical descriptions so intensely rendered that they emulate the landscape paintings of Ruskin's hero, the Romantic painter Joseph Mallord William Turner.[30] What Turner created with watercolours, Ruskin created with words, painting the Stirian mountains 'all crimson, and purple with the sunset'.[31] From atop these mountains a waterfall plunges 'in a waving column of pure gold . . . flushing and fading alternately in the wreaths of spray'.[32] As the story unfolds, Ruskin's descriptions of wild nature increasingly make use of the pathetic fallacy: 'long, snake-like shadows crept up along the mountain sides' after Hans turns his back on a dying child.[33] Whereas 'bright green moss, with pale pink starry flowers' spring up between the rocks when Gluck gives that same child 'all but a few drops' of his water.[34] Starkly contrasting with this lush atmosphere, 'the large city' to which the brothers are forced to relocate is rendered in thin,[35] threadbare sketches, amounting to nothing more than a vague locus of underhanded dealings, bouts of drunkenness, clerical corruption and labour exploitation.

If *The King of the Golden River* was composed with 'a little true Alpine feeling',[36] *A Christmas Carol* gestated while Dickens 'walked about the black streets of London, fifteen and twenty miles, many a night when all the sober folks had gone to bed'.[37] At once evoking and subverting the fairy-tale mantra 'once upon a time',[38] Stave One of this 'Christmas Carol in Prose' is set at a very particular point in time and space – 'Christmas Eve' in Victorian London's business district,[39] the City of London. Dickens's choice of the City as the opening locale forges an analogy between Scrooge and his immediate urban environment, illustrating what J. Hillis Miller has described as 'the metonymic reciprocity between a person and his surroundings',[40] which forms 'the basis for the metaphorical substitutions so frequent in Dickens's fiction'.[41] Much as the misanthropic, stingy Scrooge stands out as deviant among the good-natured Londoners of *A Christmas Carol*, so too did the City form an anomaly at the heart of Victorian London. Since the days of William the Conqueror, the formerly Roman square mile known as the City of London has preserved an administrative and managerial autonomy, closely linked with its growing wealth, and reinforced by the Roman walls that once surrounded it.[42] In the nineteenth century, as the local governments run by London's old parishes were gradually replaced by London-wide authorities, the City of London remained resolutely autonomous.[43] Then as now, its autonomy took the form of self-governance by the City of London Corporation, which consisted of members who were called the Aldermen. The Aldermen were elected by the City of London guilds, which dated back to the Middle Ages, and were also known also as the 'Livery Companies'.

Dickens regarded this arrangement as backward-looking and pernicious: 'I laugh at the sacred liveries of state, and get indignant with the corporation.'[44] In the first Stave of *A Christmas Carol*, he called attention to the discrepancy between the story's manifestations of the supernatural and the stuffy, unimaginative officials that lent this locale its character:

> Scrooge had as little of what is called fancy about him as any man in the City of London, even including – which is a bold word – the corporation, aldermen, and livery.[45]

Thus, the eruption of the supernatural into the fabric of the City in *A Christmas Carol* countervailed the pompous dullness and harsh business practices that Dickens associated with this area. One may interpret his decision to set his tale of fantastical transformations in the square mile as an assertion of the possibility of change in a London district weighted by the transformations that failed to occur in the lives of 'the multitude who are always being disappointed in the City'.[46] Setting *A Christmas Carol*'s first Stave in the City of London thus allowed Dickens to realize his aspiration of making London odd in an area that was acutely in need of such revelation.

Scrooge's redemption may be read accordingly as metonymic of the redemption of the City. From its outset, *A Christmas Carol* draws an analogy between the exceptionalism of the City and Scrooge's self-insulation. Not unlike the City with its autonomous laws, rituals and business practices that set it apart from the rest of London, Scrooge keeps his fellow Londoners at bay with his aggressive behaviour, offensive discourse, retiring habits and extreme miserliness. Dickens reinforces this analogy by likening one of the City's water-plugs to Scrooge: 'The water-plug being left in solitude, its overflowings sullenly congealed, and turned to misanthropic ice.'[47]

Consequently, when Scrooge reconnects with his fellow Londoners at the end of the book, he could also be said to reintegrate the City with the rest of London. His gift of a Christmas turkey is sent from the City to the Cratchit's lower-middle-class home in the North London area of Camden Town, which was 'a slightly dowdy, lower middle-class district' upended by the construction of the London and Birmingham Railway in the 1830s.[48] The distance between these locales is emphasized with his remark to the courier boy: 'Why, it's impossible to carry that to Camden Town. . . . You must have a cab.'[49] This resolution may be read as a redistribution of some of the City's wealth among the less affluent areas of London, reinforced by Scrooge giving Bob Cratchit a pay raise. This reading is supported by *A Christmas Carol*'s penultimate paragraph, in which Scrooge is no longer associated with the City in particular, but rather with London more broadly – he has become 'as good a friend, as good a master, and as good a man, as the good old city knew'.[50]

Where *The King of the Golden River* glorified sublime nature, *A Christmas Carol* revelled in the chaotic rhythms of London. 'They scarcely seemed to enter the city',[51] Dickens observes of Scrooge and the Ghost of Christmas Yet to Come, 'for the city rather seemed to spring up about them, and encompass them of its own act'.[52] The London of *A Christmas Carol* emerges as an actant in its own right, perhaps more so than the figures it encompasses. Cheek-by-jowl with avaricious business dealings in the Royal Exchange and pompous extravagance in Mansion House, the book showcases a gloriously personified London, teeming with energy so intense that its animation spills over and sweeps up churches and shop displays. The 'gruff old bell' of an ancient church-tower 'was always peeping slily down at Scrooge',[53] and it chimes the hour 'as if its teeth were chattering in its frozen head up there'.[54] The Spanish Onions on display wink 'in wanton slyness at the girls as they went by',[55] while 'the French plums blushed in modest tartness from their highly-decorated boxes',[56] and the Norfolk apples are found to be 'urgently entreating and beseeching to be carried home in paper bags and eaten after dinner'.[57] Everyday Londoners are so 'jovial and full of glee' that they seem to stamp the shop displays with their own corporeal and rather corpulent shapes:[58] the 'great, round, pot-bellied baskets of chestnuts' are 'shaped like the waistcoats of jolly old gentlemen',[59] much as the Spanish Onions are 'shining in the fatness of their growth like Spanish Friars'.[60] This superabundantly animate London accordingly strikes a different cord from the pathetic fallacy of *The King of the Golden River*, not least because of its excess – a lesser author might have contented himself with a single personified apple, but Dickens's metaphors spill over like the chestnuts in his baskets, 'tumbling out into the street in their apoplectic opulence'.[61] Orwell would identify this superabundance as 'the outstanding, unmistakable mark of Dickens's writing',[62] where 'everything is piled up and up, detail on detail, embroidery on embroidery'.[63]

A Christmas Carol has long been celebrated for its reworking of the countryside Christmas tale into a fantasy of Victorian London. One Edwardian critic believed that the 'strenuously modern' spirit of the tale was the key to its success: 'No picture of old times could have captured the imagination of contemporaries as did that fantasy on the actual London life of the day',[64] he contended. *A Christmas Carol* was 'the landmark for all our Christmas literature',[65] because it provided a welcome change from the 'description of country-house festivities',[66] and the 'antiquary's zest' that preceded it.[67] Present-day scholar Paul Davis has taken this argument one step further, claiming that 'in the 1840s, Dickens' story proved that urbanization had not destroyed Christmas',[68] that the spirit of 'the old Christmas could flourish in the new cities',[69] particularly in London. Ruskin, for his part, objected to Dickens's modernization of the Christmas tale: 'he had no understanding of any power of antiquity',[70] Ruskin griped, 'His Christmas meant mistletoe and pudding – neither resurrection from dead [sic], nor rising of new stars, nor teaching of wise men, nor shepherds.'[71]

Ruskin was being far from generous. *A Christmas Carol* may surely be read as valorizing the Christmas spirit, insofar as the essence of Christmas is defined by charity and forgiveness. Indeed, it readily invites Christian readings whereby Scrooge's tale allegorizes the fall and redemption of a sinner.[72] But Ruskin was right to point out that Dickens was not interested in the details and doctrines of Christian faith, Anglican or otherwise. *A Christmas Carol* has no truck with the core doctrines of the Magi or the crucifixion. This difference points up an essential divide between these two authors. Born to a stern Evangelical mother and engaged in a life-long struggle with his own faith, Ruskin refused to countenance the notion that genuine Christian faith might be experienced in any fashion other than an agonized grappling with the dogma of crucifixion and resurrection. For Ruskin, the 'total meaning' of Christianity was 'that the God who made earth and its creatures, . . . sustained the pain and died the death of the creature He had made'.[73] But for Dickens, born to parents 'not at all devout',[74] doctrine was not to be taken too seriously. The heart of Christianity was not the crucifixion, but the kindness and charity of Christ, whom Dickens envisioned as a kindly father figure with a soft spot for children, not unlike the image he cultivated of himself. Dickens's image of Christ was of a mentor, divinely sanctioned to 'teach men to love one another'.[75] Thus, *A Christmas Carol* was not merely about 'mistletoe and pudding' in Ruskin's derogative sense of hedonistic revelry. Rather, the mistletoe and pudding in *A Christmas Carol*'s are themselves imbued with religious significance. They are symbols of the redemptive power of sociability, charity and good cheer that, for Dickens, were the cardinal virtues of Christ(mas).

Dickens's and Ruskin's opposing attitudes towards fantasy were a natural outgrowth of their opposing views on Christianity – the former Ecumenical, the latter Evangelical. *The King of the Golden River* hinges on a reverse-transubstantiation whereby the flesh of the evil brothers petrifies into black stones that plunge into the roaring river, showing divine judgement to be swift, uncompromising and demanding of obeisance. In *A Christmas Carol*, the analogous transformation emphasizes the compassion and mercy of Christ, as Scrooge is spiritually transformed from a miser into a philanthropist, and the Ghost of Christmas Yet to Come, clearly the embodiment of death, stays its hand and diminishes into an everyday household object: 'It shrunk, collapsed, and dwindled down into a bedpost.'[76] Gluck's triumph is thus signified by the newly restored river; Scrooge's redemption by the newly purchased turkey.

A Christmas Carol is a confection, its supernatural tenor qualitatively different from Ruskin's tale, as can be gauged by Scrooge's reliance on household objects such as the bedpost to reassure himself that his ghostly experience was 'all true, it all happened'.[77] 'There's the saucepan that the gruel was in!',[78] Scrooge exclaims in rapture, 'There's the door, by which the Ghost of Jacob Marley entered!'.[79] It is almost as if, by becoming a bedpost, the Ghost of Christmas Yet to Come has endowed all bedposts, saucepans, doors and other household necessities with a phantasmagorical yet jubilant quality.

The fundamental differences between these two tales can be brought into sharper relief by comparing the first appearance of the King of the Golden River with that of the Ghost of Marley, because these two scenes share baseline similarities that can be used to tease out points of contrast. The King and the Ghost both manifest in household objects, the King in Gluck's golden mug, the Ghost in Scrooge's door knocker. They are both literally trammelled by wealth, the King having been transformed into the golden mug, and Marley having been clasped by a chain 'of cash-boxes, . . . ledgers, deeds, and heavy purses wrought in steel'.[80] Yet here the similarities end, for the golden mug signifies kingly treasures, whereas cash-boxes, ledgers and deeds denote affluence under a capitalist system, which was nowhere more concentrated in Victorian London than among the businesses and banks of the City.

The distinctions in function and availability between the mug in *The King of the Golden River* and the door knocker in *A Christmas Carol* are key to their symbolic significance. A mug is kept at home and used most often, if not exclusively, by its owner. A door knocker occupies the threshold between public and private space and is intended for use by outsiders seeking admittance. Ruskin's mug is handcrafted, and even within his pseudo-medieval fantasy world, it is considered 'old-fashioned',[81] underscoring Ruskin's implicit link between antiquity and enchantment. Scrooge's door knocker, in contrast, has 'nothing at all particular about' it.[82] Indeed, like a stage magician displaying the emptiness of his hat, Dickens pointedly shows that the knocker is fastened to its door with the same mechanism that one might expect of a knocker that is perfectly ordinary:

'screws and nuts that held the knocker on'.[83] These differences between Ruskin's mug and Dickens's door knocker chime audibly with a distinction that Tolkien made nearly a century later, between handcrafted items created at 'a time when men were as a rule delighted with the work of their hands',[84] and objects 'of mass-produced pattern' that were 'a product of the Robot Age'.[85] As suggested by the tenor of his remarks, Tolkien extolled the former and expressed 'a considered disgust' for the latter.[86] In stark contrast, Dickens revelled in the sheer plenitude and variety of off-the-peg objects that inundated London with the advent of mass-production. Door knockers in particular were an object of fascination: 'there is something in the physiognomy of street-door knockers',[87] Dickens asserted in one of his *Sketches by Boz* (1833–6), in the course of which he delineated 'all the most prominent and strongly-defined species' of door knockers.[88]

Ruskin's mug is not only handcrafted but a treasure worthy of a king, moulded of solid gold and crowned with a handle 'formed of two wreaths of flowing golden hair'.[89] It accordingly resembles the Holy Grail of Arthurian romance – it is a unique talismanic object whose primary purpose is to single out the worthy from those who are not, to identify a 'chosen one' who has exclusive rights to it. This one-of-a-kind treasure, destined for a single champion or a select few, which often inflicts dire punishment on any unworthy soul foolish enough to use it, has become a staple of Rural Fantasy. In a variety of permutations, one may recognize this talisman in the One Ring in *Lord of the Rings*; in Peter's sword 'Rhindon' in *Chronicles of Narnia*; in the *Sa'angreal* and variations thereof in Robert Jordan's *Wheel of Time* series (1990–2013) and in the lightsabers in the original *Star Wars* trilogy (1977–83). Whatever the overt intention of the author or director, such talismanic objects are underpinned by exclusionary assumptions about the superiority of some people to others.

Such talismans were almost entirely absent from the Urban Fantasy tradition until the late 1990s. In lieu of them, Urban Fantasy is obsessed with the natural extension of door knockers – namely, with doors, in a lineage that harks back further than *A Christmas Carol* to Dickens's 'moor eeffoc' experience, as he gazed at an oval glass plate embedded in a café door, with the words 'coffee room' embossed on it. Taking up this trope and adapting it to their purposes, the supernatural manifests in the eponymous Door in the Wall in Wells's 'The Door in the Wall' (1906) and it invades the London of *Neverwhere* in the character of 'Door', a girl whose family possesses the magical ability to open doors in London where none existed before. Dickens's Scrooge, Wells's Lionel Wallace and Gaiman's Richard Mayhew are all beholden to this threshold. Their journeys begin when they answer the call of supernatural London as it comes knocking at their door.

Where Ruskin emphasizes the preciousness of his mug, Dickens imparts a shabbiness to his door knocker. It has not been replaced in over seven years, and the door to which it is fastened fronts an inglorious house, 'a lowering pile of building up a yard',[90] which is 'old enough now, and dreary enough' that its door knocker must surely be equally dilapidated and worn.[91] By dint of this very dinginess, *A Christmas Carol* emerges as a communal, democratic, ready-to-hand fantasy, where enchantment suffuses London's bric-a-brac, touching all its objects with a ghostly light, but affording the greatest intensity to the drabbest of all. It is a fantasy geared towards inclusiveness, where even someone as surly, miserly, unimaginative and unpleasant as pre-reformed Scrooge might suddenly see a ghostly face in his door knocker, not because the door knocker is unique nor because Scrooge is extraordinary, but precisely because they are not. This insistence on the enchantment of the ordinary and the magic of the shabby forms the core of Dickens's romance of familiar things.

Indeed, the manifestation of Marley's face in Scrooge's door knocker ultimately leads to the restoration of the knocker's original, everyday function as a means of admittance into his home, across a threshold that is meant to be crossed. The symbolism of Scrooge's door knocker as the interface between Scrooge and London provides an objective correlative to his spiritual journey. Pre-reformed Scrooge slams the door on London and his fellow Londoners alike. He turns away his nephew Fred with an 'out upon merry Christmas!';[92] he chases off a carol singer with a ruler and he slams the door on his own door knocker and its apparition of Marley's face. He is a man who 'edge[s] his way along the crowded paths of life',[93] which, as Craig Buckwald suggests, evokes the image of 'him keeping to the edge of the sidewalk when he must venture out onto the London streets'.[94] Scrooge's redemption is accordingly signalled by his reparations to all the Londoners whom he had wronged. He is kind to a boy who is a variation on the carol singer; he promises to raise Bob Cratchit's wages, and he donates generously to the same portly gentleman whom he had rejected so scathingly in the first Stave. Most importantly, after turning Fred away from his counting house, he seeks admittance at Fred's door, asking with some trepidation: 'will you let me in, Fred?',[95] upon which Dickens assures us: 'He was at home in five minutes.'[96] Scrooge thereby invites back all the Londoners whom he had shut out, and is in turn invited back to the fold. The door knocker has thus done its office, as flagged up by Scrooge's exclamation on Christmas Day: 'It's a wonderful knocker!'.[97] He now confesses, 'I scarcely ever looked at it before',[98] promising to 'love it, as long as I live!'.[99]

A Christmas Carol thus closes with Scrooge's new facility for *looking* at London. Where once he edged along the London pavements, devoid of the barest touch of fancy, reformed Scrooge becomes a flâneur who takes pleasure in walking the streets of London and looking at both the cityscape and his fellow Londoners:

> The people were by this time pouring forth, as he had seen them with the Ghost of Christmas Present; and walking with his hands behind him, Scrooge regarded every one with a delighted smile.[100] . . .
>
> He went to church, and walked about the streets, and watched the people hurrying to and fro, and patted children on the head, and questioned beggars, and looked down into the kitchens of houses, and up to the windows, and found that everything could yield him pleasure. He had never dreamed that any walk – that anything – could give him so much happiness.[101]

The London of *A Christmas Carol* has remained as it was, but what has changed is Scrooge's ability to see it anew, refracted through the ghostly apparition of a face suddenly apparent in a door knocker. Hence the emphasis in this passage on scopic verbs: 'regarded', 'watched', 'looked down . . . and up'. Scrooge has discovered the romance of familiar things in London, and its concomitant revelation of the beauty that surrounds him. This revelation awakens his sociability and reconnects him with his fellow Londoners, from the hurrying pedestrians to the children to the beggars.

Scrooge himself thus becomes an oddity in the cityscape, an elderly man skipping and dashing in the streets with a youthful energy and childlike wonder. His newfound capacity to provoke others to do a double take, to look again and 'see the alteration in him',[102] brings him full circle to his creator, who sought to lend London 'an odd unlikeness of itself' and who had 'wept, and laughed, and wept again' in the streets of London as he composed his supernatural tale.[103]

'That magic lantern': Dickens's London nightscape

From his earliest sketches, Dickens's fantastical imagination fastened upon the London nightscape: its shadows, gloom, mists, indistinct shapes and fading echoes. As Matthew Beaumont puts it, Dickens's night city 'is a space of fantasy, one where "air-built castles" can be erected and maintained'.[104] 'But the streets of London, to be beheld in the very height of their glory, should be seen on a dark, dull, murky winter's night',[105] Dickens wrote in 'The Streets – Night' (1836), because then 'the heavy lazy mist, which hangs over every object, makes the gas-lamps look brighter, and the brilliantly-lighted shops more splendid, from the contrast they present to the darkness around'.[106] In London by night, he could deploy the romance of familiar things to its greatest effect, transfiguring not only the wholesomely familiar but that which is ugly and heart-breaking in its familiarity. Thus, like a fairy godmother of London, Dickens waved his pen and transformed street prostitutes into 'beautiful fairies',[107] and 'the dirty little fog-choked street over the way' into 'Fairy Land'.[108]

A pattern emerges from Dickens's written correspondences between 1843 and 1848 – the years in which he composed his five Christmas Books, out of which four were prose fantasies – that illustrates the extent to which his fantasy depended on the stimuli provided by London at night. As mentioned earlier, Dickens wrote *A Christmas Carol* while walking 'about the black streets of London, fifteen and twenty miles, many a night when all the sober folks had gone to bed'.[109] In Italy, struggling to compose the London-based fantasy that would become *The Chimes*, he complained that 'I seem as if I had plucked myself out of my proper soil',[110] and gave account that the church bells might 'clash upon me now from all the churches and convents in Genoa, [but] I see nothing but the old London belfry'.[111] 'I should not walk in them in the day time, if they were here',[112] he mused from Switzerland on his yearning for London's streets, 'but at night I want them beyond description'.[113]

Cut off for too long from London's streets at night, Dickens's powers of fantasy dried up. His mistaken notion that his fourth Christmas Book, *The Battle of Life* (1846), 'would be all the better, for a change, to have no fairies or spirits in it',[114] followed immediately upon his lament that the absence of his night walks in London made 'the toil and labour of writing, day after day, without that magic lantern [i.e. London] . . . IMMENSE!!'.[115] *The Battle of Life*, it should be noted, is widely regarded as the least of his Christmas Books,[116] and Dickens would come to regret his decision to forego 'the supernatural agency'.[117] By the time he began to contemplate his design for *The Haunted Man*, Dickens displayed an acute awareness that nocturnal London was the lifeline of his fantasy. Writing from Switzerland, Dickens knew he would need his magic lantern for the creation of the 'ghostly and wild' fantasy that was gestating in his mind.[118]

The Chimes, Dickens's second Christmas Book, opens with the proposition that 'there are not many people . . . who would care to sleep in a church'.[119] This proposition does not apply 'in the broad bold Day',[120] the narrator asserts, 'but it applies to Night' and 'must be argued by night',[121] when the church is 'wild and dreary'.[122] Viewed from the heights of a church steeple at night, London is imbued with magic and mystery, 'the smoking chimneys' and 'the blurr [*sic*] and blotch of lights' rendered in odd unlikeness of themselves,[123] 'all kneaded up together in a leaven of mist and darkness'.[124]

The Chimes tells the story of Toby 'Trotty' Veck, 'a ticket-porter' who ekes out a living by couriering letters across London but spends much of his time waiting 'just outside of the church-door . . . for jobs'.[125] He develops an abiding fascination with the chimes of this church, investing them 'with a strange and solemn character' that is borne out by his discovery that they are home to a myriad spirits who share the bells with 'gigantic, grave and darkly watchful' goblins.[126] Their church is never named, but the illustrations of Richard Doyle and Clarkson Stanfield clearly portray the then-newly rebuilt 'St Dunstan in the West on Fleet Street', in the western end of the City. Yet Doyle's and Stanfield's illustrations visibly conflict with Dickens's descriptions of the church as 'an old church',[127] crowned with a high steeple. The medieval church of St Dunstan in the West was indeed ancient, but the new church that replaced it in 1832, twelve years before the publication of *The Chimes*, was by no means old.[128] Neither the new church nor its predecessor were topped by a high steeple, rendering Dickens's specific attentions to the high steeple ascending from the church of *The Chimes* 'far above the light and murmur of the town' especially perplexing (Figures 1.1 and 1.2).[129]

Stephen Prickett dismisses this discrepancy between text and illustrations as evidence 'of the greater slackness of construction in *The Chimes*' when compared with *A Christmas Carol*.[130] But Dickens's written correspondence suggests otherwise. Upon receiving a draft of one of Doyle's illustrations, he found it 'so unlike my idea' that he requested it be done anew.[131] There is no reason to believe that such careful scrutiny was the exception rather than the rule, and that all the illustrations for *The Chimes* were not subject to similar supervision. Indeed, Jane R. Cohen suggests that such was Dickens's common practice: 'He usually inspected not only the final drawings, but the preliminary sketches as well, which he rarely returned without ideas for improvement.'[132] Prickett's contention that the incongruity between the verbal descriptions of the church and the accompanying illustrations of it was mere carelessness on Dickens's part therefore seems unlikely, particularly over such a crucial point as the prominent setting of *The Chimes*. One may therefore surmise that the discrepancy was a deliberate choice on Dickens's part.

This discrepancy may be read as the manifestation of a conflict between Dickens's political beliefs in modernity and progress, and his imaginative investment in the lost London of his childhood. In a piece titled 'Gone Astray' (1853), Dickens

Figure 1.1 'St. Dunstan in the West, Fleet Street', 1829, Drawn by Thomas Hosmer Shepherd, engraved by James Baylis Allen, published by Jones & Co, *London and Its Environs in the Nineteenth Century*, The British Museum, https://www.britishmuseum.org/collection/object/P_1880-0911-654 [accessed 16 May 2020].

recalled how he 'got lost one day in the City of London' as a child.[133] As he wanders about the City, he stops in his tracks before the old St Dunstan in the West: 'behold, I came, the next minute, on the figures at St Dunstan's!',[134] he declares breathlessly, 'Who could see those obliging monsters strike upon the bells and go?'.[135] These 'obliging monsters' were two life-sized wooden statues ensconced in an alcove of the medieval St Dunstan's, striking the bells with their rough-hewn clubs every quarter of an hour. They were removed with the demolition of the old church, giving way to a new St Dunstan's that was more architecturally sensible but considerably less arresting (see Figures 1.1 and 1.2).

Thus, when Dickens's imagination sought a London church into which he could unleash his own obliging monsters, his 'dwarf phantoms, spirits, elfin creatures of the Bells',[136] his mind harked back to the recently demolished St Dunstan's that had inspired his childish wonder. But for a writer like Dickens, who inveighed against social and artistic movements bent on 'cancelling all the advances of nearly four hundred years',[137] to privilege an old medieval church over its newer incarnation was to contravene his own political beliefs. The discrepancy between text and illustrations in *The Chimes* thus posed an

Figure 1.2 'St. Dunstan's in the West. Fleet Street' (new design), 1838, Drawn by Robert William Billings, engraved by J. Le Keux, in George Godwin and John Britton, *The Churches of London: A History and Description of the Ecclesiastical Edifices of the Metropolis*, vol. 1 (London: C. Tilt, 1838), (n.p., opposite chapter title 'St Dunstan's in the West, Fleet Street').

elegant solution, allowing him to conjure up the old St Dunstan's imprinted on his imagination while still retaining an image of the new. He thereby drew on the creative wellspring of London's past while deftly sidestepping an implicit endorsement of reactionism.

Dickens buttressed this narrative sleight of hand with more overt political statements, both fictionally within *The Chimes* and in his non-fictional commentary about the book. The 'Goblin of the Bell',[138] who secretly dwells in the titular Chimes and constitutes this Christmas Book's analogue for the Ghosts of Christmas Past, Present, and Yet To Come, provides a mouthpiece for Dickens's liberal-progressive views. 'The voice of Time . . . cries to man, Advance!',[139] the Goblin declaims, 'Time IS for his advancement and improvement; for his greater worth, his greater happiness, his better life'.[140] The Goblin likewise inveighs against reactionaries who lament 'for days which have had their trial and their failure',[141] pining for 'ages of darkness, wickedness, and violence'.[142] Dickens created a corresponding mouthpiece for such reactionary views, in the form of the odious 'red-faced gentleman' who gushes incessantly and at length on 'The good old times, the grand old times, the great old times!'.[143] As Dickens wrote to Forster, the red-faced gentleman was deliberately drawn in broad strokes to satirize 'a real good old city tory'.[144]

Compared to Dickens's full-length novels, *The Chimes* has been relatively neglected by critics, but there are several honourable exceptions. Michael Slater reads *The Chimes* as 'the most concentrated piece of socially committed fiction that he [Dickens] ever wrote',[145] noting especially its 'Chartist-style thunderings'.[146] Alexander Welsh observes that '*The Chimes* is nothing if not urban literature',[147] which in his interpretation of the book creates romanticized 'domestic havens' that foster 'the ideal of permanence'.[148] Barbara Hardy analyses the relationship between 'the dreaming state' and the 'social realities' that play off one another in *The Chimes*,[149] highlighting the book's self-reflexive ending. Jay Clayton interprets *The Chimes* as 'a powerful account of the confused affective response caused by the sound of pealing bells'.[150]

These important contributions redress the relative paucity of scholarship about *The Chimes*. But I would like to draw attention to a point that has been overlooked: it is not only the church, but London itself that remains unnamed for the better part of *The Chimes*. In relation to the old church and the chimes especially, London is quaintly referred to as 'the town' or 'the whole town'.[151] The proper name 'London' appears only thrice in the text, all three occasions close upon each other and in connection with the plight of Will Fern, a hard-up farm labourer who comes to London with his orphaned niece in search of honest work, but instead finds himself abused by a system that assumes poverty to be a mark of guilt. The MP Joseph Bowley explains that Will 'came up to London, it seems, to look for employment ... and being found at night asleep in a shed, was taken into custody'.[152] Will gives the same account from his own point of view, explaining that he arrived 'in London here' to look for a friend,[153] but having so far sought in vain, 'to-morrow will try whether there's better fortun' to be met with, somewheres near London'.[154]

Will Fern's struggles against poverty and prejudice served as a fictional rendition of 'the stern realities' to which Dickens alluded at the end of *The Chimes*.[155] A fatal combination of circumstances made the 'Hungry Forties', as the 1840s have been termed since 1904, a period of particularly acute labour depression, unemployment and famine.[156] In those turbulent times especially, the imprisonment of Will Fern for sleeping in a shed was well within the legal remit of the local magistrates, as the Vagrancy Act of 1824 outlawed 'lodging in any barn or outhouse'.[157] Dickens's outrage at such systemic injustices had reached a boiling point in the months leading up to the composition of *The Chimes*: 'I never go into what is called "society" that I am not aweary of it, despise it, hate it, and reject it.'[158] Accordingly, the named London of Will Fern is the London of social realism: it is an unfeeling city of destitution, want, oppression and conceit, on the verge of violent upheaval.

The unnamed London of the old church and its goblins, however, plays out on a different register. This alternative London is very much in keeping with Dickens's aspiration to give London 'an odd unlikeness of itself', a vision deftly achieved in *The Chimes* by striping London of its name, thereby quite literally estranging it from itself. Not unlike the London of *A Christmas Carol*, this London comes to life, literally as well as figuratively, through a transformation of objects commonly seen on the streets of the rainy capital:

> Wet days, when the rain came slowly, thickly, obstinately down; when the street's throat, like his own, was choked with mist; when smoking umbrellas passed and re-passed, spinning round and round like so many teetotums, as they knocked against each other on the crowded footway, throwing off a little whirlpool of uncomfortable sprinklings; when gutters brawled and waterspouts were full and noisy.[159]

This metamorphic cityscape takes on a life of its own with a series of wheezy metaphors, obstinate rain and uncomfortable sprinklings, a street that has throat and breath enough to choke, brawling gutters and noisy waterspouts, and umbrellas 'smoking' the mist and transmogrifying into teetotums as they knock against each other.

At the heart of this coughing and sputtering London rise the personified Chimes, first introduced by their refusal to be silenced or browbeaten:

> They had clear, loud, lusty, sounding voices, had these Bells; . . . fighting gallantly against it [the wind] when it took an adverse whim, they would pour their cheerful notes into a listening ear right royally.[160]

The Chimes are at their feistiest when they are called upon to help those in need: 'bent on being heard on stormy nights, by some poor mother watching a sick child, or some lone wife whose husband was at sea'.[161] They thus provide compassion for the dispossessed and the misfortunate that is sorely lacking from the 'realist' London that all too often turns a deaf ear to their music.

This reading of *The Chimes* as a tale of two Londons, the one realistic and dismal, the other fantastic and defiant, offers an alternative explanation to why the church is rendered simultaneously old in the text and new in the illustrations. Prior to its demolition, the medieval St Dunstan's was an increasingly obstructive protrusion into the hectic rhymes of Fleet Street, which was the centre of Victorian London's rapidly expanding news industry.[162] As described by Godwin and Britton, the church 'projected so far forward' that it became a hindrance to the 'countless throng of men, each intent upon his separate purpose' (see Figure 1.1).[163] The old St Dunstan's could thus be seen as a check on the heedless rush across the city, an arresting object that encouraged Londoners to pause and take stock of their fellow urbanites and their surroundings, as the young Dickens had done when he went astray. The new St Dunstan's posed no such obstruction – it was 'well arranged to suit its position',[164] as Godwin and Britton put it (see Figure 1.2). Yet by positioning his church indeterminately between the old and the new incarnations, Dickens endowed it with the touch of defiance that had characterized the medieval formation of St Dunstan's. Thus liminally positioned, the church of *The Chimes* emerges as an alternative locus to the callous views on time espoused by both the likes of the red-faced gentleman, who mindlessly extolls 'the good old times',[165] and the political economist Filer, who pronounces the poor to 'have no earthly right or business to be born'.[166] At once old and new, the church embodies a different timescape that inheres within London and defies the homogenization of governing powers. Its resistance to a unified temporality is made doubly potent by the paradoxes of text and illustration, which allow the church to elude even the strictures of consistent narrative. Its nexus of bubbled up time finds itself besieged by a rapidly modernizing city, but emphatically not with a view to valorizing the past. Rather, Dickens draws on the church as a pocket of time and space from which London can be re-envisioned as 'unlike itself' and thus reclaimed from the hands of the 'good old city tory' and his ilk,[167] where one may join the bells in 'fighting gallantly' against 'Wicked Cant'.[168]

'Abandoned and rejected things': Dickens's allegory

Dickens told the Earl of Carlisle that he had written *The Haunted Man* with the express intention of making the phantom 'allegorical'.[169] Ostensibly, the purport of its allegory is made plain in the story's frequent exclamation, which also closes the story: 'Lord, keep my memory green.'[170] *The Haunted Man* is thus, on its surface, a heavy-handed lesson on the importance of memory as 'the necessary basis of love and compassion in the human breast',[171] as Slater sensibly put it. Yet on a deeper level, this Christmas Book may be read as an allegory of the power of Dickensian fantasy. With this purpose in mind, some consideration may be warranted as to what Dickens meant by the term 'allegorical' in his 1849 letter to the earl.

Dickens was not prone to high-minded theorizing, but one context that probably informed his use of the term was an 1840 review of *The Old Curiosity Shop* (1840–1), written by the early-nineteenth-century essayist Thomas Hood midway through the novel's serialization. Hood was struck by the aesthetic composition of Little Nell's slumber in the eponymous Old Curiosity Shop:

> we do not know where we have met, in fiction, with a more striking and picturesque combination of images than is presented by the simple, childish figure of Little Nelly, amidst a chaos of such obsolete, grotesque, old-world commodities as form the stock in trade of the Old Curiosity Shop. . . . It is like an Allegory of the peace and innocence of Childhood in the midst of Violence, Superstition, and all the hateful or hurtful Passions of the world.[172]

Thus, for Hood, this scene presented an allegory of innocence besieged, conveyed through the stark contrast between Little Nell and the 'chaos of such obsolete, grotesque, old-world commodities' that surround her as she sleeps. His interpretation clearly struck a chord with Dickens, who thanked Hood for the review,[173] and paid it special tribute in his preface to the 1848 Cheap Edition of *Old Curiosity Shop*,[174] published contemporaneously with *The Haunted Man*.

Indeed, Dickens added several passages to the book edition of *Old Curiosity Shop*, one of which expressly described the same scene as an allegory:

> I am not sure I should have been so thoroughly possessed by this one subject [Little Nell], but for the heaps of fantastic things I had seen huddled together in the curiosity-dealer's warehouse. . . . As it was, she seemed to exist in a kind of allegory, . . .[175]

Dickens thereby confirmed Hood's reading of the book as an allegory, but his ruminations in the voice of the frame narrator Master Humphrey suggest a deeper allegorical meaning than the one mooted by Hood's review. Dickens's interpolated passage shifts the focus from Nell to the curiosities that surround her, asserting the power of 'fantastic things' to stimulate the imagination. 'Huddled together' in overflowing 'heaps', the curiosities appear to be endowed with a demonic energy that directs as well as spurs introspective thought, 'thoroughly possess[ing]' Master Humphrey's reflections.

Adorno elaborates on this theme in his own reading of *Old Curiosity Shop*, broadening the scope of its interpretation to suggest that curiosities afforded a redemptive vision that binds together the disparate fictions of Dickens's oeuvre:

> Dickens realises too that this thing world, at any rate the world of these abandoned and rejected things, contains the possibility of transition and dialectical redemption, and expresses this in a finer way than Romantic nature worship had ever been able to achieve.[176]

Building on Adorno's opposition between Dickens's 'thing world' and 'Romantic nature worship', one may observe that this redemptive vision was intensely concentrated on London. This reading is supported by Ian Duncan's observation that the 'spontaneous possession of the subjectivity by the world of objects',[177] specifically figured as a crowd in the ruminations of Master Humphrey, 'is particularly an urban effect'.[178] In this vein, Dickens's Old Curiosity Shop is expressly configured as a London phenomenon, indeed a London curiosity: 'The place . . . was one of those receptacles for old and curious things which seem to crouch in odd corners of this town'.[179] Beaumont has suggested that the London of the book emerges in its entirety as a grand curiosity shop, 'the lumber-room that is the city'.[180]

Dickens's fascination with curiosities, with material objects that had long since fallen into disrepair, was by no means limited to *Old Curiosity Shop*. Scrooge's door knocker may be regarded as another such object. An additional example may be found in Dickens's sketch, 'Meditations in Monmouth Street' (1836), set on one of the seven streets of Seven Dials in the then-notorious rookery of St Giles.[181] Three days after the publication of 'Meditations', Dickens would publish another sketch entitled 'Seven Dials' (1836), in which he described the area's 'streets of dirty, straggling houses, with now and then an unexpected court composed of buildings as ill-proportioned and deformed as the half-naked children that wallow in the kennels'.[182] But 'Meditations' eschews this journalistic realism in favour of the fanciful mode of Dickens's romance of familiar things. 'Meditations' reclaims the titular Monmouth Street, famous at the time for its second-hand clothes market,[183] as a space of fantasy where clothes spring to life. Taking its cue from the serialized version of Thomas Carlyle's *Sartor Resartus* (1833–4), which likened the second-hand suits of Monmouth Street to 'a Sanhedrim of stainless Ghosts',[184] Dickens's sketch resurrects the people from their discarded clothes. The narrator Boz, Dickens's famous alter-ego, lends a nobility and gravitas to Monmouth Street that is magnificently at odds with the grim reality of the area in the 1830s:

> We love to walk among these extensive groves of the illustrious dead, and to indulge in the speculations to which they give rise; now fitting a deceased coat, then a dead pair of trousers, and anon the mortal remains of a gaudy waistcoat, upon some being of our own conjuring up, and endeavouring, from the shape and fashion of the garment itself, to bring its former owner before our mind's eye.[185]

The second-hand clothes of Monmouth Street thus become alive enough to die, and it is the former owner who needs to be tailored to the clothes rather than vice versa. As Carey observed, this strategy of 'liken[ing] inanimate objects to people' and 'people to inanimate objects' was one of the hallmarks of Dickens's fiction.[186] What is striking about 'Meditations', however, is the extent to which these objects are worn out, the clothes threadbare and the people forsaken. As Beverly Lemire observes, by the beginning of the nineteenth century, 'pawning became less the norm for the genteel and respectable folk and was seen as the resort of the desperate, the indigent or the profligate'.[187] The loss of social status and self-esteem involved in the act of pawning one's own clothes comes to the fore when Boz resurrects the tragic life story of a single individual from 'a few suits of clothes' on which 'the man's whole life [was] written'.[188] These suits of clothes include 'a patched and much-soiled skeleton suit',[189] 'a long-worn suit . . . rusty and threadbare' and 'a coarse round frock, with a worn cotton neckerchief'.[190] They disclose the tale of a boy from a low-income family who matures into a dissolute and profligate young man and hardens into a violent criminal, meeting his end in 'A prison, and the sentence – banishment or the gallows'.[191] Dickens thereby constructs a deft analogy between discarded objects and lost souls. In so doing, he calls attention to the wider tragedy of 'the rising youth of London streets' through a fantastical vision of the city as an emporium of the cast-away,[192] the down-and-out, the threadbare and the re-circulated.

On its surface, the social purpose of 'Meditations' is entirely wholesome – it guides a middle-class readership into those areas of London that were beyond the pale of their personal experience, inviting them to identify with outcasts they were unlikely to ever add to their circle of acquaintances. Yet this sketch also discloses a more radical edge. The violent energy with which Boz invests the waistcoats that 'have almost burst with anxiety to put themselves on',[193] together with the marching rhythm that reverberates from the shoes as they alliteratively go 'stumping down the street' in Boz's fancy,[194] lend themselves to the imagining of a revolt or a strike. Beneath a cosy surface, this fantasy empowers the disenfranchised, conjuring up a vision of sartorial rebellion against the confines of the clothes shop that can easily shade into a rebellion against the confines of a society that forces people to pawn their own clothes to survive. As if to clinch this impression, this part of Boz's reverie ends with the suspicious glance of 'the policemen at the opposite street corner',[195] which resonated audibly with the jurisprudence of the times. The aforementioned Vagrancy Act of 1824, ratified twelve years before the publication of this sketch, stated that 'every person wandering abroad' and 'not giving a good account of himself or herself' could be lawfully committed to 'the house of correction'.[196] This act was aimed at beggars and prostitutes, but it implied that to be idle in Victorian London, to give oneself over to fantasy in the open streets, was an affront to the established order. Insofar as 'Meditations' is an allegory, it may be read as a challenge issued by daydreaming Londoners, particularly those audacious enough to daydream about unwanted objects and neglected people, to the conventional and legal norms of the ruling classes.

The Haunted Man: Dickens's metamorphic shadows

The Haunted Man opens with the 'gathering gloom and darkness' to which Dickens alluded in his letter to the Earl of Carlisle:[197]

> When it was just so dark, as that the forms of things were indistinct and big – but not wholly lost. . . . When people in the streets bent down their heads and ran before the weather. . . . When twilight everywhere released the shadows, . . . [that] fantastically mocked the shapes of household objects, making the nurse an ogress, the rocking-horse a monster, the wondering child half-scared and half-amused, a stranger to itself, – the very tongs upon the hearth, a straddling giant with his arms a-kimbo, evidently smelling the blood of Englishmen, and wanting to grind people's bones to make his bread.[198]

Inverting the Platonic model whereby shadows are pale imitations of ideal objects, Dickens's shadows wreak dazzling transformations on the objects that cast them. Fantasy thereby takes precedent over realism and latches onto 'the shapes of household objects'. These transformations thus distil the essence of nocturnal London's appeal for Dickens. The night makes 'the forms of things . . . indistinct and big', thereby allowing him to imagine these things anew and disclose in London 'an odd unlikeness of itself' too easily drowned in the glaring wash of daylight.[199] In *A Christmas Carol*, Scrooge's spiritual redemption endowed him with the ability to see London anew; in *The Haunted Man*, the eerie distortions wrought upon London by twilight make the child 'a stranger to itself'. In both Christmas Books, selfhood and city are mutually constitutive in a dialectic of sight and estrangement. One may further note that Dickens positions himself as both the master of the metamorphic shadows and 'the wondering child half-scared and half-amused', particularly through the detail of the nurse who morphs into an ogress. It has been well documented that Dickens's grotesque imagination was first awakened by the ghoulish tales of his nurse,[200] who nourished his childhood fancies on one 'diabolical character' after another.[201] Dickens's transformation of his nurse into an ogress was thus an apt tribute and an apt reprisal at one and the same time.

Dickens's romance of familiar things takes central stage in a scene between the titular haunted man – a renowned chemistry lecturer named Redlaw – and his ailing, impoverished student:

> The Chemist glanced about the room; . . . at those remembrances of other and less solitary scenes, the little miniatures upon the chimney-piece, and the drawing of home; – at that token of his emulation, perhaps, in some sort, of his personal attachment too, the framed engraving of himself, the looker-on. The time had been, only yesterday, when not one of these objects, in its remotest association of interest with the living figure before him, would have been lost on Redlaw. Now, they were but objects; or, if any gleam of such connexion shot upon him, it perplexed, and not enlightened him, as he stood looking round with a dull wonder.[202]

This passage is concerned with the vital role that material objects play in mediating – or obstructing – the relationships between people. The mental operation that fails Redlaw is precisely that of Dickensian fantasy, the ability to see human life projected from material objects. Redlaw loses this capacity as a result of the ill-advised bargain he strikes with his phantom double, which releases him of painful memories, but also divests him of imagination, compassion and sympathy. This premise foregrounds the connection that Dickens upholds more obliquely in his other fictions, between objects and sociability. Redlaw's maladroitness is stressed first and foremost in his incapacity to divine the social meaning of objects, to recognize in 'the little miniatures upon the chimney-piece, and the drawing of home' the student's 'remembrances of other and less solitary scenes', and still more in 'the framed engraving of himself [Redlaw]', a token of the student's 'emulation, perhaps, in some sort, of his personal attachment, too' to Redlaw himself.

Returning to Dickens's description of the phantom as 'allegorical' in his letter to the Earl of Carlisle,[203] *The Haunted Man* may be taken as an allegory of fantasy's capacity to heal what Boris Arvatov diagnoses as the 'rupture between

Things and people that characterized bourgeois society'.[204] Cut off from the Dickensian animation of objects, the world of things and people relapses into dead materiality. This denaturing is made explicit when the narrator remarks that Redlaw's 'cold, monotonous apathy, . . . rendered him more like a marble image on the tomb of the man who had started from his dinner yesterday'.[205] Thus, to lose one's ability to extrapolate the human from the object is to lose one's humanity and become object-like, 'a marble image on the tomb' of the man he once was.

This tale of the loss of fantasy and its tragic consequences is entrenched in the milieu of a rapidly modernizing Victorian London. *The Haunted Man* imparts a stronger sense of the capital as a metropolis than evident in Dickens's previous Christmas Books. The quaint 'town' of *A Christmas Carol* and *The Chimes* has become 'the great city' in *The Haunted Man*,[206] 'over-growing' and choking Redlaw's old college.[207] Where in *The Chimes* the church loomed 'far above the light and murmur of the town',[208] in *The Haunted Man* London's 'streets and buildings, . . . had been constructed above' the college,[209] reducing it to a picturesque 'nook . . . environed and hemmed in by the pressure of the town',[210] eliciting scarcely a passing glance of bemusement from 'the upper world'.[211] This shift in urban representation was reflective of real developments in Victorian London, as suggested by Dickens's particular reference to 'Oxford Street' in his letter to the Earl of Carlisle.[212] A year before the writing and publication of *The Haunted Man*, New Oxford Street was paved from Oxford Street to Holborn, providing a new and improved route that cleared much of the St Giles rookery which had featured in so many *Sketches by Boz*.[213] Dickens was acutely aware of the human cost of the slum clearance,[214] but he also took pleasure in the consequent improvement of the West End, recommending 'the tumult and bustle' of Oxford Street in an 1851 letter to a visiting friend.[215] Thus, while *The Haunted Man* never discloses the precise London location of Redlaw's college, dramatizing Dickens's contention in his letter to the earl that 'a little dreaminess and vagueness' was 'essential' to 'this sort of story',[216] Dickens integrated a series of contrasting images into the opening scenes of the book that reflected the changing character of his city. He juxtaposed the antiquated edifice, 'so remote in fashion, age and custom',[217] with the industrialized, expanding metropolis, which for all its innovations and sprawl, still cannot fully escape the phantom shadows of its gothic past.

Dickens's rendering of the London of *The Haunted Man* as a fast-growing metropolis intensifies the impact of Redlaw's blight upon the city. Redlaw emerges from his cloistered dwelling out into the London streets, infecting the Londoners around him with the curse of his forgetfulness. The sprawling metropolis thus denatures into a barren wasteland:

> The change he felt within him made the busy streets a desert, and himself a desert, and the multitude around him, in their manifold endurances and ways of life, a mighty waste of sand, . . .[218]

For Dickens, who poured into London 'all the dreaminess and all the romance with which he had invested Chatham [as a child]',[219] whose fantastical imagination restlessly craved 'the streets full of faces, at night',[220] and whose observant eye and sympathetic mind were insistently drawn to 'the multitude around him',[221] there was no more powerful emblem of the eradication of the human spirit than for a man to dismiss London and its teeming crowds as 'a mighty waste of sand'.[222] Redlaw's disavowal of the Dickensian fantasy of objects that once enabled him to relate to others by drawing imaginative connections between their cherished possessions and their emotional lives consequently involves a degradation of self and a threat to the city. It entails not only a loss of empathy and sociability, but also a loss of identity, culminating in Redlaw's exasperated cry: 'Give me back *my*self! [*sic*]'.[223]

Harry Stone has argued that in *The Haunted Man*, 'the allegory of character is intensified by the allegory of setting',[224] which together 'enforce the message . . . that good and evil are intertwined, that memories and feelings associate pain and joy'.[225] Stone therefore reads the settings as allegorical of the characters associated with them. 'The worn-out leftovers of Mr. Tetterby's defunct business' are thus interpreted as 'tokens of his ineffectual personality',[226] 'Redlaw's college' as 'a fitting representation of his mind'.[227] But I will take the opposite approach and read the characters as allegorical of their settings, specifically interpreting Milly Swidger, otherwise the book's least interesting character, as allegorical of London's capacity to heal itself.

Milly is the wife of the acting custodian of Redlaw's dwelling, and she takes on a similar custodial role with regard to London. Her role in the story is first intuited by her husband's odd remark that Redlaw's students may call her by any nickname to their liking, but that the most appropriate method would be to name her after the fashion of the bridges of London: 'London Bridge, Blackfriars, Chelsea, Putney, Waterloo, or Hammersmith Suspension'.[228] Curiously, two of the bridges on this list did not exist when Dickens wrote *The Haunted Man* in 1848. The construction of Chelsea Bridge was decreed by the 1846 Chelsea Bridge Act, but the bridge opened in 1858, whereas Putney Bridge only replaced Fulham Bridge in 1886.[229] Given Dickens's extensive knowledge of London and the frequency with which he crossed the Thames, together with the wide range of existing London bridges at the time, one may reasonably speculate that Dickens's inclusion of these two non-existent bridges was a deliberate artistic choice. This casual movement from the real bridges of London to non-existent ones and back again could therefore be read as another strategy of modulating the Victorian capital into a ghostly metropolis, akin to Dickens's deployment of twilight and shadows.

Milly's mooted nickname of 'London Bridge' bears strong allegorical significance that can be illuminated by reference to Dickens's traumatic past. Upon his father's imprisonment for debt in the Marshalsea Prison in Southwark, Dickens's family arranged for him to lodge nearby. His proximity to the Marshalsea allowed him to arrive at its gates early each morning and to wait for them to open 'in his lounging-place by London-bridge',[230] which he later crossed northward to Warren's Blacking factory. An orphan girl who worked for the Dickenses waited with him on some of these mornings, during which he would entertain her by 'telling her quite astonishing fictions about the wharves and the tower'.[231] For Dickens, this storytelling was more than a pleasant distraction – it was a strategy for survival. Dickens's greatest fear during his long days of menial labour at Warren's Blacking was that his imagination might wither away beneath the drudgery.[232] Thus, Dickens's 'astonishing fictions' were concocted to reassure himself that he was still in possession of his imaginative faculties.

This early form of storytelling could be regarded therefore as Dickens's first experiments in a potent blend of fantasy and realism spun out of ready-to-hand views and impressions of London – the London Bridge Wharf that adjoined the old London Bridge, and the Tower of London sprawling on the North Bank between London Bridge and Tower Bridge. In a variety of permutations, Dickens would develop this form of storytelling throughout his adult life. Thus, while Forster asserted that Chatham 'was the birthplace of his fancy',[233] one may posit that old London Bridge, together with the moor eeffoc café on St Martin's Lane, were the birthplace of his Urban Fantasy. The old London Bridge and its adjoining Wharf were demolished in 1832,[234] two years after the demolition of the old St Dunstan in the West. Likewise recalling his imaginative attachment to the old St Dunstan's, Dickens's fictions were drawn back to 'the innumerable veracious legends connected with old London Bridge',[235] particularly as his mind roved upon 'materials for a hundred ghost stories'.[236] Consequently, the London Bridge of Dickens's fictions could be read as a bridge between repressed memory and lived experience, the urban past and the urban present, and the fantastic and realistic dimensions of London.

It is highly fitting, therefore, that Milly becomes a symbolic 'London Bridge', a bridge between newly discontented Londoners who have fallen out with their loved ones due to Redlaw's pernicious influence. Milly sets out on Christmas Day to retrace Redlaw's journey through the city, restoring by her angelic presence the memories of all who have been infected. Heralding her journey, the dawn breaks out over London: 'the sun rose red and glorious, . . . the clear air . . . turned the smoke and vapour of the city into a cloud of gold'.[237] Yet the renewal augured by this imagery proves surprisingly qualified. Unlike Scrooge, Redlaw enjoys no redemptive walk through London, nor is there any guarantee that Milly's ailing brother-in-law will recover from his illness as Tiny Tim had done, or that the feral child who accompanied Redlaw will be saved from a life of wretchedness. Thus, the resolution of *The Haunted Man* strikes a decidedly bleaker note than the analogous ending of *A Christmas Carol*. This shift in tone accords with a change in Dickens's expressions of artistic intent: where the *Carol* was written to 'haunt their [his readers'] houses pleasantly',[238] *The Haunted Man* was pitched to a tune that was 'wilder and stranger'.[239]

Dickens's fifth and final Christmas Book thus ends not with daybreak but with twilight, ushering in the return of Dickensian shadows that 'once more stole out of their hiding-places, . . . gradually changing what was real and familiar there, to what was wild and magical'.[240] *The Haunted Man* thereby binds together all the elements that made Dickens the progenitor of the Urban Fantasy tradition: his conviction that London was a unique setting for fantasy that demanded specially tailored narrative strategies to accommodate the urban to the supernatural; his focus on the changes and modulations that rendered the familiar streets, bridges and domestic interiors of London shadowy and strange, giving the city 'an odd unlikeness of itself'; his transformation of household objects into enchanting fairy-tale figures, half-wonderful and half-menacing; and his vision of fantasy as a means by which the social bonds between Londoners were forged, maintained and articulated. It offers no permanent escape from grim realities, but it provides momentary respite in the dancing shadows on the walls that transform the 'real and familiar' into the 'wild and magical'.

'Coming from the Moon': The science fictionalization of Dickens's imagination

In the 1850s and 1860s, Dickens's imagination took a science-fictional turn, insofar as one follows Luckhurst's aforementioned definition of science fiction as 'a literature of technologically saturated societies'.[241] Luckhurst identifies the genre's full-fledged emergence in the 1880s, but he traces the roots of science fiction further back to the 1840s, when 'the railway produces new ways of reading and new forms of fiction'.[242] This view accords with Dickens's rapidly growing interest in trains from the late 1840s onwards. In *Dombey and Son*, he likened trains that arrive at their terminus to 'tame dragons',[243] and in 'Railway Dreaming' (1856), a railway journey from Paris to London takes on a more visibly science-fictional quality: 'for anything I know, I may be coming from the Moon.'[244]

The nascent generic differences embedded in this turn from draconic trains in *Dombey and Son* to a train journey returning from the moon in 'Railway Dreaming' are indicative of a wider shift in Dickens's style. Where goblins inhabit the church of *The Chimes*, a Megalosaurus waddles up Holborn Hill in *Bleak House*;[245] where *The Old Curiosity Shop* showcases 'wax-work figures',[246] *Great Expectations* is obsessed with automata;[247] where the ghost of Marley manifests in Scrooge's door knocker, the spectre of 'The Signal-Man' (1866) emerges from the red signal-light of a train junction.[248] Granted, to claim Dickens as a science-fiction author would be anachronistic, not least because the term 'science fiction' entered wide circulation only decades after his death. Yet this turn in Dickens's imaginative vision of London from gothic tropes to technological metaphors carries important implications for the Urban Fantasy tradition, particularly with regards to Wells. Thus, one may find antecedents to the solar apocalypse witnessed by Wells's Time Traveller in *The Time Machine* in the apocalyptic imagery of *Bleak House* and *Our Mutual Friend*, where the sky above London discloses 'the death of the sun',[249] or its impending demise 'as if it had gone out, and were collapsing flat and cold'.[250] Given that *Bleak House* was supposedly the most worn novel on Wells's bookshelf,[251] the similarity of these images to the solar eclipse in the farthest reaches of the future in *The Time Machine* may not be fortuitous.

Perhaps more than any other Dickens novels, *Bleak House* and *Our Mutual Friend* portray London as a cityscape of dark and alluring fantasy, 'a vampiric monster consuming the people who give it life',[252] as Rosemary Jackson put it. One may note, for example, Esther Summerson's vision of London as a cityscape burning with a Blakean intensity, no less magnificent for its promise of impending doom,[253] or Lizzie's aforementioned vision on the bank of the Thames.[254] Distilled narrative moments such as these may have spurred John Clute's contention that 'Dickens is central to the geography of sf',[255] particularly through 'the nightmarish, half futuristic, half chthonic London which figures in several of his later novels'.[256]

The emergence of a darker London in Dickens's fiction coincided with his editorship and management of his most famous periodical, *Household Words* (1850–9). From its inception, *Household Words* was conceptualized as a magazine about contemporary Victorian life, particularly life in London. As Catherine Waters observes, the Victorian periodical was inherently 'an urban form'.[257] *Household Words* was self-consciously so, an urban 'Miscellany' with a distinctively progressive ethos. Dickens's 'Preliminary Word' declared the periodical's intent to explore 'the habitations and the ways of life of crowds' and the technologies of transport that enabled these habitations and ways of life.[258] The metropolitan milieu, the ebb and flow of the city, thus became a source of exuberance and fuel for its weekly publication.

The working plans for *Household Words* capture this spirit aptly: 'No work succeeds without adopting one leading idea',[259] the notes observe, 'Let that purpose be the extraordinary condition . . . of the present day to be brought out by comparison with the past'.[260] *Household Words* would thus set forth 'the strongest arguments of social progress' with a view 'to keep the present alive'.[261] Yet its mission was to entertain as well as to instruct. 'KEEP "HOUSEHOLD WORDS" IMAGINATIVE!' was Dickens's 'solemn and continual Conductorial Injunction',[262] wedded to his determination that *Household Words* live up to its name and channel his vision for the romance of familiar things: 'familiar in their mouths as household words' was the running motto of the periodical, taken of course from Shakespeare's *Henry V*.[263]

Dickens actively solicited articles that educated the public about scientific processes and discoveries. He wrote to Michael Faraday to request his notes for his popular science lectures, for use in a series of articles in *Household Words*.[264] Faraday generously assented, and Dickens gave the notes to *Household Words* contributor Percival Leigh, chosen by Dickens for his 'practical knowledge of chemistry'.[265] Leigh proceeded to write two articles on their basis, 'The Chemistry of a Candle' (1850) and 'The Mysteries of a Tea-Kettle' (1850), both of which unfortunately proved dry and uninspired. But he had better luck with Thomas Stone, whom scholars believe to have been recruited by Dickens and his sub-editor W. H. Wills.[266] Stone contributed a piece on chemical reactions that depicted the reaction of potassium and water as 'the "death-fires" described by the Ancient Mariner, burning "like witches' oil" on the surface of the stagnant sea'.[267] This piece extolled Professor J. H. Pepper as 'an expert manipulator in such mysteries [of science]',[268] merging in his figure the images of scientist and sorcerer.

The same Pepper, in an interesting twist, would become famous for 'Pepper's Ghost', an optical illusion that he demonstrated for the first time on none other than an 1862 stage performance of Dickens's *The Haunted Man*.[269] Pepper later claimed that 'the late Charles Dickens, by his special written permission, allowed me to use [*The Haunted Man*] for the illustration of the Ghost illusion'.[270] Further evidence of this 'special written permission' has not survived, but one may imagine Dickens's enthusiasm at the prospect of his Christmas Book playing an integral role in a display of scientific wonder, not unlike a sophisticated magic lantern show, conducted by a scientist unusually gifted at communicating the marvels of science to an admiring public.

As argued in the earlier analysis of *The Chimes*, Dickens had always been a progressive writer. But the conceptualization, management and editorship of *Household Words* propelled him towards a more heightened awareness of the developing course of industrial modernity. In his new determination to instruct as well as entertain, he was no longer so quick to satirize priggish scientists as he did in *Pickwick Papers* (1836–7) and the *Mudfog Papers* (1838). This revitalized progressive spirit also fuelled his harangues across the pages of *Household Words* against reactionary idealization of the past. He thus launched a scathing attack on the 'Pre-Raphaelite Brotherhood', a coterie of poets and painters who advocated for and practiced a return to Medieval Pre-Raphael modes of art and writing, and were consequently endorsed enthusiastically by Ruskin.[271] Dickens found 'the great retrogressive principle' that governed their artistic expressions conducive to 'mean, odious, repulsive, and revolting' art.[272] 'We should be certain of the Plague among other advantages, if this Brotherhood were properly encouraged',[273] he remarked acerbically. This anti-reactionary piece resonated particularly strongly with Wells. In his own satire of conservatism, *Boon* (1915), Wells intimated that his clash with the literary establishment was 'the tail of that Pre-Raphaelite feud begun in *Household Words*, oh! generations ago'.[274]

Two regular contributors to *Household Words*, W. H. Wills and George Augustus Sala, co-authored an article in this vein, entitled 'Fairyland in 'Fifty-Four' (1853). The article reported on the new Crystal Palace that was being rebuilt in Sydenham after the Great Exhibition of 1851 had come to a close.[275] Although not written by Dickens himself, the article closely imitated his style and probably reflected his own views. Dickens had insisted a few months earlier that articles fall in line with 'opinions I am known to hold',[276] and Sala later testified to the seriousness of this policy.[277] One unintended consequence of this homogenization was Ruskin's mistaken attribution of this article to Dickens, spurring his diatribe against Dickens for 'calling the Crystal Palace "Fairyland"'.[278] Ruskin's mistake is pardonable, as 'Fairyland in 'Fifty-Four' was written very much in the vein of Dickensian fantasy. Guiding us into 'Fairy-land behind the scenes!',[279] the article revels in 'the mixture of familiar things with those that in their grandeur approach the sublime',[280] a clear and resonant echo of Dickens's romance of familiar things. In the same spirit as Dickens's articles, reviews and letters, Wills and Sala extol the new Crystal Palace only half in jest as 'a fairy palace with fairy terraces, and fairy gardens, and fairy fountains',[281] and are equally enthused by its 'marvels of what we may call scientific art'.[282] The article closes on an evocation of the liberal-democratic ideal, the hope that the Palace of the People may yet live up to its name:

> when its halls are thronged by thousands of every class and shade of class – when it shall be recognised as a palace and a pleasure ground for those whose lot it is to labour, as well as for those who sit in ivory chairs and ride in golden coaches.[283]

Then, the authors pause to reflect, 'do you think I shall have been guilty of exaggeration in calling it Fairyland?'.[284]

'Strange fancy and curious study': Dickens as midwife to the scientific romance

Would scholars be guilty of exaggeration in calling the Dickens world fairyland? Like many questions about Dickens, the answer is probably yes and no. Dickens never wrote a full-length fantasy novel like Miéville, or a full-length scientific romance like Wells. Those modes of writing had not yet crystallized in his lifetime. But one may argue that they would not have crystallized as they did if he had never put pen to paper. 'There is no getting away from the man who invented steampunk',[285] Clute once wrote, 'there is no getting away from Dickens'.[286] No author before Dickens had so successfully wedded the literature of the fantastic to the spirit of urban, liberal, progressive democracy. Dickens 'was always most accurate when he was most fantastic',[287] Chesterton observed, and one may add to this that he was also the most in tune with his convictions.

In his editorship and conduction of his final periodical, *All the Year Round* (ed. by Dickens 1859–70), Dickens became midwife to the fantasy novel in a more direct sense, and one which suggests a line of influence that runs from Dickens to Wells through Sir Edward Bulwer-Lytton. Modifying the article-based format that had governed *Household Words*, Dickens determined in *All the Year Round* on 'always reserving the first place in these pages for a continuous original work of fiction'.[288] He consequently solicited, accepted, consulted on and finally serially published Edward Bulwer-Lytton's oft-forgotten occult fantasy novel, *A Strange Story* (1861–2).

'Is there any possibility of your being induced to write a tale for All The Year Round?',[289] Dickens wrote to Lytton in 1860. Lytton proved amenable, and portions of *A Strange Story* made their way to Dickens's desk over the course of the following months. But Lytton was ill-at-ease regarding the suitability of his occult fantasy to the widespread readership of *All the Year Round*: 'much of what is called the supernatural is employed',[290] he wrote to Dickens, 'and my fear is that it may not exactly suit so wide an audience'.[291] A few weeks later he elaborated: 'The moral or phycological [*sic*] intention being necessarily subtle or somewhat bland, may not the whole awkward story appear, as addressed to a very popular class, like an appeal to superstitions.'[292] Lytton's words betray his prejudice towards this 'very popular class', disclosing his thinly concealed belief that supernatural literature should remain the remit of the upper classes. The middle and lower classes, so his argument went, lacked the sophistication necessary to pick up on subtleties, and were too susceptible to reading supernatural fiction as a confirmation of their superstitions. Given his own belief in occultism,[293] Lytton's position seems peculiar, but he evidently regarded his occultist interests as superior to the 'superstitions' of the popular class.

Dickens's response reflected his abiding belief in fantasy as a liberal-democratic genre:

> I believe that the readers who have never given their minds . . . to those strange psychological mysteries in ourselves, . . . will accept your wonders as curious weapons in the armoury of Fiction, and will submit themselves to the art with which said weapons are used. Even to that class of intelligence, the Marvellous addresses itself from a very strong position; and that class of intelligence is not accustomed to find the Marvellous in such very powerful hands as yours. On more imaginative readers, the tale will fall . . . like a spell. By readers who combine some imagination, some scepticism, and some knowledge and learning, I hope it will be regarded as full of strange fancy and curious study, startling reflections of their own thoughts and speculations at odd times, and wonders which a Master has a right to evoke.[294]

Dickens thereby expressed his conviction that fantasy literature had something to offer to everyone, from readers unaccustomed to intellectual thought, through 'more imaginative readers', to readers 'who combine some imagination, some scepticism, and some knowledge and learning', the last group overlapping precisely with the intended readership of Wells's scientific romances. Readers who were unused to speculative thought would still be stirred by the supernatural in literature, as Dickens argued, because 'the Marvellous' occupied 'a very strong position', fulfilling the cross-class need to 'submit themselves to the art . . . of strange fancy and curious study', or as Orwell and Miéville would later describe the effect of Wells's fantasies, to surrender to 'a sense of wonder'.[295]

Dickens thus championed the ability – perhaps even the right – of his readership to enjoy fantasy in a healthy and informed way. Claims of a similar tenor had been made on behalf of traditional fairy tales,[296] but one would be hard-pressed to find precedent among nineteenth-century thinkers for this vindication of a new full-length serialized fantasy novel. Dickens's publication of *Strange Story*, among the first full-length occult fantasy novels in the history of British literature, together with his championship of the readers of *All the Year Round* as a suitable audience for this fantasy, may thus be added to the myriad respects in which he was a revolutionary figure.

In the months leading up to the serialization of *A Strange Story*, Dickens offered Lytton several suggestions reminiscent of the strategies he deployed in his own urban fantasies. Twelve years after he told the Earl of Carlisle that the phantom out of Oxford Street necessitated 'the heaping up of that quantity of shadows',[297] Dickens wrote to Lytton with a similar urban metaphor: 'a serviceable concession to your misgiving',[298] he suggested, would be to choose a title 'off the stones of the gas-lighted Brentford Road'.[299] He further proposed that 'there should be no title for the town',[300] recalling his own London 'town' in *The Chimes*.[301] Dickens also made another, seemingly minor suggestion 'that after the title we put the two words – A ROMANCE'.[302] Lytton did not follow Dickens's advice in this instance and *A Strange Story* was published without the proposed subtitle. But Dickens's words may have continued to reverberate as Lytton was at work on his next fantastical novel, *The Coming Race* (1871), often credited as one of the first scientific romances in the English language and a direct influence on Wells.[303] Decades before Wells settled on the term 'scientific romance',[304] Lytton defined *The Coming Race* as 'perhaps a romance but such a romance as a Scientific [sic] amateur . . . might compose'.[305] Lytton might not have had Dickens's letter in mind when he wrote this description, though it is additionally telling that one of the earliest recorded uses of the term 'scientific romance' can be found in an 1866 popular science article in *All the Year Round*.[306]

Notwithstanding, the connective thread that this chain of events suggests between Dickens, Lytton and Wells might be entirely fortuitous. But Wells's contemporaries believed otherwise. Wells recalled with mixed feelings that 'In the course of two or three years I was welcomed as a second Dickens, a second Bulwer Lytton and a second Jules Verne.'[307] The extent to which this was the case will be the subject matter of the next chapter.

2

The Martian on Primrose Hill
Wells's scientific romances

An invention: Wells and the classification of fantasy

> Following in the wake of the sciences for half a century is a new species of literary work, which may be called the quasi-scientific novel.... The new novel is not content with presenting living embodiments of truth, but is fain to make guesses at the future. It is as yet experimental, and is quite too young to have produced an enduring masterpiece.... It is hopelessly doomed, not more by its lack of artistic breadth of treatment than by its slipshod style, which betrays all the haste of the daily 'leader' to get into type.[1]

Thus an anonymous critic in a review of Wells's *The War of the Worlds*. By then, Wells had already published *The Time Machine*, *The Island of Doctor Moreau* (1896) and *The Invisible Man* (1897) and was well on his way to proving irrefutably that the reviewer's own 'guesses at the future' fell short of the mark. But although the review failed to recognize *War of the Worlds* as the 'enduring masterpiece' it was to become, it does cast a curious light on the intellectual climate of the time. Its fatalistic tone, declaring the nascent genre of science fiction (as it would come to be known) 'hopelessly doomed', coupled with its undisguised condescension towards the genre's 'slipshod style' and its affinities with 'the daily "leader"' – a thinly guised snub at its popularity and widening appeal – forcibly testify to the degree to which the fantastic became a controversial issue at the close of the nineteenth century. Above all, it had become an issue of class, as it underwent intense 'classification' in the double sense of the term.

This chapter examines the development of the Urban Fantasy tradition in turn-of-the-century Britain. It argues that Wells's scientific romances carried on the Dickensian mode of socially engaged, liberal-progressive London fantasies, adding a pseudo-scientific rationale to the Urban Fantasy tradition and expanding its scope into deep time and deep space. The chapter reflects on Wells's developing attitudes towards turn-of-the-century London and his refractions of these views through the prism of the urban fantastic.

The 1870 Education Act, which established compulsory education for children and youth in the UK, led to a rapid increase in the rates of literacy among the new generation of working classes that were entering adulthood in *fin-de-siècle* Britain.[2] Historians of publishing identify the growth of this lower-income readership as a key factor in the disappearance of the stately 'triple-decker novel', the three-volume hardcover in which Victorian fictions were published after – and sometimes simultaneously with, or in lieu of – their serial publication.[3] Dickens's fictions were the exception to this rule in that they were reissued in 'cheap editions',[4] but for the most part, the early to mid-nineteenth-century novel was a hefty, formidable, luxury good, unaffordable to the average Briton, and designed to transmit a feeling of gravitas. The change in format from the triple-decker novel to a low-priced one-volume edition around the century's final decade led in turn to a change in publishers' expectations from new British fiction. Book publishers and editors of periodicals began to encourage authors to produce shorter and more fast-paced novels and pithy short stories.[5] It was, as Wells put it, 'an extraordinarily favourable time for new writers'.[6] Turn-of-the-century Britain marked the apex of the magazine age and the heyday of the short story.

In the 1840s, Dickens's Christmas Books had established a form of London-based fantasy that was compact and full of action and movement, geared towards daily life in Victorian London and especially tailored for a wide audience of all classes.[7] They were therefore ideally suited as models for fantasists responding to the new demands of the publishers and the public. Thus, fantasists as diverse as H. Rider Haggard, Robert Louis Stevenson and of course, Wells himself, all acknowledged Dickens's profound influence at a time when the literary fantastic flourished as never before.[8] Dickens's concern in the middle of the nineteenth century lest Britain become 'a nation without fancy' proved unwarranted by the century's end,[9] as the nation produced Stevenson's *The Strange Case of Dr Jekyll and Mr Hyde* (1886), Haggard's *She* (1886–7), Oscar Wilde's *The Picture of Dorian Gray* (1890), George Griffith's *The Angel of the Revolution* (1893), George MacDonald's *Lilith* (1895) and five of Wells's scientific romances and one of his supernatural fantasies.

This flourishing of fantasy literature aimed at a new reading public led to a backlash from the literary establishment, which derived in part from what Carey has theorized as intellectuals' 'hostile reaction' to this 'unprecedently large' readership.[10] Fantasy literature bore the brunt of their hostility, as the turn of the century saw an increasing polarization between 'highbrow' and 'lowbrow' literature, often taken to be synonymous with 'realism' and 'romance'. By this time, the process that had begun in the late 1830s, whereby the term 'romance' shifted from a label for historical romances in the vein of Sir Walter Scott to stories that 'deal in magic' and 'invest humanity with supernatural powers',[11] was fairly complete: reviews more or less took for granted that the romance was a genre that dealt in 'stories of the Impossible'.[12] Hence, when Dickens suggested to Lytton in 1861 that he subtitle his *Strange Story* as 'a romance', he was flagging its status as a fantasy. By 1887, Andrew Lang declared that 'in English and American journals and magazines a new Battle of the Books is being fought':[13]

> On one side, we are told that accurate descriptions of life as it is lived, with all its more sordid forms carefully elaborated, is the essence of literature; on the other, . . . that the great heart of the people demands tales of swashing blows, of distressed maidens rescued, of 'murders grim and great', of magicians and princesses, and wanderings in fairy lands forlorn.[14]

The very fact that 'the great heart of the people' demanded it was a black mark on fantasy literature for the more supercilious reviewers. An article in the *Dundee Courier & Argus* excoriated 'the more sensational caterers for the people in literature' for being 'quick to profit by the newly-aroused interest in the supernatural'.[15] A review in the *Pall Mall Gazette* cautioned against 'the sensational apologue' made fashionable by *The Strange Case of Dr Jekyll and Mr Hyde*,[16] regarding this new vogue as 'a path which skirts so perilously near the verge of literary vulgarity'.[17] *The Morning Post*'s review of *Dracula* (1897) remarked pointedly that 'some may regret that Mr. Bram Stoker should have employed his remarkable gifts in this particular field'.[18]

Even when they were more sympathetic, late-Victorian reviews often dismissed prose fantasies as 'inventions' not to be taken too seriously. The *Birmingham Daily Post* claimed that 'we only smile in the presence of Mr. Jekyll and Mr. Hyde, for we know they are a mere clever invention'.[19] *Blackwood's Edinburgh Magazine* remarked with more than a touch of condescension that 'invention he [Haggard] has of the most robust kind, . . . which probably impresses the masses more than the most poetic fancy'.[20] MacDonald conversely attempted to reclaim a place for fantasy as an edifying, highbrow genre by distinguishing it from 'mere inventions'.[21]

Given the critical traction of the term 'invention' across the literary debates of the time, it was surely not coincidental that the first volume editions of Wells's

The Time Machine were subtitled '*An Invention*'. As J. R. Hammond observes, the subtitle alludes to both the invention of 'the time machine itself as an artefact' and to 'the story as a fictional creation'.[22] Even before the publication of the first book editions, while *The Time Machine* was being serialized in *The New Review* (January–May 1895), Wells made the same gesture by titling the first chapter 'The Inventor',[23] and emphasizing that the Time Traveller excelled in the invention of patents and stories alike. In both the serial and the book versions, the Time Traveller refers to his Time Machine as 'my invention',[24] he reflects that 'I am naturally inventive',[25] and even admits to his guests at the conclusion: 'I cannot expect you to believe it [his tale of the future]. . . . Consider I have been speculating upon the destinies of our race[26] until I have hatched this fiction.'[27]

The Time Machine accordingly calls attention to its own ontological status as a fiction, or an invention. In this respect, it is not far from *A Christmas Carol*, where Scrooge tells the Ghost of Marley that he need but swallow a toothpick 'and be for the rest of my days persecuted by a legion of goblins, all of my own creation'.[28] Both fantasies thereby assumed an oppositional stance to the line taken up by MacDonald,[29] and later by Tolkien and Lewis, whereby supernatural fiction must justify itself by immersion in its fantasy world 'that produces . . . Secondary Belief',[30] with 'every precaution . . . taken never to break the spell'.[31] Contrary to the Rural Fantasists who aspired to 'Sub-creation',[32] Dickens and Wells shared an ethos of invention, defined by the *OED* as 'the devising of a subject, idea, or method of treatment' from materials ready to hand.[33] Thus, much as the city invents itself from the raw components of its immediate environment, so too does Urban Fantasy.[34]

The self-reflexivity of *The Time Machine* comes to the fore in one of the Time Traveller's most interesting commentaries:

> In some of these visions of Utopias and coming times which I have read, there is a vast amount of detail about building, and social arrangements, and so forth. But while such details are easy enough to obtain when the whole world is contained in one's imagination, they are altogether inaccessible to a real traveller amid such realities as I found here.[35]

This passage alludes to three key Utopian fictions of the late nineteenth century. First, Edward Bulwer-Lytton's *The Coming Race*, which as discussed at the end of the previous chapter was Lytton's next fantastical novel after *Strange Story*. Second, Edward Bellamy's *Looking Backward: 2000–1887* (1888) and third, William Morris's book-length response to *Looking Backward*, published two years later, *News from Nowhere* (1890). These three books were vastly different in the Utopias they envisioned and the ideological intent underpinning them, but they shared a common denominator in their method. They were fictions of the 'Utopian Imagination',[36] in Fredric Jameson's phrase, denoting Utopian literature that focuses its creative energies on fulfilling 'the Utopian wish',[37] the fully realized vision of an ideal world.

The Time Machine exposes the fallacy of the Utopian Imagination, suggesting in the passage quoted before that its drive to detail every aspect of 'the whole world' only underscores the Utopia's unreality. The account of a 'real' journey into the future would be fragmentary and incomplete, because (to use my own metaphor) if the past is a foreign country, then the future is a foreign planet. Thus, in the spirit of invention rather than sub-creation, the Time Traveller struggles to piece together the meaning of the future world in which he finds himself stranded, an agonizing and provisional process that strikes him rather like the process of decoding 'an inscription, with sentences here and there in excellent plain English, and, interpolated therewith, others made up of words, of letters even, absolutely unknown'.[38] 'I had no convenient cicerone in the pattern of the Utopian books',[39] he asserts pointedly, alluding to the sanguine guides who provided elaborate explanations to protagonist and reader alike in the Utopian books of Lytton, Bellamy and Morris. The Time Traveller is an inventor rather than a cicerone, offering only the working hypotheses of a scientist, rather than the perfected pitch of a guide. 'My explanation may be absolutely wrong',[40] he readily admits, but 'I still think it is the most plausible one.'[41]

The Time Machine targets *The Coming Race* in particular, by crafting a vision of the future that initially resembles Lytton's Utopia, only to gradually peel away the Utopian surface and reveal an increasingly darker dystopia.[42] *Coming Race* centres on a race of super-powerful beings called the 'Vril-ya' who live in underground cities but are expected to inherit the earth from the human race in due course. Perhaps unsurprisingly for a Utopia conceived by a bona fide baron, Lytton's society of Vril-ya resembles most visibly a polished aristocracy that conducts itself with 'exquisite politeness and refinement of manners'.[43] Lytton thus implied that the ills of humanity derived from the wane of feudal aristocracy and the rise of modern democracy, the latter of which the Vril-ya dismiss as 'one of the crude and ignorant experiments which belong to the infancy of political science'.[44]

When Wells's Time Traveller first arrives in the far future, he entertains the notion that humanity has evolved into creatures not unlike Lytton's Vril-ya: 'inhuman, unsympathetic, and overwhelmingly powerful'.[45] But these expectations are dashed by his first encounter with the 'Eloi',[46] a species that resembles the Vril-ya in their hairlessness, vegetarianism and aversion to darkness. Yet where the Vril-ya's aristocratic lifestyle led to the perfection of their species, the Eloi illustrate the opposite point: 'Under the new conditions of perfect comfort and security, that restless energy, that with us is strength, would become weakness.'[47] Thus, 'a real aristocracy, armed with a perfected science' would gradually decline into puerile imbecility.[48] Wells clinched his parody of *The Coming Race* with a final twist: where the Vril-ya will emerge triumphant from their underground cities to claim their rightful place as the new rulers of the surface, the Eloi cling to a pitiful existence on the surface as 'mere fatted cattle',[49] with no better prospects than to satiate the carnivorous appetites of the subterranean Morlocks – descendants of the working classes who devolved over countless generations due to the terrible exploitation of their labour by the Eloi's ancestors – who now gleefully devour the Eloi, in a rather gruesome staging of post-human class revenge. Thus, if *Coming Race* is a glorified hymn to aristocracy, *The Time Machine* responds to it with a cautionary tale against the dire consequences of class stratification.

In the fullness of time, Wells would become a utopianist himself, but his turn towards utopianism appears to have been a matter of self-imposed necessity rather than personal inclination. As the storm-clouds of the Great War gathered over Britain in the first decade of the twentieth century, and still more in the war-torn world of 1914–45, Wells hardly felt justified in continuing to write scientific romances: 'The world in the presence of cataclysmal realities has no need for fresh cataclysmal fantasies.'[50] But when his own inclinations were consulted, he gave account that 'I have a natural horror of dignity, finish and perfection'.[51] Thus, until the upheavals of the twentieth century wrought a change of heart, he maintained that the task of fiction was not to present blueprints of an ideal world, but to generate ideas and stimulate speculation, to offer 'comments and enhancements of the interest of life itself'.[52] In this, he surely recalled Dickens's avowal 'to bring into innumerable homes, from the stirring world around us, the knowledge of many social wonders, good and evil'.[53] The difference being that the knowledge Dickens sought to impart pertained mainly to the present day, whereas Wells was equally fascinated by the unknown vistas of deep time and deep space. Across the gamut of his scientific romances, Wells grappled with the scientific discoveries of his day that revealed an earth that was 'almost certainly more than 20,000,000 . . . years [old]' and 'a dead and empty universe' that was oddly conflated at times with 'the great vale of London spreading wide and far'.[54]

Credible and sober: Wells's fantasies of the commonplace

Echoing Dickens's romance of familiar things, Wells declared, 'I do seek . . . for the truth and beauty of things'.[55] Wells's 'gift of seeing things afresh, as though no one had ever seen them before',[56] as Arnold Bennett put it, emerged from his compounds of realism and fantasy. As Simon J. James observed,

> H. G. Wells was not the first English writer to produce fantastic fiction, but his pre-eminent success in the genre owes much to the way in which he melds with the fantastic material details of the actual.[57]

Wells thereby took up Dickens's endeavour to fuse 'the graces of the imagination with the realities of life',[58] but he developed a different narrative strategy for this amalgamation. The majority of Dickens's fictions were not overtly supernatural, but delighted rather in the fantastical imagery evoked in a figure of speech, as for example in *Our Mutual Friend*, where Mr Lammle pours himself a drink like a 'dark lord engaged in a deed of violence with a bottle of soda-water'.[59] Whereas Wells's 'method',[60] as he himself termed it, consisted of

> bringing some fantastically possible or impossible thing into a commonplace group of people, and working out their reactions with the completest gravity and reasonableness.[61]

Thus, Wells naturalized his fantastical premises through the realistic responses that they elicited from ordinary people. In *War of the Worlds*, for example, as news of the imminent Martian invasion reaches the ears of everyday Londoners, one of the fleeing news vendors takes the time to make a profit off of the crisis, 'selling his papers for a shilling each as he ran'.[62] In *Invisible Man*, the Sussex villagers respond to the revelation of Griffin's invisibility as one might expect of them: 'a crowd of perhaps forty people, . . . swayed and hooted and inquired and exclaimed and suggested'.[63]

In Wells's scientific romances, the realism invested in the responses of everyday Englishmen to the fantastical premise is compounded by the carefully unsentimental narration. Thus, the Time Traveller recounts that 'the peculiar sensations of time travelling' were 'excessively unpleasant';[64] the narrator of *War of the Worlds* remarks tersely of a woman sprawled nearby that 'she seemed asleep, but she was dead',[65] and the frame narrator of 'The Door in the Wall' reports with equal dispassion on the death of his friend: 'They found his body very early yesterday morning'.[66] Wells called attention to this narrative strategy in the frame story of *The Time Machine*, where the first-person narrator remarks of the Time Traveller's tale: 'The story was so fantastic and incredible, the telling so credible and sober.'[67] He thus inverted Dickens's 'manner of stating the truth' by way of 'fanciful treatment'.[68] For Wells, the crux of the story was the matter-of-fact stating of the fantastic.

Wells accordingly took issue with the fantasies of his time – 'the immature fantastic',[69] as he termed them – for their tendency to offer escapism and thereby serve the interests of the status quo. 'Anyone can invent human beings inside out or worlds like dumb-bells or a gravitation that repels',[70] he scoffed. At its worst, romance became a pleasant diversion for 'that tired giant, the prosperous Englishman' who 'wants to dream of the bright, thin, gay excitements of a phantom world'.[71] In the serialized version of *War of the Worlds* (April–December 1897), such 'bright, thin, gay excitements' became the target of Wells's satire, as the narrator contrasts his sombre narrative of the Martians' destruction of England with a hypothetical tale spun by 'our new romance writers'.[72] '[W]hat a fine figure they could have made of my sister-in-law',[73] the narrator muses, but his mind and pen are too preoccupied by 'the Martians, ... and the far reaching desolation and panic they created'.[74] Wells thereby followed his own injunction 'to keep everything else [except the fantastical premise] human and real'.[75] 'How would you feel and what might not happen to you' was for Wells 'the typical question'.[76]

Thus, in Wells's hands, the Urban Fantasy tradition moved from the realm of supernatural Christmas Books and Gothic London nightscapes into what he termed the 'field of scientific romance with a philosophical element'.[77] Yet Wells carried on Dickens's core mode of a fantastical yet materially grounded engagement with London, raising topical social issues through fantasies that were deeply imbricated in the London milieu. Also like Dickens, Wells crafted his fantasies into a source of oppositional values. What Dickens described as '*Carol* philosophy, ... sharp anatomization of humbug',[78] became, for Wells, 'his role as the free citizen of a new world',[79] namely 'to think, criticise, discuss, and suggest',[80] in the spirit of 'antagonism to personal, racial, or national monopolisation'.[81] Accordingly, where Dickens's fictions targeted Victorian institutions and remedial social ills, Wells targeted habits of mind and entrenched social structures, prominent among them the ossified class system of *fin-de-siècle* Britain.

The end is nigh: *The Time Machine*, *A Christmas Carol* and late-Victorian London[82]

The ways in which Wells carried on and modified the Urban Fantasy tradition from its Dickensian origins can be further illustrated by way of comparison between *The Time Machine* and *A Christmas Carol*. The two books share some interesting similarities: they are among the shortest of their authors' book-length fictions, they were both written in a flurry – *A Christmas Carol* in two months, *The Time Machine* in two weeks – they are set predominantly in London (the former in the City of London and Camden Town, the latter in a post-urban Richmond and the South Kensington area), both hinge on time travel, and both trace the journey of one man through time in fantastical circumstances. Likewise, in both stories, the flicker of London in and out of existence serves as the concrete manifestation of time travel. In *A Christmas Carol*, 'the city had entirely vanished' as Scrooge journeys back to his past and it 'spring[s] up about them' when he is led into the future.[83] In *The Time Machine*, the Time Traveller similarly sees the 'splendid architecture' of future London spring up before him and then fade away as if 'built of glimmer and mist' and upon his return he recognizes 'our own petty and familiar architecture'.[84]

In the frame narrative of *The Time Machine*, the Time Traveller and the frame narrator have constant recourse to the textures of material objects to validate what seems like an impossible event. Not unlike Scrooge who verified that 'it's all right, it's all true, it all happened' by recourse to the material evidence of 'the saucepan that the gruel was in!',[85] when the Time Traveller is seized by a spasm of self-doubt, both he and the frame narrator regain their faith in his story by interacting with the bedraggled and besmeared physicality of the time machine:

> There in the flickering light of the lamp was the machine sure enough, squat, ugly, and askew; . . . Solid to the touch – for I put out my hand and felt the rail of it – and with brown spots and smears upon the ivory, and bits of grass and moss upon the lower parts, and one rail bent awry.
> The Time Traveller put the lamp down on the bench, and ran his hand along the damaged rail. 'It's all right now,' he said. 'The story I told you was true.'[86]

Indeed, *The Time Machine* appears in one instance to directly allude to *A Christmas Carol*, by way of Scrooge's iconic cries, 'humbug, I tell you! humbug!'.[87] In the preliminaries to – and immediate aftermath of – the Time Traveller's experiment with the prototype of the time machine, his guests express their scepticism: the Psychologist declares that 'it's all humbug',[88] and the Medical Man enquires doubtfully: 'is this a trick – like that ghost you showed us last Christmas?'.[89] Given Wells's recollections of 'a complete illustrated set of Dickens [in his uncle's house] which I read in abundantly',[90] it seems probable that he was familiar with *A Christmas Carol* and that the suggestiveness of a 'Christmas ghost' was more than coincidence. In the same vein, the Time Traveller, the Morlocks, the Time

Machine and its prototype are all respectively likened to 'a ghost',[91] 'ghosts',[92] and a 'phantasm'.[93] These, too, may be subtle allusions to the *Carol*.

David Y. Hughes has analysed these references to ghosts and Christmas in *The Time Machine* as allusions to a ghost story by Grant Allen,[94] Wells's older contemporary, whose speculative fictions were widely popular with the Victorian public.[95] The ghost story in question, 'Pallinghurst Barrow' (1892), is expressly alluded to in *The Time Machine*, as the Time Traveller recounts how 'a queer notion of Grant Allen's came into my head',[96] whereby 'the world at last will get overcrowded with' ghosts from past generations.[97] Hughes persuasively argues that *The Time Machine* owes a debt to 'Pallinghurst Barrow' – both stories pit a Victorian gentleman against hordes hailing from a time period far removed from his present day, the far future in *The Time Machine*, the distant past in 'Pallinghurst Barrow'. Both describe these hordes as pale savages, both feature a scene in which the protagonist narrowly escapes by dint of simple human inventions (matches, pocket-knife), and both feature a dinner conversation about the story's fantastical conceit conducted in a respectable middle-class home. Yet these similarities begin and end with the plot, touching on neither setting nor theme. 'Pallinghurst Barrow' is a rural ghost story, set in 'a veritable waste of heath and gorse' in 'the shadowy heart of Hampshire'.[98] Its rural landscape has little in common with the suburban London of *The Time Machine*, nor does it carry social points about London's underclass in the manner of *The Time Machine* and *A Christmas Carol*. Thus, while 'Pallinghurst Barrow' assuredly influenced *The Time Machine* and was flagged up as a source by the Time Traveller himself, it is *The Time Machine*'s debt to *A Christmas Carol* that takes on greater depth, manifesting in the London setting, apocalyptic imagery and cautionary social visions shared by these two books.

Unlike 'Pallinghurst Barrow', *A Christmas Carol* and *The Time Machine* both use the mechanism of time travel to warn against the dire consequences of Victorian London's widening gap between the wealthy and the dispossessed. In *A Christmas Carol*, the Ghost of Christmas Present declaims in pre-apocalyptic tones of the allegorical children named 'Ignorance' and 'Want' as he gesticulates towards London:[99]

> 'Beware them both, and all of their degree, but most of all beware this boy, for on his brow I see that written which is Doom, unless the writing be erased. Deny it!' cried the Spirit, stretching out its hand towards the city. 'Slander those who tell it ye! Admit it for your factious purposes, and make it worse. And abide the end!'.[100]

In the dystopian future of *The Time Machine*, as Michael R. Page observes, 'the apocalypse has already happened.'[101] All that remains is for the Time Traveller to piece together the history of the future as best he can. As noted by David L. Pike, this reconstruction is attempted by 'concretely localizing the Eloi and Morlocks in terms of their temporal relation with the social space of 1895 London.'[102] Thus, in a passage strongly reminiscent of the above extract from *A Christmas Carol*, the Time Traveller reflects:

> At first, proceeding from the problems of our own age, it seemed clear as daylight to me that the gradual widening of the present merely temporary and social difference between the Capitalist and the Labourer, was the key to the whole position.... Industry... had gone deeper and deeper into larger and ever larger underground factories, spending a still-increasing amount of its time therein, till, in the end—![103]

Both passages prophesy 'the end' and predict the destruction of London as a result of its social stratification and the relentless exploitation of its working classes. They both foresee that the children of humanity will spell out its doom, be it in the form of allegorical children or devolved evolutionary descendants. The difference between these two passages is that *A Christmas Carol* holds forth the promise that disaster may yet be averted, whereas *The Time Machine* remains highly sceptical of such a possibility. Thus, Scrooge awakens with the exuberant conviction that 'the Time before him was his own, to make amends in!',[104] while the Time Traveller returns with a crushing sense of 'how brief the dream of the human intellect had been'.[105]

The Time Machine is doubtless a bleaker story than *A Christmas Carol*, but Wells's scientific romance was written at a bleaker time than Dickens's Christmas Book. Three cornerstones in the history of science contributed to this pessimistic turn. Charles Lyell's *Principles of Geology* (1830–3) had already developed the pre-existing concept of 'deep time' to show that the history of the universe was as vast as its space.[106] Darwin's *The Origin of Species* (1859) and *The Descent of Man* (1871) showed that not only was the universe vast and ancient, but that man's place within it was precariously contingent rather than divinely ordained, a result of millennia of changing environmental circumstances. As if to crown these gloomy scientific revelations, German scientist Rudolf Clausius re-formulated the Second Law of Thermodynamics in 1865, curiously coinciding with the serialization of Dickens's *Our Mutual Friend* and its urban landscape of dust-heaps. Clausius's version of the Second Law of Thermodynamics affirmed that the level of entropy in a closed system always increases; or in other words, that a closed system is constantly undergoing energy dispersal.[107] At the turn of the century, as Wells later recalled, variations on this principle took on hysterical proportions: 'the geologists and astronomers of that time told us dreadful lies about the "inevitable" freezing up of the world – and of life and mankind with it'.[108]

Wells's scientifically conditioned imagination was thus a product of its historical moment. In the decades when Lyell's, Darwin's and Clausius's insights were gaining wider traction in the scientific community, it was historically appropriate that Wells projected *The Time Machine* into the limitless reaches of deep time. The Time Traveller does not oscillate between the past, present and future of a single lifetime, as Scrooge does in *A Christmas Carol*, but casts himself into a post-human future hundreds of millennia hence. Thus, the monstrous offspring of class exploitation in *The Time Machine* are not allegorical symbols of the cast of the *Carol*'s Ignorance and Want, but evolutionary deformations springing from 'the splitting of our species along lines of social stratification'.[109] Consequently, while the ignorance and want that plague Victorian London in *A Christmas Carol* can be treated with immediate social reform, most notably the philanthropy of a reformed Scrooge and an abolishment of the workhouses, the social stratification that Wells extrapolates in *The Time Machine* is on a far grander scale, and can only be remedied by the collective effort of the entire human race, 'the responsibility of men to mankind',[110] as he put it in an 1899 interview.

The differences between Dickens and Wells can be further teased out by a closer examination of their disparate imaginative responses to the Crystal Palace in Sydenham, an area which had been largely urbanized, built over, and purchased by the London County Council (LCC) and the Lewisham District Board of Works in Wells's time.[111] Where for Dickens and his disciples, the Crystal Palace was a Fairyland, in Wells's future it becomes a wasteland, eaten away by entropy. The 'Palace of Green Porcelain' where the Time Traveller and his ward take refuge, modelled on the Sydenham Crystal Palace and what used to be called the South Kensington Museum (now the Victoria and Albert Museum), has long since been 'deserted' and is presently 'falling into ruin'.[112] Reminiscent of the Megalosaurus in *Bleak House* and more explicitly 'the megatherium' in Sala and Wills's 'Fairyland in 'Fifty-Four',[113] Wells's derelict palace features a skeleton 'standing strange and gaunt in the centre of the hall',[114] which the Time Traveller recognizes as the torso and legs of 'some extinct creature after the fashion of the Megatherium'.[115] But where Sala and Wills's megatherium, exquisitely moulded in clay 'according to some subtle theory',[116] stands as a testament to 'the marvels of what we may call scientific art',[117] Wells's megatherium has long since fallen apart, its 'skull and the upper bones lay beside it in the thick dust'.[118] The tension captured in these two very different views of the megatherium assumes an ironic social resonance when one considers that for Sala, Wills and implicitly Dickens, the Crystal Palace embodied the near-Utopian promise of a centre of learning 'thronged by thousands of every class and shade of class'.[119] For the Time Traveller, it is an armoury of deadly weapons that he wields with relish 'to kill a Morlock or so';[120] that is, to wage class warfare in the most literal sense of the term. Extrapolating from these observations, one may argue that Wells's early to mid-fictions presented a series of entropic responses to Dickens, offering fragmented portraits of a decayed, exhausted Dickens world.

Thus, Wells lent the Urban Fantasy tradition an edge of genuine scientific training and he expanded its scope into deep time, but these developments came at a cost, and that cost was a darker undercurrent of existential fear and class antipathy. Wells's lower-middle-class background, together with an episode of tedious employment as an assistant draper in his youth and his meteoric rise to literary fame, invites comparisons with Dickens's similar biographical trajectory.[121] But Wells's attitude towards the masses of lower-middle-class Englishmen who flocked to London differed considerably from Dickens's. While Dickens instinctively sided with the underclass, Wells's anger at the state of affairs in his city was directed at the Bob Cratchits of the world as well as the Lord Mayors. They did not bear the brunt of Wells's criticism, but they too were its targets. Across the gamut of Wells's writings, one finds the recurring sense that late-Victorian and Edwardian Londoners had collectively sunk into 'extreme mental immobility',[122] stultified as they were by entrenched habits, obsolete notions of propriety and the desensitizing effects of the sensational media. Thus, in *The World Set Free* (1914), he described a protest of working-class Londoners as an admission of mental inadequacy, less a demand for change as 'an appeal against the unexpected'.[123] Granted, this appeal goes unanswered, for middle- and upper-class Londoners are equally obtuse.

Given the state of London in the late nineteenth century, perhaps it was impossible to feel as hopeful about the city as Dickens had felt half a century earlier when he wrote *A Christmas Carol*. When Wells first moved to London in 1884 to begin his studies at the Normal School of Science, London had begun to sag under its own weight.[124] As its population soared to four and a half million inhabitants in 1881,[125] the inadequacy of London housing came to the fore of public discourse. Throughout the nineteenth century, until the establishment of the LCC in 1888 and the Housing of the Working Classes Act of 1890, London's building policies were starkly out of kilter with the pressing needs of the populace.[126] Adhering to the principles of the long-standing ninety-nine-year 'building-lease system',[127] Victorian entrepreneurs built fashionable houses for prospective upper-class clients, which were then left empty when these clients failed to appear. Even as 'rows of ghost houses' occupied the city's fashionable districts,[128] living conditions in London's more reasonably priced accommodations were growing atrocious. Wells laid the responsibility for this 'sustained disaster' of London housing squarely at the feet of the unscrupulous, 'recklessly unimaginative entrepreneurs' who initiated and financed it.[129] But he also suggested that their victims, the everyday Londoners who passively accepted the irresponsible housing speculation that was erupting into the fabric of the city, were complicit in their own victimization: 'To most Londoners of my generation these rows of jerry-built unalterable homes seemed to be as much in the nature of things as rain in September.'[130]

The great expansion of London was well underway in Dickens's lifetime, but in the decades immediately following his death, it accelerated to such an extent that London expanded by 119 per cent between 1881 and 1901.[131] One of Dickens's early acquaintances remarked admiringly of his familiarity with London, recalling that Dickens 'knew it all from Bow to Brentford'.[132] By the 1890s, however, it was no longer possible to know the entirety of London as Dickens had known it, nor were the boundaries of London to be drawn at Bow in the east and Brentford in the west. The scale of London's expansion may be measured by Wells's analogous and similarly alliterative line in *War of the Worlds*, whereby 'all the vastness of London from Ealing to East Ham' awakens 'to a vivid sense of danger'.[133] Ealing, north of Brentford, was part of what Jerry White has termed the 'New London' of the 1880s,[134] which came into its own as a suburb in the 1890s. East Ham, a good distance east of Bow, grew 'faster than any comparable town in England',[135] its population tripling between 1881 and 1891 and again between 1891 and 1901, so that by 1911 it 'became one of the dormitory suburbs of London'.[136]

Thus, on a grander scale than Dickens, Wells was highly attuned to distinctions of London locale. This sensitivity came to the fore in his letter to Elizabeth Healey, dated 23 February 1888, which detailed the differences between the London districts of West Hampstead and St Pancras, presumably as part of Wells's and Healey's correspondence about the Local Government Bill of 1888 that was soon to become a Government Act, establishing the LCC and dividing London into new Electoral Divisions:[137]

West Hampstead is not in St. Pancras. West Hampstead is N.W., new, respectable, conservative, articulate, detached or semi-detached, unsympathetic, and commercial. I hate West Hampstead and in fact the entire Hampstead genus, also S. Johns Wood, Regents Park and the whole of North London villadom – St. Pancras is old, dirty, immoral, drunken, radical Socialist, anarchist, inarticulate, crowded, sympathetic, starving, cheating, lurid, smoky and lovable; and yet there is a majesty also about St. Pancras that W. Hampstead has not – S. Pancras sins are deadly sins, its troubles are vital troubles; it hungers, and thirsts and longs. Hampstead's sins are social peccadillos, its troubles deal with matters such as making £150 look like £400, it dresses and performs and is satisfied.[138]

Wells's remarks were reflective of those districts at the time. In the late nineteenth century, the villas of the North London suburbs in the Hampstead area were by and large 'the homes of the middle middle-class',[139] precisely the population who might strive to make a household of £150 appear to be one of £400. Whereas the parish of St Pancras was struggling with poverty and unemployment as it took on a distinctly secular,[140] intellectual and socialist character.[141] But Wells recast these local distinctions as fundamentally opposed aspects of London life. The first aspect, incarnated in West Hampstead, was London as pretentious and false, a phoney arena that 'dresses and performs'. The second, incarnated in St Pancras, was nitty-gritty London, majestic as it viscerally 'hungers, and thirsts and longs'. He thus diagnosed an intrinsic tension within London between the material reality and the false pretence, which aligned with a distinction between the bohemia of St Pancras and the socially obsessed aspiring middle classes of 'the entire Hampstead genus'.

Wells's letter inveighed against the social pretensions of London's middling classes, but his scientific romances and social realist novels directed his criticism more broadly, at the social and political muddle of London, of which these pretensions were but one symptom. Characters such as the Napoleonic Edward Ponderevo in *Tono-Bungay* (1908–9) and the landlord of the 'ill-managed lodging-house' in *The Invisible Man*,[142] who put on airs of respectability above their station that lead inevitably to their humiliation, are at once objects of ridicule and victims of London who fall prey to the myriad ways in which the city renders its inhabitants 'invisible'.[143] The literally Invisible Man soon discovers the folly of his assumption that invisibility in London would liken him to 'a seeing man . . . in a city of the blind'.[144] 'I realized what a helpless absurdity an Invisible Man was',[145] he tells Kemp, 'in a cold and dirty climate and a crowded, civilized city' that exposes him to the elements as well as the dangers of being run over by London traffic.[146] The protagonist of *Tono-Bungay* similarly learns with time that 'London was a witless old giantess of a town' in which 'I became inconsiderable'.[147] For both characters, the experience of London hinges on 'disillusionment' and 'disappointment'.[148]

A Martian peering from the steeple:
London under an alien gaze

Wells's scientific romances were partly geared towards dispelling both the delusions of grandeur and the mental inertia that had seeped into London life. 'The War of the Worlds like The Time Machine was another assault on human self-satisfaction',[149] Wells asserted in the preface to his collection of scientific romances, assaults that were targeted particularly at Londoners. By constructing deliberately estranged versions of turn-of-the-century London, Wells opened a fictional space that called attention to the real city's social ills while jolting his readers out of their habitual treatment of these ills as an intractable part of their lives. As Simon J. James put it, 'Wells's scientific romances distort perceived reality in order to address something that he seeks to change within it.'[150] Not least among the subjects marked out for change was Londoners' attitudes towards each other and towards their city, as Wells launched his broadsides at 'an archaic system of education' that calcified 'the nineteenth-century mind' in 'profoundly retrospective . . . habits of thought',[151] rendering it ill-equipped for the challenges posed by 'the accumulation of men in cities'.[152] Wells recognized that late-nineteenth-century London was 'the most swiftly growing city in the world' and yet it was woefully underprepared to accommodate 'the multiplying multitude' that thronged its streets.[153]

Even as they highlighted the need for radical change in the social, political and managerial administration of London, Wells's scientific romances paid homage to his imperfect city of 'gas-lit winter streets'.[154] Thus, a book as proselytizing as Wells's *A Modern Utopia* (1904–5) still took a moment to reflect, in the vein of Dickens's *Haunted Man*, how 'the London air . . . makes every London twilight mysteriously beautiful'.[155] Wells thereby took on the Dickensian mantle of lending London 'an odd unlikeness of itself',[156] but where Dickens imagined a London that is 'unknown to all the people in the story',[157] Wells imagined a London that is unknown to characters who were not, strictly speaking, people. Across the gamut of his London-based fantastical fictions, his estrangement of London hinged on a careful interplay of de-familiarization and re-familiarization. When Wells cast his fantastical Londons into the distant future, the estrangement of time was balanced by familiar London topography. When he depicted a fantastical version of his present-day London, the familiar surroundings were made strange by the Othered perspective of an extraterrestrial's view of the *fin-de-siècle* metropolis.

Wells's 'The Crystal Egg' (1897) refracted London through a complex mise-en-abyme whereby a Londoner catches a glimpse of a Martian through the titular crystal egg even as, by way of analogy, a hypothetical scenario is conceived whereby the Martian catches a glimpse of London. The story centres on Mr Cave, a peculiarly Dickensian character who owns a 'little and very grimy-looking' curiosity shop 'near Seven Dials'.[158] The conditions in Seven Dials in the 1890s had scarcely improved since Dickens wrote about the area in *Sketches by Boz*,[159] and for Wells to set his fantastical story in a curiosity shop near a London slum that was made famous in large part by Dickens's journalism, was to situate his story in a Dickensian tradition. Indeed, Cave is Wells's variation on a certain type of Dickens character, the elderly owner of a curiosity shop who shuffles about among the cluttered bric-a-brac as a living curiosity among curiosities. One may recognize this figure across Dickens's writings in a variety of permutations: Nell's grandfather in *The Old Curiosity Shop*, Mr Krook in *Bleak House* and Mr Venus in *Our Mutual Friend*. Yet where Dickens's various curiosity shops operated symbolically as a microcosm for London, by reconfiguring the city as an arena of grotesque objects that metaphorically come to life, Wells's curiosity shop offers a more literal microcosm for London by opening up the city to the Martian gaze.

Cave becomes increasingly obsessed with the eponymous crystal egg, which has come into his possession through the foreclosure of another curiosity dealer's stock-in-trade. After discovering by chance that the crystal egg is luminescent, Cave performs a series of experiments that gradually reveal that the egg serves as a two-way window into a civilization on Mars. It allows the Martians to peer into his dingy shop even as he surveys their alien planet. Yet all the characters in the story, save Cave himself and a hospital employee who befriends him, are oblivious to the crystal egg's fantastical properties. Cave recounts that prior to the sudden interest of an Indonesian prince who chances by the shop, customers paid the crystal egg so little heed that he had considered lowering its price until he discovered its powers. The prince, for his part, seeks to purchase it merely out of 'curiosity – and extravagance',[160] and Mr Cave's wife treats it as an opportunity to make a profit that would allow her to purchase 'a dress of green silk for herself and a trip to Richmond'.[161] Thus, the lower-middle-class wife, the upper-class prince and the shop's ordinary customers evince neither the slightest capacity nor the inclination to grasp the extraordinary properties of the crystal egg. They collectively dramatize the small-mindedness that Wells castigated in his fantastical fictions, the stunted imaginations that 'neglected great issues' in favour of 'triumphant petty things' that he perceived as all too common in turn-of-the-century London.[162]

Mr Cave embodies Wells's meritorious exception to such meanness of spirit. Cave's receptiveness to the wonders of the universe, together with his readiness to experiment with the crystal egg and his subsequent refusal to sell it at any price after discovering its powers, despite financial and familial pressures, are rewarded by affording him a fresh view of his surroundings. Through the estrangement afforded by the crystal egg, Mr Cave experiences a widening of perspective in what had hitherto been a cramped and unfulfilling existence. From the vast distance of the red planet, he can suddenly perceive that 'the evening star that shone so brilliantly in the sky of that distant vision, was neither more nor less than our own familiar earth'.[163] Thus, from his expanded scope of deep time and deep space, Wells returned to the Dickensian vision of making London 'unlike itself', but enlarged it so that the entire planet strikes Mr Cave with its sudden distant beauty, thereby realizing Wells's aspiration to 'have the world under a totally different aspect'.[164]

In a sophisticated structure of analogies and nested visions, Wells likened Cave's revelation of the beauty of Earth from the vantage point of Mars as seen through the crystal egg, together with his other observations that form 'his report',[165] to the Martians' hypothesized impressions of London:

> Imagine the impression of humanity a Martian observer would get who, after a difficult process of preparation and with considerable fatigue to the eyes, was able to peer at London from the steeple of St Martin's Church for stretches, at longest, of four minutes at a time.[166]

Wells's choice of 'St Martin's Church', better known as St Martin-in-the-Fields, may have derived from considerations of geographical aptness – St Martin-in-the-Fields was and still is one of the most iconic steepled churches in the vicinity of Seven Dials. Yet Wells may have also chosen this church for more symbolic reasons, such as the alliterative resonance between 'Martin' and 'Martian'. Furthermore, it may be germane that St Martin-in-the-Fields was the church nearest to Dickens's 'moor eeffoc' café, which Dickens specifically mentioned in his description of this seminal experience. The recurrence of this church in two passages written by different authors in widely dissimilar contexts, yet both dedicated to the re-envisioning of London from unusual perspectives, is probably fortuitous. Indeed, the impression of London that the Martian would have received from his vantage point atop the steeple of St Martin-in-the-Fields in the 1890s would have been starkly different from Dickens's view from within the café on St Martin's Lane in the 1820s, as the area had since been transformed by the paving of Trafalgar Square and the installation of Nelson's column.[167] Yet one may also note that this same church would become one of the nodes of London's defamiliarization and re-familiarization in *Nineteen Eighty-Four*. Throughout the book, St Martin-in-the-Fields is the only London landmark that Winston successfully identifies despite the Party's best efforts to eradicate all memory of the London that preceded its rule. At the very least, this privileging of St Martin-in-the-Fields as a site of fantastical re-imaginings of London suggests that these texts were drawn to similar locales, if not actively responding to each other.

The War of the Worlds likewise opens a new perspective on London through the city's subjugation to the Martian gaze, this time by way of a full-scale Martian invasion. The unnamed narrator stands atop Putney Hill and much like Mr Cave, he is struck by the sight of a sudden otherworldly luminescence that shines against the London darkness – this time the 'pale, violet-purple fluorescent glow' of the Martian red weed rather than the light of the crystal egg.[168] Likewise harking back to 'The Crystal Egg', this luminescence opens his mind to the vastness of space, triggering his unspoken realization of the spatial and conceptual continuity between London and Mars: 'I glanced from that [the luminescent red weed] to Mars . . . and then gazed long and earnestly at the darkness of Hampstead and Highgate.'[169] Just as Cave's discovery leads him to experiment with the crystal egg and experience the beauty of planet Earth, so the narrator's revelation is accompanied by his reawakened 'sense of wonder' and propels him 'to go on into London' in the hope 'of learning what the Martians and my fellow-men were doing'.[170]

As the narrator embarks on a methodically charted journey through London, its familiar features are made strange under 'the black powder in the streets' and the writhing 'red weed [that] clambered among the ruins',[171] its sounds eerily muted in 'the closed shops, [with] the houses locked up and the blinds drawn'.[172] In 'The Crystal Egg', the Martian gaze on London was couched in hypothetical language and precariously positioned on the steeple of St Martin-in-the-Fields. In *War of the Worlds*, the uncanny gaze of the Martian is displaced onto terraformed London itself, which 'gazed at me spectrally' as the narrator recounts,[173] unsettling him with its profound strangeness to the point of insanity. Yet, not unlike the London of 'The Crystal Egg', the Martian transformation has also cast a new solemnity on London, as the narrator wonders at his surroundings: 'Why was I alone when all London was lying in state, and in its black shroud?'.[174]

The terraformed London traversed by the narrator is rendered still more eerie and strange by its implicit contrast with the everyday routines of the capital, as depicted in the story of the narrator's brother. Scholars are divided on the artistic merits of the brother's story. Tom Gibbons criticized the undifferentiated 'prose style of the brother's narrative',[175] whereas Frank McConnell argued that the 'double frame of narrative authority' constructed by the narrator's retelling of his brother's story makes 'the scenes of violence in London, ... more believable'.[176] But I would suggest that prose style and suspension of disbelief alike are secondary considerations to the main purpose of this narrative strand, namely to enable Wells to juxtapose the complacency of Londoners in the run-up to the Martian invasion and their wholesale panic when the Martians are nearly upon them. Throughout the first chapter of the brother's narrative, Wells dwells on Londoners' fatal obliviousness. Scarcely two days before the arrival of the Martians, 'there were no signs of any unusual excitement in the streets'.[177] A day before the Martian invasion, 'innumerable people walking in their best clothes seemed scarcely affected by the strange intelligence that the newsvendors were disseminating'.[178] Indeed, the precise wording used to convey the dangers of such complacency was sufficiently important to Wells that he continued to refine it across editions. In the original 1897 serialization and the 1898 first book edition, Wells described London on the night before 'the dawn of the great panic' as having 'gone to bed ... stupid and inert'.[179] In the 1924 Atlantic Edition, he altered the phrase 'stupid and inert' to read 'oblivious and inert',[180] thereby simultaneously softening the blow and sharpening its import. The brother's narrative thus allowed Wells to bring home his critique of the intransigence that had taken hold of Londoners, by showing them an unflattering portrait of themselves as oblivious, if not stupid.

The brother's story also creates a three-pronged contrast between London before, on the verge, and in the aftermath of the Martian invasion. This contrast takes on greater force through the brother's journey across London by many of the same iconic London landmarks and areas later passed or seen by the narrator. The brother walks by Regent's Park, noting that along its edge 'were as many silent couples "walking out" together under the scattered gas-lamps as ever there had been'.[181] The narrator similarly 'skirt[s] the park',[182] but in place of the silent couples, he finds 'a dog with a piece of putrescent red meat in his jaws',[183] which later proves to be a chunk of flesh torn from a dead Martian. On the eve of the Martian invasion of London, the brother watches as 'the Clock Tower and the Houses of Parliament rose against one of the most peaceful skies it is possible to imagine',[184] scarcely imagining that a day later a Martian would appear 'beyond the Clock Tower',[185] nor that by the end of the invasion all that will be left of the Palace of Westminster are 'jagged ruins'.[186] These images of devastation resonate all the more powerfully for the normalcy established in the same London locales earlier on in the brother's narrative.

In similar vein, the stillness of London after the invasion is all the more still, the silence all the more profound, the emptiness all the more hollow and echoing, for its implied juxtaposition to the tumult of 'stirring, slipping, running' Londoners that had preceded it.[187] The emptiness and silence of London strikes the keynote in the narrator's culminating vision of London in its full glory. As he stands atop the summit of Primrose Hill among the corpses of the Martians and the ruins of their base of operations, gripped by his momentous realization of the Martians' defeat, the narrator feasts his eyes upon 'the great Mother of Cities':[188]

> Those who have only seen London veiled in her sombre robes of smoke can scarcely imagine the naked clearness and beauty of the silent wilderness of houses.[189]
> Far away and blue were the Surrey hills, and the towers of the Crystal Palace glittered like two silver rods.[190]

If in *The Time Machine* the defamiliarization of deep time rendered the Crystal Palace an emblem of mankind's decline, in *War of the Worlds* the defamiliarization of deep space, through the Martian invasion, has made the Crystal Palace a beacon of hope, 'two silver rods' that glitter like a rallying point for the restoration of humanity. Yet at the height of this pathos, one may still find hints of Wells's allegiances of London locale. In the late nineteenth century, Primrose Hill was divided between Wells's hated Hampstead parish, his beloved parish of St Pancras and the parish of St Marylebone.[191] One may speculate, therefore, that Wells was motivated by more than the strict imperatives of story and geography when he chose Primrose Hill as both the central base of the Martians' conquest and the hilltop from which the narrator envisions London's salvation.

The intimation in the passage above that London is only magnificent when empty and purged of its masses has added grist to the mill of critics who accuse Wells of technocratic Malthusianism.[192] But one should not overlook the fact that Wells provided a corrective to this impression by lending his sublime vision of London a distinctively humanist timbre. Where for the Martians, London and its people are nothing more than a colony of 'ants [that] build their cities',[193] the narrator waxes lyrical on 'the innumerable hosts of lives that had gone to build this human reef',[194] conjuring up a tidal wave of human life and personalizing it with a gesture towards 'the multitudinous hopes and efforts' that are embedded in the cityscape and whose image brings him 'near akin to tears'.[195] Thus, magnificent as London may be in its solemn silence, it is the return of Londoners en masse to the public spaces of 'this dear vast dead city of mine' that will bring about London's resurrection:[196] 'the pulse of life, growing stronger and stronger, would beat again in the empty streets and pour across the vacant squares'.[197]

Wandering about: Wellsian perambulations

In addition to the epistemological estrangement wrought through the Martian perspective, Wells also defamiliarized London through acts of walking. As the nineteenth century drew to a close, London 'was no longer a walkable city',[198] at least in the sense that Dickens had walked it. Close on the heels of London's expansion, new modes of transport began competing with walking, as the London Underground expanded and began to shift from steam power to electricity in the 1890s,[199] and bicycling became prevalent among the working classes.[200] Thus, while Londoners continued to walk to a variety of destinations, they did so in more circumscribed areas, and with a heightened awareness of the differences in London locale.

Wells gave account of himself that 'London is my own particular city; all my life I have been going about in it',[201] but he never laid claim to the kind of London expertise that played such an integral part in Dickens's public image. 'If I wanted to walk from Hoxton to Chelsea without asking my way',[202] Wells wrote, 'I should have to sit down to puzzle over a map for some time.'[203] His walking knowledge of London seems to have been limited to the central areas of the city and the roads leading to the Normal School of Science, where he walked daily during his student days, first from his 'lodging in Westbourne Park across Kensington Gardens',[204] and then from his second accommodations 'at 181 Euston Road'.[205] His morning walk led him 'through the back streets as far as the top of Regent Street . . . on for all the length of Oxford Street to the Marble Arch and thence across the Park to Exhibition Road',[206] on which he continued to the Normal School of Science. Within that West End area between Hyde Park and Regent's Park, Wells took pains to chart his protagonists' journeys with precision, and to correct any errors in London geography when opportunity presented itself. Thus, in his revisions to the Atlantic Edition of *War of the Worlds*, he substituted the correct 'Portland Place' for the previous misnomer 'Portland Road' in his reference to the thoroughfare leading from Regent Street to Regent's Park.[207] Similarly, in the course of revising the serialized version for book publication, Wells changed his description of the Martian's death cry, which originated in the serialization from a vague area 'somewhere beyond Baker Street',[208] to the more precise 'district about Regent's Park',[209] thereby simultaneously clarifying the rationale of the narrator's decision to head towards Regent's Park, and drawing the reader's attention to a locale that features in both the narrator's and his brother's journeys across London.

This precision of London geography, displayed through the London walks of the narrator and his brother, is integral to what John Huntington has described as Wells's 'two world structure' that creates a 'juxtaposition of two incongruous worlds',[210] most often the world of everyday London and a fantastical, or at least outlandish, distant world. Nowhere is this two world structure more apparent than in Wells's two short stories, 'The Remarkable Case of Davidson's Eyes' (1895) and 'The Door in the Wall', both of which tell of a man who weaves his way between London and another world. The eponymous Sidney Davidson is a lab worker whose room is hit by a thunderstorm, and as a result he begins to see visions of a faraway island even as he physically remains in London. The protagonist of 'The Door in the Wall', Lionel Wallace, discovers a hidden door that leads from London to a paradisiacal garden that appears before him in pivotal moments of his life. Not unlike Mr Cave's obsession with Mars, Davidson and Wallace both develop an attachment to the other world because it offers them an alternative to the drabness of everyday London life. When Davidson's normal eyesight begins to return, he becomes 'queerly interested' in recovering his vision of the island.[211] Wallace confesses that the Door in the Wall 'made all the interests and spectacle of worldly life seem dull and tedious and vain to him'.[212]

Yet neither of these stories provides a straightforward fantasy of escape from London into a more pristine, non-urban world, because in each of them the other world is wedded to the topography of the city. Davidson's movement 'hither and thither in London' spurs his vision to move in tandem,[213] 'hither and thither in a manner that corresponded, about this distant island'.[214] Suggestively, these correspondences between London and the island resonate with Wells's dislike of Hampstead and affection for the parish of St Pancras. The upstairs floor of Davidson's home at 'Hampstead village' corresponds with 'thirty or forty feet above the rocks of his imaginary island',[215] rocks which he describes as 'white and disagreeable to see'.[216] Whereas Davidson's south-easterly journey through London on 'a bath-chair' to 'Camden Town, towards King's Cross'[217] – into what was then the parish of St Pancras[218] – corresponds with a movement from the island into the depths of the sea on 'a lovely night' with the water 'calm and shining under the moonlight'.[219]

This topographical imbrication of the metropolis with the other world imparts a new sense of wonder to London's daily life that tallied with Wells's express aim to deploy 'the modern fanciful method' in order to 'have the world under a totally different aspect'. Thus, in 'The Remarkable Case of Davidson's Eyes', Wells teased out a fantastical undercurrent from London's everyday routines through a juxtaposition of the background sounds of the city with the enchanting sights of the deep sea. As Davidson hears 'the footsteps of people going by, and a man in the distance selling the special *Pall Mall*',[220] he sees 'fish, faintly glowing, ... and things that seemed made of luminous glass; ... the seaweed became a luminous purple-red',[221] the same shade of luminescence, not incidentally, as the 'violet-purple fluorescent glow' that awakened the narrator's sense of wonder in *War of the Worlds*.[222] When Davidson's otherworldly vision begins to fade, he goes 'wandering about the low-lying parts of London',[223] traversing the Thames riverside where he believes the membrane between everyday London and his fantastical vision of the sea will be at its most permeable, in the hopes of recapturing 'the deep sea again'.[224]

The titular Door in the Wall is similarly incorporated into the cityscape of London. It manifests in specific London locations, never the same location twice, and most often in West London.[225] The Door first appears before Wallace as a young boy, when he wanders 'among the West Kensington roads'.[226] At face value, West Kensington seems an odd choice of locale on Wells's part, as it was characterized by social pretentions of the kind that Wells found profoundly distasteful.[227] Yet 'The Door in the Wall' is interested in West Kensington mainly as a transitional area situated in close proximity to both the opulent district of Kensington proper and the then-down-at-heel areas of north-west Notting Hill, enclaves known as Notting Dale and Norland.[228] Kensington and Notting Hill were topographically separated by the elevated area of Campden Hill, which is directly evoked in the second appearance of the Door in the Wall 'among some rather low-class streets on the other side of Campden Hill'.[229]

The stark juxtapositions of wealth and poverty in the Kensington area were more stridently drawn in the MSS of 'The Door in the Wall'. In one of these manuscripts, dated 1 November 1905, the first-person narrator (still unnamed) recalls that he grew up 'in a large stucco home to the south of Kensington Gardens & near the Albert Hall' (Figure 2.1), located accordingly near Kensington Palace. Yet despite his privileged upbringing, or perhaps because of it, the young narrator is drawn to the seamier areas beyond the pale of his immediate surroundings, following 'my eyes & my musings westward' (Figure 2.1).

In the MSS and the published version alike, he first discovers the Door in the Wall in an area consisting of 'mean dirty shops, and particularly that of a plumber and decorator with a dusty disorder of earthenware pipes'.[230] One would be hard-pressed to find a more striking contrast with his family mansion than this down-at-heel working-class street. Yet it is in this milieu that the young

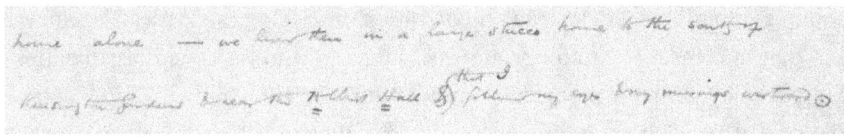

Figure 2.1 'The Door in the Wall': Wells, CB-001: *The Country of the Blind*, File 7, 'Manuscript with Author's Annotations, 1905' (dated 1 November 1905), Folder CB-147–199, leaf CB-149, the H. G. Wells papers, 1845–1946, The Rare Book & Manuscript Library, University of Illinois at Urbana-Champaign.

Wallace finds the entrance to the garden of peace and beauty to which he will yearn to return throughout his boyhood and adult life.

'The Door in the Wall' thus offers a Wellsian take on Dickens's romance of familiar things, 'even in those which are repellant on the surface',[231] with a sharper social edge that becomes pronounced with the location of Wallace's family home just south of Kensington Gardens. Wallace's literal and symbolic turn away from Kensington Gardens towards a secret garden accessible from a dilapidated street implicitly located in the Notting Hill area constitutes a temporary rejection of the life of wealth and privilege to which he was born. It is an act of defiance against his father, 'a stern, preoccupied lawyer, who gave him little attention and expected great things of him'.[232] He is rewarded for this transgression against his class and his family by 'a keen sense of homecoming' that suffuses the paradisiacal garden,[233] accentuating the depth of its absence in his actual home.

This transgressive undertow persists throughout 'The Door in the Wall'. As Wallace grows into boyhood and then adulthood, the Door's manifestations usually coincide with his impulsive deviations from the standard routes and major thoroughfares of London. The Door first materializes when 'one day he wandered',[234] much like Davidson went 'wandering about the low-lying parts of London';[235] again in Wallace's adulthood when he takes 'a short cut at a venture through an unfrequented road near Earl's Court'.[236] A particularly interesting manifestation occurs in Wallace's schoolboy years, when he plays a solitary game he has invented that he calls 'North-West Passage' after the fashion of Arctic explorers:[237]

> The way to school was plain enough; the game consisted in finding some way that wasn't plain, . . . and working my way round through unaccustomed streets to my goal.[238]

This dialectic of the subtle regional distinctions between Kensington, West Kensington and Notting Hill, coupled to the deliberate meandering whereby Wallace is 'working my way round through unaccustomed streets to my goal',[239] coheres with Michel de Certeau's theorization of walking as a 'pedestrian speech act' that 'increases the number of possibilities' within regulated organizations of space 'by creating shortcuts and detours'.[240] The 'figures of pedestrian rhetoric' that result coalesce into 'trajectories that have a mythical structure'.[241] From this theoretical standpoint, one may read the myth of the Door in the Wall as the myth of London, its prelapsarian garden a fantastical pocket of urban space that marks the genesis of an alternative, mentally liberated mode of inhabiting the city.

This reading is reinforced by the story's structural mise-en-abyme, whereby London appears to be ensconced within the garden beyond the Door even as the Door stands within the city. In the garden, the infant Wallace riffles through a book that depicts his own life in moving images, among which he notes 'the front door and the busy streets' of London.[242] Indeed, the final page of the book 'showed a long grey street in West Kensington, in that chill hour of afternoon before the lamps are lit'.[243] Wallace grieves over his return to everyday London, but the fact that the city appears as a tangible reality inside the garden, and is easily accessed from within it, suggests that these two spaces are contiguous and overlapping. The garden is thus configured as a hidden dimension simultaneously enfolded within and enfolding the cityscape, a new emancipatory mode of inhabiting urban space, rather than a pastoral respite untouched by modernity.

Young Wallace's adventure in the secret garden ends grimly with his father giving him his 'first thrashing for telling lies'.[244] A 'closer watch' is kept on him thenceforth 'to prevent my going astray' again.[245] Whether deliberately or otherwise, Wells's choice of the phrase 'going astray' calls to mind Dickens's imaginative piece 'Gone Astray', previously mentioned in Chapter 1. Notwithstanding the differences in London locale between West Kensington and the City of London, one may find curious similarities between 'Gone Astray' and 'Door in the Wall', both of which depict the wanderings of a lonely young boy across the streets of London. Wallace's game of 'North-West Passage' is anticipated by Dickens's young alter-ego,[246] who experiences the disorientation of being lost 'in the narrow, crowded, inconvenient street' as 'if I had found myself astray at the North Pole'.[247]

Dickens's piece ends with the intimation that going astray had since become a way of life.[248] Wells's story ends with going astray as a cause of death, as Wallace falls into a deep excavation site after mistaking its door for the Door in the Wall. But the closing lines of the story, articulated by a frame narrator who appears to stand in for Wells himself, suggest that Wallace's death is not necessarily the tragic result of self-delusion. 'At any rate, you will say, it [the Door in the Wall] betrayed him in the end,'[249] the narrator muses,

> But did it betray him? There you touch the inmost mystery of these dreamers, these men of vision and the imagination. We see our world fair and common, the hoarding and the pit. By our daylight standard he walked out of security into darkness, danger, and death.
> But did he see like that?[250]

Thus, not unlike *A Christmas Carol*, 'The Door in the Wall' is as much about how 'we see our world' as it is about how we inhabit it. Or more precisely, to see the world otherwise – to 'touch the inmost mystery of these dreamers, these men of vision and the imagination' – is, in this story, to inhabit the world differently.

'The strangest thing of all': Wells's future Londons

In a 1938 radio broadcast, Wells forged a link between his futurist fantasies and Dickens's historical novels. He contended that 'the best sort of futurist story . . . ought to produce the effect of an historical novel, the other way round'.[251] But so far, Wells admitted, 'none of us have ever succeeded'.[252] 'No reader has ever *lived* in a futurist novel as we have all lived in the London of Dickens' *Barnaby Rudge*',[253] he reflected, and he was surely thinking not least of his most elaborate dystopian fantasy of future London, *When the Sleeper Wakes*, which he described as 'an exaggeration of contemporary tendencies'.[254] His words intimate that however short of the mark, *When the Sleeper Wakes* was written out of a desire to create a futurist *Barnaby Rudge* (1841) 'the other way round'.

Following the pattern set out by *Barnaby Rudge*, *When the Sleeper Wakes* is the story of a mass upheaval that destabilizes social and political order in London, led by a powerful and charismatic figure skilled at manipulating the masses. In *Barnaby Rudge*, this social upheaval is a fictionalized version of a historical event, the Gordon Riots, an outburst of anger, violence, looting and destruction directed at the Catholic population of London and its environs. In *When the Sleeper Wakes*, this outburst of violence and destruction is directed at the 'White Council', a circle of trustees who rule over the future London of the year 2100 through their consolidated wealth. This uprising is instigated and led by the populist demagogue Ostrog, who pretends to fight for the people while in effect exploiting popular unrest to seize power for himself, after which the great majority of Londoners remain just as downtrodden and exploited as they were before the so-called revolution.

The solutions offered by Wells to the exploitation of workers under industrial capitalism were of a more radical tenor than those offered by Dickens. Even at his most radical, Dickens stopped short of endorsing wholesale revolution, advocating instead for an urgent change from within the existing structure of society – among individuals and institutions alike – to redress the injustice in labour conditions and labour relations. With the exception of the second French Revolution of 1848, he saw little difference between a revolution and a riot, as evident in the apocalyptic representation of the French Revolution of 1798 in *A Tale of Two Cities* (1859). Yet for Wells, apocalypse was the outcome not of revolution but of its absence. He had taken present-day social tendencies to their logical extreme in *The Time Machine* and arrived at the bleak conclusion that if society were not radically reorganized on a more egalitarian basis, then humanity was doomed. 'The whole system has to be changed',[255] Wells maintained, 'a complete change, a break with history' that was as necessary in his eyes as it was abhorrent in Dickens's.[256] The fatal danger was therefore not that revolution was imminent, but that it was not. Thus, *When the Sleeper Wakes* depicts the horrors of a prospective future in which the people's 'counter-revolution never came'.[257] A considerable portion of the book diagnoses Londoners' collective failure to act, a chronology of how the future became, in Wells's words, 'a nightmare of Capitalism triumphant'.[258]

Bernard Bergonzi's study of Wells's scientific romances argues that the main weakness of *When the Sleeper Wakes* is its embodiment of 'the radical ambiguities of its author's intellectual and imaginative attitudes',[259] especially Wells's 'dual allegiance both to the past and the future'.[260] Yet what Bergonzi construes as a weakness can be equally regarded as the most interesting aspect of the book and its two companion stories, 'A Story of the Days to Come' (1899) and 'A Dream of Armageddon' (1901). Time and again, Wells avowed his willingness to 'kick the past to pieces' in service of the future.[261] But when he conjured up London's future in his fictions, he ascribed a surprising degree of importance to the history and memories locked in London's material cityscape.

In *When the Sleeper Wakes*, the dissatisfaction of the people of London from Ostrog's revolution spurs a second, grassroots revolution led by the protagonist Graham, a Socialist from the late-Victorian past who earnestly fights for the underclass against Ostrog's autocracy. Shortly before Graham joins the revolutionary cause, Ostrog tries to get rid of him by persuading him to emigrate. Graham refuses to leave because 'the link of locality held him to London':[262]

> he found a perpetual wonder in topographical identifications that he would have missed abroad. 'Here – or a hundred feet below here,' he could say, 'I used to eat

my midday cutlets during my London University days. Underneath here was Waterloo and the perpetual hunt for confusing trains.'[263]

London topography thus forms a thread of continuity, a material link between future London and its past incarnations, which has endured despite the eroding effects of the White Council's and later Ostrog's hyper-capitalist building practices. These London localities awaken Graham's memories of everyday life in the turn of the century – eating cutlets and boarding trains – that restore his sense of belonging to the city and shadow forth his defiance of Ostrog's oppressive measures to put down the civil unrest: 'I believe in the people.'[264] The details of his recollections may have been drawn from Wells's own experiences of London in the 1890s: between 1890 and 1893, he studied and tutored at the University Correspondence College of London University;[265] in 1897, as he began writing the serialized version of *When the Sleeper Wakes*,[266] he was living in Worcester Park and commuting to London via Waterloo Station,[267] which was widely regarded as 'the most perplexing railway station in London' at the turn of the century.[268] In this respect, the significance accorded to the material cityscape of London in *When the Sleeper Wakes* tallies with Wells's more tender sympathies, almost despite himself, for his own particular city.

The most powerful moment of emotional connection between Graham and London takes place in St Paul's Cathedral, which has survived intact into the future London of 2100, albeit 'embedded out of sight, arched over and covered in among the giant growths of this great age.'[269] On the brink of the second revolution, Graham pauses in his descent into London's underworld to ascend to the dome of St Paul's. As he stands 'in the cage under the ball' and looks upward 'upon the wind-clear northern sky',[270] he reflects, 'To stand in the dome of Saint Paul's and look once more upon these familiar, silent stars' is 'the strangest thing of all'.[271] St Paul's Cathedral, seat of the bishop of London and one of the most ancient churches in the capital,[272] thus becomes a symbol of London's endurance, as steadfast and unchanging as the stars above. Wells chose St Paul's not so much for its religious significance as for its historical and personal significance. In his semi-autobiographical novel *Tono-Bungay*, the narrator openly extolls St Paul's as 'the very figure of whatever fineness the old Anglican culture achieved'.[273] On a more personal level, Wells praised St Paul's as the one place where he could 'sit and think' during his dismal Sundays as a lonely student in London.[274] Thus, contravening his own insistence that 'the past is past' and should therefore be unceremoniously discarded,[275] Wells drew the reader's attention away from 'the roar of traffic' in Edwardian London for a final look at the 'irrelevantly beautiful' cathedral as it soared up suddenly before 'dissolv[ing] like a cloud into the grey blues of the London sky'.²⁷⁶ It is curious to note that for all their progressiveness and political opposition to reactionary nostalgia, Dickens's and Wells's fantastical imaginations fixated on two of London's most enduring and ancient landmarks: London Bridge and St Paul's Cathedral.

When Wells imagined a city *without* a cultural history, his mind groped with an unpleasant, shallow spectacle anticipating the establishment of Las Vegas. In the dystopian future of *When the Sleeper Wakes* and its two companion pieces, such places are termed 'Pleasure Cities'. Simon J. James has suggested that 'Wells's "A Story of the Days to Come" and *When the Sleeper Wakes* might be seen as visions of a utopia in which no one is happy'.²⁷⁷ These stories' depictions of the Pleasure Cities, with their facile and ultimately fatal sensual gratifications, lend force to this insight. 'Dream of Armageddon' describes the Pleasure City from within as an 'enormous hotel, complex beyond explaining',²⁷⁸ followed by 'miles of floating hotels' extending as far as the eye can see.²⁷⁹ In 'A Story of the Days to Come', the recently impoverished Denton soon realizes that 'these wonderful places of delight permeated and defiled the thought and honour of these unwilling, hopeless workers of the underworld'.²⁸⁰ In the MS of 'Story of the Days to Come', recourse to Pleasure Cities marks the degradation of the rich as surely as thoughts of their hedonistic pleasures taint the poor: 'the very elaboration of sensuality that these cities displayed testified to the despair & particularly to the isolation of spirit of those to whom this alone remained' (Figure 2.2). In *When the Sleeper Wakes*, Ostrog reveals that the Pleasure Cities are 'the excretory organs of the State, attractive places' that allow the wealthy and self-indulgent to descend into 'a graceful destruction'.²⁸¹

Taken together, these three works contrast the Pleasure Cities with London in a manner that lends London a new measure of nobility. Denton's view of future London from a high balcony stirs in him inchoate thoughts of the city's history and its future ages, prompting his insight that 'whether we die or live, we are in the making'.²⁸² Graham finds beauty in 'the intricate dim immensity of the twilight buildings',²⁸³ which eases his gradual acceptance 'that this was his world, and not that other he had left behind'.²⁸⁴ As the story unfolds, this understanding underpins his resistance to Ostrog's manipulations, prompting

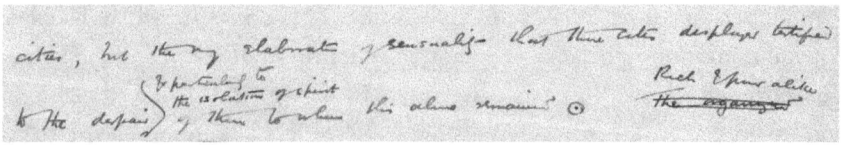

Figure 2.2 Wells, TA-001: *Tales of Space and Time*, File 5: Underneath (anno domini 2098), Folder TA-67-86, leaf TA-68, RBML, UIUC.

his assertion: 'I do not want to be King in a Pleasure City'.[285] Thus, Wells's futurist fantasies depict London and its historically embedded topography as a source of endurance rather than obsoleteness, exposing the vapidity of the Pleasure Cities as it resonates with a deeper sense of the past and the future yet to come.

'Urban tales': Wells's legacy to the Urban Fantasy tradition

Wells's London-based fantasies formed only a small part of his strikingly prolific oeuvre, created as they were over a brief period between the final years of the nineteenth century and the first part of the twentieth. By 1910, the year that Carey designates as the turning point when 'system replaced freedom as his [Wells's] ruling principle',[286] a change was discernible in Wells's writings about London.[287] This shift was captured in his extensive revisions to *When the Sleeper Wakes* eleven years after its publication, as he prepared to reissue the book under the new title, *The Sleeper Awakes* (1910). In all versions, including the original serialization (January–May 1899), the story concludes with Graham's flying contraption veering out of control and crashing to the ground. In the serialized version, Graham secures a definite victory for the people of London and dies with a 'softened' expression that the narrator glosses with the final line: 'His doubts were at an end.'[288] Wells's handwritten revisions to this scene, penned as he was reworking the serialization for book publication, added a line articulating Graham's realization that 'London was helpless no longer' (Figure 2.3). This line was discarded before publication,[289] but its appearance among Wells's manuscripts suggests that while undertaking these revisions, he intended to lend greater emphasis to the role of latter-day Londoners in the battle for their city.

The evidence provided by the handwritten revisions to *When the Sleeper Wakes* is reinforced by reference to early manuscripts of 'Dream of Armageddon', which Hammond dates contemporaneously with the serialization of *When the Sleeper Wakes* and the publication of its first book edition.[290] These manuscripts link 'Dream of Armageddon' more closely with *When the Sleeper Wakes*, recounting the aftermath of 'the battle of London' with which the book concludes (Figure 2.4):

> The ~~French & the~~ common English & Americans had it all their own way, the English engineer workers. They seemed made for flying – they stuck at nothing – they were never sick.

Thus, in the manuscripts of 'Dream of Armageddon', latter-day Londoners are expert aeroplane pilots, a skill that they had all implausibly lacked in *When the Sleeper Wakes*, all but Graham. It is these pilots, expressly described as 'the common'

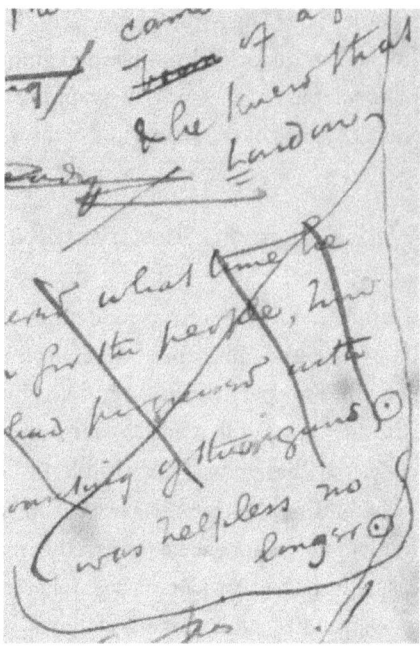

Figure 2.3 Wells, WSW-001: *When the Sleeper Wakes: A Story of the Years to Come*, Galley Proofs 1–35, leaf WSW-35, RBML, UIUC.

Englishmen and Americans, together with 'English engineer workers', who secure victory for their city. In these manuscripts, London is saved by its own people in a true grassroots revolution.

The 1899 book edition of *When the Sleeper Wakes* offers a more ambiguous conclusion – latter-day Londoners are accorded a less prominent role than afforded by the manuscript material, and the story ends with Graham's imminent crash. Yet he nevertheless consoles himself with the thought that 'he was beaten but London was saved'.[291] The 1910 edition of *The Sleeper Awakes* omitted this line entirely, and as Graham is about to crash, neither he nor the reader is given any inkling who has won the conflict. The 1921 edition, also titled *The Sleeper Awakes*, went one step further, adding a concluding sentence that turned the open-endedness of Graham's fate into a grim certainty of his death without any consolation of victory: 'Came a shock and a great crackling and popping of bars and stays.'[292] Leaving little room to mistake his intent, Wells glossed these changes in his 1910 preface to *The Sleeper Awakes*:

> I have also, with a few strokes of the pen, eliminated certain dishonest and regrettable suggestions that the People beat Ostrog. My Graham dies, as all his kind must die, with no certainty of either victory or defeat.[293]

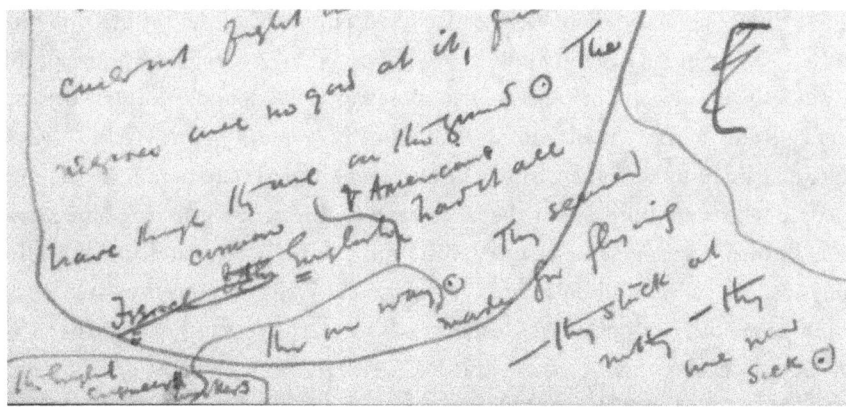

Figure 2.4 'A Dream of Armageddon (anno domini 2100)': Wells, TSD-001: *Twelve Stories and a Dream*, File 8, First Draft, 'Manuscript with Author's Annotations, Undated', Folder TSD-AI 1–24, leaf TSD/A-14, RBML, UIUC.

Thus, as the first decade of the twentieth century came to a close, Wells began to doubt whether London could be saved and whether Londoners could save it. To weigh in favour of such an outcome, even in fantasy, became 'dishonest and regrettable', for Wells saw 'either victory or defeat' equally poised on the city's horizon. If, as he contended in *The Outline of History* (1919–20), 'Human history becomes more and more a race between education and catastrophe',[294] catastrophe appeared to be in the lead. In the aftermath of the Great War, during which the German bombings of London claimed the lives of between 600 and 800 Londoners and injured up to 2,000,[295] Wells confessed that he 'had tired of talking in playful parables to a world engaged in destroying itself'.[296] 'I think I am better employed now nearer reality',[297] he contended, 'trying to make a working analysis of our deepening social perplexities'.[298]

In this prognostic spirit, London became a problem to be solved rather than a home to be cherished. Wells began to return with increasing frequency to an idea he had introduced in *Anticipations* (1901), whereby 'the "problem of our great cities"' would find resolution in 'such a process of dissection and diffusion as to amount almost to obliteration'.[299] By the time he wrote *The Shape of Things to Come* (1933), Wells could no longer imagine a future in which the major thoroughfares of the City of London and the West End, including Cornhill Street upon which Bob Cratchit slides in *A Christmas Carol*, nor even Wells's beloved St Paul's Cathedral from which Graham gazes at the stars, could be saved from ruin and flame.[300]

If the future of unity and cooperation that latter-day Wells campaigned for with increasing rancour in book after book seems only somewhat less remote in these times than it did then, Wells bequeathed a more visible legacy of a different order. As Parrinder elegantly puts it, Wells 'wished to influence the praxis of the twentieth century, but his real contribution was to its dreams'.[301] Those dreams crystallized in the Urban Fantasy tradition. Five years before Wells's death, Orwell paid him the highest tribute he had ever given a contemporary: 'thinking people who were born about the beginning of this century are in some sense Wells's own creation',[302] he asserted, 'The minds of all of us, and therefore the physical world, would be perceptibly different if Wells had never existed.'[303] In the eyes of posterity, one of Wells's most enduring legacies was the dream he most readily disavowed, that of the fantastical city. His 1921 preface to *The Sleeper Awakes* declared that 'the great city of this story . . . is a fantastic possibility no longer possible'.[304] Wells's literary heirs, however, valorized his fantastical city not for its plausibility but for its profound imaginative power. In the words of urban fantasist Yevgeny Zamyatin, Wells created the London fairy tales of the twentieth century:

> imagine a country where the only fertile soil is asphalt, where nothing grows but dense forests of factory chimneys, where the animal herds are of a single breed, automobiles, and the only fragrance in the spring is that of gasoline. This place of stone, asphalt, iron, gasoline, and machines is present-day, twentieth-century London, and, naturally, it was bound to produce its own iron, automobile goblins, and its own mechanical, chemical fairy tales. Such urban tales exist: they are told by Herbert George Wells.[305]

3

The bells of lost London
Orwell's and Peake's anti-fantasies

The open sores of London

> All the while that they were talking the half-remembered rhyme kept running through Winston's head. Oranges and lemons, say the bells of St Clement's, You owe me three farthings, say the bells of St Martin's! It was curious, but when you said it to yourself you had the illusion of actually hearing bells, the bells of a lost London that still existed somewhere or other, disguised and forgotten. From one ghostly steeple after another he seemed to hear them pealing forth.[1]

This passage from *Nineteen Eighty-Four*, capturing the thoughts of Winston Smith as he stands bemused in Charrington's junk shop, his mind groping for 'a lost London that still existed somewhere or other', can be read as a distillation of the zeitgeist of post-war London. The Second World War had induced a new epistemology, aptly summarized by British wartime writer John Sommerfield: 'The past was dead, the future would be as we made it.'[2] By the end of the war, material testaments to London's past were shattered across the cityscape, with a third of the City of London – the streets and squares traversed by Scrooge on Christmas Day – reduced to rubble.[3] St Clement Danes on the Strand, the first church alluded to in the passage quoted above, was gutted in a Luftwaffe bombing that cracked most of its bells,[4] rendering them as mute and ghostly as Winston imagines them to be. The crypt of St Martin-in-the-Fields, the second church alluded to in the passage, which had featured in both Dickens's seminal 'moor eeffoc' experience and Wells 'The Crystal Egg', was hit by a bomb while serving as an air-raid shelter.[5] The adjacent National Gallery and what was then Trafalgar Square station were likewise bombed.[6]

Thus, Londoners living through the war and its immediate aftermath could have justifiably regarded pre-war London as 'lost', many of its iconic landmarks heavily damaged or reduced to debris. Orwell's 'London Letter' of August 1941 reflected on the 'shock one would get if one could suddenly see the London of three years ago side by side with this one'.[7] A year later, he reported that 'Regency London is becoming almost ruinous',[8] and by 1944 he was positively fed up with 'this beastly town'.[9] Peake vented his feelings into a ghastly poem entitled 'London, 1941' (1941) that compared London to the corpse of a woman 'from which the plaster breaks away / Like flesh from the rough bone'.[10] This corporeal imagery recurred six years later in Peake's 'Rhyme of the Flying Bomb' (1962), where a sailor rushes with a new-born baby through a bombed-out 'London raw as an open sore'.[11] Orwell and Peake alike were struggling to maintain hope that 'presently the world would be sane again'.[12]

This chapter argues that Orwell and Peake carried forward the Urban Fantasy tradition at a time when its fundamental beliefs were shaken to the core. At a historical moment in which celebrating the urban and the modern was exceedingly difficult, Orwell and Peake devised new strategies for writing liberal-progressive, London-based fantasies. They distinguished between American and British models of modernity, to the unmistakable advantage of the latter, and developed attenuated notions of the urban, based on crowds, markets, buses, parks and the grotesque, drawing heavily on Dickensian paradigms to do so. This chapter will focus on Orwell's *Nineteen Eighty-Four* and Peake's *Titus Alone*, but it also draws on Orwell's and Peake's other writings, together with Peake's illustrations and manuscript material from the Mervyn Peake Archive at the British Library, where such evidence is deemed helpful.

Common decency and Dickensian shadows

There is no evidence to suggest that Orwell and Peake ever met. In Peter Davison's twenty-volume *Complete Works of George Orwell* (1997–8), there is only one brief reference to Peake that consists of Orwell's favourable opinion of Peake's illustrations for a book. Yet the two authors shared some interesting resemblances. They were both born before the two world wars and lived through them. They died young and, unlike Dickens and Wells, achieved fame too late to enjoy it. Both moved to the London area in the late 1920s, and both worked for the Ministry of Information during the Second World War. As the war dragged on, they grew weary of Nazi bombardments and the city's wartime grimness, but endured the bombs and rockets and daily discomforts until the Allies had achieved a decided victory. Both wrote about London during the war and its aftermath, both looked back to Dickens as their model and inspiration, and for both, their first book of Urban Fantasy proved their last.

Orwell shared with Dickens an 'attraction of repulsion' to the seamier sides of London,[13] likewise recalling Wells's soft spot for the 'old, dirty, immoral, drunken' district of St Pancras.[14] His colleague, George Woodcock, thus recounted that Orwell was particularly fond of 'marginal districts like Islington and the less respectable fringes of Hampstead'.[15] Given Wells's hatred of the 'Hampstead genus' on account of its being 'respectable',[16] Woodcock's remarks speak to the changes in London locale since Wells's heady days in the late-Victorian capital, as the outlying areas of Hampstead took on an edgier cast.[17] These areas became the basis for Orwell's depictions of the down-at-heel districts of future London in *Nineteen Eighty-Four*. Orwell's fifth-floor flat in Langford Court afforded a clear view on the Ministry of Information that was housed in the nineteen-storey triangular building of Senate House in Bloomsbury that was the inspiration for Orwell's Ministry of Truth.[18] This flat has been further identified by W. J. West as the basis for Winston's flat in Victory Mansions,[19] 'seven flights up',[20] with a view on 'vistas of rotting nineteenth-century houses',[21] dwarfed by the 'enormous pyramidal structure' of the Ministry.[22]

In Islington, a north London area closer to the city centre, Orwell frequented a nearby 'working-class tavern',[23] where he seemed 'out of place' among the working-class patrons.[24] This experience was recognizably transposed to *Nineteen Eighty-Four*, as Winston enters 'a dingy little pub' in an unnamed prole quarter,[25] prompting the voices around him to lower noticeably. Orwell situates this prole quarter 'somewhere in the vague, brown-coloured slums to the north and east of what had once been Saint Pancras Station',[26] a description that fitted Islington's geographical location if not its social milieu. As Woodcock concluded, in *Nineteen Eighty-Four* Orwell envisaged 'the dread world of the future' as 'an even more decayed version' of 'wartime London'.[27]

Yet in the spirit of Dickens's romance of familiar things, Orwell took pleasure in discovering the beauty in these otherwise unprepossessing milieus. 'Suddenly, towards the end of March, the miracle happens and the decaying slum in which I live is transfigured',[28] he recounted, remarking with exaltation that 'not even the narrow and gloomy streets round the Bank of England are quite able to exclude' the advent of spring.[29] His admiration for 'a brighter blue between the chimney pots' in 'the most sordid street ... in the very heart of London' found its way into the London of *Nineteen Eighty-Four*,[30] where Winston's experience of 'mystical reverence' intermingles with 'the aspect of the pale, cloudless sky, stretching away behind the chimney pots'.[31]

Orwell's debt to Dickens was also deeply political. Orwell valorized |Dickens as the embodiment of 'common decency', a key term in his oeuvre that he also used to gesture towards the quality that was being systematically eroded by the forces of fascism. The *OED* defines 'decency' chiefly as a pragmatic trait, a kind of social decorum: an 'appropriateness or fitness to the circumstances'.[32] But what Orwell meant by 'decency' was rather different. He used the term to capture a particularly English (in Orwell's opinion) |inter-subjective social quality that occupies the liminal space between the external attribute of 'honour' and the internal property of 'virtue'. Decency, for Orwell, was 'the feeling that one is always on the side of the underdog'.[33] In the arena of international politics, common decency was signalled by the 'non-acceptance of the modern cult of power worship' that was characteristic of 'the English common people'.[34] Orwell never explicitly equated the 'English common people' with the English working classes, but such an equation was implied when he contrasted them with 'the British intelligentsia' and the 'middle class' to the unmistakable advantage of the working classes.[35] This association led in turn to his championship of Dickens's writings as consummate expressions of 'the native decency of the common man',[36] underpinned by Dickens's acute sensitivity to the everyday life of 'the ordinary, decent, labouring poor'.[37]

The political valence of Dickens's social perspective was a topic of lively debate between Orwell and Humphry House, as House was putting the final touches to *The Dickens World* (1941), arguably the most important book-length study of Dickens since Gissing's and Chesterton's studies of 1898 and 1906. The cover picture of its second edition of 1960, in a pleasing coincidence, was drawn by Peake.[38] House had read Orwell's article on Dickens with interest, and was sufficiently impressed by it to write him a seven-page letter in response, in which

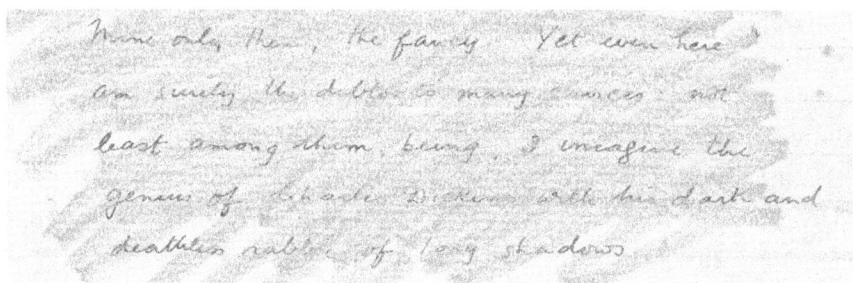

Figure 3.1 Peake, '"Ideas for Book Two" (*Titus Groan* chapters 60–61)', written *c.* 1939–43, 2 (paginated erratically), MPA, BL. © The British Library Board Add MS 88931/1/3/9.

he disputed Orwell's claim for Dickens's political radicalism on the basis that Dickens's ideas were superficial.[39] Orwell's interest lay not in Dickens's ideas, however, but precisely in the fact that where Dickens's analytical faculties fell short, his heart was sound, as evident in 'his quasi-instinctive siding with the oppressed against the oppressors'.[40] For Orwell, Dickens embodied a spirit of dissent, all the more enduring for its refusal to peddle political nostrums: 'the strongest single impression one carries away from his books is that of a hatred of tyranny.'[41]

Peake was less politically outspoken than Orwell, and his interest in Dickens was first and foremost aesthetic. Perhaps more than any other author, Peake recognized and celebrated the fact that Dickens's Urban Fantasy relied on cascading images of shadows. In a working notebook for *Titus Groan*, he wrote the following acknowledgement of his debt to Dickens (Figure 3.1):

> I am surely the debtor to many sources: not least among them, being, I imagine[,] the genius of Charles Dickens with his dark and deathless rabble of long shadows[.][42]

Dickens's 'dark and deathless rabble of long shadows' was discussed at length in Chapter 1. As shown, Dickens consciously deployed the imagery of shadows in order to craft his own brand of specifically London-based fantasy, because 'the heaping up of that quantity of shadows' was 'absolutely necessary' in a tale about the Phantom out of Oxford Street. The fact that Peake not only picked up on this quality in 'the genius of Charles Dickens', but directly acknowledged its influence on his own fantasy novels, emphasizes the extent to which Dickens and Peake were bound by a shared crepuscular vision of the fantastical city. Further supporting this point is Peake's unusual use of the term 'rabble' to describe 'shadows', for a few years later he would allude to 'my Gormenghast rabble'.[43]

Dickensian shadows permeate the *Gormenghast Trilogy*, from 'the shadows of time-eaten buttresses' of Gormenghast Castle,[44] to 'the shadows that hung like black water against the walls' in the unnamed city.[45] Indeed, the first figure to detach itself from Peake's Gormenghastian shadows in *Titus Groan* is Rottcodd, the curator of Gormenghast Castle's Hall of the Bright Carvings. The inspiration for Rottcodd's name came to Peake at a decidedly 'moor eeffoc' moment – Peake named him after seeing the word 'doctor' on the windscreen of his father's car: from inside the vehicle it read 'rotcod'.[46]

Orwell's and Peake's views on fantasy may be neatly related to the two figures that coalesce from the transformations wrought by the shadows of Dickens's *Haunted Man*, which make of tongs the 'straddling giant . . . smelling the blood of Englishmen' and of 'the rocking-horse a monster'.[47] Orwell declared that 'the basic myth of the Western world is Jack the Giant Killer',[48] which for him was emblematic of the 'good-tempered antinomianism rather of Dickens's type'.[49] Orwell celebrated this myth as a distilled dramatization of 'common decency': 'until recently the characteristic adventure stories of the English-speaking peoples have been stories in which the hero fights *against odds*',[50] he asserted. Jack the Giant Killer was the myth that underpinned 'the popular protests . . . against imperialism' in Britain,[51] together with the rejection of fascism by the majority of the British public. Yet as the war dragged on, he was concerned to see this myth turning against itself: 'to be brought up to date this [myth] should be renamed Jack the Dwarf Killer'.[52] The new myth seemed disconcertingly in line with the rising ideologies of the time, as Orwell discerned its underlying currents of 'sadism, . . . nationalism, and totalitarianism'.[53]

Peake was fascinated by the rocking-horse-turned-monster, an object of delight suddenly made terrible, channelling the darkness that lurks at the heart of every childhood. In *Titus Alone*, he made an elegiac variation on that same image, in what may have been an oblique allusion to Dickens: 'A rocking-horse, festooned with spiders' rigging, sways where there's no one in a gusty loft.'[54] By 'how small a twist might she not suddenly have become beautiful,'[55] he wrote of his heroine Fuchsia Groan, but by the same token by how small a twist might not innocence suddenly become terror, as Titus discovers to his dismay when confronted by a devastating farce of his childhood home in the tellingly named 'Black House'.[56]

Peake's illustrations for *Bleak House* – made for an edition that eventually fell through but not before he drew a host of Dickens characters as marvellous grotesques – share more than a passing resemblance to his illustrations of his own grotesque characters in the *Gormenghast Trilogy*. His illustration of Mr Chadband (Figure 3.2) – a clergyman in *Bleak House* who preaches to Jo about his 'state of sinfulness',[57] but fails to offer him the slightest compassion or aid – is a case in point. The illustration portrays Chadband with a large abdomen and small head, in keeping with Dickens's descriptions of the clergyman as a man of voracious appetite but weak intellect. His body and clothes melding in a flabby texture of undifferentiated whiteness, Peake's Chadband is separated from his grey background by a fuzzy black line that renders his body porous almost to the point of gelatinousness.

Peake's full-page drawing of Swelter (Figure 3.3), the chef of Gormenghast Castle, bears visible resemblances to both his illustration of Chadband and Dickens's descriptions of the clergyman. Swelter is similarly portrayed as a grotesquely large-bodied man awash in white, whose flesh is barely contained by the thinnest of black lines against a swirling grey background. Furthermore, a section from one of Peake's working notebooks for *Titus Groan* that predates his illustrations for *Bleak House* contains a sketch of Swelter threatening a boy with a kitchen cleaver.[58] But the published drawing shows Swelter embracing a boy in a manner scarcely less threatening for the absence of a cleaver, but which aligns him more closely with Chadband who in a patronizing gesture lays 'his flabby paw' on 'Jo's arm'.[59] Indeed, the visual correspondences between Chadband and Swelter seem to have spilled over from Peake's illustrations to his text. Dickens repeatedly likened Mr Chadband to 'a vessel',[60] 'a consuming vessel',[61] 'a gorging vessel',[62] or with heavy irony, an 'exemplary vessel'.[63] Peake likened Swelter's chef hat to 'a vague topsail half lost in a fitful sky',[64] observing that 'the total effect' of Swelter's appearance 'was indeed something of the galleon'.[65]

Peake even tried his hand at a Dickensian Christmas tale, 'Danse Macabre' (1963), which was written during the early stages of his work on *Titus Alone*.[66] 'Danse Macabre' reworked the premise of Dickens's 'Meditations in Monmouth Street' into a satirical horror story. The protagonist of the tale discovers that his formal attire comes to life each night to escape his wardrobe and dance in the woods with the evening gown of his estranged wife. Unlike Boz, who was swept up in the excitement of the sartorial uprising taking place in his mind's eye, Peake's narrator responds with indignation at the spectacle of his clothes 'trying to dislodge themselves from the hanger'.[67] His most pressing concern proves to be that his public reputation might suffer as a result: 'I would never have

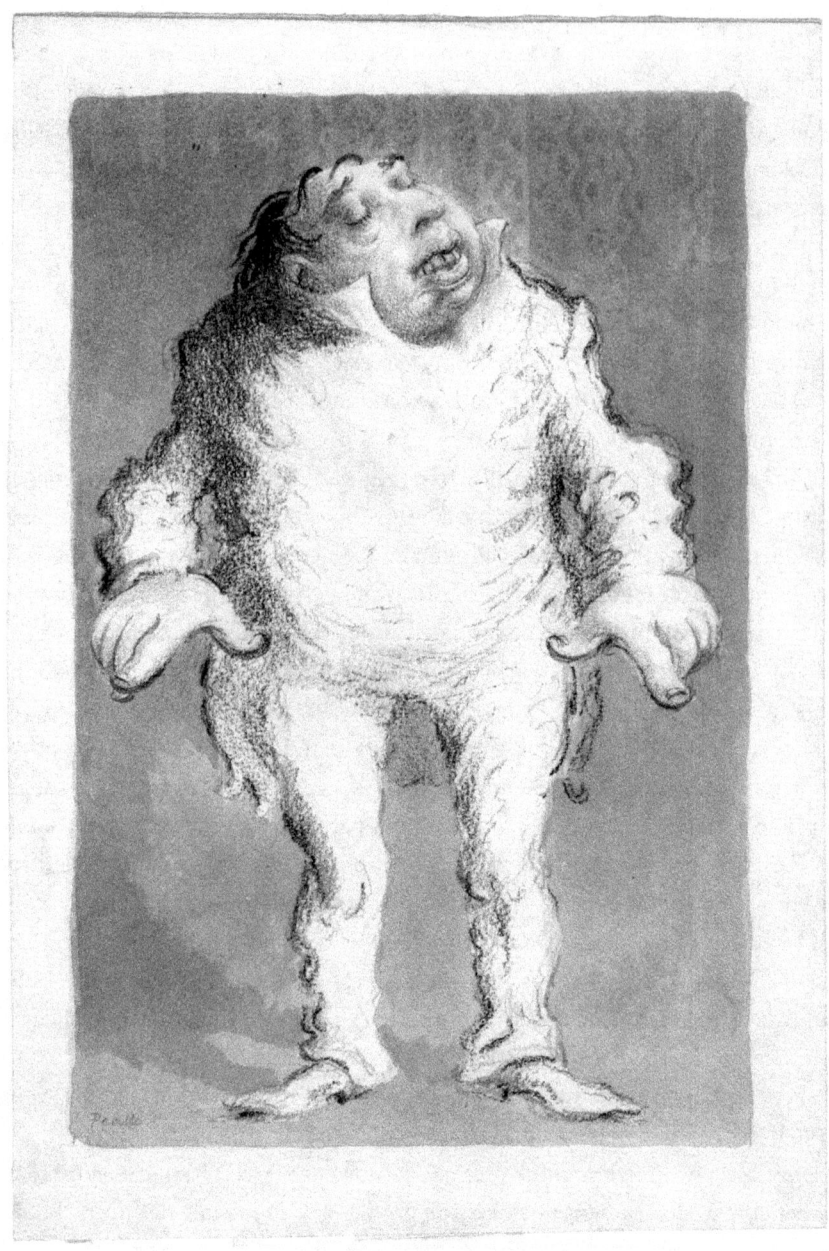

Figure 3.2 Drawn by Mervyn Peake, 'Mr Chadband', c. 1945, in *Sketches from Bleak House*, 47.

Figure 3.3 Drawn by Mervyn Peake, 'Swelter with Kitchen Urchin' (captioned 'Abiatha Swelter'), *c.* 1968, in *Titus Groan* (1946), 2nd edn (London: Eyre & Spottiswoode, 1968), opposite 368 (n.p.).

lifted my head again in public if I knew myself to be regarded as some kind of metaphysical crank.'[68] Thus, where Dickens used the premise of resurrected clothes to restore visibility and humanity to the social outcasts of Victorian London, Peake used it to satirize post-war Englishmen whose priggish sense of propriety left them imaginatively and emotionally stunted, scarcely more than empty suits and deflated gowns longing for meaningful human connection but unable to offer it themselves.

Where Orwell expressed a Dickensian fascination with London's squalor, Peake shared Dickens's love of London grotesquery. Ernest Everon wrote of Dickens that his characters were drawn from 'the streets of a great city',[69] which showcase 'those circumstances which are strange, and those individual peculiarities which are odd and singular'.[70] The same could be said of Peake, whose London escapades in the early 1930s were recalled by his close friend Gordon Smith in decidedly Dickensian terms:

> From the tops of buses, from circuses, and foreign restaurants; out of a wild variety of lodgings and town houses and dance-halls, Mervyn took his spoils: little men with placards proclaiming 'The End is Nigh!', waiters in sleazy bars,

grotesque but pitiful women saying goodbye at railway termini to fantastic men,
. . . On an old envelope from his pocket or on a sketching-pad, he took them: strangely transformed, yet always real and convincing.[71]

Thus, while Orwell was drawn to the rougher haunts of north London, Peake preferred the artistic bohemia of Soho. His experiences of London, as described by Smith, formed a breathless diorama of idiosyncratic characters, unusual vantage points, startling juxtapositions, dazzling variety and tragic vignettes glimpsed from afar that, taken together, were nothing if not Dickensian. Yet these experiences were also firmly grounded in Peake's 1930s London and filtered through his artistic sensibility. The enticing 'foreign restaurants' that had caught his eye had sprung up in Soho after the First World War, as 'the decline in the numbers of domestic servants increased the habit of "eating out"'.[72] Dance-halls were likewise a distinctive feature of London's nightlife in the interwar years,[73] celebrated in Peake's poem 'Palais de Danse' (1937). Peake was in his element among the Soho crowd, meeting his fellow art students at local cafés where he sketched the clientele and contributed to local exhibitions.[74] In the early 1930s, he joined a coterie of artists who took their name from the area, 'the "Soho Group"',[75] even as he planned a book of artwork based on his London sketches, to be entitled *Head-Hunting in London*.[76] The book failed to materialize, but Peake's sketches developed and honed his acute sensitivity to the idiosyncrasies of London.

For all his apparent bonhomie, Peake was not blinkered to the tragedies of London. The 'little men with placards proclaiming "The End is Nigh!"' that he had sketched in Smith's company were later reworked into a drawing that adorns Peake's aforementioned imaginative piece, 'London Fantasy'. This drawing portrays a man in profile sandwiched between two plaques – one above his head proclaiming 'prepare to meet thy God',[77] the other draped over his front declaiming 'repent o ye who sin'.[78] Peake emphasized the soft features of the man's face, which are tenderly sketched down to the small scar by his ear and the hint of stubble beneath his chin. This figure is never directly referenced in the written piece, but its defeated posture and sad eyes suggest that it typifies the everyday casualties of London, 'those who have given up'.[79] According to his wife, Peake had met such people at close quarters. On the first Christmas of the war, he made his way down to the arches beneath Waterloo Bridge where he knew that 'the derelict and the homeless congregated' to distribute packets of cigarettes among them.[80] Although he lamented in 'London Fantasy' that 'the eye can cease to respond, the brain to absorb, the heart to miss a beat',[81] Peake remained sensitized to the pain of his city, chronicling in paint, poetry and prose 'the story that is told by the tilt of a hat, the torn sleeve, the stare that is out of focus, the humped shoulders'.[82]

'Poisonous rubbish': Orwell, Peake and American modernity

The 1930s and 1940s did not provide a climate conducive to writing in the Urban Fantasy tradition that was underpinned by a liberal-progressive world view and celebrated the city even while critiquing it. Writing contemporaneously in this period, Orwell and Peake were living through a time in which it was more difficult to believe in the ethos of progress, or even to define it, than ever before or since. As Orwell observed, 'when Wells was young, the antithesis between science and reaction was not false',[83] but in the throes of the Blitz it no longer held true. The Great War and the Second World War had shattered the naïve belief in progress that had been the prevailing ethos of nineteenth-century left-wing intellectualism, proving that technological progress did not lead inevitably to moral progress or to the betterment of the human condition. Rather, in its fascist incarnation it went hand in hand with the resurgence of moral primitivism, 'a ghost from the past',[84] which progressive intellectuals such as Wells had believed to have long since been laid to rest.

Celebrating London proved equally difficult, scarcely less in the immediate aftermath of the Second World War than it had been during wartime. Post-war London was pockmarked with bombsites and covered in rubble, and the flagging spirits of Londoners who were recovering from the Blitz and mourning loved ones were dampened still further by the continued rationing of food and other necessities that was imposed during the war and maintained well into the 1950s.[85] London was, as Orwell's friend Cyril Connolly described it, 'the largest, saddest and dirtiest of great cities'.[86]

Yet Orwell and Peake were broadly committed to an ideal of progress and a belief that the future of humanity lay in the city. Time and again, Orwell voiced the unpopular claim that 'men are only as good as their technical development allows them to be'.[87] Even in the throes of the Blitz, he continued to insist on the positive impact of science and technology on the lives of Britons, particularly the working classes.[88] He praised Zamyatin's *We* (1924), an acknowledged influence on *Nineteen Eighty-Four*, for taking account of 'the tendency to return to an earlier form of civilization which seem[s] to be part of totalitarianism'.[89] In this respect, Orwell viewed totalitarianism as the enemy of progress rather than its culmination. While taking advantage of surveillance technology and modern weaponry, the totalitarian Party in *Nineteen Eighty-Four* makes strenuous efforts to ensure that 'the world is more primitive today than it was fifty years ago'.[90]

Unlike Orwell, Peake was a 'non-political animal' by nature,[91] as attested by Gordon Smith. But his writings had political underpinnings that disclosed something of his world view. In the *Gormenghast Trilogy*, Titus's distaste for the empty rituals of Gormenghast Castle and his especial aversion towards the degradation of the local peasantry involved in these ceremonies, all suggest liberal-progressive undercurrents. Indeed, the case can be made that the *Gormenghast Trilogy* stages the futility of attempts to turn back the clock or arrest time. The creed of Gormenghast Castle is 'No Change!',[92] but change arrives without the slightest regard for the Gormenghastians' objections. The greatest change is ushered by Titus himself, who abdicates the throne and leaves his ancestral home, arriving at a futurist, modern city that has never heard of Gormenghast Castle. Moorcock went so far as to argue that of the 'living English writers' of the 1950s,[93] 'only Mervyn Peake seemed to have an interest in contemporary life'.[94]

One of the principal ways in which Orwell and Peake grappled with their conflicted notions of liberal-progressiveness was to define these notions against a brand of modernity often identified with the United States and the Americanization of Britain. By the end of the Great War, the British Empire was on the wane and the United States was coming into its own as the leading global power of the Western world. In 1919, New York superseded London as the financial capital of the world,[95] and from the 1920s onward, American culture began to be exported rapidly and en masse into Britain, a process of cultural osmosis that accelerated during the Second World War and beyond it to the post-war era.[96] Some British authors resented this process of Americanization, whether for cultural, ideological or professional reasons (or a blend thereof), and singled out qualities in American culture that they found particularly objectionable.

Orwell defined British modernity as a new iteration of the enduring British trait of common decency, which was modern insofar as it was marked by 'a general softening of manners' enabled 'by the fact that modern industrial methods tend always to demand less muscular effort'.[97] He defined American modernity by the opposite character, by a culture of 'masochism, success-worship, power-worship',[98] and a queasy atmosphere where 'everything [is] slick and shiny and streamlined'.[99] 'One periodical reminder that things *have changed* in England since the [Second World] war is the arrival of American magazines',[100] Orwell observed with evident regret, 'with their enormous bulk, sleek paper and riot of brilliantly coloured adverts'.[101] American magazines were indeed widely exported into Britain in the 1940s and American science-fiction pulps in particular had increased in popularity since Hugo Gernsback began editing the first pulp exclusively devoted to fantastical fiction.[102] As Gary Westfahl argues, Gernsback played a seminal role in 'the continuing prominence of melodrama in written and filmed science fiction'.[103] John W. Campbell, often regarded as Gernsback's successor in the 1940s and 1950s, steered American science-fiction pulps away from Gernsbackian melodrama into what Mike Ashley has termed 'the world of "modern" sf' that explored 'social and political issues'.[104] But Orwell and his British contemporaries were responding less to Campbell than to Gernsback's earlier and still highly influential iteration.

Orwell unceremoniously declared the American science-fiction pulps to be 'poisonous rubbish'.[105] He was particularly grieved to see 'the genuine scientific interest of the H. G. Wells stories' denuded into 'a riot of nonsensical sensationalism'.[106] Not only were these stories rubbish, but they were toxic: 'they tend to stimulate fantasies of power'.[107] The pulps' professions to anti-fascism were all but lip service, Orwell contended, because it was precisely in their most avowedly anti-fascist issues that they gave themselves the greatest licence to glorify violence with 'the frankest appeal to sadism'.[108] He was dismayed to see that the American 'doctrine that might is right' was supplanting the British 'tendency to support the weaker side merely because it is weaker'.[109] Thus, in defiance of this glorification of violence, Orwell affected a return to the local and provisional, to the Dickensian fascination with streets, inns, crowds and stalls. He celebrated 'the open-air market',[110] 'the cabbage-littered alley between the stalls',[111] 'pubs, fried-fish shops, picture-houses',[112] 'the vivid green of an elder sprouting on a blitzed site' and 'a first-rate performance by a blackbird in the Euston Road'.[113]

Peake's aversion to the form of modernity most readily associated with the United States is evident in Titus's response to the Americanized centre of the unnamed city in *Titus Alone*, which features a cluster of high-rises not unlike Wells's vision of the 'Pleasure Cities' that defiled the honour of ordinary Londoners in his dystopian imaginings of the future. 'Had Titus come across a world of dragons he could hardly have been more amazed than by these fantasies of glass and metal',[114] the narrator observes, but 'he suffered at the same time a pang of resentment'.[115] These lines plainly express British resentment of the American culture of skyscrapers and glass towers that had sprung up in Chicago and New York at the turn of the century, anticipating an analogous boom in London that would begin in the mid-1960s,[116] scarcely five years after the publication of *Titus Alone*'s first edition. A similar distaste for high-rises may be found in *Nineteen Eighty-Four*, where the four government Ministries 'dwarf the surrounding architecture'.[117] As aforementioned, Orwell's Ministry of Truth was inspired by the high-rise of Senate House, then the tallest skyscraper in London.[118]

Recalling Dickens's penchant for the obsolete curiosity, Orwell and Peake aligned themselves with the time-worn, rough-hewn object against the slick and shiny product. This was (and still is) a very British attitude, articulated by Orwell as he complained that 'the majority of English people' now prefer 'the shiny, standardised, machine-made look of the American apple' to 'the superior taste of the English apple'.[119] Titus, for his part, cherishes 'an egg-shaped flint' that is knobby, rough and uncouth, its abrasive touch reminding Titus 'that his boyhood was real'.[120] Taken from the Tower of Flints in Gormenghast Castle that forms 'a mutilated finger . . . pointed blasphemously at heaven',[121] the flint becomes a symbolic correlative of Titus's own untethered state: 'He was a chip of stone, but where was the mountain from which it had broken away?'.[122] Titus eventually sacrifices the flint to destroy a surveillance globe that represents everything that is hateful about the Americanized section of the city. Forming a fractal of the 'crystal buildings' in the 'glassy region',[123] the surveillance globe is a 'glassy sphere',[124] 'glittering',[125] 'exquisite',[126] and 'something quite hideously efficient'.[127] Titus shatters it into 'a cascade of dazzling splinters' with a well-aimed throw of 'his knuckle of flint'.[128]

This opposition between the glittering globe and the knobby flint extends to characters as well as inanimate objects. Titus's false admirer Cheeta is 'slick as a needle to the outward eye',[129] aligning her firmly with the glassy region. His mysterious pursuers, two silent helmeted men reminiscent of Orwell's Thought Police, are depicted 'not so much walking as gliding, so smoothly they advanced'.[130] The steadfast Muzzlehatch, by contrast, boasts a 'huge, craggy head' that calls to mind 'the inordinate moon with its pits and craters'.[131] Muzzlehatch thereby embodies the abrasive and down-to-earth section of the city that he describes as 'the slums that crawl up to my courtyard'.[132] In the MSS of *Titus Alone*, Titus explicitly reflects on the comforting familiarity imparted by Muzzlehatch's unruliness, noting that contrary to the glass-and-metal centre of the city, 'Muzzlehatch . . . was not a building, or a flying needle. & his dark untidy home was something T[itus] could understand'.[133] The MSS likewise dwell on the 'rough-hewn sanity' of three vagrants from the Under-River,[134] a hidden realm of outcasts beneath the city. These vagrants are gradually introduced among piles of detritus and bric-a-brac (Figure 3.4):

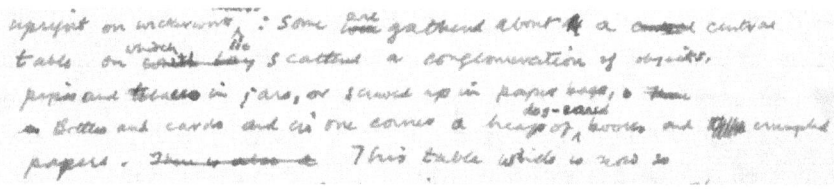

Figure 3.4 Peake, '"Titus 3" (*Titus Alone* chapters 51–63 (a))', dated 1956, 2 (paginated erratically, strikethrough in original), MPA, BL. © The British Library Board Add MS 88931/1/3/31.

> Some ~~were~~ are gathered about ~~a~~ a ~~central~~ central table on ~~which lay~~ which lie scattered a conglomeration of objects, pipes and tobacco in jars, or screwed up in paper bags, . ~~There~~[?] ~~is~~[?] Bottles and cards and in one corner a heap of dog-eared books and ~~torn~~ crumpled papers.

Thus, Orwell and Peake formulated a strategy for celebrating urban life at a time when such a celebration was exceedingly difficult. They did so by contrasting British urbanism with an image of American urbanism as 'slick and shiny and streamlined' and full of 'glass and metal'. They could thereby define British urbanism by way of contrast, aligning it with 'the spoor and gristle' of the detective's 'hound-like job',[135] with 'the crowds by the river' and especially 'the old and the worn' among them,[136] with 'the stink' and the 'old black pipe' lit from 'the night-old shadows' on 'the bank of the river' in the slum district of Peake's unnamed city.[137] Or in Orwell's formulations, 'the barges on the miry river, the familiar streets, . . . the men in bowler hats, the pigeons in Trafalgar Square'.[138] Little did they know that slick and shiny and streamlined glass and-metal corporate skyscrapers would soon dominate London's skyline in the City of London and Canary Wharf.[139] In this respect, Wells's futurist fictions of the London of the year 2100 were more prophetic of the twenty-first-century cityscape than Orwell's depictions of the London of the near future. Orwell's and Peake's visions were residual and attenuated, but however shrill and small, they valorized urban life at a time when grave doubt was cast on the value of continued dwelling within the forms and fashions of the city.

'Only a city': Orwell's and Peake's fantastical Londons

Nineteen Eighty-Four and *Titus Alone* are both set in a future London (in *Titus Alone*, a recognizable variation thereof), but it is a future of an altogether different timbre from Wells's rendition in *When the Sleeper Wakes*. Orwell's writings suggest that *When the Sleeper Wakes* was his favourite among Wells's scientific romances,[140] and its influence on *Nineteen Eighty-Four* has been well documented.[141] But the imagined futures of *When the Sleeper Wakes* and *Nineteen Eighty-Four* differed significantly in the measure of their remoteness from their respective present-days. *When the Sleeper Wakes* is set in the London of 2100, more than two centuries into the future from the year of its publication, whereas *Nineteen Eighty-Four* is set in the London of its titular year of 1984, a mere thirty-five years from the date it was published, famously inverting the last two digits of the year it was finalized (1948/1984).

This condensation of time speaks to the urgency of Orwell's vision. *When the Sleeper Wakes* and *Nineteen Eighty-Four* are both cautionary tales of a nightmare future. But the temporal remoteness of this future in *When the Sleeper Wakes* allows readers to take comfort in the thought that the nightmare lies far ahead. Orwell allowed for no such consolations. As he told Fredric Warburg, *Nineteen Eighty-Four* was not intended as 'a book of anticipations' in the Wellsian spirit of prognostication.[142] Rather, it was a call to immediate action, more in the nature of an air-raid siren than of Wells's meditations on 'Things to Come'. As Orwell affirmed in a Press Release issued shortly after the book's publication: 'The moral to be drawn from this dangerous nightmare situation is a simple one: *Don't let it happen. It depends on you.*'[143]

Nineteen Eighty-Four is consequently shot through with a heightened sense of historical rupture, as it hypothesizes that in the span of three and a half decades the entire population of Britain will forget its history in a wilful act of collective amnesia termed '*doublethink*'. *Titus Alone* manifests a similar temporal incongruity, transporting the reader from the ancient world of Gormenghast Castle to a modern setting of urban high-rises, aeroplanes, cars, futuristic surveillance equipment, telecommunications and death-rays, with scarcely a pause for reorientation.

These vertiginous shifts were reflective of the historical moment. Orwell and Peake were living through a rupture with the past. When Wells wrote *When the Sleeper Wakes* at the turn of the century, it was reasonable to assume that the future would roughly resemble the present, which had roughly resembled the past, and consequently to spin a cautionary tale against mental intransigence. Ironically, by the early 1940s, it was Orwell's turn to accuse Wells of intransigence, on the grounds that history had ruptured, and that Wells was still clinging to now-debunked Victorian and Edwardian frames of thought.[144] *Nineteen Eighty-Four* and *Titus Alone* are consequently suffused with the fear that the past might be irrevocably lost. The motto of the totalitarian Party in *Nineteen Eighty-Four* reads:

'who controls the past controls the future: who controls the present controls the past',[145] and Winston suspects they may be right. By ceaselessly altering historical records, newspaper reports and language itself, as well as conditioning human memory, the Party ensures that 'the past is whatever the Party chooses to make it'.[146] Accordingly, a crucial step in Winston's surrender involves his acceptance of O'Brien's diagnosis: 'You suffer from a defective memory'.[147]

Titus is subject to a similar diagnosis, after he correctly introduces himself as the Seventy-Seventh Earl of Gormenghast. After being told repeatedly that his 'title belongs to another age' and subjected to interrogations to the effect of 'have you lapses of memory?',[148] Titus too begins to doubt himself, confessing to the local Magistrate: 'I have lost my bearings, sir'.[149] Lest this suggest nostalgia for the glory days of the British Empire, which was on its last legs during the post-war years, one should recall that Gormenghast Castle is decadent and stifling to the core, and that while yearning for home as he wanders in exile, Titus was desperate to leave when he was being groomed for Earldom. Titus's longing for 'the kingdom in my head' is thus not so much a desire to turn back the clock,[150] but the search for a new kind of stability that has slipped away with his abdication.

For Orwell and Peake alike, the crisis of history was centred upon London, explicitly in *Nineteen Eighty-Four* and implicitly in *Titus Alone*. London was the natural choice, as nowhere in Britain were the effects of the Second World War more starkly visible. 'London looked like the moon's capital',[151] Elizabeth Bowen wrote grimly in 1944, it was 'shallow, cratered, extinct'.[152] Orwell and Peake both experienced the bombings at first-hand. 'The whole house shakes',[153] Orwell reported in 1941 of 'the mere passage of a bomb',[154] and in 1944 he and his family were bombed out of their Kilburn flat.[155] Peake's Soho studio remained intact by sheer luck: 'the V1s ... buzzed ominously overhead, and then cut out, above the glass roof of the studio'.[156]

Orwell's vision of dystopian London in *Nineteen Eighty-Four* was therefore substantively different from Wells's in *When the Sleeper Wakes*. Wells's vision may have been 'a nightmare',[157] but it was a sublime and glorious one, a breathtaking evocation of 'overwhelming architecture'.[158] Orwell's future London, by contrast, is dreary, spent and dilapidated. Its elevators malfunction and its sinks clog on a regular basis, its underground trains are overcrowded and its interior hallways smell perennially of cabbage. If the dystopian London of *When the Sleeper Wakes* is magnificent, the dystopian London of *Nineteen Eighty-Four* is underwhelming, irritating and uncomfortable:

> The plaster flaked constantly from ceilings and walls, the pipes burst in every hard frost, the roof leaked whenever there was snow, the heating system was

usually running at half steam when it was not closed down altogether from motives of economy.¹⁵⁹

This downscaled vision of future London was a direct corollary of the historical moment. Orwell's London was not Wells's 'seat of world Empire',¹⁶⁰ but a vulnerable city under nightly attacks, suffering from constant scarcity and disruption in transport, the plaster peeling off the walls of its buildings and 'disgusting scenes' unfolding in its 'Tube stations at night'.¹⁶¹

The city that forms the setting of the better part of *Titus Alone* remains unnamed, but as Tanya Gardiner-Scott points out, it resembles from above 'an aerial view of London' defamiliarized by its placement on a mountainside.¹⁶² Peake himself attested that 'London, famous for its eccentrics, was at my elbow' in a BBC talk contemporaneous with the earlier stages of his composition of *Titus Alone*.¹⁶³ In the MSS of *Titus Alone*, Peake's descriptions of the subterranean Under-River hidden away in tunnels and caverns beneath the city are lifted almost verbatim from 'London Fantasy'. In 'London Fantasy', the narrator ruminates on the 'delirium of heads',¹⁶⁴ 'the endless, generous profligacy' of London.¹⁶⁵ 'There is no end to it. The Invention is so rapid, various, profluent',¹⁶⁶ the narrator exclaims, until finally

> Each desperate moment, clutching Entirety, sinks with a smouldering fistful of raw plunder; sinks into nullity while time slides on, and the heads move by and are huge: . . . huge, as they turn and stare . . . ¹⁶⁷

In a section of the MSS, dated 21 November 1956, nearly the exact same phrases recur in a scene in the Under-River, with handwritten corrections – probably Peake's – altering these phrases from the present to the past tense (Figure 3.5):

> It was a delirium of heads: and every one one an original. An endless, gen profligacy. There is was no end to it. The invention is was so rapid, various, profluent. [illegible word] Each mo moment sinks sank away, sinks sank with a smouldering fist-ful of raw raw plunder plunder; sinks sank into nullity while time slid slides[?] on & the heads grew huge as they stared.

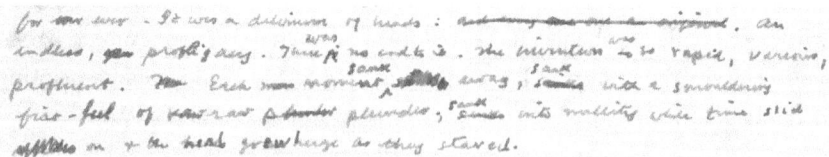

Figure 3.5 *Titus Alone* chapters 51–63(b) (paginated erratically, strikethrough in original), MPA, BL. © The British Library Board Add MS 88931/1/3/31, 17.

Peake's verbatim transposition of substantial sections from a sketch about the fantastical qualities of London to a description of the underworld beneath the surface city of *Titus Alone* suggests at the very least that he had London in mind when he designed his unnamed metropolis. Doubly so given the topical resonances of the Under-River – Londoners had sheltered in the subterranean spaces beneath their city, in Tube stations, crypts and deep-level shelters, on a nightly basis during the Blitz and the Little Blitz,[168] scarcely a decade before Peake began his work on *Titus Alone*. Peake expressly associated the London eccentrics that inspired his visual art, and by implication his writing, with the London Underground: 'The Red Queen, or nearly the Red Queen, bumped into me in Holborn Underground.'[169]

If the London of *Titus Alone* remains unnamed, the London of *Nineteen Eighty-Four* is the only geographical location that has not undergone a name change under the rule of the totalitarian Party, prompting Winston to wonder 'whether London had always been quite like this'.[170] Orwell's longer-lived contemporary, Wyndham Lewis, observed in his assessment of *Nineteen Eighty-Four* that its 'lost London' of the past resembled 'the London of Charles Dickens'.[171] Given that Orwell's lost London is evoked through the ghostly peals of church bells, and given that, as discussed in Chapter 1, Dickens's *The Chimes* was his most overtly political London fantasy, Lewis's observation seems apposite. Orwell's fantastical London gestured back to Dickens's – most visibly to the London of *The Chimes*, with its supernatural goblins and 'clear, loud, lusty' chimes, 'fighting gallantly' against adversity with 'their cheerful notes' of irrepressible verve[172] – because for Orwell, Dickens's London was a distillation of the London he feared might be irrevocably lost. It was the London of 'the bells of St Martin's' that were within earshot of Dickens's moor eeffoc café,[173] which toll away in Winston's and Orwell's minds as if they had never cracked and the Blitz had never happened. It was the London of 'an armchair beside an open fire' and 'the friendly ticking' of 'an old-fashioned glass clock with a twelve-hour face' that paint a consummate picture of Dickensian domesticity;[174] of '*a time when thought is free, when men are different from one another and do not live alone*' that could easily be a distillation of Dickens's social vision.[175] Lest readers mistake his intent, Orwell cemented this connection between Victorian London and his lost London of the past as Winston's discerns 'a message from a hundred years ago' inside his glass paperweight,[176] a past more precisely defined in the extant manuscript of *Nineteen Eighty-Four* as 'the nineteenth century'.[177]

Lawrence Phillips argues that 'the material fabric' of London in *Nineteen Eighty-Four* defies the Party's erosion of history,[178] because it refracts the city's piecemeal development across the centuries. As Phillips contends, London's quilted cityscape, made up of a medley of buildings from previous eras jostling with 'the contemporary material experience of the city',[179] undermines the Party's endeavour to homogenize the semiotics of London topography into 'an endless present in which the Party is always right'.[180] Despite its systematic alteration of 'statues, inscriptions, memorial stones, the names of streets',[181] London locales are still recognizable through their material presence, and thus capable of disclosing the city's past. The Party might claim that the 'statue of a man on horseback' in 'Victory Square' represents 'Oliver Cromwell',[182] but the reader recognizes Trafalgar Square and its statue of King George IV, not least because Victory Square has retained 'the lions at the base of the monument'.[183] Furthermore, some London institutions have retained their function if not their name – the National Gallery is still a 'picture gallery'[184] – and others, such as 'Paddington Station',[185] have retained both. Likewise, St Martin-in-the-Field's might have become 'a museum used for propaganda',[186] but its iconic appearance has remained unchanged: 'A building with a kind of a triangular porch and pillars in front, and a big flight of steps.'[187] In these respects, at least, traces of Dickens's and Orwell's Londons are detectable in the eroded London of *Nineteen Eighty-Four*. Phillips's point is well-taken, but one should note that unlike Graham's epiphanies in *When the Sleeper Wakes* as he discovers 'a perpetual wonder in topographical identifications',[188] in *Nineteen Eighty-Four* Winston partakes of this pleasure only once: on his way to meet Julia in Victory Square, 'he . . . got a sort of pale-coloured pleasure from identifying St Martin's church'.[189] A 'pale-coloured pleasure' is a far cry from Graham's 'perpetual wonder', and even this pleasure is largely foreclosed to Winston. Throughout the bulk of *Nineteen Eighty-Four*, he must content himself with a vague, fleeting echo of lost London, 'a sort of nostalgia, a sort of ancestral memory'.[190]

Orwell's and Peake's celebration of London is thus attenuated and residual, focusing chiefly on the local and provisional aspects of urban life. The first volume of Henry Lefebvre's *The Critique of Everyday Life* (1947), published at approximately the same time as *Titus Groan* and *Nineteen Eighty-Four*, pitted everyday life against 'nostalgia for the past or dreams of a superhuman future'.[191] For Lefebvre, 'the rejection of everyday life' led to 'the Hitlerian "mystique"',[192] whereas 'all the acts of our everyday lives' had the redemptive quality of making 'the human being . . . more social'.[193] Notwithstanding that Lefebvre was a French philosopher and they were British authors of Urban Fantasy, Peake's and Orwell's visions took on a similar tenor. Their progressiveness was genuine, but they ended up celebrating London on a reduced scale, fastening on markets, buses, parks, the crowd and minute acts of interpersonal kindness, in an ever-increasing distance from the modern and the technological.

In *Nineteen Eighty-Four*, Winston and Julia are only ever safe from the Party when they venture outside of enclosed office or domestic spaces into the crowded cityscape. With the dubious exception of the countryside, where 'you could not assume that you were much safer ... than in London',[194] the only place in which they can find temporary relief is in 'the heart of the [London] crowd'.[195] Inverting the conventional division between public and private spaces, the Party exerts absolute control over the interior spaces of the city – the flats,[196] bedrooms and bathrooms – whereas the teeming streets and squares of London afford a modicum of freedom and privacy. In the MS of *Nineteen Eighty-Four*, Julia is said to 'have a complete map of London inside her head',[197] which dovetails with the book's observation that 'she obviously had a practical cunning which Winston lacked'.[198] A significant component of this cunning is her familiarity with London and her understanding that there is safety in its crowds. Winston and Julia thus set the location for their first meeting at Victory Square, and when Winston objects that 'it's full of telescreens',[199] Julia responds: 'It doesn't matter if there's a crowd.'[200]

Calling to mind Orwell's assertion in *Keep the Aspidistra Flying* that 'whenever you see a street-market you know that there's hope for England yet',[201] they meet again in 'an open market which was generally crowded and noisy',[202] acting on the hope that 'with luck, in the middle of the crowd, it would be safe'.[203] They thus develop a rhythm of doomed romantic *flânerie*, drifting 'down the crowded pavements, not quite abreast and never looking at one another'.[204] They are not caught during any of these rendezvous in London's crowded public spaces. It is only when Winston and Julia discard the protective mantle of the London crowd in favour of the empty and therefore exposed room of Charrington's faux-junk shop that the Thought Police descend upon them.

Peake was equally fascinated by the London crowd, but his milieu was less the open market and more the streets around Cambridge Circus where 'The crowd collects.'[205] When depicting confrontations between the metropolitan authorities and the urban underclass, his sympathies invariably lay with the latter. In 'London Fantasy', a huckster who must constantly relocate his trade, because like Jo the crossing-sweeper in *Bleak House*, 'the police move him on',[206] elicits Peake's admiration:

> Neither too good nor too bad, he must walk the tightrope, gauging the width of the street, the proximity of the police, the varying size of the crowd as he clangs his spoons, or wakes the yearning handsaw of the kerb.[207]

In *Titus Alone*, the positive forces of change that inhere within the city manifest in arbitrary acts of kindness performed by urban mendicants. The book's earliest depictions of poverty and hardship centre on the riverside, to which the fishermen arrive at the break of dawn, 'some on foot hugging themselves in the cold; some in ramshackle mule-drawn carriages',[208] while beggars linger among them, some so cold that they are liable to seek warmth in 'the mouldering stern' of Muzzlehatch's car.[209] These depictions may have drawn on Peake's experiences living in rooms in 'a warehouse just over Battersea Bridge' in 1936,[210] which as his wife later recalled, had 'patches of damp' on their walls and were infested by 'large river rats'.[211] Battersea featured explicitly in the title and verses of Peake's whimsical poem, 'The Dwarf of Battersea' (1937), in which a lecherous dwarf is captured in a tin of linseed oil and cast into the Thames on a papier-maché boat. Peake's aforementioned poem, 'The Cocky Walkers', which depicts the tragic bravado of loitering youth, was originally titled 'Battersea'.[212] Indeed, Moorcock remarked that 'the picture of "Cardboard City" on the South Bank' – a homeless encampment near the southern end of Waterloo Bridge that had become a symbol of London poverty in the 1980s and 1990s – 'could have come straight from a Peake story'.[213]

In *Titus Alone*, the riverside is not only the focus of poverty but also of arbitrary acts of unrequited kindness. Titus drifts unconsciously in a boat towards the city, oddly restaging the journey of the Dwarf of Battersea in reverse, when a humpbacked fisherman catches the boat and extracts him, an act of kindness that 'never afterwards failed to amaze him and amaze his friends, for they knew him to be clumsy and ignorant'.[214] Titus is thence transferred to the hands of 'two beggars',[215] who presumably help him for no better reason than that he seems 'as ragged a creature as themselves'.[216] Later on in the book, the denizens of the Under-River, 'the failures of earth',[217] instinctively side with Titus against the sadistic Veil and toss him 'a hundred' weapons,[218] despite the fact that 'Not one of the great conclave of the displaced had ever seen Titus before.'[219] In the scenes that unfold between the riverside and the Under-River, Titus is rescued countless times by Muzzlehatch, who pays dearly for his kindness, as his erstwhile lover Juno falls in love with Titus, his entire zoo – all but the ape – is slaughtered by scientists wielding death-rays in reprisal for Titus's destruction of their surveillance globe, and he too finally meets his death at the hands of Titus's pursuers. In the MSS of *Titus Alone*, Muzzlehatch wonders at his own actions in rescuing Titus: 'There must be something normal in my bones', he concludes.[220] These accumulated acts of kindness, performed without self-interest or even reasoned justification, dramatize Orwell's claim for the enduring quality of common decency in the British view of life, the tendency to be 'on the side of the underdog, always and everywhere'[221] – to have something normal in one's bones.

As these observations suggest, Orwell and Peake had less confidence than Lefebvre that everyday life would prevail. The most distilled act of common decency in *Nineteen Eighty-Four* is followed by its most searing display of violence. As Winston awaits torture in the Ministry of Love, he shares his cell with several inmates, among them a 'chinless man' and a 'skull-faced man',[222] the latter dying of starvation. When the chinless man registers the condition of the skull-faced inmate, he timidly approaches and 'held out a grimy piece of bread'.[223] The Thought Police instantly recognize this act of compassion as a threat to everything they stand for, guards burst into the room, and in the first prolonged scene of violence in the book, they beat the chinless man to the point of shattering his dental plate. Perhaps most terrifying of all, the skull-faced man shows not the least bit of gratitude, attempting rather to send the chinless man to Room 101 in his place.

By the end of *Titus Alone*, all the main characters have left the city, and there is little to indicate that the beggars and the vagrants left behind have improved their own lot through their acts of kindness and compassion towards Titus. Indeed, even the extent to which their intervention really helps Titus remains questionable, at least so far as his duel with Veil is concerned. Titus picks up one of the hundred weapons they have tossed him, only for the sword to fly 'hurtling from his grasp' on Veil's first blow.[224] Ironically, Veil himself then 'picked up a couple of knives from the wet ground',[225] with the intention of murdering Titus with the weapons tossed to his aid. Thus, the predominant atmosphere that pervades this book is helplessness and bemusement in the face of an inscrutable world, one which affords the dubious insight that 'a jack-knife at the ribs can cause as terrible a sensation as any lurking gas or lethal ray'.[226] Titus himself turns his back on both the jack-knife and the lurking gas or lethal ray, on both Gormenghast Castle and the unnamed city, rejecting these two spaces that respectively embody the violence of the past and the violence of the future, and proceeds down a new track 'that he had never known before'.[227]

In this open-ended dénouement, Peake proved more sensible to the emerging realities of his time than Orwell was in *Nineteen Eighty-Four*. Orwell, for all his objections to Dickens's and Wells's privileging of London as 'the centre of the earth' and their 'complete unawareness of anything outside the contemporary English scene',[228] hardly ventured outside of London in his own literary fantasy, still less outside of Britain. Peake, writing *Titus Alone* in the 1950s in an emergent post-imperial Britain and postcolonial world, broke free of this narrowness. The world of the *Gormenghast Trilogy* is bound neither by Gormenghast Castle, nor by the unnamed London. Titus is besieged by women who try to persuade him otherwise: his mother tells him that he 'will only tread a circle',[229] and his spurned lover Cheeta makes a mockery of his journey: 'He does not realize that he is treading water.'[230] But he defies them by venturing into the unknown, thereby heeding the sounder advice of his true friend, Muzzlehatch: 'Get on with life. Eat it up. Travel. . . . This is only a city. This is no place to halt.'[231]

The reader shares in Titus's exhilaration as the world opens up to him. And yet, one cannot help but feel that from the bird's-eye view of 'new cities and new mountains; new rivers and new creatures',[232] the unnamed London of *Titus Alone* appears rather small, a speck of light receding into the distance.

Giant killer and abdicator: *Nineteen Eighty-Four* and *Titus Alone* as anti-fantasies

In an aforementioned letter to his publisher, Orwell wrote that *Nineteen Eighty-Four* 'is in a sense a fantasy, but in the form of a naturalistic novel'.[233] The terms of his description gesture towards a tension that runs through the book between a fantastical premise and a naturalistic social and materialist approach. *Nineteen Eighty-Four* is a fantasy insofar as it posits a political and social state of affairs drastically different from the reality of its readers and postulates the existence of non-existent technologies such as telescreens, floating fortresses and automated book-writing machines. But it is naturalistic in form insofar as it places a great deal of emphasis on realistic material details and plausible social and political processes, which evoke the atmosphere of wartime and post-war London.

Yet the tension between fantasy and naturalism in *Nineteen Eighty-Four* runs deeper than the disjunction between hyper-advanced technologies and the chronic shortage of razor blades. The novel is profoundly concerned with fantasy as a political tool for the formation of public opinion and the distortion of reality. The word 'fantasy' appears three times in the book, and in each appearance it refers to the systematic lies and fabrications spun by the Party. Winston notes that 'statistics were just as much a fantasy in their original version as in their rectified version';[234] during his daily work at the Ministry of Truth he realizes that 'what was needed was a piece of pure fantasy',[235] and he speculates on whether 'literally every word in the history books, even the things that one accepted without question, was pure fantasy'.[236]

Where the Party deals in pure fantasy, Winston is fighting for empirical reality, as his reflections make clear: 'The obvious, the silly and the true had got to be defended. Truisms are true, hold on to that!'.[237] Winston desperately maintains that 'the solid world exists, its laws do not change',[238] while O'Brien unremittingly plies loose his grasp on reality until he finally persuades him that 'Reality is inside the skull'.[239] This clash between Winston's stubborn belief in an external reality outside the purview of totalitarianism and the Party's sustained endeavour to remake the world in the image of its power fantasy is neatly captured in an exchange between Winston and O'Brien in the torture chambers of the Ministry of Love. Desperately trying to draw limits on the Party's sphere of influence, Winston exclaims: 'You don't even control the climate or the law of gravity'.[240] O'Brien responds: 'There is nothing that we could not do. Invisibility, levitation – anything. I could float off this floor like a soap bubble if I wished to'.[241]

O'Brien's casual assertion of his own supernatural powers invites a reading of *Nineteen Eighty-Four* as a satire on the American science-fiction pulps. In this reading, Orwell's choice of levitation to symbolize O'Brien's power fantasies can be related directly to his criticism of the juvenile power fantasies propagated across the pulps' gaudily coloured pages. The ability to defy gravity was precisely the plot device that epitomized, for Orwell, the tenor of American 'scientifiction': 'You can hardly look at a page without seeing somebody flying through the air (a surprising number of the characters are able to fly).'[242] In this vein, O'Brien's inflated view of himself chimes audibly with Orwell's remarks on 'Superman [who] whizzes through the clouds',[243] an 'all-powerful character who dominates everyone about him'.[244]

Critical consensus reads the totalitarian society of *Nineteen Eighty-Four* as a composite of the USSR and the Third Reich.[245] These are no doubt its obvious models, but one must not let this point undercut Orwell's own explanation: 'the scene of the book is laid in Britain in order to emphasize that the English-speaking races are not innately better than anyone else.'[246] Building on this statement, and given Orwell's aversion to the Americanization of Britain, it may be not insignificant that Oceania is an amalgam of the British Empire and the United States, rather than, as might be expected for the ease of geographic continuity, of the British Isles and the European Continent. Orwell believed that the war against totalitarianism was to be waged not only on the battlefield but across popular literature. In this respect, Britain's greatest ally on the battlefield was its greatest enemy on the cultural front, for it was 'the American ideal' that was eroding British culture, 'the "he-man", the "tough guy", the gorilla who puts everything right by socking everybody else on the jaw',[247] and who 'is intended as a superman'.[248] As Orwell pointed out with distaste, at least one of the American pulps actually portrayed its super-powerful hero 'swinging a rubber truncheon'.[249] Thus, Orwell wrote *Nineteen Eighty-Four* in part as a fantasy against fantasy, a novel set in the future that targeted the American science-fiction pulps of its time, by laying bare their sadistic underpinnings and re-casting their 'superman' hero as the front-man of a totalitarian nightmare.

It is tempting to read *Nineteen Eighty-Four* as Orwell's revival of what he regarded as the Dickensian fantasy idiom of Jack the Giant Killer, 'the hero [who] fights *against odds*'.[250] Certainly, the odds are stacked against Winston – he is 'the Last Man in Europe', as the book was nearly titled,[251] clinging to the belief that 'sanity is not statistical'.[252] But such a reading is problematized by the fact that O'Brien lures Winston into a trap by playing on this very idiom, conjuring up a tale of espionage in which Winston plays the role of self-sacrificing agent in a brave and tragically doomed conspiracy of 'the Brotherhood'.[253] The naturalistic dimension of *Nineteen Eighty-Four* ruthlessly dismantles this fantasy when O'Brien proves to be an entirely loyal high-ranking official of the Inner Party and claims to have co-written the book that guides the Brotherhood himself. In this light, it seems probable that the Brotherhood is nothing more than a cover organization for Big Brother, a lightning rod to attract and neutralize potential threats to the Party. This suspicion is strengthened, of course, by the resonance between the names 'Big Brother' and 'Brotherhood'. Moreover, Orwell's Jack by no means kills the Giant. Winston breaks completely under O'Brien's torture, the depths of his defeat plumbed by his new acceptance of O'Brien's claim to supernatural powers:

> 'If I wished,' O'Brien had said, 'I could float off this floor like a soap bubble.' Winston worked it out. 'If he *thinks* he floats off the floor, and if I simultaneously *think* I see him do it, then the thing happens.'[254]

Thus, even the fantasy that Orwell cherished was not immune from his self-reflexive irony.

Furthermore, the trap that the Thought Police set for Winston strongly alludes to Dickens's *Old Curiosity Shop* and Wells's 'The Crystal Egg', discussed respectively in Chapters 1 and 2. In his essay 'Just Junk – But Who Could Resist It?' (1946), Orwell made an interesting distinction between antique shops and junk shops. He defined an antique shop as 'clean, its goods are attractively set out and priced at about double their value',[255] whereas a junk shop 'has a fine film of dust over the window, . . . and its proprietor . . . displays no eagerness to make a sale'.[256] By this logic, Orwell aligned the junk shops of his time, and by extension Charrington's junk shop in *Nineteen Eighty-Four*, with Dickens's Old Curiosity Shop, notable for its 'dust and rust',[257] where no business seems to be conducted in any form.

A comparison between the Old Curiosity Shop and Charrington's junk shop yields some interesting results. Both shops are located in an off-beat, crepuscular nook in a poor quarter of London. Both are owned by a reticent, unmarried elderly man, who strikes the visitor as 'haggard' or 'faded',[258] a curiosity among curiosities. These proprietors elicit sympathy by telling the visitor of the death of a loved one, in both cases a woman – the proprietor's daughter in *The Old Curiosity Shop*, his wife in *Nineteen Eighty-Four* – and recounting their subsequent descent into poverty. Dickens's Old Curiosity Shop showcases 'distorted figures in china' and 'strange furniture';[259] Charrington apologizes for the absence of 'furniture, china, glass' from his shop,[260] as if it were a given that these elements should be present.

These similarities give rise to three different interpretations. First, they might arise simply from Dickens's and Orwell's shared cultural images of London curiosity shops. Second, they may derive from Orwell's deep familiarity with Dickens and Dickens's London, which may have led him, consciously or unconsciously, to model his fictional shop on Dickens's. Third, the Thought Police may be deliberately playing upon Winston's fantasy of a Dickensian world, 'of a lost London that still existed somewhere or other',[261] a cross between *The Old Curiosity Shop* and 'The Cricket on the Hearth', where one can go scavenging for treasures among the junk and return home to 'an open fire with your feet in the fender and a kettle on the hob'.[262]

A character like Charrington, who knows the words to a range of old English nursery rhymes and is capable of recognizing, naming and locating the former sites of London's old churches, may have read Dickens. After all, Orwell's appendix to *Nineteen Eighty-Four* reports that Dickens is among the writers who are being ideologically and linguistically translated into Newspeak.[263] If one entertains this possibility, then it would not be unreasonable to speculate that the Thought Police designed Charrington's junk shop in distorted imitation of Dickens's Old Curiosity Shop. The Party would thus be appropriating Dickens, Orwell's champion of common decency, in order to destroy that very quality in Winston. In this respect, O'Brien's promise to Winston, 'We shall squeeze you empty, and then we shall fill you with ourselves',[264] can be equally applied to the Party's misuse of Dickens, as they empty Dickens's Curiosity Shop of its actual meanings, and fill it with their power games. Ironically, had Winston himself been versed in Dickens, he might have seen through Charrington's act. In the course of *The Old Curiosity Shop*, the proprietor reveals himself to be more sinister than initially suggested, his mild-mannered countenance melting into a 'white face pinched and sharpened by the greediness which made his eyes unnaturally bright'.[265] Charrington undergoes an analogous transformation from 'a man of perhaps sixty, frail and bowed',[266] to 'a man of about five-and-thirty',[267] whose 'body had straightened',[268] and 'the wrinkles were gone, the whole lines of the face seemed to have altered'.[269] It is probable that Orwell, who unlike Winston knew Dickens's fiction to the hilt, planted this final irony deliberately.

While Charrington's junk shop most visibly alludes to Dickens's *Old Curiosity Shop*, its description as 'a frowzy little junk-shop in a slummy quarter of the town' also resonates with Wells's 'The Crystal Egg' and its 'little and very grimy-looking shop near Seven Dials'.[270] Orwell was never shy of acknowledging Wells's influence on his work, their personal differences notwithstanding. By his own account, at the age of 'ten or eleven' he obtained a copy of a collected edition of Wells's short stories,[271] which included 'The Crystal Egg', 'The Door in the Wall' and 'The Remarkable Case of Davidson's Eyes', all three of which were discussed in Chapter 2.

One may reasonably speculate, therefore, that Winston's fantasy of a secret world encapsulated inside the glass paperweight that he purchases at Charrington's junk shop, 'a sort of eternity at the heart of the crystal',[272] could be an allusion to Wells's titular Crystal Egg that discloses a world of its own, which turns out to be Mars. This speculation is reinforced by reference to the closing remarks of 'The Crystal Egg' that ruminate on the possibility that the Crystal Egg 'may at the present moment be ... serving as a paperweight'.[273] In *Nineteen Eighty-Four*, the bedroom above Charrington's shop is at once inside and outside the paperweight, rather like the London of Wells's 'The Door in the Wall' that is both within and without the pages of a book in the paradisiacal garden, except that the world of the paperweight has a domestic familiarity for the readers that makes its strangeness to Winston all the more poignant:

> He had the feeling that he could get inside it, and that in fact he was inside it, along with the mahogany bed and the gateleg table, and the clock and the steel engraving and the paperweight itself. The paperweight was the room he was in, and the coral was Julia's life and his own.[274]

Winston struggles to maintain a vision of past and present simultaneously, a double perspective which Orwell expressly associated with Wells in his satirical novel, *Coming Up for Air* (1939). The protagonist of *Coming Up for Air* returns to the village of his youth to find it utterly changed. The dissonance that results from this discrepancy between his present environment and his recollections of how it once appeared is illustrated by way of reference to Wells's 'The Remarkable Case of Davidson's Eyes':

> Did you ever read a story of H. G. Wells's about a chap who was in two places at once – that's to say, he was really in his own home, but he had a kind of hallucination that he was at the bottom of the sea? . . . Well, it was just like that.[275]

Unlike Wells in 'The Remarkable Case of Davidson's Eyes', however, Orwell was less concerned in *Nineteen Eighty-Four* in revealing the hidden beauty of London, as he was in cautioning against what London might become. Thus, unlike the Martian world glimpsed through the Crystal Egg, and the island and watery depths seen by Davidson's eyes – both of which Wells had used to cast London 'under a totally different aspect'[276] – Winston's 'eternity in the heart of the crystal' is a tragic illusion.[277] Charrington's junk shop is revealed to be a honey-trap for Thought Criminals, Charrington himself a member of the Thought Police. Building on these revelations, one may plausibly assume that the glass paperweight is a fake replica manufactured by the Party. Thus, *Nineteen Eighty-Four* ultimately forecloses Wells's doubled ontology much as it foreclosed the Dickensian fantasy idiom of Jack the Giant Killer: fantasies of escape and of agency, even self-reflexive ones, are shown to be wholly co-opted to serve the interests of totalitarian power. In this respect, Orwell's vision of totalitarianism was truly total, encompassing Britain and the United States, past and present and realism and fantasy.

Titus Alone is an anti-fantasy of a different order, as its target is not so much the American science-fiction pulps as it is Tolkienian escapism and, more generally, the pastoralism of Rural Fantasy. Peake read the first volume of *The Lord of the Rings*, *The Fellowship of the Ring*, shortly after it was first published in 1954.[278] As aforementioned in the introduction to this study, he was unimpressed by it, mocking it as 'rather twee' and singling out 'Goldberry, Tom Bombadil's lady-friend' for particular ridicule.[279] Given that *The Fellowship of the Ring* was published contemporaneously with Peake's composition of *Titus Alone*, Peake's dislike of it may serve as an illuminating context for his own fantasy writing at the time.[280] His especial distaste for the Goldberry and Bombadil episode can be palpably felt in the imagery that Peake deployed in Muzzlehatch's satirical description of the terrain that lies beyond the city, a description that can be traced back to a working notebook dated 1957 – three years after the publication of *Fellowship of the Ring*.[281] This description forms part of Muzzlehatch's response to Titus's decision to depart the city and abandon his friends to their fate:

there are forests like the Garden of Eden where you can lie on your belly and write bad verse. There will be nymphs for your ravishing, and flutes for your delectation.[282]

Laden with the irony of a scorned friend, Muzzlehatch's description of the vistas that await Titus can be read as a synoptic parody of the conventions of the Arcadian pastoral, more specifically targeted at the Tom Bombadil and Goldberry episode in *Lord of the Rings*. Goldberry is nothing if not a ravishing nymph-figure: 'Her long yellow hair rippled down her shoulders; her gown was green, green as young reeds'.[283] Given Tolkien's emphasis on Goldberry's 'yellow hair', it is germane that the MS of Muzzlehatch's speech includes a half-formed sentence that characterizes the nymphs as blond.[284] She is first alluded to in what might be unkindly described as Tom Bombadil's 'bad verse': '*There my pretty lady is, River-woman's daughter, / Slender as the willow-wand, clearer than the water.*'[285] And as the hobbits follow this song to its source, the menacing Old Forest gives way to a grassy knoll 'like the Garden of Eden'.[286] The only element missing from the Bombadil and Goldberry episode to complete Muzzlehatch's picture is the flute, whose musical notes sound elsewhere in *The Lord of the Rings*.[287] Needless to say, Titus encounters nothing of the sort: in place of a nymph for his ravishing, he finds himself pursued by the controlling and vindictive Cheeta 'who was dangerous as black water';[288] in place of an Edenic forest, he finds a forest of chimneys belching 'thin columns of green smoke';[289] in place of the flute, he hears 'an endless impalpable sound that, had it been translated into a world of odours, might have been likened to the smell of death'.[290]

Titus's escape from the frying pan that is the city into the fire that is Cheeta's home serves as an object lesson for him. His flight from the city marks the culmination of his disgraceful pattern of behaviour towards his friends, whereby he abandons them at their hour of need after taking advantage of their compassion and generosity. Titus's first encounter with Muzzlehatch, who rescues him from the clutches of his pursuers, provokes him to lash out at the older man with the agreeable words 'I will never thank you.'[291] This is then followed by several variations on the same theme, whereby Titus gets into scrapes and is extracted by Muzzlehatch and by Muzzlehatch's erstwhile lover Juno. Titus acknowledges his accruing debt of gratitude towards Muzzlehatch by physically assaulting him, and after a short period of respite in the arms of the enamoured Juno, he deserts her as well with the flimsy excuse that 'our love is too intense. I am a coward. I cannot take it.'[292] Thence he descends into the Under-River and rescues a dying girl, only to leave her to the care of Muzzlehatch and Juno with the explanation that 'her suffering is far too clear to see. There is no veil across it: no mystery: no romance.'[293] If all this sounds faintly ridiculous and Titus comes across as a selfish brute, it is intentionally so, for Peake was launching a concentrated attack on escapist fantasy. His targets were, inter alia, those who required a veil of 'romance' and 'mystery' to sugar-coat the suffering of the world, lest it become 'far too clear to see'.

Yet Peake's critique of escapism in *Titus Alone* was directed no less at himself than at Tolkien and the pastoral brand of fantasy that Tolkien came to represent. Peake was not immune to the allure of Secondary-World fantasy and the escape it afforded, as he demonstrated in a letter to Smith, dated 24 October 1943:

> What was I after anyway [in *Titus Groan*]? I suppose, to create a world of my own in which those who belong to it and move in it come to life and never step outside into either this world of bus queues, ration books, or even the upper Ganges – or into another imaginative world.[294]

In this letter, Peake expressed his intention to make Gormenghast Castle the centre of a closed fictional realm in the vein of Tolkien's contemporaneously developed theory of Secondary Worlds. This intention was reinforced by Peake's specific rejection of elements from his everyday life in wartime London – indeed, precisely those elements that Orwell brought to the fore – namely, 'bus queues' and 'ration books'. It is thus unsurprising that C. S. Lewis wrote to Peake to congratulate him on *Titus Groan* and *Gormenghast* (1950), the first two volumes of the *Gormenghast Trilogy*, praising them as fine additions to the 'class of literature' typified by '*The Faerie Queene* or *The Lord of the Rings*'.[295] In the terms of this study, Lewis claimed Peake as a Rural Fantasist.

Yet even as Peake's American publishers concurred with Lewis and tried to capitalize on the success of *The Lord of the Rings* by advertising their second editions of the *Gormenghast Trilogy* as 'a vast Tolkienesque adventure',[296] perspicacious reviewers were quick to point out their mistake:

> With Tolkien, imagination fused with scholarship to create a neat, orderly, eminently manageable fantasy. With Peake, imagination fed on something darker; the result was artistic chaos, deliberate disorder for effect.[297]

By thus pinpointing the core differences between Tolkien's and Peake's fantastical imaginations, this review anticipated the division made by this study between the 'neat, orderly, eminently manageable' Rural Fantasy and the darker, deliberately disordered Urban Fantasy.

By the time he set out to write *Titus Alone*, Peake had revised his conceptualization of Titus and his world. Contrary to his previous insistence on keeping Gormenghast insulated, he told Smith that 'he wanted . . . to include in this volume more of the modern world'.[298] By removing Titus from his ancestral home and the shelter of its ponderous walls, and relocating him to a modern-day city reminiscent of London, Peake turned his back on the consolations of Secondary-World fantasy. *Titus Alone* thus became a sustained meditation on the imperative of facing evil, however tempting the prospect of flight. So long as Titus flees the scientists and their death-rays, the helmeted men and their foreboding silence, they continue to pursue him like a shadow attached to his person. His coming of age is signalled by his decision to stand his ground and remain at Muzzlehatch's side at a time of crisis, because 'there is loyalty in dreams, and beauty in madness, and he could not turn from the shaggy side of his friend'.[299] Peake's choice of words is telling – Titus and Muzzlehatch are bonded not by harsh circumstances but by shared 'dreams' and the 'beauty in madness'. In this vein, *Titus Alone* does not disavow fantasy altogether. Rather, it dramatizes a shift from Rural to Urban Fantasy, from fantasy as escape to fantasy that uses 'dreams' and 'madness' as a source of camaraderie and a spur to action.

'A boot stamping on a human face – for ever': Tyranny, totalitarianism, laughter

In a key scene in *Nineteen Eighty-Four*, O'Brien instructs Winston: 'tell me *why* we cling to power.'[300] Winston's reply strongly recalls Ostrog's speeches in *When the Sleeper Wakes*: 'You are ruling over us for our own good, . . . You believe that human beings are not fit to govern themselves, and therefore—'.[301] O'Brien silences Winston with a jolt of pain and a reproach:

> That was stupid, Winston, stupid! . . . The Party seeks power entirely for its own sake. We are not interested in the good of others; we are interested solely in power. Not wealth or luxury or long life or happiness: only power, pure power.[302]

This insight into the totalitarian mind was where Orwell was at his furthest from Wells. Wells's scientific romances grapple with problems that have rational causes and consequently rational solutions. The societies of *The Time Machine* and *When the Sleeper Wakes* are the result of labour exploitation, exacerbated by evolutionary deterioration; the invasion of the Martians in *War of the Worlds* serves the time-honoured purpose of conquering territory, and the atrocities committed by the Invisible Man and Doctor Moreau are fables of scientific ambition gone wrong. Accordingly, these problems can and sometimes are overcome by rational thinking, brute force or natural causes, as is suggested in one form or another in all of these works.

In Orwell's and Peake's fantasies, however, evil is largely its own cause. Orwell complained that the depiction of authoritarian power in *When the Sleeper Wakes* was unconvincing, because 'the upper castes for whom the workers toil are completely soft, cynical and faithless'.[303] 'No society of that kind would last more than a couple of generations', he opined of the dystopian London of *When the Sleeper Wakes*,[304] 'A ruling class has got to have a strict morality, a quasi-religious belief in itself, a *mystique*.'[305] Accordingly, while O'Brien might superficially resemble Doctor Moreau in his megalomania and readiness to inflict pain, these two characters are crucially different. Moreau concentrates his efforts on obedience to 'the Law', whereas O'Brien is fully committed to his own mystique and to the exercise of psychological power, asserting that 'The Party is not interested in the overt act: the thought is all we care about.'[306] Orwell drew on Wells's half-civilized Beast Folk, the 'Sayers of the Law' in *The Island of Doctor Moreau*, for his own half-civilized farm animals in *Animal Farm* (1945), who chant and bleat the increasingly distorted Seven Commandments.[307] But O'Brien's will to power is of a different order from both Moreau's and Napoleon the pig's in *Animal Farm*, because his vision is relentless and total: 'It is intolerable to us that an erroneous thought should exist anywhere in the world, however secret and powerless it may be.'[308]

In this respect, one may postulate that Wells explored the workings of tyranny, which compels outward obedience, whereas Orwell explored the makings of totalitarianism, which compels inner belief; one local and rational, the other total and fanatical. This distinction coheres with the theories of philosopher Leo Strauss, writing contemporaneously with Peake, who made the case that 'modern science' and 'modern technology' had enabled the transformation of 'classical tyranny' into the all-encompassing totalitarianism that came to power in the first half of the twentieth century.[309] It was in this sense that Orwell believed Wells to be 'too sane to understand the modern world'.[310] Orwell observed that 'Wells, like Dickens, belongs to the non-military class' of 'a non-military nation',[311] both Dickens and Wells being embodiments of 'the nineteenth-century Liberal'.[312] Consequently, as Orwell argued, Wells could not understand the scale of the totalitarian threat, which was of an entirely different order from 'the military adventurer, Napoleon' or 'fox-hunting Tories'.[313] Ambitious French generals of the previous century and land-owning Tories were not armed with modern technologies of warfare and the insights of modern science, and therefore unlike them, Hitler could actually effect 'an impossible reversal of history'.[314] Thus, in his 1910 preface to *The Sleeper Awakes*, Wells articulated what he saw as the fundamental question of the novel: 'Who will win – Ostrog or the People? A thousand years hence that will still be just the open question we leave to-day.'[315] Less than forty years thence, Orwell closed that question and sealed it with 'a boot stamping on a human face – for ever.'[316]

The villains of *Titus Alone* do not cut as memorable a figure as O'Brien, perhaps because the qualities concentrated in O'Brien are scattered across multiple figures in Peake's book. The main antagonists are a mysterious cabal of scientists, ominously nicknamed 'the dedicated men,'[317] who work 'to the glory of science and in praise of death.'[318] They are aided by other malevolent characters, such as the aforementioned Cheeta – daughter of the lead scientist – and the pair of helmeted men who are evidently colluding with the scientists in some mysterious way. The indictment of science that arises from these figures highlights the extent to which the Urban Fantasy tradition was under special pressure in the mid-twentieth century. It would have been well-nigh impossible for Peake and Orwell to celebrate the achievements of science with the same exuberance as Wells's utopias or the articles that Dickens commissioned for *Household Words*. For Orwell and Peake, having lived through the Great War and the Second World War, science had become 'something that created bombing planes and poison gas.'[319] That being said, they still rejected the model typified by the fantasies of Tolkien and Lewis, where the heroes wage war in the name of a pastoral, pseudo-medieval world against the forces of modernity, be it the orcs and their factories in Middle Earth, or the false prophet Shift in Narnia. While Tolkien's hobbits return to the familiar comforts of the Shire and rebuild it after the devastation wrought by modern warfare, Peake's Titus never returns to his ancestral home of Gormenghast Castle, which is 'never seen by him again' as he shakes 'off his past from his shoulders like a heavy cape.'[320]

As the Second World War came to a close, Peake undertook the grim resolution 'to make records of what humanity suffered through war.'[321] To this end, he travelled through war-torn Europe in the company of a war correspondent, eventually arriving at Belsen and the hospital wards attached to it, which were caring for the camp's recent inmates. The experience left an indelible mark on Peake's art and writing, darkened still further by a crushing sense that he could not live up to the task he had set for himself. 'I think I could only do justice to what I felt in the most powerful poem I have written,'[322] he wrote to his wife in the immediate aftermath, 'certainly it would have to be finer than anything I've done otherwise I would not want to write it.'[323] Peake did write a poem about Belsen, plainly titled 'The Consumptive. Belsen 1945' (1945), which self-reflexively articulated the ethical problematics of fashioning art out of the Holocaust. Standing before a dying girl in Belsen, the speaker reproaches himself for seeing 'the ghost of a great painting, . . . / In this doomed girl of tallow'.[324] Peake was thus torn by contradictory impulses: on the one hand, the imperative to record human suffering; on the other, as his biographer John Watney put it, the feeling 'as if he were intruding on something too terrible and too sacred to be the subject of public curiosity'.[325]

The antagonists of *Titus Alone* may be construed as Peake's attempt, not altogether successful, to reconcile these feelings. Dissatisfied with poetry and sketches, Peake finally turned to prose fantasy in an attempt to capture the enormity of the Holocaust, while preserving a respectful distance by mediating reality through the conventions of fantasy literature. Thus, the scientists' massacre of Muzzlehatch's zoo is twice referred to as a 'holocaust',[326] and Muzzlehatch's shock in the aftermath gestures towards more than the mourning of his wildlife: 'Dazed by the enormity of his loss, he had for a time refused to believe'.[327] The 'prison camp' of which Veil was a former guard is a place 'of official cruelty',[328] where the inmates 'grew thinner and thinner' and their 'head was shaved'.[329] An instant before attacking Titus, Veil makes a gesture reminiscent of the fascist salute: 'It is loyalty that fills him, as he lifts his long right arm'.[330] These attempts to integrate Holocaust allusions into a fantasy novel may account for the fact that the villains of *Titus Alone* oscillate between tragedy and farce.

Titus Alone offers a strategy of resistance, however, that plays upon its farcical elements in a way entirely foreclosed to the nightmare vision of *Nineteen Eighty-Four*. If there is one recourse that never occurs to Winston as he is tortured in the Ministry of Love it is to burst out laughing. Yet that is precisely Titus's response under mental torture in Cheeta's 'Black House':

> But what no one expected, least of all Titus or Cheeta herself, was that it should be on the ludicrous and not the terrifying that Titus should fix his attention.
>
> Such a sensation can become too powerful for the human body. . . . It is laughter. Laughter when it stamps its feet; when it sets the bells jangling in the next town. Laughter with the pipes of Eden in it.[331]

Greater emphasis is given to the subversive edge of Titus's laughter in the MSS, which added the line, subsequently crossed out: 'There is Anger; there is Fear; there is Love, but the most devastating of all is Laughter.'[332] Such laughter, the MSS suggest, 'is a fabulous beast: it tramples upon shrines'.[333] Furthermore, in an earlier MS, one finds the beginning of a description of Titus's 'terror' upon encountering an automated plane, while he is strutting around the city stark naked. Peake apparently changed his mind mid-sentence, because the struck-out description cuts off abruptly: '~~and terror took hold of Titus for the nakedness which he had so recently rejoiced in~~'.[334] The description begins again in the next paragraph:

> Instead of being terrified, Titus began to laugh. To be sure ~~the sudden~~ it had been horrible, & it may be that to some degree his laughter had been the result of the shock for it was high & uncontrolled – but there was something of the lud [*sic*] ludicrous that touched the laughter off & set it flying.[335]

Thus, bolstered by material from its earlier drafts, *Titus Alone* suggests that perhaps the best answer to terror and cruelty is to laugh in its face.

The farcical undertones of Titus's outbursts of laughter may give some indication as to why a number of critics regard Peake as a proto-postmodernist.[336] Granted, there is also a postmodernist quality to the way in which the apparatus of torture in the Black House – designed by Cheeta to derange Titus through a grotesque parody of Gormenghast – falls apart like cheap stage props: 'the battered masks, the hanks of hair; the Countess breaking in half, dusty and ludicrous; the sawdust; and the paint'.[337] But Peake was never as iconoclastic as, for example, the postmodernist novelist Don DeLillo, whose extremes of comedy and tragedy interrogate the cultural meaning of the Holocaust for a twenty-first-century readership.[338] In *Titus Alone*, the reader is left not so much with the splattered paint and gritty sawdust as with Peake's mournful aside, inserted parenthetically: '(how horrible and multifarious are the ways of modern death).'[339]

But the bleakness and despair of Orwell's and Peake's fantasies did not strike the final note of the Urban Fantasy tradition. Nor had the bells of lost London fallen entirely silent. A decade later, Moorcock would assert, with a renewed vigour and a Dickensian celebration of the urban, how joyous and multivalent are the ways of modern life.

4

A pyramid of flesh on Villiers Street
New Worlds magazine and the Jerry Cornelius myth

'The new breed of urban man': Moorcock's editorial vision

The 1960s was a watershed decade in the history of British fantasy. *The Lord of the Rings* garnered enthusiastic reviews from the early days of its publication,[1] but it was the 1960s that witnessed the trilogy's unprecedented commercial success.[2] *Lord of the Rings* sold 1 million copies by 1966 and 3 million by 1968 and gave rise to a cult following. Among American college students especially, proclamations of the Age of Aquarius were accompanied by the slogans 'Frodo lives' and 'Gandalf for President' and inscriptions in Elvish adorned the walls of New York subway stations.[3] The Tolkien Society was founded in London in 1969,[4] and by 1971 London counterculture movements held meetings in Covent Garden basements christened 'Middle Earth'.[5]

Yet as multitudes of British and American readers fell under the spell of the Shire, voices of dissent and criticism of the 'Tolkien phenomenon' rose with mounting force from within the coteries of British fantasy.[6] One of the most vocal organs denouncing Tolkien and the brand of fantasy for which he stood was the avant-garde magazine *New Worlds*, which was injected with a new radical spirit when Michael Moorcock took over its editorship between 1964 and 1973, with M. John Harrison joining his team as books editor in 1968. During this period, *New Worlds* defined itself against the rising vogue for Tolkienian Rural Fantasy, which was castigated by Moorcock and Harrison across multiple issues as juvenile escapism,[7] derivative formula,[8] and cheap comfort literature.[9] Moorcock's attacks on *Lord of the Rings* focused particularly on its 'refusal to face or derive any pleasure from the realities of urban industrial life'.[10] 'THE LORD OF THE RINGS is a pernicious confirmation of the values of a morally bankrupt middle-class',[11] Moorcock contended, 'a fearful, backward-yearning class' to which Tolkien belonged and pandered by constructing a neat opposition in which 'the Shire is a suburban garden',[12] whereas 'Sauron and his henchmen' embody 'the worst aspects of modern urban society represented as the whole'.[13] Thus, 'the fantasies of people like Tolkien' were 'aimed at reinforcing opinions rather than analysing them, at preserving conventions rather than expanding them'.[14]

Moorcock's criticism was unfair – as recent scholarship has demonstrated, *The Lord of the Rings* is a more sophisticated work of literature than his attacks allowed for.[15] But his reading of *The Lord of the Rings* was deliberately distorted in order to create a starker rival paradigm of fantasy literature against which *New Worlds* could redefine itself and thereby reissue Urban Fantasy's perennial challenge to its Rural counterpart. Moorcock thereby fashioned *New Worlds* as a platform for fantasy and science fiction that was expressly opposed to an idealization of the past and a demonization of urban modernity. Under his editorship, the magazine promoted science fiction and fantasy that was 'unconventional in every sense',[16] addressed to 'the new breed of urban man',[17] and 'trying to tackle real issues'.[18] To this end, *New Worlds* magazine concerned itself with developing 'a new mythology' for the twentieth century,[19] one that was urban and progressive in its sensibilities.

New Worlds magazine accordingly nailed its colours to the mast of Wells's progressiveness. Wells divided human thought into 'two divergent types':[20] the first, 'retrospective in habit',[21] interpreting the present 'entirely with relation to the past';[22] the second, 'constructive in habit',[23] 'perpetually attacking and altering the established order of things'.[24] Needless to say, he declared himself wholly of the constructive type, maintaining that 'If the world does not please you, *you can change it*.'[25] This position was reiterated almost verbatim in *New Worlds*:

> All fictions tend towards either a retrospective or a prospective mode, towards understanding the present either in terms of the past or of the future. . . . The fiction that has appeared in *New Worlds* since its inception has been almost invariably prospective.[26]

In Moorcock's hands, *New Worlds* wrenched the Urban Fantasy tradition back to life with a call for metropolitan, socially progressive fantasies engaged with the present and the future and disavowing Rural Fantasy's pining for an idealized past.

This chapter draws on a range of editorial prefaces, literary manifestos, book reviews and polemical pieces across the 1960s issues of *New Worlds* magazine and the 1970s issues of its reincarnation as *New Worlds Quarterly*. It examines the rejuvenation of the Urban Fantasy idiom in *New Worlds*, centring on Moorcock's homespun myth of the assassin-cum-rock star 'Jerry Cornelius', which he opened up to riffs penned by the magazine's regular contributors. This chapter explores the parallel and fluctuating Londons that come to life through Jerry's misadventures, focusing on Moorcock's novels and Harrison's short stories and the changes in Jerry's character as he moves away from Moorcock's bohemian West London to Harrison's North London bedsitter belt. The chapter concludes with an examination of Moorcock's and Harrison's changing attitudes towards London in the late 1970s.

A new wave looking back at the old: *New Worlds* and the Urban Fantasy tradition

The leading article for the July 1967 issue of *New Worlds* set forth the magazine's manifesto as a rallying cry to face the modern urban reality from which Tolkien and his followers had shirked. '[T]he human condition is changing,'[27] the article declared, a change wrought by urban life and especially by London:

> the urban dweller is becoming more and more independent of the basic rhythms of night and day and of the seasons. It is possible – and often necessary – to live out a year in a metropolis like London without significantly adjusting the pattern of ones' life to the great, mythic dichotomy of winter and summer, of death, re-birth and harvest.[28]

Given Moorcock's valorization of Dickens's novels as 'the finest London fiction we have',[29] it is unsurprising that this leading article shares some striking similarities with Dickens's 'Preliminary Word' (1850). Much as Dickens had celebrated 'the mightier inventions of this age',[30] this *New Worlds* piece declares its intention to engage with 'an environment of artifacts and artifices'.[31] Where Dickens declared the focus of his new periodical to be urban and concerned 'with the habitations and the ways of life of crowds',[32] the *New Worlds* article asserts that man has become 'an urban dweller' and that 'the countryside . . . [has become] a stage-set for occasional "outings"'.[33] While Dickens aligned *Household Words* with Victorian modernity, the *New Worlds* article announces the magazine's intention to address 'these elements of modern life' of the second half of the twentieth century,[34] 'our technological world',[35] with which 'literary art has characteristically lagged behind in dealing'.[36]

Most significantly of all, this *New Worlds* article followed in the footsteps of Dickens by asserting that the best way to engage with urban modernity is through the fantastical imagination. Dickens had called for a romance of familiar things that would transform objects as 'repellant [sic]' as 'the towering chimneys' into 'swart giants'.[37] *New Worlds* took up this vision and carried it forth into the second half of the twentieth century, declaring the magazine's raison d'être to be the cultivation of 'an act of sustained and informed imagination' that would help readers engage imaginatively with the present and the future,[38] 'to handle experiences and ideas for which nothing in our past lives has prepared us'.[39]

It would be overstating the case to suggest that *New Worlds* was a twentieth-century reincarnation of *Household Words* – *Household Words* had a sizeable non-fiction component, whereas *New Worlds* was primarily a magazine of fantasy and science fiction. But this comparison highlights how *New Worlds* channelled certain aspects of Dickens's ethos, calling for a renewal of fantasy literature that was Dickensian insofar as it was positively engaged with urban modern life and committed to a social vision. Or as Moorcock put it,

> a [fantasy] literature of acceptance, delighting in the changes and possibilities of modern society while still concerned with the need to find a new set of morals and ethical principles that will make that society a just one.[40]

Notwithstanding that *New Worlds* enshrined newness in its title, Moorcock and Harrison envisioned the magazine as a return to what I have been calling the Urban Fantasy tradition. They were sceptical of the 'new wave' label that their American counterparts pinned upon *New Worlds*,[41] preferring to regard the magazine as heir to an already-existing line of socially engaged, London-based, liberal-progressive British fantasies. In a retrospect on his editorship, Moorcock asserted that the magazine had built on an older tradition of the British fantastic, naming two authors of Urban Fantasy: 'the English tradition of Wells, Huxley, Orwell, etc'.[42] For Moorcock, this was essentially a 'Wellsian tradition coupling naturalistic narrative and characters with romantic imagery and idealism'.[43] Harrison emphasized the Wellsian roots of their project still further, arguing that *New Worlds* was 'a belated attempt at growth by the stunted, abandoned trunk of Wellsian science fiction' that privileged 'the old virtues of imagination, exercises in speculation and social comment, and that condition of fantasy which engenders a fresh viewpoint'.[44]

Thus, Moorcock and Harrison were driven by a desire to revive the Urban Fantasy tradition, to restore to the British fantastic an edge of social radicalism that, in their view, had been traded away for Tolkien's 'Literature of Comfort',[45] as Harrison called it, or in Moorcock's blunter appellation after the fashion of A. A. Milne, 'epic pooh'.[46] They were exquisitely attuned to the key traits that distinguished the Urban Fantasy tradition from its Rural counterpart: 'exercises in speculation' rather than all-encompassing fantasy worlds; 'social comment' rather than escapism; and, most crucially, cultivating 'that condition of fantasy which engenders a fresh viewpoint', implicitly channelling Dickens's vision of making London 'unlike itself'.

Moorcock and Harrison valorized Dickens, Wells, Orwell and Peake across the pages of *New Worlds* magazine and *New Worlds Quarterly*, as authors who embodied the spirit of innovation, defamiliarization and social engagement they sought to revive. In the December 1967/January 1968 issue of *New Worlds*, Moorcock issued a call for 'truly popular but uncompromising literature',[47] describing the author he sought as 'our new Dickens'.[48] In the first paperback instalment of *New Worlds Quarterly* (1971), Harrison hailed Wells as 'the primogeniture of science fiction',[49] declaring that 'if science fiction is to regain the direction given to it' by Wells and other early practitioners,[50] it must also 'take on the maturity hinted at by Orwell'.[51] Moorcock ran multiple tributes to Peake across a range of *New Worlds* issues, including Langdon Jones's 'A Reverie of Bone' (1967) and 'The 77the Earl' (1968), Harrison's 'Mr. Throd and the Wise Old Crocodile' (1969), 'The Boy from Vietnam' (1969) and 'By Tennyson Out of Disney' (1971), and his own 'Gormenghast; Mervyn Peake' (1969) and 'Mervyn Peake – An Obituary' (1969). He published Peake's art on the front covers of issues and within their pages,[52] and he solicited 'imaginative fantasies' closer to Peake 'than to, say, the work of Heinlein or Asimov'.[53]

These observations speak to the extent to which Moorcock and Harrison had begun to realize that Dickens, Wells, Orwell and Peake formed a continuous line of influence to which they were heirs. Across Moorcock's writings, one finds an increasingly tangible sense of a tradition that ran from Dickens's 'durable images of Victorian London',[54] to Wells's writings as 'an affectionate observer of suburban London',[55] to 'the London in which Orwell wrote *1984*',[56] to Peake's 'hallucinatory vision of the city'.[57] Thus, for Moorcock, it was 'their own British tradition' that the writers of *New Worlds* were in the febrile process of 'rediscovering'.[58]

Cornelius of London: *The Final Programme*

The *New Worlds* vision of facilitating 'a literature of acceptance' that 'relished and embraced change' was nowhere more apparent,[59] nor more concentrated, than in its eclectic array of 'Jerry Cornelius' stories, extracts and serializations. Jerry Cornelius, a physicist, rock star and assassin rolled into one, is a child of the Swinging Sixties, who 'was born in the modern city' and thrives in its 'comforting familiarity'.[60]

Moorcock originally conceptualized the character and world of Jerry Cornelius 'in late 1964',[61] several months into his tenure as editor of *New Worlds*, and with a similar purpose:

> I was casting around for a means of dealing with what I regarded as the 'hot' subject matter of my own time – stuff associated with scientific advance, social change, the mythology of the mid-twentieth century.[62]

His first Jerry Cornelius book, *The Final Programme* (1968), extracts of which were first published in *New Worlds* issues between 1965 and 1966, was thus a modernization and urbanization of Moorcock's already-existing mythology of Elric of Melniboné. Moorcock transformed Elric, the 'last son of Melniboné's sundered line of kings' whose tragedies play out in ancient cities and otherworldly citadels,[63] into Jerry Cornelius, the dimension-hopping pop star who swaggers out of a 'Shaftesbury Avenue garage' into a London of flashing neon,[64] men and women in drag, pinball machines and live pop music dominated by Beatles' hits. This staggering change of milieu follows the same pattern as the *Gormenghast Trilogy*, where Titus escaped the ancient towers of Gormenghast Castle into the unnamed city of modern skyscrapers. Consciously imitating Peake, Moorcock released his 'Eternal Champion' from the exotic trappings of sword-and-sorcery set 'on a far-away world' and recast him 'in a contemporary setting',[65] a fictionalized version of his own London.

The inspiration for the name and appearance of Jerry Cornelius came from a street view of 1960s Notting Hill, as glimpsed from within a café:

> This beautiful young man, with his ascetic features, elegant clothes and floating long hair, had suddenly appeared as I looked up. Behind him was the name of one of our local greengrocer's shops, Cornelius of London.[66]

This moment of epiphany from within a London café looking outward at the city recalls Dickens's formative 'moor eeffoc' experience. But where Dickens's coffee room was on St Martin's Lane, Moorcock's café was in Notting Hill. As Moorcock observed, the Jerry Cornelius myth was a product of the Notting Hill area,[67] where Moorcock had lived throughout most of his tenure as editor of *New Worlds*,[68] where he held 'virtual open house for his contributors in the living-room-office of his London flat',[69] where many of the contributors occupied 'the rooming house around the corner' from Moorcock,[70] and where the offices of *New Worlds* were based from late 1965 until 1971 (excepting several months in Bloomsbury in 1968).

In *The Final Programme*, Jerry Cornelius lives on Holland Park Avenue, an opulent thoroughfare in Notting Hill, where he occupies the entirety of a luxurious 'hotel-sized building'.[71] One would be hard-pressed to find a starker contrast with Moorcock's own home in the same area at the time: a 'tiny flat' on 'Colville Terrace',[72] 'then an infamous slum'.[73] Furnishing his protagonist with a glamorous townhouse an easy walking distance from his own cramped flat is obvious wish fulfilment, as Moorcock would openly acknowledge in the fourth Jerry Cornelius book, *The Condition of Muzak* (1977). But Jerry's opulence in *The Final Programme* also emphasized a point that Moorcock made in an article published shortly after extracts from the book appeared in *New Worlds* magazine: 'Affluence and poverty are here in their extremes.'[74] As discussed in Chapter 2, Wells made a similar point in 'The Door in the Wall' with regard to the same West London area. For Wells, Campden Hill formed the border between wealth and poverty in West London; for Moorcock, wealth and poverty were mapped out along the length of Portobello Road.

When Moorcock first moved to Notting Hill in 1963, the area was beginning to see a change in its social makeup. The north-western enclaves of Notting Dale and Norland had been down-at-heel since the late nineteenth century, while the 'half-mile radius of the junction of Talbot and Ledbury Roads' to the east of these enclaves,[75] which covered Moorcock's flat on Colville Terrace, had been taken over by the sex industry. But Notting Hill was also 'one of the earliest sites of post-war gentrification',[76] and the London Government Act 1963, which established the Greater London Council (GLC) and created thirty-two new London Boroughs, forged stronger affinities between Notting Hill and the then-bohemian Chelsea by encompassing both areas in the newly formed Royal Borough of Kensington and Chelsea.[77] Bolstered by the Notting Hill Carnival, Notting Hill developed into 'a new bohemia for white and black intellectuals' in the decade that came to be known as the 'Swinging Sixties'.[78]

Following the end of post-war food rationing in the mid-1950s, booms in domestic manufacturing and a rise in London property values prompted a surge in the economic prosperity of Londoners that particularly benefited the younger generation, many of whom saw their wages doubled.[79] This increase in affluence gave rise to an effervescent youth culture of fashion, drugs, clubs, parties, free love and pop music that went hand in hand with progressive legislation legalizing abortion and decriminalizing homosexuality.[80] The early years of Moorcock's tenure as editor of *New Worlds* were thoroughly in tune with the zeitgeist, which he defined as a time 'when popular music was growing more complex and interesting, . . . when it really did seem that "popular" and "quality" and "enlightened" could prove themselves compatible'.[81] In this spirit, the Jerry Cornelius of *Final Programme* wields gun and guitar with equal virtuosity.

In keeping with the greengrocer's sign that inspired his name, Jerry Cornelius is thoroughly 'of London'. He is a man-about-town, who 'never felt really comfortable unless he had at least fifteen miles of built-up area on all sides',[82] and who is happiest 'walking towards Leicester Square and the Blue Boar Tavern for a quick cocktail'.[83] Thus, Jerry epitomizes 'the new breed of urban man' whose advent was hailed in the July 1967 issue of *New Worlds*.[84] His 'natural habitat' consists of the casinos and clubs of Swinging London,[85] 'a world ruled these days by the gun, the guitar, and the needle, sexier than sex'.[86] Jerry's London stretches from Notting Hill to what he refers to as 'the Area' of the West End:[87] Shaftesbury Avenue, Leicester Square, Trafalgar Square, Piccadilly Circus and Tottenham Court Road.

The London of *The Final Programme* is a city of rock 'n' roll beats and opulent consumption, of 'Beat City showrooms',[88] dance clubs lit by 'an old-fashioned dance-hall globe',[89] guitars 'studded with semi-precious gems',[90] private wine cellars and vulgar cocktail bars, Duesenberg limousines upholstered with blue silk and neon signs blazing across the streets. In the febrile excitement that fuels its treatment of 'the hot, bubbling core of the city',[91] the book illustrates Moorcock's contention that 'there is an increasing atmosphere of positive and hopeful thinking in the world of art'.[92] For Moorcock, *The Final Programme* was 'a way of celebrating the modern age: using the new world of electronics and technology as toys'.[93] Its penultimate line thus affirms that the world of Jerry Cornelius is 'A very tasty world.'[94]

The 'tastiness' of this London is captured in one of Mal Dean's illustrations for the first British edition that does not so much depict a scene from the story as convey its mood. In this illustration (Figure 4.1), Jerry looms over a map of central London with poker chips scattered upon it seemingly at random. Four of the chips create a rectangle around Jerry's beloved Leicester Square; two of these flank Shaftesbury Avenue where he parked his car; the third sits squarely on Piccadilly Circus, where Jerry has another parking space 'in the Piccadilly Sky Garage'.[95] Diminishing horizontal lines emanate from two poker chips, marking Jerry's swaggering stroll to the Blue Boar Tavern and his walk down Tottenham Court Road back to the Shaftesbury Avenue garage in the company of the indomitable computer programmer Miss Brunner. Another poker chip placed where Farringdon Street becomes Blackfriars Road makes a subtler reference to a journey undertaken by one of the characters 'down Farringdon Street towards the [Blackfriars] bridge',[96] a journey from which that character never returns. The other chips are strategically placed before London landmarks – the British

A Pyramid of Flesh on Villiers Street   139

Figure 4.1 Drawn by Mal Dean, 'London Fun Machine', 1969, in Moorcock, *The Final Programme* (London: Allison & Busby, 1976), (n.p., opposite page 67).

Museum, Buckingham Palace, the Houses of Parliament – all suggesting that Jerry regards London as his personalized boardgame. The sinister expression on his face intimates that his next move will be far from benevolent.

As implied by the nuances of Dean's illustration, *The Final Programme* is by no means a naïve perpetuation of the glitzy image of Swinging London. Indeed, the iconic trappings of the 1960s – the beat club's oscillating floor lights, its whirling discs and globes and its ample supply of recreational drugs – are subjected to scathing parody as they morph into horrifying weapons. The lethal defences that protect the Cornelius family château include hallucinatory gases, a mesmeric 'huge back-and-white disc [that] began to whirl',[97] and paralysis-inducing searchlights whose 'colour changed to red, then yellow, then lilac ... in garish primary colours, fizzing like neon',[98] creating what is essentially a nightmare version of a dance floor.

Jerry's favourite West End club, the fictional 'Friendly Bum' on Villiers Street, likewise becomes a grotesque parody of itself. As atrophy takes hold of London, the Friendly Bum's 'beautiful blend' of instruments playing live music,[99] its catchy beats and refracted lights and its inducement of a 'delicious feeling' of dancing as 'part of the mass' all turn languid and horrible.[100] Its music becomes 'dragging, monotonous',[101] its 'dead neon sign drooped',[102] its band 'moulded on to or around its instruments' and its dancers fuse together into 'a tired pyramid of flesh that moved to the slow rhythm, near quiescent'.[103] According to Moorcock, this cumulative portrait of a London sinking into entropy envisages 'an "alternative" near future',[104] in which the 'idealism of the '60s' had given way to narcissistic self-indulgence.[105] In such a future, it is only a matter of time before the swings of London come to a halt.

The final scenes of *The Final Programme* cohere with Moorcock's aspirations for *New Worlds* magazine to promote a speculative fiction 'concerned with the need to find a new set of morals and ethical principles' suitable to the modern world.[106] While Jerry is distinctly amoral, the story gestures towards an ethical way of life. The ethical vision set forth at the end draws on the anarchist philosophy of Peter Kropotkin, which Moorcock expressly cited as an influence on the book.[107] Kropotkin made the case, *contra* Social Darwinism, that within members of the same animal species and in human society alike, 'Better conditions [of life] are created . . . by means of mutual aid and mutual support'.[108]

In *The Final Programme*, Kropotkin's ethics of mutuality are dramatized in the physical merger of Jerry Cornelius with the aforementioned Miss Brunner, a brilliant if ruthless computer programmer who possesses a determination and purposefulness that Jerry sorely lacks. This unity creates 'a tall, naked, graceful being' christened 'Cornelius Brunner' that is greater than the sum of its parts.[109] Thus, Miss Brunner's red hair, described initially as 'nice red hair, but not on her',[110] has no such qualifications when adorning the head of Cornelius Brunner. Her 'predatory jaw' is likewise 'softened by Jerry's aesthetic mouth',[111] and they enjoy a single body with 'breasts and two sets of genitals'.[112] Far from a sacrifice of individuality, the merge of Cornelius and Brunner brings together two personalities who share an overwhelming, vampiric lust for life, but remain distinct from each other and individualistically minded. The two personalities that were once Jerry and Miss Brunner accordingly debate their next destination from within their shared body, each expressing their own preferences and referring to themselves as 'I' and the other as 'you'.[113] It is the fact that Cornelius Brunner does not speak with one voice that makes it a more compelling figure, one that is wholly different from the writhing pyramid of flesh on Villiers Street. Where the pyramid of flesh was sluggish and atrophying, Cornelius Brunner crackles with renewed energy, a 'self-fertilising and thus self-regenerating' force capable of 're-creating itself over and over again'.[114]

This is not to say that Cornelius Brunner heralds a promise of redemption, as Jerry Cornelius and Miss Brunner are insufficiently principled for their unification to embody an ethical vision of the future. But Moorcock nevertheless celebrates their merger as the first step towards a mutuality liberated from both a loss of self and a desire for control, as Miss Brunner's grandiose plans for 'a fantastic programme' that would bring order to the world morph into an ecstatic consumption of life.[115] Cornelius Brunner thus emerges from its metal chamber like a rock star stepping into the spotlight for a long-anticipated gig. The first words to issue from its mouth are, appropriately enough, 'Hi, fans!'.[116]

An 'unbordered world': *A Cure for Cancer*

If *The Final Programme* culminated in the potent melding of Jerry Cornelius and Miss Brunner, then the *New Worlds* magazine saw an analogous process on the metafictional level, whereby its contributors collaborated on the expansion and enrichment of the Jerry Cornelius myth following Moorcock's decision to open it up to his coterie of writers. Precisely three years elapsed between the publication of the last extract from *The Final Programme* in the March 1966 issue of *New Worlds*, and the publication of the first instalment of Moorcock's second Jerry Cornelius novel, *A Cure for Cancer*, in the issue of March 1969. By his own account, Moorcock completed the manuscript of *Cure for Cancer* 'by 1967',[117] but its serialization began two years later. In the interim, Moorcock began to publish short stories in the Jerry Cornelius world and he concomitantly gave the *New Worlds* writers his blessing to write their own Cornelius tales. 'It was the closest a group of aggressively individualistic writers came to collaboration',[118] Moorcock recounted proudly, 'I was delighted by what they [the *New Worlds* contributors] produced'.[119] As Rob Latham has argued, 'Jerry became something of an informal mascot for the magazine, as other hands took up the picaresque chronicle of his wayward adventures'.[120]

Jerry Cornelius thus played a pivotal role in the endeavours of *New Worlds* writers 'to find a viable myth figure for the last half of the 20th century'.[121] As a Protean figure who was constantly in flux, who 'can crop up in any situation, any guise and any sex',[122] he was as much 'a literary technique' as a literary character.[123] His stories thereby became 'a form in themselves',[124] retaining 'relevance to our immediate situation' and 'carry[ing] levels of satire, parody, lampoon and self-satire'.[125] Jerry's oscillation between different gender, sexual, racial and class identities dramatized what Clute has described as the desperate search for 'an identity strategically capable of constituting urban life'.[126] For the writers of *New Worlds* magazine, he formed the locus for fictional explorations, elaborations, variations and permutations on the urbanite who 'cannot avoid a consciousness of his own essential mutability'.[127] By embracing this mutability, Jerry became 'the paradigmatic native of the inner city',[128] his connection with London the single immutable constant in his otherwise infinitely elastic identity:

> He is sometimes described as being white, sometimes black, and a whole cycle of myths have it that 'he' was a woman. All sources are agreed, however, that Cornelius was born in the notorious Ladbroke Grove area of London between the years 1900 and 1950.[129]

The Jerry Cornelius stories thus became the cast into which Urban Fantasy was moulded in the 1960s and 1970s.

The first three Cornelius stories to be published in *New Worlds* recast Jerry as a displaced person not unlike the forlorn figure who had once haunted his decadent parties on Holland Park Avenue.[130] No longer swaggering in the clubs and casinos of the West End, the Jerry of these stories has lost wife, son and home, and is drifting through countries once colonized by the British Empire or its imperial neighbours, grappling with the febrile memories of a London consumed by flames. Obliquely allegorizing the decline of post-imperial Britain, Jerry has been shorn of his wealth, stripped of his glamour and reduced to the status of those who were once on the receiving end of his self-indulgent magnanimity. By the end of Moorcock's 'Delhi Division' (1968), Jerry is 'weeping uncontrollably';[131] by the end of his 'Tank Trapeze' (1969), Jerry is dead;[132] and by the end of James Sallis's 'Jeremiad' (1969), we discover that London has been destroyed by American airstrikes.[133] Thus, if Jerry Cornelius was originally conceptualized 'as a way of celebrating the modern age',[134] then by the closing years of the 1960s, his adventures had taken a darker turn, one which was postcolonial and anti-American in its sensibilities.

This bleaker cast is markedly discernible in *Cure for Cancer*, serialized in *New Worlds* magazine in four parts. The first instalment offers a biting satire on class exclusion, focused on Jerry's and Moorcock's home turf of North Kensington. It is prefaced by an epigraph lifted verbatim from a real brochure for *Derry & Toms Famous Roof Gardens* (1966), an iconic stretch of pleasure gardens on the roof of what was then the Derry and Toms department store on Kensington High Street.[135] Moorcock set the scene with a brief description of the roof gardens that closes with a rhetorical question: 'Who better to describe this roof garden than those who built it?'.[136] This question prompts a lengthy quotation from the same brochure, detailing the roof gardens' history, dimensions, views and special attractions. But where the brochure emphasizes the roof gardens' open pastoral spaces,[137] the narrator points out that 'There are walls about the retreat.'[138] Where the brochure boasts of the gardens' 'magnificent views' on 'the spires and towers of the Kensington Museums, the great Dome of St Paul's,'[139] the narrator calls attention away from these London landmarks to the contrast between the opulent department store and its less salubrious surroundings: 'Derry and Toms faces towards North Kensington, . . . the most delicious slum in Europe.'[140]

This sardonic interplay between the brochure's promotional material and the wry descriptions that follow it is particularly effective in the original *New Worlds* serialization. Across the pages of a magazine that featured its own inset advertisements among articles, reviews, conference reports and fictional pieces, this narrative strategy gains a self-reflexive frisson that is diminished in book publication. The original serialized version therefore provides the best context for fully appreciating the effect of the epigraphs and embedded quotations peppered across *Cure for Cancer*. Latter-day Moorcock might claim that the revised editions of the *Michael Moorcock Collection* (2013–15) are definitive,[141] but one should not downplay the significance of the fact that *Cure for Cancer* was initially crafted for consumption in serialized form. Granted, the revised book editions from 1979 onwards are superior to the original serialization in some important respects – they provide fuller explanations for the characters' motivations, and they substitute the more thematically appropriate character of Una Persson for Captain Brunner in the penultimate scenes of the story. But readers should bear in mind that this increased clarity and greater thematic cohesion come at the expense of the richer contextualization provided by the original serial publication in *New Worlds*.

Moorcock's choice of Derry and Toms roof gardens was far from incidental. By his own account, this pastoral spot was one of his 'secret boltholes' in North Kensington in the 1960s.[142] Moorcock was thoroughly incensed when the roof gardens underwent a process of gentrification, which began with a solicitor inviting him 'to a newly formed "gardens committee"' and ended with the roof gardens becoming 'a private club' by 1980.[143] He regarded this gentrification as nothing short of 'the beginning of the end' of the 'golden age' that was the 1960s,[144] a symptom of wider transformations in the area whereby the opulent 'South Kensington helped polarise and ghettoise North Kensington in the '60s and '70s'.[145] Indeed, the sociologist Ruth Glass, who coined the term 'gentrification' in 1963,[146] singled out 'North Kensington' and 'the "shady" parts of Notting Hill' as contemporary examples of 'the upper-middle class take-over' of London.[147]

These transformations culminated in Moorcock's sense of becoming 'a stranger in my own city'.[148]

He took his revenge in a satirical sequence in *Cure for Cancer*, where well-heeled ladies discover the disadvantages of the roof gardens' increasing exclusivity. Strolling along 'the pleasant paths',[149] their leisure activities are interrupted by a shoot-out between Jerry and a helicopter. Attempting to flee the scene, they find 'the lift out of order and the emergency exits blocked' on the instructions of Jerry himself,[150] with no one willing to assist them. Left behind as Jerry commandeers the helicopter and departs in it, the ladies remain trapped on the roof but are unwilling to call attention to themselves and 'start a fuss',[151] and they consequently die of starvation. Their reluctance to appear unladylike, however, does not extend to their conduct towards Jerry, at whom they hurl racist abuse: 'Hooligan! Go back to your own country!'.[152]

As suggested by this scene, *Cure for Cancer* turned its attention to the weightier issues of the time, the undercurrents of racism in England that had found virulent expression in Enoch Powell's 'Rivers of Blood' speech in April 1968,[153] and the ongoing international crisis of the Vietnam War. Accordingly, the Jerry of *Cure for Cancer* is no longer the fair-skinned cross between Mick Jagger and James Bond that he had been at the opening of *Final Programme*.[154] Reversing Elric's albino complexion, Jerry's skin begins to darken in 'Delhi Division',[155] and by *Cure for Cancer* he has become a photographic negative of his former self: 'his skin was ebony and his hair not blond but milk white'.[156] No longer able to play the sahib in Cambodia and Delhi, he is instead mistaken for 'a dandified negro' by the middle-class ladies on the roof gardens.[157] The racial slurs that they hurl at him carry echoes of the 1958 Notting Hill Race Riots that had erupted a short walking distance north of Derry and Toms. Instigated primarily by local young white men, known as 'Teddy Boys', Notting Hill suffered from a series of violent attacks targeted at the local dark-skinned immigrant population from the West Indies.[158] *Cure for Cancer* tacitly alludes to these events, as Jerry's American contact casts doubt on his British citizenship and speculates instead that he must have arrived from 'the West Indies'.[159] The antagonist Bishop Beesley, who mistakes Jerry for 'an Indian',[160] owns a yacht pointedly christened '*Teddy Bear*'.[161]

The most concentrated scenes of racism and violence in *Cure for Cancer* are perpetrated not by white Englishmen in West London but by Americans. In the second instalment, Jerry travels to a dystopian 'Amerika' after the fashion of Kafka,[162] a spelling that Moorcock glossed as shorthand for 'the imperialist, bullying, unjust aspects' of the United States.[163] In a nice Dickensian touch, Jerry gives his name as 'Chuzzlewit',[164] and his experience of America is scarcely less dismal than that of his Dickensian counterpart. American bureaucrats address Jerry as 'bwah',[165] American police officers call him 'sonny' and 'boy',[166] and even an Indian war chief apologizes to Jerry for attacking his car because 'we didn't know you was a schvartze'.[167] With the exception of 'Captain Brunner' who appears to be as Protean as Jerry himself,[168] all the characters whom Jerry meets in the United States relate to him first and foremost by the colour of his skin.

This emphasis on American rather than British racism may strike one as a too-convenient displacement of home truths. But it takes on fresh merit when considered as part of Moorcock's broadside against the Vietnam War, which he castigated as 'real evil' furthering the cause of 'American imperialism'.[169] This interpretation is reinforced by Moorcock's suggestion in the December 1967/January 1968 issue of *New Worlds* that 'the Vietnam War and race riots' were the primary manifestations of contemporary 'society's ills' and thus different facets of 'the problem' that mature science fiction was called upon to refract rather than evade.[170] The war had been raging for some time, but the late 1960s saw an escalation in the conflict, together with an expansion of the targets from 'strictly military' to 'farms, factories, and transportation lines'.[171] As Moorcock recalled, the images that reached London were shocking: 'I'd just seen these pictures of [Vietnamese] children on fire'.[172] In *Cure for Cancer*, he dislocated these images from Vietnam to London. This '"Vietnamisation" of Ladbroke Grove',[173] as he described it, comes into play when Jerry returns home to find that the north wall of his house – no longer an opulent mansion on Holland Park Avenue but a 'high walled fortress in Ladbroke Grove'[174] – has been vandalized with graffiti reading 'Vietgrove'.[175]

The third instalment features an American napalm airstrike on London that takes place during Jerry's second visit to Derry and Toms roof gardens. At its most overt, this scene inveighs against the horrors of the Vietnam War by 'substituting England for Vietnam, to bring the war home'.[176] Yet beneath this political broadside lies a pattern of London history endlessly repeating itself. As he pulls up by Derry and Toms and watches 'a boy and a girl . . . on fire',[177] Jerry obliquely reflects that 'The fire would probably help cope with the plague.'[178] This off-hand comment refers to the Great Fire of London of 1666, which brought an end to the Great Plague of 1665.[179] But one may also discern the contours of more recent London history in 'the sound of falling buildings, the scream of rockets, the boom of the bombs' that Jerry hears around him on Kensington High Street.[180] Moorcock grew up in London at the height of the Luftwaffe air raids, his childhood unfolding to 'the sound of the aircraft siren, warning us of an attack'.[181] His boyhood experiences of the Blitz and the Little Blitz instilled in him a life-long sense of London as intrinsically fantastical, a metamorphic city 'of almost constantly changing landscapes'.[182] For a young boy eager for adventure, London's blitzed ruins became a freewheeling playground:

> The world was unbordered. All its walls had been smashed down. . . . We ranged through glass-roofed conservatories. . . . We learned to walk on roofs.[183]

This rubble-strewn London of 'glass-roofed conservatories' where children 'learned to walk on roofs' chimes with Jerry's 'glass conservatory' on 'the roof of the Angkor Hilton' in the opening scene of *Final Programme*,[184] as well as the twin scenes on Derry and Toms roof gardens in *Cure for Cancer*. The analogy between these roofscapes becomes explicit in *Condition of Muzak*, where 'the department store [of Derry and Toms] . . . had come to resemble the forgotten ruins of Angkor Wat in Cambodia'.[185] With his characteristic iconoclasm, Moorcock has asserted that the 'bombed buildings' of London are among 'the happiest impressions from my childhood'.[186] 'I long to find them again',[187] he wrote wistfully. His Cornelius books thus draw on his childhood escapades in an 'unbordered' London, reworking his experiences through the rose-tinted filter of nostalgia. In this respect, one may read *Cure for Cancer* as an elegy for the 'unbordered world' of Moorcock's youth where 'walls had been smashed down', composed at a time when class borders and their correlative walls were being shored up across London, not least on the roof gardens of Derry and Toms.

Moorcock has tellingly described the second scene on Derry and Toms roof gardens as 'the grand finale [that] takes place in the middle of the book'.[188] His comment reinforces the wider impression instilled by *Cure for Cancer* that its central conflict is not so much between London and the American aggressors who bomb it, as between the 'locked gate' of Derry and Toms roof gardens and the 'unbordered' London across which the young Moorcock 'learned to walk on roofs'.[189] Thus, the metaphorical 'cancer' that spreads through London is the obsession with regulation, segregation, separation and order. This obsession is nourished by the antagonists: Jerry's brother Frank, who in *Cure for Cancer* commits himself to 'tidying the world',[190] and Bishop Beesley, who believes that 'We are put on this earth to order it.'[191] Jerry, for his part, 'see[s] it another way'.[192] 'I don't like the way you and your allies slice up time',[193] he tells Frank, and remarks in a similar vein to Beesley's wife Karen: 'We merely serve the people, Karen. . . . Beesley knows what's good for them.'[194] 'We are all offered a selection of traditional roles',[195] he elaborates in *Condition of Muzak*, 'we attempt to console as many actors as possible by finding them the parts in which they can be as happy as possible.'[196] Thus, Jerry strives for what Moorcock termed, in a line added to the 1979 revised book edition of *Cure for Cancer*, 'The equilibrium of anarchy'.[197]

The clash between Frank's and Beesley's authoritarianism and Jerry's 'anarchic individualism' plays out symbolically in the pastoral spaces of London.[198] Between the two scenes on Derry and Toms roof gardens, Jerry visits a subtly altered Kew Gardens in West London. Several years before Moorcock began writing *Cure for Cancer*, the real Kew Gardens underwent renovations that tamed its wilder patches. The unruly 'petrified forest' was replaced by the well-kept 'Heath Garden' just east of Kew's famous Pagoda at the south-eastern corner of the gardens.[199] Jerry wreaks havoc on such immaculate stretches of Kew: he 'gunned through flower beds and lawns' on his motorcycle,[200] 'his bike leaving a churned scar across the autumnal lawns' as he cuts across the gardens to his meeting at the Pagoda.[201] He thereby literally etches a mark of chaos into the neat and tidy landscape of trimmed lawns and lined flower beds.

Jerry enters the Pagoda with an insouciance wholly unconcerned with the fact that the real Pagoda was closed to the public in the 1960s.[202] Indeed, the Pagoda and the entirety of Kew Gardens appear to have been abandoned in *Cure for Cancer*, by all save the man whom Jerry has come to meet, a flasher ironically named 'Flash Gordon' after the popular comic book hero created in the 1930s.[203] Flash Gordon is in possession of the key to Kew's Australian House, and Moorcock heavily implies that he exploits his unfettered access to expose himself in the variety of exotic buildings and greenhouses afforded by the Gardens. All of this suggests that any semblance of order has long since dissipated in Kew, but Moorcock gives the screw another turn by endowing the Pagoda with a borderline-fantastical element drawn directly from its history. Originally built with eighty wooden dragons poised to take flight on the corners of each of its ten balconies,[204] the real Pagoda was stripped of its dragons within a few decades of its completion.[205] Yet when Jerry arrives, the dragons stand 'at each corner of each of the octagonal roofs' as if they had remained in their posts since the eighteenth century.[206] But this nominal restoration of past glories is itself subject to subversion – where the original dragons were made of wood, these dragons are 'bronze',[207] belying the narrator's claim that they are identical to the dragons 'placed [on the Pagoda's balconies] in 1761'.[208] Thus, an ostensible return to architectural order is undercut by subtle changes, an effect all the more unsettling for the minuteness of its alterations and the fantastical quality of its subject matter.[209]

Cure for Cancer's dénouement takes place in Holland Park, the park nearest to Jerry's home on Ladbroke Grove. With the help of a mysterious black box that 'breaks down the barriers' between dimensions and thereby literally demolishes borders,[210] Jerry foils Bishop Beesley's plans and creates a new version of London where the Bishop and his daughter have petrified into marble statues on the cricket pitch of Holland Park, fixed in permanent stasis as 'they would have wanted'.[211] Jerry takes quiet pleasure in this new London enabled by his destruction of physical barriers such as the 'steel door' through which he bore a hole in order to gain access to the park.[212] The collapse of metaphysical, biological and social borders follows shortly, as Jerry resurrects his dead sister Catherine and the siblings make love on the snow-covered grounds of the park, with 'the sharp outlines of Holland House' looming disapprovingly in the background.[213] By the end of the story, Jerry is pregnant with their baby and he 'could feel it stirring'.[214]

Moorcock himself lived near Holland Park, which he once named as the place in which he was happiest,[215] but he surely chose this setting for more than personal reasons. The once-stately Holland House that looms behind Jerry's and Catherine's lovemaking has a venerable history as a social centre for literary figures from Byron to Wordsworth to Dickens.[216] Less amicably, the headquarters of the White Defence League, later the British National Party, stood just off of Holland Park.[217] For Moorcock to choose Holland Park as the grounds for Jerry's ultimate act of transgression against death, conventional morality, social taboo and the dictates of human reproductive systems was therefore to fly in the face of social decorum and to challenge authoritarian fascism on its doorstep.

Yet this dénouement also carries problematic racial overtones that countermand its valorization of sexual and social freedoms. Once Jerry revives Catherine, the story is inundated by images of whiteness. He awakens to a view of 'The towers of the [Oxford] Cathedral [that] were white against the white sky'.[218] 'It was snowing',[219] Moorcock notes, weather that 'was only to be expected'.[220] This whiteness of environment leads up to the revelation that Jerry too has once again become Caucasian not in the manner of Elric the Albino but in the manner of a man who has regained his 'true' form. 'They were very much alike',[221] Moorcock remarks of Jerry and Catherine, and Catherine herself comments: 'You've turned quite pale, Jerry'.[222] To which Jerry replies: 'It's for the best, I suppose'.[223] This sense that Jerry's restored whiteness 'is for the best' sits uncomfortably with Moorcock's stalwart claims for the emancipatory possibilities encoded in the Cornelius myth.

This pervasive whiteness expands from Oxford to London. Jerry's and Catherine's lovemaking is preceded by their romantic stroll 'hand in hand' through a 'Holland Park [that] was covered in snow'.[224] The snow takes on conventional symbolic connotations of purity and renewal, as 'the trees cast clean, black shadows on the white ground' and Catherine lies 'in the snow amongst the snowdrops'.[225] This strenuous emphasis on whiteness, particularly on the backdrop of a park near the headquarters of the White Defence League and well within the area of the 1958 Notting Hill Race Riots,[226] is a questionable artistic choice for a self-proclaimed 'committed anti-racist' like Moorcock.[227] *Condition of Muzak* exacerbates this problem when it revisits the events of *Cure for Cancer* and suggests that Jerry was never a black man in the first place – he was in blackface, having smeared black greasepaint on his face and hands.[228] Thus, in Jerry's 'unbordered world', one border remains firmly in place – the border of race. Jerry would undergo many alterations in the course of his adventures, into a woman and a transvestite,[229] a Jew,[230] and a black-and-white cat,[231] but the closing scene of *Cure for Cancer* leaves the impression that however much he celebrates the fluidity of his identity, his happiness is bound up with the whiteness of his skin.

'The landscape *is* the fiction': Harrison's Cornelius stories

New Worlds magazine published a variety of Jerry Cornelius fiction concurrently with, and in the months following upon, its serialization of *Cure for Cancer*. Moorcock, Harrison, Sallis, Jones, Brian Aldiss, Norman Spinrad and Maxim Jakubowski all spun different riffs on the elastic Cornelius myth. Asked for his thoughts on the Cornelius stories penned by other hands, Moorcock replied that they 'helped me broaden the myth, and Harrison's were the best of them, as far as I was concerned'.[232] Harrison has penned three Cornelius stories to date, all with alliterative titles suggesting a cyclical structure: 'The Ash Circus' (1969), 'The Nash Circuit' (1969) and 'The Flesh Circle' (1971).

'Ash Circus' was first published in the same *New Worlds* issue as the second instalment of *Cure for Cancer*. From its opening note, it strikes up a dialogue with Moorcock.[233] The second instalment featured an exchange between Jerry and Karen, where Jerry replies to Karen's query with the enigmatic remark: 'I'll probably die. I almost always do.'[234] Several pages earlier in the same issue, 'Ash Circus' opened with the sub-header 'Jerry is dead'.[235] Where the second instalment charted Jerry's journey away from London to an authoritarian America, 'Ash Circus' followed Jerry's return to London on an American nuclear submarine. Harrison's images of a post-apocalyptic London further echo the second instalment where wrecks of tankers float through oil on the Thames.[236]

'Ash Circus' similarly showcases 'the whole smashed London basin',[237] leaving Jerry feeling 'depressed',[238] 'disturbed',[239] and 'struggling with his malaise of the head'.[240] The story tacitly suggests that Jerry has returned to the wrong London, a city where others are welcome and where others find beauty and wonder, but where he feels out of kilter, subject to a 'process of dislocation'.[241]

'Ash Circus' may be read, therefore, as a metafictional meditation on the complexities of identity in a shared myth. With tongue firmly lodged in cheek, Harrison implies that Jerry's attenuated sense of self derives from the fact that he is a riff in an open-ended myth already mined by Moorcock and Sallis. Thus, Harrison's Jerry suffers from the ennui of a character who has arrived too late to the party. He finds himself in an England already occupied by Moorcock's Jerry from *Final Programme*, as suggested by an off-hand exchange with one of his enemies:

> 'I don't know what you're after, but Cornelius and Brunner aren't going to like this – '
> 'Ho ho,' said Jerry, 'Pardon?'[242]

Lest this metafictional play be lost on the reader, Harrison reinforces his point in a section entitled 'Jerry Is Unoriginal'.[243] Jerry ends up travelling with Miss Brunner, a reunion that at once echoes their merger into Cornelius Brunner at the end of *Final Programme* and anticipates his reunion with the now-male 'Captain Brunner' at the end of the second instalment of *Cure for Cancer*.[244] Given that Brunner was mentioned neither in the first instalment nor in the Cornelius stories that Moorcock had published hitherto in *New Worlds* magazine,[245] her sudden reappearance in both 'Ash Circus' and the second instalment lends further irony to her acerbic remark, which closes Harrison's story: 'I'd have expected something more original from you, Mr Cornelius.'[246]

Harrison's London comes into its own in his second Cornelius story, 'Nash Circuit'. This title tacitly alludes to John Nash's Park Crescent in Regent's Park,[247] where Jerry now lives 'in his Nash Crescent house' within earshot of 'the wild animals collecting in the park'.[248] Harrison moved to London from Warwickshire in 1966 to become a professional writer and enjoy 'the many benefits of an alienated & intellectualized modernity'.[249] He found what he sought, residing 'on a long sweep of bedsitters running down from Tufnell Park station towards Holloway',[250] which he described elsewhere as 'an area of one-roomed cold-water apartments full of Irish expatriots'.[251] Working through the night and sleeping through the day, Harrison felt 'little connection with the scenes in which I found myself'.[252] Yet these scenes inspired his imagination as well as his alienation: 'I still find the area fascinating,[253] he has asserted, 'the landscape *is* the fiction; all else devolves from it'.[254]

In 'Nash Circuit', Harrison began to chart his own London territory for Jerry Cornelius, changing the scene from the bohemia of West London and the West End to the middle-class suburbs of North London. The Jerry of this story is thus spun from the landscape of 'the deserted, stinking streets of Barnet',[255] the 'demolished hospital' off of 'the Holloway Road' and 'the greenery' that graces 'Barnet Lane and Totteridge'.[256] This Jerry prefers a friendly chat with 'a plump waitress' at a diner on Haverstock Hill to sleeping with the female staff in the private room of a Soho club.[257] He is thus a gentleman of moderate appetites and stolid tastes, a North London suburbanite who gazes out of 'French windows' and appreciates the well-kept 'tennis courts',[258] who wields a 'tape machine' rather than a gem-studded guitar,[259] and who orders a pisco rather than a Pernod.

Harrison recalled that during his time 'living frugally in the bleak "bedsitter" belt of London's Tufnell Park and Camden Town',[260] 'everything that happened there made me anxious'.[261] Accordingly, 'Nash Circuit' is permeated with existential dread. Jerry's chronic identity problems have now become acute, as he hears another 'Jerry Cornelius moaning softly' in the pub.[262] The story's set piece takes place in Madame Tussauds, unfolding a sequence so rich in symbolism and sociopolitical undercurrents that Harrison reworked it for a Jerry Cornelius comic strip published the following month.[263] The sequence begins at 'the Battle of Trafalgar',[264] a real waxworks tableau of the most famous battle in the Napoleonic Wars.[265] This setting is used for parodic effect, as Jerry's accomplice merrily shoots down floorwalkers 'from the bridge of the [HMS] *Victory*',[266] to the triumphant tune of *Rule Britannia*. Harrison ratchets up his satire with the wholesale destruction of waxwork models of Winston Churchill, 'HRH Queen Elizabeth II',[267] 'HRH Prince Philip',[268] 'HRH Princess Margaret' and even 'the Royal Corgis'.[269] 'Nash Circuit' thereby gleefully reduces Britain's patriotic emblems, its war heroes and its royal family into lumps of molten wax. Given Harrison's reading of *The Final Programme* as a book that raises 'not social but personal' questions,[270] this scene may have marked his attempt to create a more overtly sociopolitical riff on the Cornelius myth.

The sequence at Madame Tussauds enfolds an existential dimension as well as a sociopolitical one. When Jerry reaches a captive Albert Einstein, he finds him strapped to a dentist's chair and staring at a cast of 'his own face'.[271] Einstein is so profoundly shaken by this likeness of himself that he is unsure where he ends and the waxwork begins: 'I can't get out of my . . . head',[272] he murmurs, as if his own head and the head of clay were one and the same. Thus, Harrison anticipated

Baudrillard's concept of 'the body being serially reproduced' until 'there is no possibility of a return to an original being'.²⁷³ As argued by Uta Kornmeier, the waxworks of Madame Tussauds provide a particularly compelling instance of such corporeal simulacra, because they 'consist primarily of a component that is very similar in color and substance to human skin and body tissue'.²⁷⁴ To apply Walter Benjamin's theoretical paradigm, the human body thus loses its aura, its originality and uniqueness dissipating as it becomes an infinitely reproducible model.²⁷⁵

This sequence culminates in a confrontation between Jerry and his own waxwork models, who have been upgraded into walking and speaking automata. The waxwork Corneliuses, who 'wore identical velvet frock coats and mazarine hipsters',²⁷⁶ instigate an immediate crisis of identity. Foreclosing any possibility of separating the 'real' Cornelius from among them, they cast doubt on the very existence of the original:

> 'Jerry Cornelius! Jerry Cornelius!' shouted Jerry. He screamed. They screamed. They were him. His power leaked away into them. . . .
> Jerry got one foot under him, raised his heavy head. He shot himself.²⁷⁷

This encounter swerves vertiginously between the perspectives of the waxworks and the putatively human Jerry, each of them referred to by the pronoun 'he', as Jerry kills himself and is killed by himself time and again. These waxworks are unconvincing simulacra – 'waxen-faced, they clicked and whirred as they moved'²⁷⁸ – but it is precisely their robotic qualities that point up the automation in Jerry himself, triggering the collapse of his selfhood.

Forming the core of 'Nash Circuit', this mise-en-scène suggests that the gamut of characters in this story are little more than waxwork models. London's streets are patrolled by 'groups of . . . automata',²⁷⁹ and children pleading for food in the diner appear carved of a material other than flesh. A group of Irish girls touring the London Zoo wear identical 'print dresses' and make 'winking, clicking' sounds with their box-Brownie cameras that echo the clicking and whirring of the wax-Jerries.²⁸⁰ Even the Zoo's seals cannot distinguish reality from simulacrum in their own pool, 'as they dived for imitation polythene fish'.²⁸¹ 'Nash Circuit' thus reimagines the suburbs and inner districts of North London as a series of Madame Tussauds showrooms that have been temporarily 'switched on',²⁸² the people within them more wax than otherwise.

This theme is developed further in Harrison's third and final Cornelius story to date, 'The Flesh Circle', which focuses on Jerry's agonized grappling with mental instability and a loss of self as he visits several mental hospitals and rest homes. Failing to save his friend from a mental hospital nestled among 'the terrible brightnesses of Knightsbridge',[283] Jerry eventually finds himself driving northward 'down Watford Way',[284] and 'into Barnet Way',[285] reversing the route he had taken in 'Nash Circuit'. He speeds across the North London suburbs, past a landscape of science- fictional transonic planes and decaying buildings from 'the forties and early fifties',[286] patches of urban blight that Harrison described elsewhere as emblematic of aborted futures.[287] The headlights of Jerry's motorcycle 'whitened the bemused eyes of accountants and headmasters',[288] all as one walking 'their cocker spaniels' towards 'the golf course, for a pee'.[289] This golf course is similarly occupied by teachers who all wear undifferentiated 'prim, long-suffering expressions' on their faces,[290] and Jerry fancies that he can hear their complaints about his noise and intrusion uttered in one voice. By the end of the story, this milieu has defeated him. As he enters 'a double door beaded with imitation rosewood, smelling of Johnson's wax' that recalls the imitation polythene fish and the waxwork models of 'Nash Circuit',[291] Jerry confesses: 'I didn't calculate on that much inertia.'[292] The story's concluding sentence is identical to the opening sentence of 'Ash Circus': 'Jerry Cornelius was buried at sea without honour, although Captain Vassily personally draped the coffin with a Hungarian flag.'[293] It thereby bears out the cyclical intimations of the titles 'Ash Circus', 'Nash Circuit' and 'Flesh Circle'. Harrison thus implies that like a rebooted waxwork tableau in Madame Tussauds, Jerry's nightmare of North London lassitude will restart presently.

Where Blenheim Crescent met Ladbroke Grove: *The English Assassin*

Moorcock's third Cornelius novel, *The English Assassin*, is titled after Jerry's sobriquet, but it revolves around his conspicuous absence. Jerry has fallen into a deep coma, in which he remains for the better part of the book, and the narrative consequently splinters into multiple vignettes in scrambled chronological order that shuttle across the points of view afforded by the other characters in the Cornelius myth. This kaleidoscope of focalization enabled Moorcock to write a more aesthetically ambitious and emotionally sensitive book, disclosing a vision of London that is at once more raw and more tender than Jerry's distancing tone would have allowed for.

The English Assassin brings a new set of concerns into the Cornelius myth – the struggles of everyday life in a low-income household. Starkly contrasting with Jerry's opulent mansion on Holland Park Avenue, Jerry's mother Honoria lives in a damp and gloomy basement on Talbot Road, a moment's walk from Moorcock's erstwhile flat on Colville Terrace and in much the same milieu. Honoria works as a maid in the houses of upper-class women who entertain themselves by trying to humiliate her. Thus, while *The English Assassin* contains apocalyptic vignettes in the vein of Moorcock's previous Cornelius books, it is far more concerned with the soul-crushing effects of poverty. Moorcock resurrects Jerry for a shoot-out on Ladbroke Grove every so often, but the images that stay with the reader are of 'the glazed look of the really poor'.[294]

Jerry's brother Frank is accordingly no longer a caricature villain who hatches devious schemes from his office in Buckingham Palace, but a dutiful son who takes care of his mother in Jerry's absence, paying her gas bills and arranging replacements for her broken furniture. The conversations among Jerry's family members afford a new perspective on Jerry quite different from the messianic image of him in *Final Programme* and his heroic depiction in *Cure for Cancer*. 'Well, at least yer 'elp out sometimes',[295] Honoria tells Frank, 'I don't see 'im [Jerry] one year ter the next.'[296] 'Jerry's far too involved in the affairs of the world to spare time for the simple things of life',[297] Frank scoffs later on in the book. *The English Assassin* thus produces its own self-critique, casting a critical light not just on Jerry but on the exclusions that underpin boys' adventures in his vein. It calls attention to the grimy realities of life carefully bracketed out by thrilling adventure tales, reminding us that the true struggles of London inhere not in the shoot-outs of the gun-toting action hero but in the council flats where exhausted mothers fail to keep up with their gas bills.

The most touching scenes in *English Assassin* centre on Honoria's unnamed child, referred to only as 'the boy' and 'her son'.[298] Dejected and lonely, the boy wanders the less salubrious streets around Ladbroke Grove after his mother evicts him in preparation for a night of sexual activity. He is narrowly missed by passing cars and jeered at by local children, and he responds to his dismal situation by escaping into flights of fancy. He imagines that his 'parlour was a dark jungle of aspidistra and mahogany',[299] a fancy curiously reminiscent of both the rooftop conservatory in *Final Programme* and Derry and Toms roof gardens in *Cure for Cancer*. He likewise 'pretended he was a fighting aeroplane making a death dive on its enemies',[300] recalling a scene in *Cure for Cancer* where Jerry pilots a '95 ft. aircraft' and angles it downward towards an attacking pirate ship.[301] These resonances cumulatively suggest that the entire Cornelius myth may be nothing more than stories made up by an imaginative boy seeking escape from his intolerable reality. Lest the reader miss the import of these clues, the boy encounters the jeering children as he 'rushed panting into Blenheim Crescent' to the corner 'where it met Ladbroke Grove'.[302] There he sees the group 'by the wall of the newly-built Convent of the Poor Clares'.[303] This encounter is followed by an apocalyptic vignette that depicts an adult Jerry heading to the same spot from the other direction, walking 'into Ladbroke Grove . . . until at last he reached the corner of Blenheim Crescent and realised with a shock that the Convent of the Poor Clares was down'.[304] It is at the Convent of St Clares, Jerry's headquarters in nearly all of Moorcock's Cornelius fictions since *Cure for Cancer*,[305] that the pitiful boy and the swaggering Jerry become one, a confluence of character and setting that forms the heart of the fourth and final book of the Cornelius Quartet, *The Condition of Muzak*.

'Yer orlways did 'ave yer 'ead in the clards': *The Condition of Muzak*

By the mid-1970s, little remained unchanged of the bohemian Notting Hill in which Moorcock first settled in 1963. The 1970s saw a sharp rise in unemployment as manufacturing jobs were lost across England, not least in London, which lost a third of its manufacturing jobs by the early 1970s,[306] and another third between 1973 and 1983.[307] North Kensington had a sizeable population of manual workers whose jobs were at risk,[308] and Notting Hill became a hotbed of tensions that erupted into violence as black residents were scapegoated for socio-economic problems.[309] Further exacerbating matters, the council housing sector was rapidly overtaking privately rented flats,[310] but council subsides were cut by the 1972 Housing Finance Act.[311] Consequently, as Geoffrey Evans observed, 'lower income group residents' were liable to find themselves priced out of their newly refurbished flats.[312] Thus, as Frank remarks in *Condition of Muzak*, 'multiple tenancies are giving way to one-family houses',[313] creating a gentrified middle-class Notting Hill that had lost its bohemian edge.

The landmarks of Jerry Cornelius's London were likewise in the throes of change. Derry and Toms was sold to Biba's in 1971, and their roof gardens closed for three years as the interior of the shop was being remodelled.[314] The real Convent of St Clares, which had stood opposite the corner of Blenheim Crescent and Ladbroke Grove, was demolished in 1970 to make way for new council flats.[315] Small wonder, perhaps, that the Jerry of *Condition of Muzak* curls up on the abandoned overgrown roof gardens of Derry and Toms and gives in to despair, reflecting that 'the seventies were proving an intense disappointment'.[316]

'When they began to destroy his city he lost his bearings completely',[317] Major Nye remarks of a catatonic Jerry. *The Condition of Muzak* is thus permeated with Moorcock's own sense of loss, dramatizing his realization that 'the best time we ever had in London, the sixties and early seventies' was well and truly over.[318] Not unlike Dickens's attachment to the old St Dunstan in the West and the old London Bridge, for all Moorcock's progressiveness, his fantastical renditions of London became increasingly invested in reclaiming the past.

Condition of Muzak is concerned with demythologizing the Cornelius myth in response to what Moorcock perceived as a pernicious mythologization of London by the heritage industry. The 1960s and 1970s saw London's transition from light manufacturing and riverport trade to an economy based around finance, services and tourism,[319] prompting a rapid growth in its heritage industry.[320] 'The docks disappeared with astonishing speed',[321] Moorcock recalled, 'One day the ships were shadows honking out of the smog and the next they were gone.'[322] With their disappearance, he lost the locales of his boyhood, across which he had 'wandered… vast acreages of docks, still full of the world's ships'.[323] He thus reflected mournfully that 'the London I loved and grew up in' had become 'fleeting, mysterious, torn down or buried'.[324] His sense of loss was underwritten by his conviction that Londoners collectively relied 'on the geography of our cities for the myths and rituals by which we live',[325] in lieu of which memory denatures into 'some vague ideas of what still lies under the steel-and-concrete cladding'.[326]

Diagnosing an etiolated London where 'sentiment and pastiche replace London's original identity to facilitate the appetites of heritage investors',[327] Moorcock lamented 'the heritaging up of every obscure nook and idiosyncratic cranny Londoners used to think of as their own'.[328] Harrison similarly observed that 'it's the future of Heritage to replace the past',[329] and thus 'the Heritage experience becomes in itself heritage, as authentic as the real thing',[330] thereby rendering the past and its heritage experience equally inauthentic. This heritagization of London was perhaps nowhere more visible than in the decision taken by urban developers to repurpose the waterfront area of the closed St Katherine Docks as a leisure complex themed around Dickens's London – 're-creations of Dickensian streets and workshops' were to occupy this newly vacated space.[331] Moorcock was particularly incensed by these plans because they aimed to supplant the working riverside areas of London that, for him, captured the true spirit of Dickens's London: 'the city of Dickens, who had turned London into a character, a monstrous entity',[332] had dwelt in the places 'where great warehouses had loomed over black water'.[333] Now, 'the dark mysteries of Dickens's Thames have gone',[334] he wrote wistfully.

Moorcock and Harrison, who expressly saw themselves as heirs to a Dickensian tradition of London-based fantasy literature, were personally affronted by this prospective transformation of the Docklands into a money-making simulacrum of Dickens's London. Harrison inveighed against 'Britain's ridiculous heritage industry':[335] 'We had ceased to be a live culture,'[336] he recalled, as England became 'RetroLand' and London adopted a 'studiedly retro' posture.[337] Moorcock was outraged that London 'was being dismantled into a kind of Disneyland before our eyes,'[338] and he could naught but hope that 'when fashions such as Dickens World cease to satisfy the tourists, we'll have another city standing by'.[339] Hence the title of *Condition of Muzak* – a riff on Walter Pater's assertion that '*all art constantly aspires towards the condition of music*'.[340] Moorcock used this title to imply that all London aspires towards the condition of muzak, 'a trade name for piped music used in restaurants, supermarkets, bars and other public places'.[341] It is thus the musical equivalent of a Disneyfied London,[342] an ersatz imitation pandering to the lowest common denominator and thereby cheapening the original.

Yet even as he excoriated the transformation of London into a Victoriana theme park, Moorcock was acutely aware that he too was spinning fantasies out of the bricks-and-mortar of his city. 'I wanted to write about the mythology of London,'[343] he reflected back on the Cornelius stories, but 'I invented a mythology more than I examined one.'[344] Thus, *Condition of Muzak* interrogates the foundations of Urban Fantasy – it subjects the Cornelius myth to intense scrutiny and strips it away to reveal the worm-eaten woodwork beneath the stage.

Condition of Muzak unrolls an intricate tapestry of interwoven narrative threads that come together in their deconstruction of the Cornelius myth. Jerry has returned from his absence in *English Assassin*, but he is neither the 'messiah to the Age of Science' that he was in *Final Programme* nor the champion of anarchy that he was in *Cure for Cancer*.[345] Revisiting key scenes from the previous books, the messianic Cornelius Brunner is now exposed as nothing more than Jerry in drag.[346] As aforementioned, the black-skinned Jerry from *Cure for Cancer* is now in blackface, his emancipation of Londoners merely a way of earning 'flat commission'.[347] The family château from *Final Programme* is now a rundown house fronted by a 'weed-grown drive';[348] the Friendly Bum is nowhere to be seen on Villiers Street, and all that is left of the adjacent Charing Cross Station is a 'ruined wall'.[349] Even Jerry's daring escapades to rescue Catherine are now performed 'in grubby underpants',[350] instilling the impression that Jerry is nothing more than a 'wailing barbarian'.[351]

The penultimate sections of *Condition of Muzak* draw heavily on Dickens's and Wells's Urban Fantasy in order to lay bare their own fictionality. This strategy allowed Moorcock to wear his influences on his sleeve and pay homage to the milestones of the Urban Fantasy tradition. In the first of these two consecutive scenes, Moorcock reimagines Graham's awakening in *When the Sleeper Wakes* with Jerry in Graham's place. Much like Graham, Jerry awakens in a future London after a prolonged coma to discover that 'I get the whole of London'.[352] This 'City of the Future' is on the cusp of becoming the future London of *When the Sleeper Wakes*:[353] already an independent city-state, it looms with 'skyscrapers' that will 'have high-level moving platforms going between them eventually'.[354] To which Jerry adds with a knowing wink at the reader: 'Is it going to have a dome over it, too.'[355] This scene follows Wells's example to the hilt, down to its culmination with Jerry standing on a balcony and surveying the future architecture of London to the shouts of a galvanized crowd. 'Just like the Jubilee!',[356] Jerry exclaims with a final allusion to *When the Sleeper Wakes* where Graham falls asleep shortly before '[Queen] Victoria's Jubilee'.[357]

In the style of a pantomime flitting from one act to the next, Moorcock shifts the allusive framework from Wells to Dickens, conjuring up an extravagant Christmas celebration that weds the panoply of seasonal decorations, the overwhelming sensory enticements and the pervasive good cheer of *Christmas Carol* with the 'overhead pedestrian galleries' and 'moving sidewalks' of *When the Sleeper Wakes*.[358] Jerry darts across the bedecked streets of West London to the calls of 'Merry Christmas!' and 'Plump turkeys',[359] past 'stalls piled with vegetables, with meats, toys and sweets; stalls burdened with fowl and game, . . . heather, holly and laurel'.[360] He registers the Dickensian touches of 'friendly intercourse' between 'men and women of every nationality' and 'mouth-watering smells' of 'pie-shops, whose windows are heaped with beef puddings, steak and kidney pies',[361] as he makes his way to his destination. No longer merely an opulent town house on Holland Park Avenue or a high-walled fortress on Ladbroke Grove, Jerry now celebrates Christmas in a veritable fairy-tale castle, 'Of porphyry and jade and marble and lapis lazuli'.[362] The castle is so marvellously enchanting, the narrator so obviously ensorcelled, that the reader harbours little doubt that like the Ghost of Christmas Yet to Come, it too shall dwindle into mundanity.

In keeping with all the permutations of Jerry's London headquarters in Moorcock's stories since *Cure for Cancer*, this fairy-tale castle is 'erected on the site of the legendary Convent of the Poor Clares Colettine'.[363] This convent features at the beginning and end of *Condition of Muzak*, bookending the story and knitting together its various narrative strands. 'For those residents of Blenheim Crescent,

Ladbroke Grove and Westbourne Park who found themselves with time on their hands,[364] Moorcock observes in the 'Prelude' section, 'the convent represented a regular diversion'.[365] One such resident is the real Jerry Cornelius, whose infinite permutations, gadgetry and wit were all fantasies born in the mind of 'a young man [who] had lived most of his life in the three room apartment' in 'a wretched tenement in Blenheim Crescent'.[366]

The real Jerry of *Condition of Muzak* is the older version of the dejected boy in *English Assassin*, now a young man bitter with failed aspirations. This Jerry still lives with his mother; he is surly and sullen, a foundering musician and a failure with the opposite sex. His guitar is no longer gem-studded but a second-hand loan from a friend that Jerry wrecks in a fall through a makeshift stage. As Clute has observed,[367] the conservatories on Angkor Hilton and Derry and Toms roof gardens have now dwindled into 'the tiny balcony formed by the house's front porch'.[368] To a certain extent, this Jerry is a send-up of the stereotypical adolescent male fantasy reader, spending his days moping around the house and his rare moments of socialization making snide comments about Stanley Kubrick. Moorcock's readers are thus invited to see in Jerry an unflattering portrait of themselves.

The host of other characters that populate the Cornelius myth are similarly stripped of their glamour, becoming stock types in a low-income neighbourhood of West London. Frank is now a seedy antiques dealer on Portobello Road; Miss Brunner a teacher who sexually abuses the children in her care, Jerry included; Bishop Beesley a drunkard named Dennis with a scandalous past that probably also involved sexual misconduct. Honoria Cornelius is the sole exception, as she was never glamorized in the first place. As Paul March-Russell has argued, Jerry's mother 'embodies Moorcock's faith in a proletarian vulgarity' that holds forth a greater hope for London than any of Miss Brunner's increasingly authoritarian schemes.[369]

Struggling to cope with life among these sordid people in these dilapidated surroundings, Jerry fixates on the Convent of St Clares: 'It was almost as if, for a few hours, an aura spread from the convent and made the world outside as tranquil as the world within.'[370] The convent thus endows his unprepossessing area with a measure of nobility. It exerts an endless fascination on Jerry, not least because as a man he can never set foot within its walls, allowing him to project his fantasies upon it with no risk of disillusionment. Jerry knows the nuns' schedule intimately, down to the moment when 'all the Poor Clares would emerge together' from 'the door of the chapel'.[371] He watches them avidly, assigns them nicknames and feels moved to acts of heroism on their behalf. Initially, he aspires to 'buy that bloody nunnery' and thereby preserve it in perpetuity.[372] But Moorcock implies that once the convent is demolished by the GLC, Jerry's imagination untethers from the real building and soars to ever greater heights, spinning increasingly more extravagant fantasies.

The Convent of St Clares is thereby revealed as the core of Jerry's homespun myth, the epicentre from which his alternate Londons unfold. It remains the single recognizable coordinate across multiple dimensions, time periods and apocalypses. In some iterations it still functions as a convent, into which Jerry is not only permitted but greeted by 'the Mother Superior';[373] in others it has been refitted as Jerry's headquarters with 'electrified barbed wire' on its gates and a 'recognition plate' for his palm;[374] in others still it has become the site of 'Hearst's monstrous white castle' transposed from California to Ladbroke Grove;[375] it conceals an 'ancient tunnel' that sometimes 'led into all sorts of other dimensions',[376] and sometimes merely 'to the Belvedere restaurant' in Holland House.[377] In these permutations and others, it is the one metamorphic fixture in Jerry's metamorphic London. Thus, in the tradition of Dickens's romance of familiar things, Jerry spun his fantasies from the landmarks of his London environment. He thereby came back in a full circle to his creator who, while living around the corner in Colville Terrace, had drawn Jerry's likeness from a passer-by and plucked his name from a local greengrocer's shop.

Condition of Muzak ends with the dissipation of the Cornelius myth. The death of Jerry's mother, brutally depicted in its agonies and indignities, is bound up with Jerry's acceptance that the convent is gone, replaced not by Jerry's fortress but by 'the fortress of the new housing estate'.[378] Immediately upon Honoria's death, Jerry turns from her body to face the housing estate for the first time: 'He looked out, over the top of the area, through railings at the block of new flats.'[379] The loss of his mother thus reverberates with the loss of the convent and the relinquishment of his fantasies. Jerry can no longer evade the harsh realities of his city, its lost landmarks, its smashed-up parking metres and his mother lying dead in the bedroom of her cluttered council flat. The final word thus seems to be Honoria's, not in her death scene but in a rare moment of tenderness towards Jerry. 'Yer orlways did 'ave yer 'ead in the clards',[380] she observes, 'Come darn ter Earf a bit now, eh?'.[381] Jerry and his readers are brought down to earth and invited to smell its rot.

Yet Moorcock did not repudiate his mythologization of London altogether. He continues to write riffs on the Cornelius myth and has integrated it into his ever-expanding multiverse.[382] Taken together, his Cornelius stories of the 1960s and 1970s chart his search for a mode of fantasy writing that could reclaim his

London without blinkering the reader to the hard truths of his city. Even as he decried the cynical mythologization deployed by arrivistes of various stripes, Moorcock readily acknowledged that to live in London is to mythologize it. The degree to which this mythologization is coercive depends on its transparency. Thus, one may posit that the final word is not Honoria's but Moorcock's:

> We create virtual identities for London. We create them for ourselves. . . . Jerry Cornelius knows, as he strolls – in clothes that have just recently come back into fashion – through virtual ruins, virtual futures, that it's the only way we'll survive, *as long as we're fully conscious*.[383]

From London to Viriconium: Harrison's dented bins and dancing snowflakes

Harrison left London in the late 1970s and returned in the mid-1980s.[384] His desperation to leave found expression in his semi-autobiographical novel *Climbers*:[385] 'anything to get away from Camden Town where in summer the Irishmen sleep the day away in parks'.[386] He recalled that 'the real reason I left London was that I felt I had come to a cul-de-sac'.[387] As Mike of *Climbers* lyrically puts it: 'I was aware that the life was leaking tragically out of all these things.'[388]

In Harrison's fantastical and borderline-fantastical short stories of the mid to late 1970s, London is not just a veritable wasteland but one from which the romanticizing filters of fantasy literature have been studiously removed. Harrison's 'Running Down' (1975) follows the narrator Egerton who, recently returned from Kenya, finds it 'almost as difficult to adjust to the dirty chill of late Autumn in the city as to accept bacon at a hundred pence a pound'.[389] Egerton drifts across a London that is 'indescribably cheerless',[390] 'wondering grimly if I could afford to go into a cinema and waste another evening'.[391] His former classmate Lyall, whose toxic behaviour propels the story, lives in 'two poky, unwelcoming rooms' in Harrison's patch of 'Holloway'.[392] The interior and exterior of his house are equally dingy. Egerton registers 'a sink, a filthy gas-stove and some carpets glazed with ancient grease'.[393] An 'ominous pall of sodium light' filters in from the street,[394] and after fleeing Lyall's flat, Egerton finds himself 'among the dented bins and rotting planks of the concrete area'.[395] This post-apocalyptic vision of North London has no redeeming features in the manner of 'Nash Circuit', no cosy diner nor amiable waitress on Haverstock Hill.

For Harrison, 'the setting is the story',[396] and his fantasies accordingly foreclose any escape from their setting, persistently returning to 'that warren of defeated streets which lies between Camden Road and St. Pancras.'[397] Drooping with 'forgotten net curtains' and traces of better days 'before the war',[398] these defeated streets become emblematic of what Harrison perceived as the 'long declining dream' of England.[399] His stories portray Londoners who at once haunt and are haunted by the culs-de-sac of North London, increasingly aware that 'In some places we're all ghosts.'[400] But Harrison allowed a moment's grace in London, albeit in its southern inner-city districts in which he has shown increasing interest since his return to the capital in the mid-1980s.[401] Should the reader 'look away from the [television] screen' and its cheap fantasies,[402] he may yet catch a glimpse of what Harrison described elsewhere as 'the substrate of mystery which underlies all daily life'.[403] The reader who turns his gaze down 'Peckham High Street' may behold 'an old black man staring into a shopfront full of winter woollens' lit up by the sparks from the television set 'amid dancing snowflakes'.[404]

Even as his borderline-fantastical fictions persistently returned to the bedsitter belt of Tufnell Park, Harrison withdrew from London in his overtly fantastical short stories and novels that are set in his invented city of 'Viriconium'. Harrison's first Viriconium story, 'Lamia Mutable' (1972), was written shortly after he moved to London.[405] It thus chimes with the heady days of *New Worlds* magazine, concluding with a wry dedication 'to Jerry Cornelius',[406] and an 'Afterword' explicating the story 'as a snide parody of London intellectual life'.[407] Yet Harrison increasingly distanced Viriconium from London throughout the 1970s and early 1980s. His first Viriconium novel, *The Pastel City* (1971), bore scant traces of the affectionate send-up of Swinging London that had characterized the earlier story. To the extent that Viriconium is London in *The Pastel City*, it is a London where 'a change had come about in the essential nature of things',[408] and 'they could never be the same again'.[409] In 1980, Harrison asserted that 'Paris may very well be Viriconium, or Vienna may be',[410] but he made no mention of London. Two years later, he mooted that 'Viriconium is all the cities there have ever been'.[411]

Harrison's turn from London to Viriconium reversed the trajectory more common in the Urban Fantasy tradition from invented worlds to fantastical Londons, as in Peake's turn from Gormenghast to the London-based city and Moorcock's turn from Melniboné to London. Yet even as his 1970s Viriconium fantasies expanded and enriched this Secondary World,[412] Harrison redoubled his harangues on Secondary-World fantasy across the pages of *New Worlds Quarterly*. His second Viriconium short story (in order of writing) was published in the same issue of *New Worlds Quarterly* as his article that excoriated fantasy novels which 'take you out of yourself for a couple of hours and then put you back together in exactly the same mental shape'.[413] His third Viriconium short story was published contemporaneously with his polemical piece that inveighed against the 'complete "world"' of Tolkien,[414] 'of *Dune* and of *Star Trek*',[415] and even 'of Michael Moorcock'.[416] This tension between Harrison's fictional and non-fictional outputs underscores the difficulty of writing Urban Fantasy in the 1970s and 1980s. As London came to resemble a 'Dickensland' theme park for Moorcock and Harrison,[417] so it became proportionally more challenging to use it as a setting for their fantasy literature.

This problem of representation was highlighted by Harrison himself, in a change that he made to the title and the name of the titular city in 'A Young Man's Journey to Viriconium'.[418] Harrison changed the name of the city to 'London' in his revisions for the story's reissue in a 2003 short-story collection. Thus, Viriconium became London once more, but in a manner very different from the parodic identification underlying 'Lamia Mutable'. The identification of Viriconium with London in 'Young Man's Journey' renders London a city out of reach, ever-beckoning yet obscured in the fogs of time and myth. In both versions of the story, the narrator desperately tries to learn the truth about Viriconium/London, only to be left with gaps, conflicting versions and a bleak sense that what knowledge he has gained has only made matters worse, for he will never act upon it. As Miéville observed, Harrison changed the name of the city because 'it is London which is actually unattainable not the fantasy'.[419]

Yet the choices available to London fantasists who were grappling with an increasingly unrecognizable image of their city were not as stark as Harrison's uncompromising stance sometimes implied. There was middle ground between 'a writer or a hack',[420] to use Harrison's dichotomy, and between derivative Secondary-World fantasy that offered the cheap nostrum of an 'easily-grasped handle by which to pick up the universe' and unremittingly bleak fiction stripped of all vestiges of escapism.[421] As discussed in Chapter 5, that middle ground was partly filled by Secondary-World Urban Fantasies, fantastical fictions that drew on the narrative strategies theorized and perfected by Tolkien in order to create fully fleshed alternative Londons.

5

'My home, the city'
Secondary-World London

'A golden age'

'Something is happening in the literature of the fantastic,'[1] Miéville declared in 2003, 'Particularly in Britain, where we are being reviewed *in the papers*, of all things, and selling copies, and being read and riffed off by yer actual proper literary writers.'[2] The late 1990s to early 2000s marked a fluorescence of fantasy literature, particularly London-based fantasy. The two decades between 1996 and 2016 saw the publication of Gaiman's *Neverwhere*, George R. R. Martin's epic fantasy series *Song of Ice and Fire* (1996–present), J. K. Rowling's *Harry Potter* books (1997–2007) and their film adaptations (2001–11), Christopher Priest's *The Separation* (2002), Peter Ackroyd's *The Clerkenwell Tales* (2003), Susanna Clarke's *Jonathan Strange & Mr Norrell* (2004), Iain M. Banks's *The Algebraist* (2004), Conrad Williams's *London Revenant* (2004), Tim Lebbon's *Echo City* (2010), Tom Pollock's *Skyscraper Throne* trilogy (2013–15), Miéville's *King Rat* (1998), *The Tain*, the Bas-Lag trilogy (2000–4), *Un Lun Dun* (2007) and *Kraken* (2010), the 1998 knighting of Terry Pratchett and the renewal of *Doctor Who* (2005–present). *Publishers Weekly* observed a 'Fantasy Explosion' in the literary market,[3] *The Guardian* declared 'a golden age for British science fiction,'[4] and *The Times* announced that we live in 'an age which loves science fiction and fantasy'.[5]

For many left-leaning British intellectuals, this literary fluorescence dovetailed a change in the political climate. The eighteen years between 1979 and 1997 saw a period of uninterrupted conservative government dominated by Prime Minister Margaret Thatcher and to a lesser extent her successor John Major. Thatcher was criticized by her opponents for, among other things, dismantling the GLC and implementing policies that led to a steep rise in homelessness, which was especially visible in Greater London.[6] Her premiership rarely found favour among British fantasists of the period, who often lampooned her in their fantastical fictions. In Moorcock's latter-day Cornelius stories, Miss Brunner became 'Baroness Brunner' after the manner of Baroness Thatcher,[7] her ageing mind wholly preoccupied with 'her old power'.[8] Harrison's Viriconium stories saw a change in the female monarch of their titular city from a kind-hearted queen to one who was sadistic and power-hungry and who resembled Thatcher in appearance as well as conduct.[9]

As Luckhurst argues, the 'British Boom' in speculative fiction roughly coincided with Tony Blair's election in 1997 and the rise of New Labour.[10] The late 1990s saw a cultural rebranding of London, a 'Swinging London Mark II',[11] as the 1997 issue of *Vanity Fair* had called it. The period saw a resurgence of optimism, energy and chic, but even as *Newsweek* declared London 'the coolest city on the planet',[12] many London-based fantasists felt less at home in their city than ever before. The sense that underneath the hype London had lost its homeliness and denuded into a simulacrum, which had found early expressions in the fantasies of Moorcock and Harrison in the late 1970s, had all but redoubled in the 1990s. As Moorcock wrote of Thatcher in 1993 under the guise of discussing latter-day Miss Brunner: 'For a while she succeeded in turning Britain into a theme park with what was left of our history blown to bits, mocked into oblivion or hived off to heritage developers.'[13]

As London completed its transition from a manufacturing to a service-based economy and expanded its finance and business sectors in the 1980s, its iconic landmarks were repurposed as office space, residential housing and entertainment complexes.[14] The Black Eagle Brewery (now known as Truman's Brewery),[15] Old Billingsgate Fish Market and Battersea Power Station all suffered a similar fate.[16] Concurrently, the 1980s and 1990s saw large-scale construction of high-rises that transformed London's skyline, especially in the City of London that comprised London's most ancient district, and the newly opened Canary Wharf that formed a vast complex of office blocks, hotels and restaurants on what was once the West India Docks.[17] Thus, by the close of the twentieth century, parts of London had begun to resemble Wells's vision of 'Titanic buildings' and 'overwhelming architecture',[18] as well as the enormous hotel complexes of his 'Pleasure Cities'. These eruptions into the fabric of London were accompanied by shifts in the makeup of its population. The gentrification process that had taken hold of Notting Hill in the 1970s expanded into other areas of London in the 1980s, and by 1991 Hammersmith & Fulham, Tower Hamlets, Islington and Wandsworth all underwent demographic changes that displaced the working-class locals with middle-class professionals.[19]

Consequently, far from a restored sense of belonging to London, the new surge of prosperity and chic in the late 1990s led to what Phil Baker described as 'an alienation of an almost unprecedented kind from the built environment'.[20] Luckhurst contends that this alienation stemmed in part from 'the full opening of London markets to the borderless flows of international capital and their final severance from the social fabric of London itself'.[21] In the throes of these transformations, London fantasists voiced a sense of dislocation not only from the London of their present day but also from their past, even a past as recent as the 1980s. In 2005, the same year that saw the publication of the revised 'Author's Preferred Text' of *Neverwhere*, Gaiman remarked that 'the London I remember' from the 1980s seemed 'already to be retreating into myth'.[22] Thus, the London fantasists of the late 1990s and early 2000s were less concerned with celebrating London in the manner of Moorcock and his *New Worlds* coterie in the early to mid-1960s than they were with creating alternative fantastical Londons that offered an escape from their denuded city.

This chapter anatomizes the relatively recent turn in the Urban Fantasy tradition towards fantasies set in fully fleshed alternative Londons or recognizable variations thereof. These fantastical fictions rework Tolkien's paradigm of Secondary-World fantasy to fit a metropolitan milieu, but in so doing, they also encode an escapism that runs counter to the political and social engagement that had been at the heart of this tradition hitherto. This shift will be explored more fully by comparing the fantastical estrangements of London in representative short fictions by Wells, Harrison and Miéville. The chapter then presents a close reading of Gaiman's *Neverwhere* as a case study in the strengths and limitations of Secondary-World fantasy set in London. It subsequently analyses Miéville's metropolitan world-building in a range of his fantasies that reflect London's ascendance as a global cosmopolitan city. The chapter concludes with a retrospect on the Urban Fantasy tradition, contextualized by T. S. Eliot's essay, 'Tradition and the Individual Talent'.

Mirror, mirror: From 'moor eeffoc' to nodnoL

Wells's 'The Door in the Wall', Harrison's 'A Young Man's Journey to Viriconium/London' and Miéville's *The Tain* each tell the story of a man who discovers a portal from England into another realm. But in a subversion of the conventions of 'Portal Fantasy' where the action typically takes place primarily in the other world,[23] these stories focus on the crossing between worlds that thematizes the act (or failure) of escape.

As discussed at greater length in Chapter 2, the titular Door in the Wall appears at certain moments in unremarkable London streets and leads to a paradisiacal garden. The protagonist Lionel Wallace discovers the Door in the Wall as a young boy and crosses over to the other world, only to be sent back to everyday London shortly thereafter. He encounters the Door again at life-changing crossroads throughout his life, but on each occasion reluctantly prioritizes worldly matters over the enchanted realm. At the story's conclusion, Wallace is found dead on the other side of a door resembling his descriptions of the Door in the Wall. It is left to the reader to decide whether Wallace was deceived or whether his death signals a release, a final 'going astray' in London that liberates him from the 'dull and tedious' routines of 'worldly life'.[24]

Harrison has expressly named Wells as one of his 'short story heroes' and 'the door in the wall' as a specific inspiration.[25] Nowhere is this influence more apparent than in his 1985 short story, 'A Young Man's Journey to Viriconium', which as discussed in Chapter 4 changed its title to 'A Young Man's Journey to London' in 2003, with the name of its titular city altered accordingly.[26] In both versions of the story, the narrator accuses his interlocutor of squandering his opportunity to cross over to the mythical Viriconium/London in a phrase that alludes strongly to 'The Door in the Wall': 'You had the clue as a child. You found the doorway but you never went through it.'[27]

'A Young Man's Journey' can therefore be read as a re-envisioning of 'The Door in the Wall' on the backdrop of the 1980s. The story is pervaded by an atmosphere of quiet despair characteristic of the London-based fantasies of the time. Thus, where Wallace led a glamorous if unsatisfying life as a bright and promising schoolboy, a successful politician and a less than scrupulous womanizer, the characters of Harrison's tale drift through life across a dismal landscape well past its glory days. The narrator works in a tourist café and whiles away his spare time by dreaming about Viriconium/London and watching the news. His neighbour is 'a middle-aged man in a dirty suede coat' who obsessively collects the post addressed to 'the previous tenants of the house'.[28] His third interlocutor gives off the impression that 'something had gone wrong with him',[29] suffers from bouts of illness and drifts miserably 'from cafe to cafe in Huddersfield'.[30] They criss-cross each other on streets 'daubed with political slogans',[31] on buses 'full of old women' and railway carriages full of 'old people',[32] in cafés where 'damp thickened in the corner by the coats',[33] by apple trees which have 'not flowered for ten years',[34] and in homes infested with 'vigorous houseflies' that 'pour in and cluster on any warm surface'.[35]

Wells's titular Door in the Wall also made its first appearance in drab surroundings, but Harrison's story takes the dinginess a good measure further. In a rather iconoclastic homage to Lewis Carroll's *Through the Looking Glass*, the portal to Viriconium/London is a mirror in 'the lavatory of the Merrie England cafe',[36] ingloriously hanging 'above the sink with its flake of yellow soap'.[37] The specificity of 'the Merrie England Café' in Huddersfield resonates with Harrison's *Climbers*, published four years after the first version of 'A Young Man's Journey'. *Climbers* likewise features a scene in 'the Merrie England [café]'.[38] As Mike sits in the café and looks out onto the street, he registers that 'all the women shoppers on New Street seemed to be dressed in imitation of Margaret Thatcher, Princess Diana or Princess Anne'.[39] Thus, if Dickens looked through the glass darkly of a coffee room and saw London through the estranging medium of 'moor eeffoc', Harrison looked out of the Merrie England café and saw the prime minister that he loathed duplicated again and again along the street.

'A Young Man's Journey' and *Climbers* share another café scene that resonates still more strongly with Dickens's 'moor eeffoc' fantasy, although they differ in the location of the café. Dickens's coffee room was on St Martin's Lane in London, the café scene in 'A Young Man's Journey' is in Manchester and the analogous scene in *Climbers* is in Bradford. Allowing for the difference in locale and small variations in detail, the two scenes in 'A Young Man's Journey' and *Climbers* are virtually identical.[40] In both scenes, a young Petromax and a young Mike look out through 'the plate glass window' of the café and see the interior reflected back at them,[41] not reversed and shocking in 'moor eeffoc' fashion, but sad and underwhelming: 'a big plain patient girl of seventeen or eighteen with chipped nail varnish and a tired back from sorting cutlery all morning' is superimposed upon the glass.[42] In both *Climbers* and 'A Young Man's Journey', Petromax and Mike respectively rush headlong into the plate-glass window expecting to cross from one world to another. Their expectations are literally dashed – they both hit the glass painfully and suffer a concussion. Asked about these corresponding scenes, Harrison replied that his characters 'are constantly running into that plate glass window' in their failed attempts to escape their unfulfilling lives,[43] attempts that occasionally take the form of rock-climbing, 'but could equally be fantasy [literature]'.[44] While he has expressed sympathy for this desire to escape, confessing that he spent much of his youth with 'this sense I had of a plate glass window between me and everything else',[45] Harrison has no patience for the fantasy literature that fulfils it, denouncing 'that sort of escapism' as 'rubbish'.[46]

Thus, Harrison foreclosed what Miéville has described as 'the sense of the numinous'.[47] In the desolate vision of 'A Young Man's Journey', fantasy is as bland and dilapidated as reality, and neither discloses any untapped dimensions of beauty. Characters who successfully cross over to the mythical Viriconium/London discover to their dismay that the otherworldly city merely reproduces the dinginess of an urban slum, as if Viriconium/London were indeed nothing more than a smeared reflection on a grimy mirror. The fantasy of escape into another world is thereby exposed as a sham, the depth of disappointment it instils increasing exponentially with the name change of the otherworldly city from Viriconium to London. Commenting on this name change, Harrison asserted that its purpose was to 'undermine Viriconium as a credible fantasy destination, by calling the city London'.[48] The implication of this statement being that Harrison does not regard London as 'a credible fantasy destination', reflecting the extent to which he believed London to be tainted by what he termed 'Thatcherland'.[49] While in the 1970s he had claimed that 'the landscape *is* the fiction',[50] by 1989 he felt that there was no longer an '"English" landscape' to speak of,[51] but 'only a palimpsest of agricultural and industrial usage',[52] devastated by Margaret Thatcher's political fantasies and remade into 'perilous seas and fairy lands forlorn'.[53]

Miéville published *The Tain* in 2002, as a stand-alone novella prefaced with an introduction by Harrison. The following year saw the publication of Harrison's 'A Young Man's Journey to London' in its revised version in a short-story collection for which Miéville wrote the introduction. As Miéville indicated in a 2002 conversation with Harrison, he had read both versions of 'A Young Man's Journey' by the year of *The Tain*'s composition and publication.[54] Small wonder, then, that the influence of 'A Young Man's Journey' on *The Tain* is palpably felt, particularly in a scene where Miéville apparently tried to beat Harrison at his own game, by making a vampire burst out of a mirror at an even dingier spot than Harrison's Merrie England café: 'in the toilet of a hospital, near my ward of melancholics and hysterics'.[55]

Recalling Wells's *The War of the Worlds* that shuttled between the first-person narration of the unnamed protagonist and the third-person perspective of his brother, *The Tain* is divided into two narrative strands, narrated in the first and third person respectively. The first-person narrative visibly alludes to Harrison's 'A Young Man's Journey', particularly when the narrator crosses 'beyond the mirror'.[56] The third-person narrative is focalized through Sholl, a Londoner who wanders through the post-apocalyptic capital in a journey strongly reminiscent of the final chapters of *War of the Worlds*.

Sholl's journey northward across a silent, empty, smouldering London parallels the journey undertaken by Wells's narrator. Beginning at Grosvenor Bridge rather than Putney Bridge, Miéville charts a trajectory for Sholl that is east of Wells's, but it follows similar geographic and narrative beats. Wells's narrator first hears the Martian howling 'near South Kensington',[57] and Sholl hears the 'high mewing sound' emanating from the 'imagos'[58] – vampires who originated as reflections newly escaped from their mirrors – 'from the direction of South Kensington'.[59] Wells's narrator discerns 'a haze of smoke to the north-west',[60] and Sholl similarly registers that 'trees of poisonous smoke grew over north London'.[61] Both journeys end on hills of Hampstead Heath – Wells's narrator discovers the dead Martians 'on the summit of Primrose Hill',[62] Sholl concludes the first phase of his plan on 'the trails of Parliament Hill, with London behind him'.[63]

These similarities between *War of the Worlds* and *The Tain* throw into relief important differences. Wells's narrator suffers a mental breakdown because his London has become uncanny. No longer masked by the smoke, fog and gaslight of Victorian life, the London of *War of the Worlds* discloses 'a blot of the Real',[64] to use Slavoj Žižek's Lacanian phrase. Žižek describes the Real as an interruption in the exchange between subject and object, as in a typical Hitchcock scene where 'the subject's eye sees the house, but the house – the object – seems somehow to return the Gaze'.[65] In *War of the Worlds*, London itself becomes the object that returns the Gaze: 'London about me gazed at me spectrally'.[66] Yet the London of *The Tain* undergoes the opposite process – it loses its realness, flattening out into 'a cutout of London',[67] its colours faded, its 'architecture brittled by war'.[68] Having lost the reflective and refractive properties of light with the escape of the imagos from their mirrors-cum-prisons, Sholl's London is literally depthless. 'London was never so alien as after the rain',[69] Sholl reflects as he walks through 'water-blackened streets',[70] musing that the absence of reflections and of refracted light made it appear 'as if London were an etching'.[71] Nor is it granted any reprieve in the manner of Wells's 'great Mother of Cities'.[72] Echoing Wells's famous description of the Martians as 'intellects vast and cool and unsympathetic',[73] Sholl's story concludes with his encounter with the 'vast, unsympathetic' imago leader,[74] to whom he tenders London's unconditional surrender.

This act of surrender takes place in the British Museum, a setting that Andrew M. Butler has related to Britain's imperial history and the museum's special role in that history as 'the center of the spoils of the British empire'.[75] His reading is reinforced by *The Tain*'s depiction of a massacre of British soldiers on the museum's doorstep in a grotesque enactment of the revenge of the ancestors of colonized people upon the heirs of Empire, the imagos taking the forms of 'pharaohs, . . . American shamans and Phoenicians and Byzantines'.[76] *The Tain* thus reworks the anti-imperial theme of *The War of the Worlds* with a post-imperial and postcolonial sensibility. Where Wells criticized the Empire when it was at the height of its power, Sholl envisions a future for London as '*A little colony of the imago empire*',[77] tolerated only on account of its insignificance. Miéville thereby reconfigured the tropes and themes of *The War of the Worlds* to suit the geopolitical situation of the twenty-first century.

The Tain harks back not only to Wells but also to Dickens, albeit more obliquely. Its first-person narrative stages a return to Dickens's 'moor eeffoc' idiom, offering the escape that Harrison had denied his readers in 'A Young Man's Journey'. Fleeing the ravages of war, the unnamed first-person narrator ends up in 'nodnoL',[78] the London 'beyond the mirror',[79] built by the imagos in what was once their homeland and prison. 'nodnoL' is the next link in the chain of reversals that was also taken up by Peake with the name 'Rottcodd' that reversed the word 'doctor' from his view of a car sticker through the inner side of a windshield. In certain respects, nodnoL marks the restoration of London at the end of *The Tain*, as the narrator observes: 'This place is more like London than London now'.[80] Yet nodnoL also heralds the promise of a utopian London superior to the original, a safe haven for 'rebel imagos' and 'escaped humans' alike,[81] who come together as 'fellow citizens'.[82] As the narrator knows instinctively, 'we are all safe here'.[83] It is a city newly born, 'all unlit and coursed through with wind',[84] and thereby free of power structures, government regulations and deep-seated prejudices. Road signs that had once circumscribed movement and access to space have lost their original meaning and become cyphers of a new language and thus a new beginning, reading 'YRTNE ON and YAW EVIG'.[85] The narrator, once the inmate of a mental asylum where he was vilified as 'a monster' and cast out onto the streets,[86] can now entertain the possibility that 'I have come home'.[87] Even class distinctions, the most intractable of all divisions in British society, have little to no bearing on this city. The first-person narrator concludes his tale on the verge of contact with a man 'wrapped in what was once an expensive coat',[88] embedding the implicit promise of a classless society: 'We stand at opposite ends of the street, . . . and it is as if we are in the same room, about to meet'.[89]

To call nodnoL a full-fledged Secondary World in the Tolkienian sense would be an exaggeration. But *The Tain* certainly goes further in this respect than either 'The Door in the Wall' or 'A Young Man's Journey'. Where 'The Door in the Wall' left ambiguous the Door's ontological status as either a portal to a different world or a figment of Wallace's imagination, and 'A Young Man's Journey' asserted that the mythical London beyond the mirror was inaccessible to narrator and reader alike, Miéville created nodnoL as a fantastical city autonomous from everyday London and accessible from it that provided an enticing escape from the faded, depthless, war-torn capital. nodnoL is expressly depicted as 'a natural formation' in the manner of Tolkien's organic Secondary World,[90] and it showcases an 'inner consistency of reality' in Miéville's attention to its details:[91] the wares in abandoned shops feature labels 'printed in mirror-writing',[92] the sun rises 'on the wrong side of the sky',[93] the skyscrapers loom 'on the wrong side of the city'.[94]

The Tain is undoubtedly more hopeful than 'A Young Man's Journey'. Harrison's fantasy was determined to work against itself, to frustrate the reader's desire for escape by tantalizing him with the promise of another world and then slamming him against grimy bathroom mirrors and reflective café walls as he attempts to pass through them to access it. Miéville's fantasy is more forgiving, electing rather to readjust the refractive angles of fantasy in order to create a utopian nodnoL as an alternative to a ruined and spent London. Yet it is a hope tinged with loss. There is no sense in *The Tain*, as there was in *The War of the Worlds*, that the real, everyday London may yet be redeemed. The utopian promise lies rather with a new London, a fantastical double of the everyday city that is also framed as an infinitely preferable alternative. This impetus to escape London into a fantastical version of itself, to turn one's back on the everyday city and give it up as a lost cause, resonates persistently across Secondary-World urban fantasies, as exemplified in the discussion that follows.

Making it mythic: *Neverwhere*

A year before the publication of the 'Author's Preferred Text' of *Neverwhere*, Gaiman made a declaration that Moorcock, Harrison and Miéville would have found appalling: '[At thirteen years old] I came to the conclusion that *Lord of the Rings* was, most probably, the best book that ever could be written',[95] and therefore 'I wanted to write *The Lord of the Rings*',[96] but 'The problem was that it had already been written.'[97] The book he wrote instead was *Neverwhere*, arguably the first sustained attempt to compose a London-based fantasy that would be to Urban Fantasy what *Lord of the Rings* was to its Rural counterpart. For Clute, *Neverwhere* created 'a world too copious, too subaqueous and mazed, to be exhausted in a single tale',[98] thereby providing what Clute regarded as 'the bones of the best and purest London fantasy yet written'.[99]

Neverwhere has a long compositional history spanning fourteen years that played a key role in the shaping of its fantastical London. Broadly speaking, the more Gaiman distanced himself from the real London, the richer, more immersive and more detailed his fantastical London became. *Neverwhere* began life as a BBC television series of the same name, consisting of six episodes written by Gaiman between 1991 and 1996. As Gaiman recalled, he wrote the first episode shortly after he 'moved to the US',[100] followed by the next five episodes, all written from across the Atlantic. He then returned to London for the filming and began writing the novelization in January. He finished the 1996 British edition 'in southern California',[101] while the 1997 American edition was written from 'the World Trade Centre'.[102] The 2005 'Author's Preferred Text' was 'assembled from the various drafts of the book' after Gaiman had been an expat living in the United States for fourteen years.[103]

Reflecting back on *Neverwhere*'s gestation and development, Gaiman emphasized his ever-increasing distance from London as a factor that inspired rather than hamstrung his work on the novel:

> it's almost as if one is recreating England in one's head, seeing it from a long way away and picking those elements one likes. . . .
>
> . . . creating a sort of mythic London was in many ways much easier, writing it in places like a hotel room in Galveston, Texas or sitting around at home in Minneapolis. One could isolate why one wanted to make it mythic, what one was going for.[104]

These comments illustrate the turn in the Urban Fantasy tradition away from refracting the lived realities of London towards 'mak[ing] it mythic', recreating London fantastically 'in one's head'. Urban Fantasy had come a long way since Dickens lamented the difficulties of writing fantasy while away from his 'magic lantern' of London's streets at night.[105] Gaiman drew inspiration from 'seeing it from a long way away', a distance that facilitated the creation of 'a sort of mythic London'. '[*Neverwhere* is] very much my view of London',[106] he asserted in a 1996 interview, but his view was starkly different from Dickens's: 'I infinitely prefer London as a stranger. I love London as Oz, as Narnia.'[107] *Neverwhere* thus reimagines London as a Secondary World, one whose analogues are as much the Rural Fantasies of Narnia and Oz as the Londons of Chesterton and Dickens. Its fantastical rendering of London is thus fundamentally different from Dickens giving the city 'an odd unlikeness of itself'. To adapt the distinctions made by Irvine, Dickens writes from the street level of London and pens 'stories of real or almost-real cities in which fantastic events occur';[108] Gaiman writes about London from afar by bringing 'the tropes of pastoral or heroic fantasy . . . into an urban setting'.[109]

Neverwhere takes up the fantastical recreation of London as its central theme, structuring its narrative on the opposition of two representational modes of the city: the Urban Fantasy novel and the London Underground map. The map of the Tube was central to *Neverwhere* from its first incarnation as a BBC series, with each episode opening with a mock-interview (or monologue) on the backdrop of a slightly blurred, tilted map of the London Underground that remains in the background through the opening credits. The 1997 American edition opens with a two-page spread of the Tube map, and the 1996 British edition uses the iconic symbol of the London Underground – a circle bifurcated by a horizontal line – as the marker separating different sections of the story. Yet the centrality of the Tube map in *Neverwhere* is by no means an endorsement of it. Quite the contrary, in all the book editions, a key part of the acclimatization of the protagonist Richard Mayhew to life in London consists of his realization that the Tube map is a false representation of the city: 'Gradually he realized that the Tube map was a handy fiction that made life easier, but bore no resemblance to the reality of the shape of the city above'.[110]

Richard's insight that the Tube map distorts the lived reality of London has been ably expanded upon by urban scholar Janin Hadlaw:

> Because the places on the various lines were no longer distinguishable from each other, the map's representational priority essentially shifted from the particularity of the *places* the Underground linked to the *idea* of the Underground as a *conduit* for the flow of trains and people, and ultimately, capital itself.[111]

Hadlaw's analysis highlights the extent to which the Tube map is not an innocent heuristic. Designed by Harry Beck in 1931, the contemporary Tube map has some problematic consequences: it reduces the experience of London to an assembly line commute made up of unswerving lines and right angles, homogenizing travel, distorting and condensing distance, fragmenting the city and aligning geographic locations in a way that does not correlate with the actual places on the surface. The London encoded in the Tube map is a city enframed by the rhythms of work and efficiency, paying little heed to the lived experience, the locales, particularities, sights, sounds, irregular rhythms and colourful idiosyncrasies of the real city. Furthermore, it imposes a grid on an organic, teeming, chaotic, hodgepodge metropolis that is fundamentally resistant to this kind of schematic rigidity. This false representation is rendered doubly problematic by the fact that, as Janet Vertesi has observed, the Tube map has become a totalizing representation of London, 'representing not just the subway but even the city itself'.[112] *Neverwhere* is centrally concerned with contravening this semiotic power of the London Underground map and offering a historically eclectic, fantastical, but equally totalizing alternative vision of the city.

Not unlike *The Tain*, *Neverwhere* is a tale of two Londons, divided not by verbal slight-of-hand but by vertical space, with the fictionalized version of everyday London designated as 'London Above' and the fully fleshed fantastical London designated as 'London Below'. This schism between a visible surface London and a hidden subterranean one has a long and rich history in London-based fantastical literature, which can be traced back to Wells's *The Time Machine*, together with *When the Sleeper Wakes* and its companion pieces, and indeed further back still to Bulwer-Lytton's *The Coming Race* (though not expressly set in London), and forward to the Under-River in *Titus Alone*, Bruce Graeme's *Blackshirt the Adventurer* (1936), Nigel Kneale's *Quatermass and the Pit* (novelization 1960), Terrance Dicks's *Doctor Who: Web of Fear* (novelization 1976) and William Corlett's *The Secret Line* (1988).[113] Yet *Neverwhere* distinguishes itself from these earlier examples by creating London Below as a full-fledged, autonomous Secondary World, one that is infinitely more vibrant, colourful, lively and desirable than its surface counterpart.

Echoing the transformations that reshaped London in the late 1990s and early 2000s, London Above is a soulless city ruled by the interests of global finance. Richard works in 'one of the finest investment analysts in London',[114] his best friend is 'Gary-from-work' who invites him to drinks at the end of the day not so much to unwind as 'to talk about the Merstham Account'.[115] His fiancée Jessica Bartram works for a man who is 'a corporate entity in his own right',[116] and she soon reveals herself as another Thatcher-figure in a long line of cold, domineering women who feature in the London-based fantasies of the 1980s and 1990s.[117] Jessica is wealthier and more successful than Richard, her salient characteristic being that she is 'certainly going somewhere'.[118] Her London is as schematically overdetermined as the Tube map, its pathways rigidly laid out towards her career advancement, success, wealth and conspicuous consumption. Like a train speeding onwards, she walks 'as fast as her heels permitted',[119] dragging Richard along on her race to success and resolutely bracketing out those lived realities of London that do not fit her rigid world view. Thus, notwithstanding its designation as 'above', Jessica throws into relief the close correspondences between London Above and the capitalist-driven logic of the Tube map.

Neverwhere enacts what David Ashford has described as 'resisting the panoptic rational pattern embodied by the Underground Map'.[120] Pitting itself against this grid-based version of London, London Below is constantly shifting and unmappable, scrambling the Tube map and undermining its claims to be a reliable representation of the city. In London Below, Tube stations and trains are not where they should be, and every time Richard relies on the Tube map as his ready-to-hand reference for understanding London, he is proven wrong and ridiculed. When Richard points out, in the course of his adventures in London Below, that 'Earl's Court station isn't on the Central Line',[121] which in reality it is not, his reluctant companion the Marquis de Carabas responds with 'There really is nothing quite like total ignorance'.[122] In London Below, Earl's Court *is* on the Central Line when it needs to be, and it literally assumes the form of 'a small medieval court'.[123] The presiding Earl mocks Richard for his conviction that 'there isn't a British Museum station',[124] which in reality closed in 1933 but is operative in London Below.[125] Thus, Richard is made all the more risible for his stubborn insistence that 'like all Londoners, he knew his Tube map'.[126] In the scornful tones of the Marquis and the Earl, *Neverwhere* chides domestic and international readers alike for believing that to be a Londoner is to know one's Tube map.

The Earl's court is not only on the wrong London Underground line, but it is held on a dysfunctional train carriage, a glitch in the transport system that punctures its homogeneity and efficiency. The court is uniquely accessible from 'Bank station' at the heart of the City of London,[127] which primarily serves financiers and business people during the week, represented in *Neverwhere* by Jessica and her boss, their office 'halfway up a large crystalline, mirrored structure in the City of London'.[128] Thus, the earl's court disrupts the flow of commuters into and out of the City, implicitly disrupting the flow of global capital. It pointedly delays the Londoners who benefit most from dogmatic adherence to the world view encoded in the Tube map. This quaint medieval court thereby challenges the steel-and-chrome skyscrapers of corporate finance that tower above Bank Station and the powers that they represent.

As typified by the earl and his court, the locals and locales of London Below are crafted out of the fantastical literalization of the names of London landmarks and especially London Underground stations, names that predate the Tube map by centuries.[129] In *Neverwhere*, Old Bailey is the name of a 'kind and creased' elderly man who lives on London's rooftops;[130] the West London area of Hammersmith becomes embodied in an actual blacksmith hammering away on molten metal;[131] Knightsbridge station is accessed via the haunted 'Night's Bridge';[132] Blackfriars station is home to a group of black-robed friars;[133] Angel station in the Borough of Islington conceals the 'Great Hall'-cum-prison of an actual angel named Islington,[134] and 'the Raven's Court',[135] 'Olympia, the Shepherd Queen, the Crouch Enders',[136] and 'shepherds in Shepherd's Bush' are all mentioned in passing.[137] *Neverwhere* thereby champions the fantasy novel as an alternative mode of representing London. It creates a full-fleshed mythology of the city that replaces the schematic grid of the Tube map with shifting verbal playfulness, exceeding and disrupting strict functional denotations by conjuring up the literal referents of London place names. *Neverwhere* thus breathes new life into signifiers that habit has made trite, and by extension, lays a new enchantment on the places that they signify.

Even as it absorbs roofscapes, forgotten buildings and abandoned rooms, London Below regularly commandeers the most famous buildings of London Above as venues for its 'Floating Market'[138] – an itinerant market of goods and services that strikes a distinctively Dickensian chord. Gaiman's descriptions of the Floating Market recall both 'the heaps of fantastic things' in Dickens's *Old Curiosity Shop* and the resurrected clothes in 'Meditations in Monmouth Street':[139]

> One stall was piled high with bottles, full bottles and empty bottles of every shape and every size, . . . another sold lamps, and candles, made of many kinds of wax and tallow; . . . others that sold clothes – old clothes patched, and mended, and made strange.[140]

Gaiman added a layer of contemporary social criticism to this Dickensian fascination with outmoded objects, which chimes with Lefebvre's spatial theory in *The Production of Space* (1974), translated from French into English just as Gaiman began work on *Neverwhere*. Lefebvre distinguished between '*representations of space*',[141] a term which denotes the layout and function of a particular space as envisioned by 'scientists, planners, urbanists, technocratic subdividers and social engineers',[142] and 'spatial practice',[143] a term which refers to 'a specific use of that space'.[144] He used this distinction to argue that *contra* the assumptions of some urban planners, 'relations between . . . the perceived, the conceived and the lived are never either simple or stable'.[145] The tensions and disjunctions between representations of space and spatial practice can therefore produce space that is resistant to totalizing systems, global capitalism not least among them. In *Neverwhere*, the Floating Market constitutes a paradigmatic instance of spatial practice that defies representations of space. Its venues are famous London landmarks, none intended for use as indoor markets, and most centres of political, religious or economic power. The earliest Floating Market mentioned in the book was held in Elizabeth Tower;[146] a recent one took place in Westminster Abbey,[147] and the last on the decks of the HMS *Belfast* in its contemporary incarnation as a museum ship run by the Imperial War Museum.[148] Floating Markets are boisterous affairs, 'loud, and brash, and insane',[149] but they are not lawless. A 'Market Truce' prohibits violence in the market outside of formal competitions;[150] the tolling of 'a huge brass bell' signals the closing of the market,[151] and Richard pointedly observes that even as the market is in full swing, 'no one was looting'.[152] Thus, the Floating Markets exhibit a form of spatial practice with its own internal and consistent set of codes that offer an alternative to the rigid strictures of global capitalism.

The Floating Market that receives the greatest authorial attention in *Neverwhere* occupies the interior rooms of Harrods, London's fashionable and opulent department store. Harrods has long been regarded as 'one of the world's largest and most exclusive emporia'.[153] It held a Royal Warrant for the better part of the twentieth century and recently made headlines by restricting access to its Christmas grotto to customers who had spent a minimum of £2,000 at the store.[154] In the London of *Neverwhere* as in real London, Harrods constitutes a bastion of wealth and privilege in the upper-class district of Knightsbridge. Jessica shops there regularly and instructs Richard to purchase her engagement ring from 'Harrods' many jewellery concessions',[155] notwithstanding that it costs him 'the largest amount of money Richard had ever spent on anything'.[156] The Floating Market accordingly forms a striking contrast to its opulent surroundings, as Harrods's lush displays are submerged under a sweeping aggregate of market stalls 'next to, or even on, counters that, during the day, had sold perfume, or watches, or amber, or silk scarves'.[157] Vendors and shoppers alike pay no attention to these luxury items as the market stalls hawk 'Rubbish! ... Garbage! Trash!',[158] taking special pride in merchandise judged worthless by London Above. In this vein, money has no value in this market, as purchases are made by an ad hoc system of barter and exchange,[159] with Richard trading a ballpoint pen and a book of matches for a sandwich and lemonade, and a handkerchief for information.

The spatial practice of the Floating Market thereby rejects the assumptions of global capitalism, defying the representations of space encoded in the layout and displays in Harrods's 'huge rooms' and sumptuous halls.[160] The Floating Market sets forth an alternative value system that favours substance over style. Shoppers gravitate towards 'the smells of grilling meats and mushrooms' emanating from the stalls while 'Harrods' Fish and Meat Hall' is converted into an arena for auditioning bodyguards.[161] A deaf and dumb 'iron-haired woman' sells 'small, nutty biscuits',[162] whereas 'Harrods' gourmet jellybean stand' serves merely as structural support for the bell that tolls the closing of the market.[163] 'Lost Property' is treasured in consummate Dickensian fashion,[164] even as Harrods's display-room 'selling sunglasses and figurines' remains dark and empty.[165] The Floating Market's open disdain for the opulence that surrounds it may partly account for Harrods's denial of Gaiman's request to film in their store. As a result, in the BBC series of *Neverwhere*, the Floating Market's location was changed from Harrods to Battersea Power Station (exterior shots) and the then-Black Eagle Brewery (interior shots),[166] both of which had ceased operation in the 1980s and could therefore serve for location filming in the 1990s. Thus, the forced change of location inadvertently shifted the thematic subtext from the vacuity of capitalist opulence to the decline of London's manufacturing industry.

Chiming with the conclusion of *The Tain*, *Neverwhere* ends with Richard's decision to depart London Above and cast his lot with London Below. Upon realizing that the soulless corporate life of London Above no longer suits him, Richard turns his back on everyday London and escapes into a magical doorway leading back to London Below, 'leaving nothing behind'.[167] His escape dramatizes the readerly pleasure of Secondary-World fantasy, a pleasure described by Tolkien as fulfilment of 'the desire to escape, not indeed from life, but from our present time and self-made misery'.[168]

Gaiman has defended this form of escapism by claiming that it can 'give you knowledge about the world and your predicament'.[169] Yet one might question the extent to which this argument applies to *Neverwhere*. The book's very title suggests the problem that attends it – while it purports to engage with the social ills of London, it ends up presenting a tale of 'Neverwhere', a kind of urban Neverland. The original BBC series was pitched by co-creator Lenny Henry as a fantasy series 'about tribes of homeless people in London'.[170] Gaiman was reluctant to tackle the subject, 'because that could make it really cool to be homeless in London'.[171] It was this reluctance that prompted his creation of London Below as a plainly fictional 'world that exists in the cracks' which he populated with 'the people who fell through the cracks in the world'.[172] Yet in its very efforts to avoid romanticizing homelessness, *Neverwhere* ends up doing just that. The allure of London Below is so great that it leaves the reader with the indelible impression that the homeless and the dispossessed living within this fantasy world are better off than the everyday Londoners fortunate enough to hold down a job in London Above. This impression is redoubled in the final pages of the book, as Richard openly disparages his 'nice normal life'.[173] His choice to return to London Below is thus tantamount to Peter Pan's decision to remain in Neverland – Richard remains in Neverwhere, choosing a life of adventure, danger and freedom from adult responsibility over the daily challenges of a nice normal life.

Furthermore, the success of Gaiman's world-building effectively blunts the social edge of his fantasy. Whatever 'knowledge about the world and your predicament' that may have been gleaned from *Neverwhere* is lost in the sheer attractiveness and vivacity of London Below. Gaiman spends so much time thickening the textures of his fantasy world that one is liable to forget that London Below was intended as a 'metaphor'. Thus, for example, a sisterhood of 'Velvet Children' live in a cavern and prey upon innocent men;[174] 'a ghost-thing, the colour of black smoke' is one of many monsters who 'live in the gaps' between the platforms and the trains;[175] 'a fat man in chain-mail' commissions 'a perfect black rose' made of metal;[176] the Marquis brokered a 'peace treaty' between Earl's Court and Raven's Court;[177] the Old Bailey owes the Marquis an unspecified 'big favour';[178] Hunter was employed by the menacing 'Seven Sisters' who 'hadn't spoken to each other for, oh, at least thirty years'.[179] With the accumulation of detail upon tantalizing detail, *Neverwhere* invites the readers to forget the social ills of real London for the duration of the reading and enjoy their stay in the bewitching world of London Below.

This tension between the dictates of world-building and Gaiman's earnest desire to make social points finds stark expression in the character of Anaesthesia. A homeless girl who has fled an abusive household in London Above, Anaesthesia's story takes on tragic overtones reminiscent of Tiny Tim, but these are attenuated by her visible contentment among her adopted community of rats in London Below and the pride that she feels in her role as 'a rat-speaker'.[180] The social criticism conveyed through her backstory is thus undercut by the world-building that necessitates the fleshing out of a society in which rats not only speak but are held in high regard and treated with reverence. This tension between Anaesthesia as a vehicle for social criticism and Anaesthesia as a vehicle for world-building exemplifies the conflict at the heart of Secondary-World fantasy set in London. The richer and more immersive its Secondary-World London, the greater the pressure on the fantasy novel to release its grip on the splintered and slippery realities of the everyday city.

Christmas Carol had inspired Robert Louis Stevenson to 'make it a little better for people',[181] and it caused Thomas Carlyle to be 'seized with a perfect *convulsion* of hospitality'.[182] One would be hard-pressed to imagine such a reader response to *Neverwhere*. Far easier to imagine, as Clute had done in his review, the reader who exclaims: 'Let me alone for a moment, I want to read the *story*.'[183] Gaiman himself seems to have, on occasion, forgotten the social impetus of London Below. Asked about the possibility of a sequel, he replied without any reference to the social valence of his envisioned fantasy: 'it's a huge and wonderful world, and there are other places and cities I want to visit with it'.[184] Thus, Secondary-World fantasy forecloses the reality outside of it regardless of the author's intentions.

Or as Mark Bould observed, it is a fantasy that 'disavows the very possibility of a territory which is not its map'.[185]

'This is totality': Miéville's Bas-Lag trilogy

Miéville's *Perdido Street Station*, the fantasy novel that catapulted him to fame, ends its acknowledgements with a tribute 'to M. John Harrison, and to the memory of Mervyn Peake'.[186] The influence of Peake and Harrison on *Perdido Street Station*, particularly of Harrison's second Viriconium novel, *A Storm of Wings* (1980), is indeed palpably felt. *Perdido Street Station* features the actual title phrase 'a storm of wings' twice,[187] and its species of insect-headed women called the '*khepri*' may well have been inspired by the striking image of 'an insect-headed woman' in Harrison's book.[188] Peake's influence on Miéville, by Miéville's own account, stems from his 'organic relationship with the language',[189] evident for example in Peake's descriptions of a 'morning that was . . . fructified and like a grape of air',[190] and a drop of lake water that 'burgeoned the vast summer'.[191] *Perdido Street Station* accordingly evinces a Peakean luxuriance in language: 'Time was stretched out and sickly in this endless corridor, like rancid treacle.'[192]

These influences notwithstanding, *Perdido Street Station* reworks earlier paradigms of the Urban Fantasy tradition in ways that do not fully cohere with any single previous model. Where Peake's fantasies disclosed a deep suspicion towards science and technology, *Perdido Street Station* is very much at home with intricate engines, sentient robots and jerry-rigged machinery. The protagonist Isaac is a scientist, for whom a material-scientific approach to 'the fabric of ontology' is a point of pride.[193] Granted, Wells's scientific romances featured a range of scientists, sometimes heroes as in *The Time Machine* and sometimes villains as in *The Invisible Man* and *The Island of Doctor Moreau*. But Miéville does not treat science with quite the same gravitas as Wells. If for Wells literature had an important role to play in cultivating 'the taste for good inductive reading',[194] Miéville regards the rhetoric of pseudo-science as literary trappings of the same basic timbre as those of undisguised fantasy: '"scientism" is just sf's mode of expression of the fantastic'.[195]

As previously discussed, Dickens and Wells were never particularly invested in creating stories that were immersive enough to elicit in their readers a suspension of disbelief, an effect that was far more vital to the tradition of Rural Fantasy. The same can be said of Orwell and Peake, though in Peake's case this was truer of *Titus Alone* than of the first two volumes of the *Gormenghast Trilogy*.

Orwell was surely not one to encourage suspension of disbelief, given that the term bears a disconcerting similarity to his concept of *doublethink*, the operation of 'consciously to induce unconsciousness'.[196] Miéville, in contrast, is deeply committed to 'the particularly strong kind of suspension of disbelief that fantasy involves'.[197] He thus champions the same quality that Tolkien celebrated as key to Secondary-World fantasy, namely the inducement of 'Secondary Belief'.[198]

Where Gaiman openly acknowledged his debt to Tolkien, Miéville harangued Tolkien with a vehemence matching Harrison's and Moorcock's.[199] But Miéville's fantasies have more in common with *The Lord of the Rings* than he would care to admit. Their debt to Tolkien may be brought into sharper relief by way of comparison with Harrison's *Viriconium* saga. In his 1980s Viriconium stories, Harrison made a sustained effort to ensure that his fantastical city of Viriconium did not cohere with Tolkien's concept of a Secondary World, namely an immersive environment with an 'inner consistency' that enables and encourages 'Escape'.[200] 'Viriconium was never intended to be the same place twice',[201] Harrison asserted, observing that 'The very streets shift, from story to story'.[202] He thus injected details that flatly contradict each other across the saga, and inexplicably changed the name of a central location from 'the Plaza of Unrealised Time to the Plaza of Realised Time'.[203] Even the name of the city changes with no apparent rhyme or reason, featuring variously as Viriconium, 'Uroconium',[204] 'Vriko',[205] 'Vira Co',[206] and eventually, 'London'.[207] Thus, if Tolkien made the case for the creation of self-contained and immersive Secondary-World fantasies, Harrison championed a self-aware strain of fantasy that flaunted its own fictiveness.

Miéville, by contrast, conceded in an unusually sanguine mood that 'Tolkien's most important contribution by far, and what is at the heart of the real revolution he effected in literature, was his construction of a systematic secondary world'.[208] Miéville certainly objects to Tolkien's politics, which he has excoriated as 'resolutely rural, petty bourgeois, conservative, anti-modernist, misanthropically Christian and anti-intellectual',[209] thereby pinpointing the qualities that this study has identified with Rural Fantasy. But when Miéville asserted that *Perdido Street Station* was 'a deliberately anti-Tolkienesque fantasy',[210] he did not mean this in the same sense that Harrison, Moorcock or Peake would have meant it. 'I kind of made a checklist',[211] Miéville recounted, 'Tolkien is rural and bucolic, so let's make it urban and shitty; Tolkien is feudalism lite, so let's make it capitalism dark, and you go through like that'.[212] This checklist places Miéville squarely in the Urban Fantasy tradition, but one can hardly fail to notice that he excluded Tolkien's key concept of Secondary-World fantasy, which would have made the top of Harrison's list. In this vein, few fantasy worlds are as fully fleshed and vividly rendered as Miéville's world of 'Bas-Lag', particularly the London-based metropolis at its heart, 'New Crobuzon'. New Crobuzon is first introduced in *Perdido Street Station*, and further developed in its two sequels, *The Scar* (2002) and *Iron Council* (2004). These three fantasy novels are known collectively as the 'Bas-Lag trilogy'.

Perdido Street Station follows certain genre conventions of Secondary-World fantasy, which were established by *The Lord of the Rings* and which Harrison staunchly disavowed, namely fleshing out the fantasy world with 'its own maps, its histories and technologies'.[213] Thus, the novel is prefaced by a meticulous map of the city of New Crobuzon that details the names of its boroughs, bridges, landmarks, twin rivers and the titular station at its heart, as well as the numerous railways and 'skyrails' that expand out of it and across the city. Nearly all of its vast array of place names appear in the novel and it is broadly possible to follow the protagonists' journeys across the city on foot, rail and cab, by cross-referencing them against the map. In this vein, the narrative point of view constantly oscillates between the street level of the local borough and the bird's-eye view of the city from above, never letting the reader forget, in the words of one of the characters, that 'This is totality.'[214]

The totality is reinforced by the kaleidoscopic vision of New Crobuzon as filtered through a khepri woman's multiple insect-eyes:

> A million tiny sections of the whole, ... Within each segment, . . . a precise story was told. Each visual fragment, each part, each shape, each shade of colour, differed from its surroundings in infinitesimal ways that told her about the state of the whole structure.[215]

This fraught dynamic between the 'visual fragment' and the 'whole structure' builds up to a diorama of mass, breadth and most importantly overwhelming presence. Through an accumulation of 'a million tiny sections of the whole', in each of which 'a precise story was told', New Crobuzon becomes not only immersive but so immersive as to be regarded as the paradigmatic setting for the 'New Weird [type of] urban, secondary-world fiction' for which Miéville is famed.[216]

Miéville was aware of the problems that attend his chosen mode of Secondary-World fantasy, and the Bas-Lag trilogy tries to avoid the pitfalls of escapism by presenting multiple and pliable narratives that do not fully correlate, thereby disrupting the reader's immersion in their Secondary World. It provides a plethora of viewpoints, identities and opinions, and even conflicting accounts of the same event. Thus, in *The Scar*, the human boy Shekel and the 'Remade' human-amphibian Tanner bond by exchanging different versions of a folktale. This folktale is predicated upon the rejection of a master narrative in favour of ad hoc oral improvisations: 'even those that Shekel had heard before Tanner knew variations of, and he narrated them all well.'[217] Shekel's reaction to the first of Tanner's stories is telling: 'I always preferred them stories without the morals.'[218] Shekel is dissatisfied with the story's moral because it dismisses the value of narrative approximation, claiming that it is 'better to have none' than to settle for the 'nearly right'. Whereas he displays a preference for the unofficial, rough-hewn and probably apocryphal story.

As Shekel and Tanner exchange their tales, they gradually cultivate a friendship that defies New Crobuzon's rigid social order. The Remade, whose bodies have been violently refashioned by the state as punishment for criminal or political dissidence, are at the very bottom of the social scale, reviled and ostracized, and often used as slave labour by the state as well as by the various criminal organizations that are rife in Bas-Lag. Fraternization between 'normal' Crobuzoners and the Remade is not only a social taboo but is viewed as undesirable by the totalitarian authorities who might easily punish all the parties involved. But Shekel and Tanner develop a bond nonetheless, one which rejects the doctrine that positions the Remade as Other, valorizing the oral story as a conduit for friendship. Thus, multiple, conflicting stories build a plateau for social camaraderie and resistance, if only in the modest scope of burgeoning friendship between two very different but kind-hearted men.

In *Iron Council*, narrative multiplicity takes on a broader political meaning in the context of national myths. A puppet show titled 'The Sad and Instructional Take of Jack Half-a-Prayer' presents a subversive account of the death of the legendary outlaw Jack who featured as a minor character in *Perdido Street Station*.[219] According to the official statement issued by the New Crobuzon militia, Jack was 'a bandit and a murderer',[220] caught by the authorities and killed by a family member of one of his victims in an act of grief-fuelled revenge. An alternative version claims that Jack's death was actually 'a *mercy* killing' carried out by a close friend of Jack to save him from public execution.[221] But the 'Instructional Take' offers a different take altogether, presenting a scenario in which Jack and his companion survive, 'still fighting, still trying to win'.[222] As Henry Farrell observes, this last version 'is clearly intended to inspire solidarity, to suggest that there is hope for those struggling against the city's government'.[223] Yet while Farrell locates the source of resistance in the performance's content, it also inheres in the very co-existence of contradictory versions, in the self-referential acknowledgement that this performance is one 'take' among many, which undercuts the definitiveness of New Crobuzon's official annals. This is supported by yet a fourth version, Miéville's retelling of Jack's capture and its aftermath in a separately published short story, 'Jack' (2005), told from the perspective of the man who originally Remade Jack and now exacts his revenge on Jack's betrayer. The multiplicity of versions thus fulfils a twofold role – it subverts the totalitarianism of the New Crobuzon government and it obviates the danger of Miéville's own totalization becoming fully immersive and thereby more deeply escapist.[224]

Miéville argues strenuously for the transformative potential of Secondary-World fantasy, contending that the fantastical 'construction of a paranoid, impossible totality is at least potentially a subversive, radical act'.[225] His argument turns on two major points. First, according to Miéville, the creation of 'an internally coherent but actually impossible totality . . . mimics the "absurdity" of capitalist modernity' in its Marxist formulation.[226] Secondly, as Miéville contends, the immersion of the reader in a fantastical yet totalizing Secondary World can trigger a renegotiation of the interface of the possible and the impossible, thereby creating a 'mental space redefining – or pretending to redefine – the impossible'.[227] By this logic, Secondary-World fantasy can provide an especially potent framework for the subversion of the status quo, because it creates a robust alternative reality that brings home the fantasist's vision of political and social change. It is in this sense that Miéville has asserted: 'we need fantasy to think the world, and to change it.'[228]

But Miéville's theoretical assertions do not square with his Secondary-World fantasies, to which, one may assume, they were meant to apply. Rather than dramatizing his far-reaching aspirations for Secondary-World fantasy, Miéville's Bas-Lag trilogy suggests that there may be an element to this mode that narrows the scope of its remit for social change, at least when it is underpinned by Marxist ideology.[229] In *Perdido Street Station*, the protagonists defeat the monstrous slake-moths that threatened to destroy all sentient life in New Crobuzon, but the city's despotic government continues to rule as strong as ever. The main source of hope at the end of the novel lies in the successful self-transformation of the first-person narrator, 'Yagharek',[230] a member of an avian desert-dwelling species called the 'garuda'.[231] In line with the endings of *The Tain* and *Neverwhere*, *Perdido Street Station* closes with Yagharek turning his back on his erstwhile home. But unlike Richard and the narrator of *The Tain*, Yagharek does not turn his back on everyday life in the city. He tears off his feathers and attempts to snap off his beak in order to become human and more importantly, urban: '*I turn and walk into my home, the city, a man.*'[232] Echoing the narrator of *The Tain*, the garuda who initially felt lost and adrift at the port of '*this great wen*' can now regard the Crobuzoners as '*my citizen fellows*'.[233] This marks a triumph of urban identity, the fluidity of the self and the power of the individual to bond with the city, but it is hardly a triumph of social change.

Iron Council revises the ending of *Perdido Street Station* in such a way that it at once expands and contracts its remit of social change. In the classic fashion of the *Bildungsroman*, the fearless Ann-Hari arrives at New Crobuzon as a wide-eyed girl from a parochial village. But rather than transforming into an urbanite like Yagharek, or even undergoing the bitter disillusionment of Dickens's Pip or Wells's George, Ann-Hari merely departs New Crobuzon after a time and returns to her previous occupation of selling sexual favours to a railroad construction team. 'She has liked New Crobuzon, has looked on it with passion and interest',[234] the narrator glosses her decision, 'but for her all its mass and history – its accreted stones and struggle – could only ever be an adjunct to the iron road'.[235] The metaphor of the railway as an open future and an escape from 'mass and history' is in keeping with the slightly proselytizing tone of *Iron Council*, Miéville's most overtly political novel to date. But the book culminates with hope deferred, as the titular Iron Council – a train gone rogue that temporarily forms a self-contained utopia – is caught on the threshold of New Crobuzon by a 'time golem' that preserves it from harm but also freezes it in place.[236] This narrative crux brings to a head the overdetermined clash between Ann-Hari and the golemist Judah Low, who unlike his Jewish namesake is a born and bred urbanite, a Crobuzoner with an acute sensitivity to the social and material constraints that limit the scope of human agency. The clash between Ann-Hari, who regards the city as nothing more than 'an adjunct to the iron road',[237] and Judah, who 'sees everything as a city',[238] is resolved by Ann-Hari's execution of Judah as a punishment for his creation of the time golem. Thus, if *Perdido Street Station* concluded with a desert-dweller making the city his home, *Iron Council* concludes with the thorough-going urbanite shot at point-blank by a woman who turned her back on the city. The Iron Council itself remains perpetually in stasis, the people of New Crobuzon risking their lives in surreptitious pilgrimages to its frozen form, chanting that the train '*is coming, is still coming*'.[239] *Iron Council* thereby subverts the trope of individual self-transformation in the city and allows for only a deferred possibility of collective social agency.

One may read this ending as emblematic of the way in which social idealism and Secondary-World fantasy scrape against each other. Miéville's belief that fantasy literature can change the world by offering a new and radical mode of thought runs counter to the fundamental tendency of Secondary-World fantasy to resist radical change. Secondary-World fantasy, whether urban or rural, depends on the consistency and coherence of its fantasy world. At the heart of a Secondary-World fantasy novel, by definition, lies its world-building – its meticulous mapping out of the fantasy world's geography, history, society, politics, races and monsters, together with a codification of its magic or its pseudo-science. A radical change in this world, of the scope to which Miéville alludes, effectively undercuts the very world-building upon which the fantasy book is premised. As Mendlesohn has observed, Secondary-World fantasies commonly follow an arc of decline rather than progressive or radical change: 'They rarely tell of building, because building is a venture into the unknown.'[240] Thus, Secondary-World fantasies tend towards a reconfirmation of their own status quo or an attenuated version thereof. Consequently, the ideology embedded in this form will, by implication, affirm the ineluctability of the status quo outside of the book. This is a paradox that Miéville has been thus far unable to resolve, and it may partly explain his recent ambivalence towards Bas-Lag. He has written no Bas-Lag fantasies for over a decade, and when asked if he planned to return, he responded: 'I will be staying away for a while yet.'[241]

The 'most successfully multicultural city': Miéville's cosmopolitan London

Setting aside their ideological ambiguities, Miéville's totalizing fantasies refract the totality of contemporary London as a global world city. Spanning roughly 1,600 square kilometres, Greater London encompasses a population that grew from 6.77 million to 8.2 million between 1983 and 2001,[242] but the most radical change during this period was the diversification of its population. According to Jerry White, 'London was, indeed, greatly more foreign in the 1990s than ever before',[243] and by the end of the twentieth century it had become 'one of the world's greatest cosmopolitan cities'.[244] In this respect, many Londoners felt – and still feel – that their city is a microcosm of the world, a totality onto itself.

If there is a single thread that runs through the entirety of Miéville's oeuvre – his London-based fantasies, his Secondary-World fantasies and his non-fiction – it is his endorsement of urban inclusivity and cosmopolitanism. Miéville grew up in Willesden, an area in north-west London that he describes as 'working-class, ethnically-mixed'.[245] This upbringing may account in part for Miéville's view of London as congenitally multicultural: 'to Londoners' joy and fortune, London is the most and most successfully multicultural city in Europe'.[246] His London-based New Crobuzon is accordingly made up of a rich medley of species, languages and cultures, a *'mongrel city'* that relies on *'the immigrants, the refugees, the outsiders who remake New Crobuzon every day.'*[247] The pirate city of Armada, which forms the principal setting of *The Scar*, likewise thrives on pressganging the crews of captured ships in order to renew and enlarge its population: 'That, after all, was what Armada was – a colony of the lost, the renegade, the absent without leave, the defeated.'[248]

Miéville's first fantasy novel, *King Rat* (1998), is set in the Willesden area where he grew up, which he has since claimed as 'the zone that defines London for me',[249] not only for personal reasons but also on account of its liminality, as 'a very large ring that's neither central nor suburban'.[250] This liminality is ethnic as well as spatial, it is 'a London of council estates and dirty walls, black youth and white youth, Armenian girls'.[251] This vision of London is under threat from the antagonist of *King Rat*, the genocidal Pied Piper of Hamelin, who is intent on purifying the city of every person who, in his judgement, 'don't belong in this world'.[252] He assumes the role of an insanely zealous urban planner, seeking to empty London of its people much as he had emptied Hamelin of its rats. The hypnotic music of his flute is thus figured as 'an intruder in the city that shaped it contemptuously',[253] his musical number conjuring up 'a huge metropolis, deserted and broken, alone, entropic, . . . cleared of all its rubbish'.[254]

Miéville's choice of the well-known German folktale of the Pied Piper as the major intertext of *King Rat* tallies closely with his celebration of diversity. The folktale of the Pied Piper is, at its most basic, an allegory on the fatal consequences of intolerance, in which the destruction of the Other – the rats of Hamelin – leads to the destruction of the self, the village children. Unlike Browning's poem 'The Pied Piper of Hamelin' (1842), which may be seen as another, more submerged intertext, the satirical target of *King Rat* is less the Malthusian ideal of depopulation upheld by the 'Mayor and Corporation',[255] and more the genocidal impulse embodied in the blond-haired, blue-eyed, unmistakably Aryan Piper. Indeed, the Piper's machinations are at one point expressly likened to a 'holocaust',[256] lending a further suggestiveness to the fact that Miéville chose a German folktale and harkening back to the 'holocaust' that was the massacre of Muzzlehatch's zoo in *Titus Alone*.[257]

Anticipating the Bas-Lag trilogy, *King Rat* also ends with a social revolution deferred and a restoration of the everyday. In tune with the novel's valorization of cosmopolitanism, the protagonist Saul defeats the Piper by virtue of his mixed blood as a half-man, half-rat: 'I'm not rat plus man, get it? I'm bigger than either one *and I'm bigger than the two. I'm a new thing. You can't make me dance.'*[258] In the aftermath of the battle, he abdicates the throne of King Rat, whom he has succeeded, declaring 'Year One of the Rat Republic'.²⁵⁹ He thinks of himself as 'an agent of history',²⁶⁰ but Miéville himself cast a dampening light on Saul's self-aggrandizement in response to an interview question about the book's ending: 'it is a bourgeois revolution, rather than a socialist one.'²⁶¹ Thus, the true victory in *King Rat* lies in the fact that Londoners of all backgrounds, cultures, nationalities and ethnicities may continue 'making tea and writing reports and having sex and reading books and watching TV and fighting and expiring quietly in bed'.²⁶²

Miéville's London-based fantasies appear altogether more reconciled to this restoration of the status quo than his Bas-Lag trilogy. Yagharek bitterly resents the obliviousness of the New Crobuzon public in the aftermath of his agonized struggle to save the city: '*the city squats fatly in its freedom, brazen again and fearless. It ignores us. It is an ingrate.*'²⁶³ Saul, however, feels oddly consoled by the realization that 'London slept, fat and dangerous and blithely unaware of what had happened'.²⁶⁴ 'It carried on whatever',²⁶⁵ he reflects, 'There was a great comfort in that.'²⁶⁶ Miéville's *Un Lun Dun*, an open tribute to *Neverwhere* that substituted the hapless Richard for the canny adolescent girl Deeba,²⁶⁷ went so far as to posit that there may yet be hope for everyday London. Where Richard and the narrator of *The Tain* abandoned everyday London for its fantastical mirror city, Deeba returns to London from the fantastical 'abcity' of 'UnLondon'.²⁶⁸ While 'she felt the lack of UnLondon like a loss',²⁶⁹ she refuses to be forgotten by her family and resumes her life with them on a Kilburn council estate, embracing the everyday routines of a young girl from a low-income family while reassuring her friends in UnLondon that 'I'll be back all the time'.²⁷⁰ Deeba's choice is not motivated solely by homesickness – she is determined to fight for 'London and UnLondon' against government corruption and exploitation,²⁷¹ regarding both cities as her 'home front'.²⁷² Thus, Miéville reconsidered the resolutions of both Gaiman's *Neverwhere* and his own *The Tain* and revised their finality by ending *Un Lun Dun* with a compromise between the fantastic and the everyday. In the final analysis, he has become more accepting of everyday London, celebrating 'the metal tines',²⁷³ the 'plate and cutlery',²⁷⁴ as much as the grotesque forms and deep dark histories of '*this great wen*'.²⁷⁵

'A default cultural vernacular': Ben Aaronovitch's *Peter Grant* series

As delineated in the opening of this chapter, the past ten years have seen a veritable explosion in London-based fantasy, from Kate Griffin's *Matthew Swift* series (2009–present), to Paul Cornell's unfinished *Shadow Police* (2012–16), to V. E. Schwab's *Shades of Magic* trilogy (2015–17), to name but a few. Asked in a survey, 'What do you think have been the most significant developments in British science fiction and fantasy over the past twenty years?',[276] Miéville replied that the genres of science fiction and fantasy had become 'a default cultural vernacular'.[277] Nowhere is this development more apparent than in Ben Aaronovitch's *Peter Grant* series (2011–present) that follows the titular PC Peter Grant as he joins the Metropolitan Police's special unit for containing supernatural threats, known from the fourth book onward as the 'Special Assessment Unit'.[278] Aaronovitch is hardly the first author to combine London-based fantasy with the police procedural, but the *Peter Grant* series is unusual in the degree to which it treats fantasy and science fiction as 'a default cultural vernacular'. The books are replete with allusions to *Harry Potter*, *Twilight*, *Doctor Who*, *Blade Runner*, *X-Files*, *Star Wars*, *Firefly*, *Battlestar Galactica*, *Dungeons & Dragons* and *Avatar: The Last Airbender*, to name a few. Its Urban Fantasy influences are flagged up emphatically. The second book explains the rationale for a police interrogation technique by asserting that 'we were aiming for a cross between Kafka and Orwell',[279] the third features an underground community hidden in the tunnels beneath Notting Hill, described by one character as 'A race of people living under West London like Morlocks',[280] and the seventh remarks upon 'what made Dickensian London Dickensian'.[281]

The overarching story arc from the second novel to the seventh dramatizes the clash between Urban Fantasy and its Rural counterpart in the ongoing battle of wits between Peter and his nemesis. Peter is a Londoner born and bred, who is fascinated by the idiosyncrasies of London, exhibiting a deep familiarity with its geography, culture, architecture and local history, and resenting police duties that require him to leave the city. His nemesis is 'a Dark Ages enthusiast' whose favourite author is Tolkien,[282] who owns 'five or six different editions of *The Lord of the Rings*' and a 'signed first edition of *The Hobbit*',[283] and who hatches a scheme to magically regress Britain into a pastoral Arthurian landscape purged of urban modernity. Peter accordingly defeats him by drawing on London's deeper past and rallying a Roman legion to defend 'early Londinium'.[284] Thus, the clash between Urban Fantasy and Rural Fantasy plays out across a pastiche of London history. While the champions of Urban Fantasy prevail in this instance, their victory is tempered by the books' tacit acknowledgement that Londoners are not altogether blameless for the hostility levied at their city. Peter's world view is circumscribed by the M25, to the extent that he describes Hertfordshire as 'what Londoners like to think of as "everywhere else"'.[285] The detrimental effects of this London-centrism are brought to the fore when he asks one of his enemies, 'What's the city ever done to you?',[286] to which she replies indignantly that London 'sucks the rest of the country dry.... All the jobs, all the money goes to London.'[287] Thus, for all its celebration of London life, the *Peter Grant* series urges a reconsideration of the power imbalance and unequal resource distribution between London and the rest of the United Kingdom. In the wake of the EU referendum and the debates it has provoked, this call rings with renewed urgency.

'No city like London': A tradition made visible

T. S. Eliot's essay, 'Tradition and the Individual Talent' (1919), has made a fine point about the bi-directionality of literary influence:

> what happens when a new work of art is created is something that happens simultaneously to all the works of art which preceded it. The existing monuments form an ideal order among themselves, which is modified by the introduction of the new (the really new) work of art among them. The existing order is complete before the new work arrives; for order to persist after the supervention of novelty, the *whole* existing order must be, if ever so slightly, altered; and so the relations, proportions, values of each work of art toward the whole are readjusted; and this is conformity between the old and the new. Whoever has approved this idea of order, of the form of European, of English literature, will not find it preposterous that the past should be altered by the present as much as the present is directed by the past.[288]

Eliot's point gestures towards the extent to which a literary tradition may only be recognized in retrospect, by examining a literary expression in the present that in its very innovation spurs a search for the antecedents that led up to its particular turn. Thus, it was only when writers like Moorcock began to hail Miéville as the head of 'the modern school of urban fantasy ... the gritty opposite of the Tolkien school',[289] that one could begin to question whether this opposition is truly new, or whether it had earlier iterations in the oppositions between Peake and Tolkien, Wells and MacDonald and Dickens and Ruskin. The reconstruction of any line of influence therefore depends on the last link in this line so far, 'the new (the really new) work of art' that affects an alteration in 'the *whole* existing order'.

The fact that Miéville so unabashedly, joyously and self-consciously writes urban fantasies celebrating metropolitan life and the social and technological potentialities of the city, coupled with the fact that he expressly names Dickens, Wells, Peake and Harrison as his predecessors and strongly alludes to Orwell, enables scholars to read these earlier authors in turn as urban fantasists themselves, in a way that might not have been possible before Miéville. When Miéville named 'Charles Dickens's London' as a prominent model for New Crobuzon,[290] he reconfigured Dickens's London into a setting of urban fantasy. This is not to say that Dickens's London is not endemically fantastical – this study has insisted that it is – but rather that it could only be seen as the ur-city of Urban Fantasy once that Urban Fantasy was written and could project back upon it. In this respect, Miéville is not only the latest addition in a continuous line of influence but the addition that allows the line to become visible. By being the latest author in a history of writers who sought to positively engage with London through urban, liberal-progressive, materially saturated fantasies, Miéville bound these authors together, or enabled scholars to see the tradition that was already there, which amounts to the same thing.

The crux of the Urban Fantasy tradition lay in the fact that it insisted on maintaining a positive engagement with London, even when that positive engagement was exceedingly difficult to justify. The Urban Fantasy tradition offered new visions of London through fantasies of what Adorno described as 'the negative knowledge of the actual world',[291] but it also celebrated London as much for what it is and was as for what it could be. In stark contrast to its rival tradition of Rural Fantasy, the Urban Fantasy tradition refused the temptation to return to the past and to a simpler world without cities, technology or industrialization. Instead, it strived to find beauty in the present and the future, in a world in which urban modernity was a permanent fixture of human life. 'Ours is the age of cities',[292] Wells wrote in 'A Story of the Days to Come', 'In the city – that is the life to which we were born.'[293] These lines were as much a statement about Wells's present day as a description of his imagined future, and they may be taken as the motto of the entire Urban Fantasy tradition.

Dickens's social criticism of Victorian London never stopped him from celebrating it as the wellspring of his fantasy, the site of the animated clothes on Monmouth Street, the transformative shadows of *The Haunted Man*, and the 'ugly, handsome, crippled, exquisitely formed' goblins of *The Chimes*.[294] Dickens's London was brimming with enchantment, 'all kneaded up together in a leaven of mist and darkness' where 'all common things become uncommon and enchanted'.[295] Thus, when he cast his thoughts into the far future and imagined 'the race of men then to be our successors on the earth' exerting 'the utmost force of the human intellect' to piece together human history,[296] Dickens's imagination placed these intellectuals of ages yet to come on the same route that he took on his 'street expedition' in London,[297] 'hard by Temple Bar' and not far from where he had conjured up a Megalosaurus when he cast his thoughts in the opposite direction back to the antediluvian past.[298] Past, present and future were for Dickens all equally bound up with London, the city into which he channelled 'all the dreaminess and all the romance' of his imagination.[299]

In Wells's hands, Urban Fantasy took a darker turn. With the widespread acceptance of Darwin's evolutionary theory and a newfound understanding of the Second Law of Thermodynamics, Wells's vision of the future was not of Dickens's 'race of men to be our successors on the earth' applying their intellect to good purpose,[300] but an entropic world in which the human intellect had 'committed suicide',[301] urban modernity had disappeared, the glorious architecture of London had crumbled with neglect and disuse and even the Crystal Palace, Dickens's fairyland in its Sydenham incarnation, was 'deserted and falling into ruin'.[302]

Wells fervently wished he could celebrate the 'fitful indignations and fantastic and often grotesque generosities, which this dear London life of ours exudes' with the same unqualified love of the city as Dickens had shown.[303] But the unchecked expansion of London at the turn of the century, coupled with his bleak sense that there was no reason 'to suppose that this continuous muddle of partial destruction and partial rebuilding is not to constitute the future history of London',[304] made it difficult for him to imagine such a future history as terminating in anything other than 'the ultimate eating away and dry-rotting and dispersal of all our world'.[305]

With the ever-lengthening shadow of the Great War looming before him, Wells disavowed his fantasies of future London altogether. In *Anticipations*, he declared that he was telling 'the story of his own disillusionment',[306] the implication being that the object of this disillusionment was, among other things, 'his own particular city'.[307] *Anticipations* pronounced his fantastical visions of 'the future of London' to have been misguided:[308] 'gigantic tenement houses, looming upon colossal roofed streets' and automated 'moving ways' made good material for fantasy,[309] but their 'plausibility crumbles away' on rigorous analysis.[310] In the fullness of time, so Wells's new argument went, 'the city will diffuse itself' until it was absorbed into hybrid rural-urban regions and faded like 'the blot on the map' that it had become in Wells's increasingly proselytizing forecasts.[311]

The trials and tribulations of twentieth-century history made celebrating the city still more difficult for Orwell and Peake. They were writing Urban Fantasy at a time in which technology had culminated in the atom bomb and the discoveries of science led to the refinement of Zyklon B, and in which London life came to mean air-raid sirens, blackouts, shelters, nightly fear of death, bombed-out buildings, scarcity and austerity. In such a world, Orwell and Peake could hardly celebrate urban life as unambiguously as Dickens or embrace scientific and technological progress with the same fervour as Wells. Yet they were not ready to give up on 'this dark hive called London' altogether and refused to pen fantasies that glorified a return to a pre-industrial rural past in the vein of Tolkien's and Lewis's Rural Fantasy.[312] Rather, Orwell and Peake turned to more attenuated versions of urban life in the spirit of Dickensian locality, valorizing crowds, markets, buses, parks and small acts of kindness in the fabric of the everyday.

Thus, Orwell and Peake kept the Urban Fantasy tradition alive at a time when it was under imminent threat, but in the final analysis they left the genre in abeyance. Peake set the keynote in the words of one of his best-formed characters, Muzzlehatch, who articulated a sentiment that would have left Dickens stunned: 'This is only a city.'[313] Had the Urban Fantasy tradition ended with Orwell and Peake, it may well have been the story of a genre that had struggled to celebrate London but was left with the sense that it was 'only a city'; a genre that believed in science and technology but saw it put in the service of the worst kinds of moral and social atavism, of 'creatures out of the Dark Ages [who] have come marching into the present'.[314] In other words, it may well have been the story of a genre that was overwhelmed by history and petered out.

But that is not the end of the story. Under the editorship of Moorcock and his books editor Harrison, *New Worlds* magazine carried on the Urban Fantasy tradition in the second half of the twentieth century, particularly through the shared mythos of the 'Jerry Cornelius' stories, extracts and serializations. Through this Protean figure, the stable of *New Worlds* writers experimented with new forms of fantasy fiction to express the lived realities of a London in the throes of change, faced with an uncertain future. In the later decades of the twentieth century, these fantasists expressed the sense that London was becoming a denatured version of itself, that 'life was leaking tragically out of all these things'.[315] Many of them left London, and some took to writing totalizing Secondary-World fantasies set in cities that were at varying degrees of remove from London. Urban Fantasy thus became increasingly distanced from the socially engaged street-view of lived London experience. In Gaiman's own words, it was easier to write about London fantastically 'as a stranger',[316] opting for a view of 'London as Oz, as Narnia'.[317]

At the dawn of the twenty-first century, Miéville revived Dickens's celebration of London as a source of fantasy, a nexus of liberal-progressive and radical imaginings, and the very centre of 'a kind of magical merging of things'.[318] Having matured in the late twentieth century, Miéville does not suffer from the ambivalences and struggles that plagued Orwell's and Peake's engagements with the city. 'Cities are fantastic',[319] he has announced unapologetically, playing on both meanings of the word 'fantastic'. London especially so, because it is 'a more or less unplanned chimera, and the chimera is also a default figure of the fantastic'.[320] There 'was no city like London',[321] he asserted in *Kraken*. Miéville ended *Perdido Street Station* with the line '*my home, the city*' because he truly feels more at home in the city than any of his predecessors in the Urban Fantasy tradition since Dickens.[322] In this respect, Miéville's fantasy is a return to the beginning, to Dickens's Fairyland of London. But in Miéville's vision, London's fantastical qualities derive from a different source than Dickens's twilight city and its attendant shadows and spectres. Miéville's London is fantastical by virtue of its vibrant, teeming and aggregative multiculturalism, a 'chaotic aggregation of ideas that's going to translate into a sensation of the fantastic'.[323]

Miéville's substantively different vision of London is crucially informed by the stretch of history that unfolded between Dickens's Victorian, imperial London and the global, cosmopolitan London of the twenty-first century. But the differences between Dickens and Miéville also speak to the extent to which the Urban Fantasy is an active tradition. It is not merely a line of authors imitating one another, but an ongoing project in which each author has wilfully reread, manipulated and overmastered his predecessors. It is no coincidence that Orwell's favourite among Wells's scientific romances was the atypical *When the Sleeper Wakes*, which dealt exclusively with London and celebrated 'midday cutlets' and 'the perpetual hunt for confusing trains',[324] thereby dovetailing with Orwell's valorization of common decency in everyday life, the redemptive quality that seeped through the cracks of totalitarianism. By the same token, Peake's favourite Dickens novel was *Bleak House*,[325] because more than any other of Dickens's fictions save perhaps *The Haunted Man*, *Bleak House* is permeated with Dickens's 'dark and deathless rabble of long shadows',[326] and could thereby serve as the prominent inspiration for Peake's return to a Dickensian gothic mode of prose fantasy. Chiming with Eliot's essay, each link in the chain of the Urban Fantasy tradition affected a shift in the value and meaning of the links that preceded it. The next link and its attendant shift await the forge.

Recent days have marked an uncertain moment for London cosmopolitanism as well as for the Urban Fantasy tradition, with the United Kingdom's vote to leave the European Union. This vote has been interpreted as a vote against globalization, urbanization, multiculturalism, immigration, the predominance of the metropolis in British life, and what is often perceived to be Britain's London-centred self-image. In other words, it was a vote against the ideals that form the core of the Urban Fantasy tradition. In this respect, it may not be entirely whimsical to regard the vote metaphorically as a sudden blow that Rural Fantasy has struck against Urban Fantasy. The question of whether London will be able to retain its status as a global, multicultural and multiracial city has been posed. But recent events notwithstanding, it seems reasonably clear that the future of human affairs – and thus the future of literature – is urban. Not only are cities the centre of social, cultural and economic life, but they have also recently proven more environmentally sustainable than rural communities in the long term.[327] Where cities flourish, urban literature will continue to flourish alongside them, and urban fantasies of a variety of shades and contours will rise to the challenge of reflecting, refracting, critiquing and joyously celebrating the metropolis, with a finely tuned sensibility towards the tradition from whence they hail and the fantasies yet to be written.

Notes

Introduction

1 China Miéville, *Perdido Street Station* (London: Pan, 2000), 1-2. Italics in original. Henceforth all italics in quotations are in the original unless otherwise stated.
2 Miéville and Joan Gordon [interviewer], 'Reveling in Genre: An Interview with China Miéville', special issue on The British SF Boom, ed. Istvan Csicsery-Ronay, Jr., *Science Fiction Studies* 30, no. 3 (November 2003): 362 (355-73).
3 Sherryl Vint, 'Introduction: Special Issue on China Miéville', special issue on China Miéville, ed. Vint, *Extrapolation* 50, no. 2 (2009): 197 (197-9).
4 Ibid.
5 Miéville and Mark Bould [interviewer], 'Appropriate Means: An Interview with China Miéville', *New Politics* 9, no. 3 (Summer 2003): 171 (169[-176]).
6 Miéville, A. C. Thompson and David Martinez [interviewers], 'The *Lit* Interview: China Miéville; A Young British Writer Dons the Robes of the Un-Tolkien', *San Francisco Bay Guardian Online*, August 2004, http://www.sfbg.com/38/48/lit_mievi lle.html [accessed 9 May 2015].
7 Ibid.
8 This is surely not to suggest that these were the *only* strands at work within British fantasy, which from its inception has been multiform and polyphonic.
9 Roger Luckhurst, *Science Fiction* (Cambridge: Polity, 2005), 3.
10 Ibid.
11 Adam Roberts, *The History of Science Fiction* (2006), 2nd edn (London: Palgrave, 2016), 20.
12 Lucie Armitt, *Fantasy Fiction: An Introduction* (London: Continuum, 2005), 8.
13 Farah Mendlesohn, *Rhetorics of Fantasy* (Middletown: Wesleyan UP, 2008), xiii.
14 Guy Debord, 'Introduction to a Critique of Urban Geography' (1955), in *Situationist International: Anthology*, ed. and trans. Ken Knabb (Berkeley: Bureau of Public Secrets, 1981), 5.
15 Miéville, 'Editorial Introduction', *Historical Materialism* 10, no. 4 (January 2002): 48 (39-49).
16 Juliet John, *Dickens's Villains: Melodrama, Character, Popular Culture* (Oxford: OUP, 2001), 3.
17 Ibid.

18 See John Clute, 'Urban Fantasy', in *The Encyclopedia of Fantasy*, eds Clute and John Grant (1997; repr., New York: Griffin, 1999), 975–6; Alexander C. Irvine, 'Urban Fantasy', in *The Cambridge Companion to Fantasy Literature*, eds Edward James and Farah Mendlesohn (Cambridge: CUP, 2012), 200–13; and Elana Gomel, *Narrative Space and Time: Representing Impossible Topologies in Literature* (New York: Routledge, 2014).

19 Gomel, *Narrative Space and Time*, 52. See also Clute, 'Urban Fantasy', 975; Clute, 'Dickens, Charles', in *Encyclopedia of Fantasy*, 268–9 and Michael Dolzani, 'Introduction' (2004), in *Northrop Frye's Notebooks on Romance*, vol. 15 of *Collected Works of Northrop Frye*, ed. Dolzani (Toronto: University of Toronto Press, 2004), xxvii (xxi–lvii).

20 Charles Dickens, *Our Mutual Friend* (1864–5), ed. Michael Cotsell (Oxford: OUP, 2008), 74.

21 Dickens, *Little Dorrit* (1855–7), ed. Harvey Peter Sucksmith (Oxford: OUP, 2008), 23.

22 Dickens, *Bleak House* (1852–3), ed. Stephen Gill (Oxford: OUP, 1998), 11.

23 Dickens, *Dombey and Son* (1846–8), ed. Alan Horsman (Oxford: OUP, 2001), 234.

24 Ibid., 508.

25 George Gissing, '*Oliver Twist*' (1899), in *Essays, Introductions and Reviews*, vol. 1 of *Collected Works of George Gissing on Charles Dickens*, ed. Pierre Coustillas (Surrey: Grayswood, 2004), 93 (87–95).

26 V. S. Naipaul, *The Enigma of Arrival* (London: Penguin, 1987), 122–3.

27 Salman Rushdie, 'Influence' (1999), in *Step across This Line: Collected Non-fiction, 1992–2002* (London: Cape, 2002), 71 (69–76).

28 Ibid.

29 Ibid.

30 See Rushdie, *The Satanic Verses* (London: Penguin, 1988), 422.

31 See Gary K. Wolfe, 'Fantasy from Dryden to Dunsany', in *Cambridge Companion to Fantasy Literature*, 11.

32 See Mike Ashley and Robert A. W. Lowndes, *The Gernsback Days: The Evolution of Modern Science Fiction from 1911–1936* (Holicong: Wildside Press, 2004).

33 George Moir, 'Modern Romance and Novel' (*c.* 1830–42), in *Victorian Criticism of the Novel*, eds Edwin M. Eigner and George J. Worth (Cambridge: CUP, 1985), 40 (39–57).

34 Ibid.

35 David Masson, *British Novelists and Their Styles: Being a Critical Sketch of the History of British Prose Fiction* (Cambridge: Macmillan, 1859), 239–40.

36 G. H. Lewes, 'Dickens in Relation to Criticism', *Fortnightly Review* 11 (February 1872): 147 (141–54).

37 Donald Hawes, *Charles Dickens* (London: Continuum, 2007), 9.

38 John, *Dickens's Villains*, 20.
39 Harry Stone, *Dickens and the Invisible World* (London: Macmillan, 1979), 147.
40 Ibid.
41 Elaine Ostry, *Social Dreaming: Dickens and the Fairy Tale* (London: Routledge, 2002), xii.
42 Dickens, 'Preface to the Charles Dickens Edition' (1867), in *Martin Chuzzlewit* (1843–4), ed. Margaret Cardwell (Oxford: OUP, 2009), 719 (719–20).
43 See Lewes, 'Literature', *Leader* 3, no. 142 (11 December 1852): 1189 (1189).
44 Dickens, 'Preface to the First Edition' (August 1853), in *Bleak House*, 6 (5–6).
45 Dickens, 'All the Year Round', *Household Words* 19, no. 479 (28 May 1859): 601 (601).
46 Ibid.
47 Dickens, qtd. in John Forster, *The Life of Charles Dickens* (1871–3), ed. J. W. T. Ley, one-volume memorial edn (London: Cecil Palmer, 1928), 727.
48 Ibid.
49 Theodor Adorno, 'Reconciliation Under Duress' (1961), in *Aesthetics and Politics*, trans. Rodney Livingstone, and ed. Ronald Taylor (1977; repr., London: Verso, 1992), 160 (151–76).
50 Adorno, *Aesthetic Theory*, trans. C. Lenhardt and eds Gretel Adorno and Rolf Tiedemann (1970; repr., London: Routledge and Kegan Paul, 1986), 192.
51 Dickens, qtd. in Forster, *Life of Charles Dickens*, 728.
52 Dickens, 'A Preliminary Word', *HW* 1, no. 1 (30 March 1850): 1 (1–2).
53 Ibid.
54 Ibid.
55 Forster, *Life of Charles Dickens*, 11.
56 Dickens, note 67 (1857), in Dickens, *Charles Dickens' Book of Memoranda: A Photographic and Typographic Facsimile of the Notebook Begun in January 1855*, transcribed and annotated by Fred Kaplan (New York: New York Public Library, 1981), 14.
57 Ibid.
58 Ibid.
59 G. K. Chesterton, *Charles Dickens* (1906), in *Chesterton on Dickens*, ed. Alzina Stone Dale, vol. 15 of *The Collected Works of G. K. Chesterton* (San Francisco: Ignatius, 1989), 65 (29–209).
60 Ibid.
61 Ibid.
62 See F. S. Schwarzbach, *Dickens and the City* (London: Athlone, 1979).
63 Chesterton, *Charles Dickens*, 65.
64 J. R. R. Tolkien, 'On Fairy-Stories', in *Essays Presented to Charles Williams*, ed. C. S. Lewis (London: OUP, 1947), 74–5 (38–89).

65 Ibid., 44.
66 H. G. Wells, 'A Chat with the Author of *The Time Machine*' (1895), ed. David C. Smith, *The Wellsian*, no. 20 (Winter 1997): 6 (3–9).
67 Wells, *The War of the Worlds* (1897), ed. Parrinder (London: Penguin, 2005), 161–2.
68 George Orwell, 'Charles Dickens' (1940), in *A Patriot After All: 1940–1941*, ed. Davison, vol. 12 of *The Complete Works of George Orwell* (London: Secker & Warburg, 1998), 20 (20–56).
69 Orwell, 'Wells, Hitler and the World State' (1941), in *A Patriot After All*, 539 (536–41).
70 Orwell, 'Charles Dickens', 44.
71 Ibid., 52.
72 Orwell, 'Review of *Criticisms and Opinions of the Works of Charles Dickens* by G. K. Chesterton' (1933), in *A Kind of Compulsion: 1903–1936*, ed. Davison, vol. 10 of *The Complete Works of George Orwell* (London: Secker & Warburg, 1998), 326 (324–6).
73 Orwell, 'Censorship in England' (1928), in *A Kind of Compulsion*, 118 (117–19).
74 Orwell, 'Review of *Jules Verne: A Biography* by Kenneth Allott' (1941), in *A Patriot After All*, 368 (367–9).
75 Ibid.
76 Orwell, 'Review of *Angel Pavement* by J. B. Priestley' (1930), in *A Kind of Compulsion*, 186–7 (186–8).
77 Ibid.
78 Ibid., 187.
79 Ibid.
80 Orwell, *Keep the Aspidistra Flying* (1936), ed. Davison, vol. 4 of *The Complete Works of George Orwell* (1987; repr., London: Secker & Warburg, 1998), 267.
81 Orwell, *Nineteen Eighty-Four* (1949), ed. Davison, vol. 9 of *The Complete Works of George Orwell* (1987; repr., London: Secker & Warburg, 1998), 229.
82 Ibid., 228.
83 Mervyn Peake, qtd. in Hadas Elber-Aviram, 'Dark and Deathless Rabble of Long Shadows: Peake, Dickens, Tolkien, and "This Dark Hive Called London"', *Peake Studies* 14, no. 2 (April 2015): 7 (7–32).
84 Peake, 'Book Illustration, a Radio Talk' (1947), *Mervyn Peake Review* 9 (Autumn 1979): 16 (14–22).
85 Gordon Smith, *Mervyn Peake: A Personal Memoir* (London: Gollancz, 1984), 100.
86 Peake, qtd. in Elber-Aviram, 'Dark and Deathless Rabble of Long Shadows', 7.
87 See John Watney, 'Introduction', in *Peake's Progress: Selected Writings and Drawings of Mervyn Peake*, ed. Maeve Gilmore (1978; repr., London: British Library, 2011), 20 (13–33).
88 Peter McKenzie, 'Memories of Mervyn: A Review of John Watney's Biography with Reminiscences and Other Contributions', *MPR* 4 (Spring 1977): 22 (17–26).

89 Ibid.
90 Peake, *Titus Alone* (1959), rev. edn 1970, in *The Illustrated Gormenghast Trilogy*, one-volume edn of *The Gormenghast Trilogy* (1992; repr., London: Vintage, 2011), 770 (749–943).
91 Maeve Gilmore, *A World Away: A Memoir of Mervyn Peake* (London: Gollancz, 1970), 18.
92 John Carey, 'Deadly Slapstick', *New Statesman*, 26 July 1974, 121 (121–2).
93 Peake, 'London Fantasy' (1949), *PS* 9, no. 4 (April 2006): 5 (3–7).
94 Ibid.
95 Peake, *Titus Alone*, 848.
96 Ibid.
97 Dickens, *Bleak House*, 677.
98 Ibid.
99 G. Peter Winnington (ed.), *Mervyn Peake: The Man and His Art* (London: Peter Owen, 2006), 165.
100 Peake, 'The Cocky Walkers' (1937), in *Mervyn Peake: Collected Poems*, ed. R. W. Maslen (Manchester: Carcanet, 2008), 32 (31–2).
101 Ibid.
102 Peake, 'London Fantasy', 3.
103 Michael Moorcock (writing as 'James Colvin'), 'A Literature of Acceptance', *New Worlds*, no. 178 (December 1967/January 1968): 60 (59–61). The title of *New Worlds* altered over the course of its publication, from *New Worlds Science Fiction* to *New Worlds Speculative Fiction* to *New Worlds* to *New Worlds Quarterly*. The first three titles are shortened as *New Worlds* and abbreviated as *NW*. *New Worlds Quarterly* is abbreviated as *NWQ*, because it marked a change in format and a resetting of the magazine's issue numbers.
104 Ibid.
105 M. John Harrison, 'By Tennyson Out of Disney', *NWQ* 2 (1971): 181 (181–5).
106 Ibid.
107 Moorcock, 'Mervyn Peake – An Obituary', *NW*, no. 187 (February 1969): 57 (57–8).
108 Ibid.
109 Neil Gaiman, 'A Speech I Once Gave: On Lewis, Tolkien and Chesterton', delivered 2004, posted 2012, blog post, *Journal* [Neil Gaiman's personal website], http://journal.neilgaiman.com/2012/01/speech-i-once-gave-on-lewis-tolkien-and.html [accessed 26 December 2019].
110 Gaiman, 'Neil Gaiman Introduces Neverwhere', *The Telegraph*, posted 3 January 2010, https://www.telegraph.co.uk/expat/expatlife/6915542/Neil-Gaiman-introduces-Neverwhere.html [accessed 8 August 2019].
111 Chesterton, *Charles Dickens*, 64.
112 Ibid., 65.

113 Gaiman, qtd. in 'Down Town', *GQ Magazine*, 1 October 1996, 46 (46).

114 Gaiman, and Jayme Blaschke [interviewer], 'Voices of Vision: Neil Gaiman', conducted 2002, in *Conversations with Neil Gaiman*, ed. Joseph Michael Sommers (Jackson: UP of Mississippi, 2018), 103.

115 Gaiman, *Neverwhere* (1996), rev. edn retitled *Neverwhere: Author's Preferred Text* (London: Headline, 2005), 19.

116 Gaiman, 'Chat with Neil Gaiman', 'weekly chats', conducted 22 October 1998, *Event Horizon*, http://www.astralgia.com/sfzine/chats/transcripts/102298.html [accessed 10 August 2019].

117 Miéville, 'Reveling in Genre', 369.

118 Miéville, 'Introduction' (2011), in *Illustrated Gormenghast Trilogy*, x (ix–xii).

119 Miéville, 'Author Q&A', posted 2010, *Random House* http://www.randomhouse.com/rhpg//rc/library/display.pperl?isbn=9780345497529&view=qa [accessed 10 August 2019].

120 Miéville, *The Tain* (2002), in *Looking for Jake and Other Stories* (2005; repr., London: Pan, 2011), 292 (225–300).

121 Ibid.

122 Ruskin, '*To* Charles Eliot Norton' (19 June 1870), in *The Letters of John Ruskin,* vol. 2, *1870–1889*, eds E. T. Cook and Alexander Wedderburn, vol. 37 of *The Works of John Ruskin*, library edn (London: George Allen, 1909), 7 (7).

123 Ruskin, 'Fiction Fair and Foul' (June 1880), part 1, in *The Storm-Cloud of the Nineteenth Century; On the Old Road; Arrows of the Chace; Ruskiniana*, eds Cook and Wedderburn, vol. 34 of *The Works of John Ruskin* (London: George Allen, 1908), 276 (263–397).

124 Ruskin, '*To* Charles Eliot Norton' (8 July 1870), in *The Letters of John Ruskin*, vol. 2, 10 (9–10).

125 Ruskin, '*To* Charles Eliot Norton' (19 June 1870), 7 and Ruskin, '*To* Charles Eliot Norton' (8 July 1870), 10.

126 Ruskin, '*To* W. H. Harrison' (17 July 1870), in *The Letters of John Ruskin*, vol. 2, 12 (11–12).

127 Ruskin, *The Stones of Venice*, vol. 3 (1853), in *The Stones of Venice, Volume III and Examples of the Architecture of Venice*, eds Cook and Wedderburn, vol. 11 of *The Works of John Ruskin* (London: George Allen, 1904), 173 (1–307).

128 Ibid., 169.

129 Ruskin, '*To* Charles Eliot Norton' (8 January 1876), in *The Letters of John Ruskin*, vol. 2, 189 (188–9).

130 Ibid.

131 Dickens, 'Old Lamps for New Ones', *HW* 1, no. 12 (15 June 1850): 265 (265–7).

132 Dickens, *Little Dorrit*, 264.

133 Dickens, *Dombey and Son*, 407.

134 Jay Clayton, *Charles Dickens in Cyberspace* (Oxford: OUP, 2003), 3.

135 Wells, qtd. in [anonymous], 'Mr. H. G. Wells on Socialism', *Science Schools Journal* 18 (February 1889): 153 (152–5).
136 Wells, *Joan and Peter: The Story of an Education* (1918), part 1, vol. 23 of *The Works of H. G. Wells, Atlantic Edition* (London: T. Fisher Unwin, 1927), 153.
137 Wells, 'Is Life Becoming Happier?' (1927), in *The Way the World is Going: Guesses & Forecasts of the Years Ahead* (London: Benn, 1928), 191 (190–9).
138 Wells, *The Outline of History; Being a Plain History of Life and Mankind* (1919–20), 4th revision, vol. 2 (1920; repr., London: Cassell, 1925), 603.
139 Ibid., 604.
140 George MacDonald, 'The Imagination: Its Function and Its Culture' (1867), in *The Princess and the Goblin and Other Fairy Tales*, eds Shelley King and John Pierce (Toronto: Broadview, 2014), 339 (327–55).
141 MacDonald, 'The Fantastic Imagination' (1893), in *The Princess and the Goblin and Other Fairy Tales*, 326 (321–7).
142 Ibid.
143 Ibid., 323.
144 MacDonald, 'A Journey Rejourneyed', part 1, *The Argosy: A Magazine of Tales, Travels, Essays, and Poems* 1, no. 1 (December 1865): 59 (53–63).
145 MacDonald, 'The Imagination', 333.
146 Ruskin, 'Fiction Fair and Foul', part 1, 297.
147 Ibid., 294.
148 Ibid., 293.
149 MacDonald, *The Marquis of Lossie* (1877; repr., London: Cassell, 1927), 57.
150 Wells, *'42 to '44: A Contemporary Memoir Upon Human Behaviour During the Crisis of the World Revolution* (London: Secker & Warburg, 1944), 139.
151 Ibid.
152 Ibid.
153 Tolkien, 'On Fairy-Stories', 60.
154 Ibid., 67.
155 Ibid., 60.
156 Ibid.
157 Ibid., 44.
158 Ibid.
159 Ibid., 75.
160 Ibid., 65.
161 Ibid.
162 Ibid.
163 Ibid.
164 Lewis, 'To Jane Gaskell' (1957), in *C. S. Lewis: Collected Letters,* ed. Walter Hooper, vol. 3, *Narnia, Cambridge and Joy 1950–1963* (London: HarperCollins, 2006), 880 (879–82).

165 Ibid.
166 Ibid., 880–1.
167 Lewis, *The Magician's Nephew* (1955), in *The Chronicles of Narnia* (1950–6; repr., London: HarperCollins, 2004), 12 (7–106).
168 Ibid., 64.
169 Lewis, 'Is Theology Poetry?' (1952), in *C. S. Lewis: Essay Collection and Other Short Pieces*, ed. Lesley Walmsley (London: HarperCollins, 2000), 13 (10–21).
170 Lewis, letter to Robert Lancelyn Green (28 December 1938), in *C. S. Lewis: Collected Letters*, vol. 2, *Books, Broadcasts and War 1931–1949*, ed. Hooper (San Francisco: HarperCollins, 2004), 236–7 (236–7).
171 Ibid.
172 Orwell, 'As I Please' (1944), in *I Have Tried to Tell the Truth: 1943–1944*, vol. 16 of *The Complete Works of George Orwell*, ed. Davison (London: Secker & Warburg, 1998), 440 (439–45).
173 Orwell, 'Review of *That Hideous Strength* by C. S. Lewis' (1945), in *I Belong to the Left: 1945*, vol. 17 of *The Complete Works of George Orwell*, ed. Peter Davison (London: Secker & Warburg, 1998), 251 (250–2).
174 Orwell, *The Lion and the Unicorn* (1941), in *A Patriot After All*, 407 (391–434).
175 Orwell, *The Road to Wigan Pier* (1937), ed. Davison, vol. 5 of *The Complete Works of George Orwell*, (1986; repr., London: Secker & Warburg, 1998), 109.
176 Peake, qtd. in Moorcock, 'An Excellence of Peake', *PS* 6, no. 4 (April 2000): 9 (7–13).
177 Ibid.
178 Peake, qtd. in John Wood, 'Mervyn Peake: A Pupil Remembers', *MPR* 12 (Spring 1981): 25 (15–28).
179 Ibid.
180 Tolkien, 'On Fairy-Stories', 81.
181 Peake, 'Introduction', in *Drawings by Mervyn Peake* (London: Grey Walls, 1949), 11 (7–11).
182 Ibid., 11, 9, 8.
183 James Gifford, *A Modernist Fantasy: Modernism, Anarchism, & the Radical Fantastic* (Victoria, Canada: ELS, 2018), 123. I am indebted to Erin Horáková for calling my attention to this piece and generously supplying me with a copy of it.
184 Moorcock, 'An Excellence of Peake', 9.
185 Michael Moorcock and Charles Platt, 'Barbarella and the Anxious Frenchman', *NW*, no. 179 (February 1968): 21 (13–23).
186 Moorcock, *Epic Pooh* ([Dagenham]: British Fantasy Society, 1978), [5].
187 Ibid.
188 Ibid., [4].
189 Ibid.
190 Ibid.

191 Moorcock, 'Starship Stormtroopers', *Anarchist Review* 1, no. 4 (1978): 41 (40–4).
192 Harrison, 'By Tennyson Out of Disney', 184.
193 Ibid.
194 Ibid., 183.
195 Ibid.
196 Ibid.
197 Harrison, 'A Literature of Comfort', *NWQ* 1 (1971): 167 (166–72).
198 Ibid., 172.
199 Ibid., 171.
200 The original source has been taken down, but not before it was quoted in numerous other sources. Original reference: 'Debate', *China Miéville Official Website, Panmacmillan*, http://www.panmacmillan.com/features/china/debate.htm. For a partial reprint, see Henry Farrell, 'Socialist Surrealism: China Miéville's New Crobuzon Novels', in *New Boundaries in Political Science Fiction*, eds Donald Hassler and Clyde Wilcox (South Carolina: University of South Carolina Press, 2008), 272 (272–9).
201 Miéville and John Newsinger [interviewer], 'Fantasy and Revolution: an interview with China Miéville', *International Socialism Journal*, no. 88 (Autumn 2000), http://pubs.socialistreviewindex.org.uk/isj88/newsinger.htm [accessed 2 May 2015].
202 Miéville, 'Appropriate Means', (172).
203 Ibid.
204 Ibid., (171).
205 Ibid., (175).
206 Ibid., (171).
207 Gaiman, 'A Speech I Once Gave', (n.p.).
208 Ibid.
209 This discussion of the term 'urban fantasy' and its vicissitudes owes a debt to Stefan Ekman, 'Urban Fantasy: A Literature of the Unseen', *Journal of the Fantastic in the Arts* 27, no. 3 (2016): 452–69.
210 David Langford, addendum (2012) to Clute, 'Urban Fantasy' (1997), *The Encyclopedia of Fantasy*, rev. edn online, entry updated 2012, http://sf-encyclopedia.uk/fe.php?nm=urban_fantasy [accessed 15 May 2015].
211 Irvine, 'Urban Fantasy', 200.
212 Mendlesohn and Edward James, *A Short History of Fantasy* (London: Middlesex UP, 2009), 26.
213 Helen Young, *Race and Popular Fantasy Literature: Habits of Whiteness* (New York: Routledge, 2016), 141.
214 Ibid. Emphasis mine, H-EA.
215 James, 'Tolkien, Lewis and the Explosion of Genre Fantasy', in *Cambridge Companion to Fantasy Literature*, 62.

216 Fredric Jameson, *Archaeologies of the Future: The Desire Called Utopia and Other Science Fictions* (2005; repr., London: Verso, 2007), 67.
217 Brian Atterbery, *Strategies of Fantasy* (Indianapolis: Indiana UP, 1992), 14.
218 Darko Suvin, 'Considering the Sense of "Fantasy" or "Fantastic Fiction": An Effusion', *Extrapolation* 41, no. 3 (Fall 2000): 236 (210–47).
219 Moorcock, 'Metropolitan Dreams: Review of *The Portrait of Mrs Charbuque* and *The Physiognomy* by Jeffrey Ford' (2003), in *Wizardry & Wild Romance: A Study of Epic Fantasy* (1987), rev. edn (Austin: MonkeyBrain, 2004), 171 (171–3).
220 Moorcock, 'Facing the City: Review of *Veniss Underground* by Jeff VanderMeer' (2003), in *Wizardry & Wild Romance*, 183 (183–5).
221 Dirk Vanderbeke, 'The Sub-Creation of Sub-London: Neil Gaiman's and China Miéville's Urban Fantasy', in *From Peterborough to Faëry: The Poetics and Mechanics of Secondary Worlds; Essays in Honour of Dr. Allan G. Turner's 65th Birthday*, eds Vanderbeke and Thomas Honegger (Zurich: Walking Tree, 2014), 142 (141–65).
222 Ibid.
223 See special issue on The British SF Boom, *SFS*, 30, no. 3, particularly Andrew M. Butler, 'Thirteen Ways of Looking at the British Boom', 374–93 and Bould, 'What Kind of Monster Are You?: Situating the Boom', 394–416.
224 Parrinder, 'The Age of Fantasy' (1982), in *The Failure of Theory* (Sussex: Harvester, 1987), 109–14.
225 Germaine Greer, 'Books of the Century: Germaine Greer on Our Readers' Poll', *W: The Waterstone's Magazine* 8 (Winter/Spring 1997): 4 (2–9).
226 John Mullan, qtd. in Alison Flood, 'Science Fiction Author Hits Out at Booker Judges', *The Guardian*, 18 September 2009, https://www.theguardian.com/books/2009/sep/18/science-fiction-booker-prize [accessed 13 August 2019].
227 Jonathan Jones, 'Get Real. Terry Pratchett Is Not a Literary Genius', *The Guardian*, 31 August 2015, https://www.theguardian.com/artanddesign/jonathanjonesblog/2015/aug/31/terry-pratchett-is-not-a-literary-genius [accessed 13 August 2019].

Chapter 1

1 Raymond Williams, *The Country and the City* (London: Chatto & Windus, 1973), 1.
2 Ibid., 2.
3 [Anonymous], 'A Parthian Glance at '56', *The Building News* 3 (1857): 1 (1–2).
4 See Jerry White, *London in the Nineteenth Century: A Human Awful Wonder of God* (London: Jonathan Cape, 2007), 50.
5 See Christopher Chalklin, *The Rise of the English Town, 1650–1850* (Cambridge: CUP, 2001), 9.

6 See Tyler Edward Stovall, *The Rise of the Paris Red Belt* (Berkeley: University of California Press, 1990), 18.
7 See Richard Lawton, 'Census Data for Urban Areas', in *Census and Social Structure: An Interpretive Guide to 19th Century Census for England and Wales*, ed. Lawton (Abingdon: Frank Cass, 1978), 82 (82–145).
8 See Chalklin, *Rise of the English Town*, 9.
9 Masson, *British Novelists and Their Styles*, 238.
10 Ibid., 239.
11 See Edwin Chadwick, *Report on the Sanitary Condition of the Labouring Population of Great Britain* (1842; repr., Edinburgh: EUP, 1965), 232.
12 See ibid., 231.
13 William Cobbett, 'To Mr. Canning' (1823), in *The Opinions of William Cobbett*, eds James Grande, John Stevenson and Richard Thomas (Surrey: Ashgate, 2013), 84 (84).
14 Daniel Defoe, *A Tour through the Whole Island of Great Britain* (1724–6), vol. 1, rev. edn (London: Dent, 1966), 323.
15 Roger Luckhurst, 'The Contemporary London Gothic and the Limits of the "Spectral Turn"', *Textual Practice* 16, no. 3 (2002): 531 (527–46).
16 Ibid.
17 Dickens, *Dombey and Son*, 480.
18 Ruskin, 'Lecture I: Work' (1865), in *The Crown of Wild Olive* (1866), in *Sesame and Lilies; The Ethics of the Dust; The Crown of Wild Olive; with Letters on Public Affairs, 1859–1866*, eds Cook and Wedderburn, vol. 18 of *The Works of John Ruskin* (London: George Allen, 1905), 406 (401–32).
19 Wells, qtd. in R. Thurston Hopkins, *H. G. Wells: Personality, Character, Topography* (London: Cecil Palmer, 1922), 52.
20 MacDonald, *The Marquis of Lossie*, 111.
21 Dickens, '*To* the Earl of Carlisle' (2 January 1849), in *The Letters of Charles Dickens*, vol. 5, *1847–1849*, eds Graham Storey and K. J. Fielding (Oxford: OUP, 1981), 466–7 (466–7).
22 Ruskin, vol. 2 of *Praeterita* (1886, 1887), in *Praeterita and Dilecta*, containing all three vols of *Praeterita* (1886–9), eds Cook and Wedderburn, vol. 35 of *The Works of John Ruskin* (London: George Allen, 1908), 304 (1–562).
23 See Suzanne Rahn, 'The Sources of Ruskin's *Golden River*', *Victorian Newsletter*, no. 68 (Fall 1985): 1–9.
24 Ruskin, *The King of the Golden River* [written 1841] (1851), in *Early Prose Writings: 1834 to 1843*, eds Cook and Wedderburn, vol. 1 of *The Works of John Ruskin* (London: George Allen, 1903), 313 (305–54).
25 Ruskin, 'Fairy Stories' [written 1868] (1869), in *The Cestus of Aglaia and The Queen of the Air; with Other Papers and Lectures on Art and Literature, 1860–1870*, eds

Cook and Wedderburn, vol. 19 of *The Works of John Ruskin* (London: George Allen, 1905), 236 (232–9).
26 Ruskin, *King of the Golden River*, 313.
27 Ibid., 331.
28 Ibid., 313.
29 Ibid., 325, 314.
30 See Ruskin, vol. 2 of *Modern Painters* (1846), eds Cook and Wedderburn, vol. 4 of *The Works of John Ruskin* (London: George Allen, 1903), 259–61.
31 Ruskin, *King of the Golden River*, 327.
32 Ibid.
33 Ibid., 338.
34 Ibid., 345, 344.
35 Ibid., 326.
36 Ruskin, *Praeterita*, vol. 2, 304.
37 Dickens, 'To C. C. Felton' (2 January 1844), in *The Letters of Charles Dickens*, ed. Kathleen Tillotson, vol. 4, *1844–1846* (Oxford: OUP, 1977), 2 (2–5).
38 Dickens, *A Christmas Carol in Prose: Being a Ghost Story of Christmas* (1843), in *A Christmas Carol and Other Christmas Books*, ed. Robert Douglas-Fairhurst (Oxford: OUP, 2006), 10 (5–83).
39 Ibid.
40 J. Hillis Miller, 'The Fiction of Realism: *Sketches by Boz, Oliver Twist*, and Cruikshank's Illustrations', in *Dickens Centennial Essays*, eds Ada Nisbet and Blake Nevius (Berkeley: University of California Press, 1971), 97.
41 Ibid.
42 See Mary Cathcart Borer, *The City of London: A History* (London: Constable, 1977).
43 See Liza Picard, *Victorian London: The Life of a City 1840–1870* (2005; repr., London: Phoenix, 2006), 73–4.
44 Dickens, 'Gone Astray', *HW* 7, no. 177 (13 August 1853): 554 (553–7).
45 Dickens, *A Christmas Carol: A Facsimile of the Original Manuscript* (1843; repr., London: Cassell, 1897), 8. Douglas-Fairhurst's edition is based on the 1868 Charles Dickens Edition, which Dickens revised slightly to read 'the city of London' (16).
46 Dickens, 'Gone Astray', 554.
47 Dickens, *A Christmas Carol*, 15.
48 Andrew Sanders, *Authors in Context: Charles Dickens* (Oxford: OUP, 2003), 4. See also Edward Cornelius Osborne, *Osborne's London and Birmingham Railway Guide* (London: Simkin, Marshall & Darton & Clark, 1840), 50–1.
49 Dickens, *A Christmas Carol*, 79.
50 Ibid., 83.
51 Ibid., 64.

52 Ibid.
53 Ibid., 14–15.
54 Ibid., 15.
55 Ibid., 46.
56 Ibid., 47.
57 Ibid., 46.
58 Ibid.
59 Ibid.
60 Ibid.
61 Ibid.
62 Orwell, 'Charles Dickens', 48.
63 Ibid., 50.
64 W. T. H. [Full name unknown], 'Ideas Xmas Number' (December 1905), [n.p.]. Scrapbook in the Charles Dickens Museum, uncatalogued collection.
65 Ibid.
66 Ibid.
67 Ibid.
68 Paul Davis, *The Lives and Times of Ebenezer Scrooge* (London: YUP, 1990), 13.
69 Ibid.
70 Ruskin, '*To* Charles Eliot Norton' (19 June 1870), 7.
71 Ibid.
72 See Joshua Taft, 'Disenchanted Religion and Secular Enchantment in *A Christmas Carol*', *Victorian Literature and Culture* 43 (2015): 659–73.
73 Ruskin, *Praeterita*, vol. 2, 351.
74 Edgar Johnson, *Charles Dickens: His Tragedy and Triumph*, vol. 1 (London: Gollancz, 1953), 19.
75 Dickens, *The Life of Our Lord* [written 1849] (1934), in *American Notes; Pictures from Italy; A Child's History of England; The Life of Our Lord*, vol. 1 of *The Nonesuch Dickens*, eds Arthur Waugh, Hugh Walpole, Walter Dexter and Thomas Hatton (Bloomsbury: Nonesuch, 1938), 859 (855–91).
76 Dickens, *A Christmas Carol*, 77.
77 Ibid., 78.
78 Ibid.
79 Ibid.
80 Ibid., 19.
81 Ruskin, *King of the Golden River*, 325.
82 Dickens, *A Christmas Carol*, 16.
83 Ibid., 17.
84 Tolkien, 'On Fairy-Stories', 79.
85 Ibid., 76.

86 Ibid.
87 Dickens, 'Our Next-Door Neighbour' (1836), in *Sketches by Boz: Illustrative of Every-Day Life and Every-Day People* (1833–6), ed. Thea Holme (Oxford: OUP, 1997), 40, 41 (40–6). This reference owes a debt to J. Hillis Miller, 'The Genres of A Christmas Carol', *Dickensian* 89, no. 3 (Winter 1993): 195 (193–206).
88 Ibid.
89 Ruskin, *King of the Golden River*, 326.
90 Dickens, *A Christmas Carol*, 16.
91 Ibid.
92 Ibid., 11.
93 Ibid., 10.
94 Craig Buckwald, 'Stalking the Figurative Oyster: The Excursive Ideal in *A Christmas Carol*', *Studies in Short Fiction* 27, no. 1 (Winter 1990): 3 (1–14).
95 Dickens, *A Christmas Carol*, 81.
96 Ibid.
97 Ibid., 79.
98 Ibid.
99 Ibid.
100 Ibid., 80.
101 Ibid., 81.
102 Ibid., 83.
103 Dickens, 'To C. C. Felton' (2 January 1844), 2.
104 Matthew Beaumont, *Nightwalking: A Nocturnal History of London, Chaucer to Dickens* (London: Verso, 2015), 387.
105 Dickens, 'The Streets – Night' (1836), in *Sketches by Boz*, 53 (53–8).
106 Ibid.
107 Dickens, 'Where We Stopped Growing', *HW* 6, no. 145 (1 January 1853): 362 (361–3).
108 Ibid.
109 Dickens, 'To C. C. Felton' (2 January 1844), 2.
110 Dickens, qtd. in Forster, *Life of Charles Dickens*, 345.
111 Ibid.
112 Ibid., 424.
113 Ibid.
114 Ibid., 423.
115 Ibid.
116 See Michael Slater, 'The Christmas Books', *Dickensian* 65 (1969): 22 (17–24).
117 Dickens, qtd. in Forster, *Life of Charles Dickens*, 426.
118 Ibid., 422.
119 Dickens, *The Chimes: A Goblin Story of Some Bells that Rang an Old Year Out and a New Year In* (1844), in *Christmas Carol and Other Christmas Books*, 87 (85–161).

120 Ibid., 87.
121 Ibid.
122 Ibid.
123 Ibid., 124.
124 Ibid.
125 Ibid., 89.
126 Ibid., 91, 126.
127 Ibid., 88.
128 See George Godwin and John Britton, *The Churches of London: A History and Description of the Ecclesiastical Edifices of the Metropolis* (London: C. Tilt, 1838), vol. 1, 1–14 [paginated erratically].
129 Dickens, *The Chimes*, 88.
130 Stephen Prickett, *Victorian Fantasy* (Sussex: Harvester, 1979), 74, endnote 39.
131 Dickens, 'To Mrs Charles Dickens' (2 December 1844), *Letters of Charles Dickens*, vol. 4, 234 (234–5).
132 Jane R. Cohen, *Charles Dickens and His Original Illustrators* (Columbus: Ohio State UP, 1980), 5.
133 Dickens, 'Gone Astray', 553.
134 Ibid., 554.
135 Ibid.
136 Dickens, *Chimes*, 125.
137 Dickens, 'Old Lamps for New Ones', 267.
138 Dickens, *Chimes*, 128.
139 Ibid.
140 Ibid.
141 Ibid.
142 Ibid.
143 Ibid., 101.
144 Dickens, qtd. in Forster, *Life of Charles Dickens*, 355.
145 Slater, 'Introduction', in *Dickens 1970*, ed. Slater (London: Chapman & Hall, 1970), xii (ix–xiii).
146 Slater, 'The Christmas Books', 21.
147 Alexander Welsh, 'Time and the City in *The Chimes*', *Dickensian* 73 (1977): 12 (8–17).
148 Ibid.
149 Barbara Hardy, *Dickens and Creativity* (London: Continuum, 2008), 43, 44.
150 Clayton, 'The Dickens Tape: Affect and Sound Reproduction in *The Chimes*', in *Dickens and Modernity*, ed. Juliet John (Suffolk: English Association, 2012), 22 (19–40).
151 Dickens, *Chimes*, 88, 122.
152 Ibid., 112.

153 Ibid., 118.
154 Ibid.
155 Ibid., 161.
156 See Gail Turley Houston, *Consuming Fictions: Gender, Class, and Hunger in Dickens's Novels* (Carbondale and Edwardsville: Southern Illinois UP, 1994), 8.
157 'Vagrancy Act 1824', *Official Home of UK Legislation; National Archives,* http://www.legislation.gov.uk/ukpga/Geo4/5/83/section/4 [accessed 3 December 2015].
158 Dickens, qtd. in Forster, *Life of Charles Dickens*, 324.
159 Dickens, *Chimes*, 90.
160 Ibid., 88.
161 Ibid.
162 See Peter Ackroyd, *London: The Biography* (London: Chatto & Windus, 2000), 401–4.
163 Godwin and Britton, *Churches of London*, vol. 1, [2] [paginated erratically].
164 Ibid., [11].
165 Dickens, *Chimes*, 101.
166 Ibid., 104.
167 Dickens, qtd. in Forster, *Life of Charles Dickens*, 355.
168 Dickens, '*To* Douglas Jerrold' (16 November 1844), in *Letters of Charles Dickens*, vol. 4, 218 (218–20).
169 Dickens, '*To* the Earl of Carlisle' (2 January 1849), 467.
170 Dickens, *The Haunted Man and the Ghost's Bargain* (1848), in *Christmas Carol and Other Christmas Books*, 408 (323–408).
171 Slater, 'Christmas Books', 24.
172 [Thomas Hood], 'Master Humphrey's Clock', *Athenaeum* (7 November 1840): 887 (887–8).
173 See Dickens, '*To* Thomas Hood' (late February 1841), in *Letters of Charles Dickens*, vol. 2, *1840–1841*, eds Madeline House and Graham Storey (Oxford: OUP, 1969), 220 (220).
174 See Dickens, 'Preface to the Cheap (1848), Library (1858), and Charles Dickens (1867) Editions', in *The Old Curiosity Shop* (1840–1), ed. Elizabeth M. Brennan (Oxford: OUP, 1997), 610 (609–10).
175 Dickens, *Old Curiosity Shop*, 19.
176 Adorno, 'An Address on Charles Dickens's *The Old Curiosity Shop*' (1931), trans. Michael Hollington, *Dickens Quarterly* 6, no. 3 (September 1989): 101 (95–101).
177 Ian Duncan, *Modern Romance and Transformations of the Novel: The Gothic, Scott, Dickens* (Cambridge: CUP, 1992), 217.
178 Ibid.
179 Dickens, *Old Curiosity Shop*, 9.
180 Beaumont, *Nightwalking*, 385.

181 See Ackroyd, *London*, 136–43.
182 Dickens, 'Seven Dials' (27 September 1836), in *Sketches by Boz*, 71 (69–73).
183 See Vivienne Richmond, *Clothing the Poor in Nineteenth-Century England* (Cambridge: CUP, 2013), 76.
184 Thomas Carlyle, 'Sartor Resartus', *Fraser's Magazine* 10, no. 56 (1834): 78 (77–87).
185 Dickens, 'Meditations in Monmouth Street' (24 September 1836), in *Sketches by Boz*, 75 (74–80).
186 Carey, *The Violent Effigy: A Study of Dickens' Imagination* (1973), 2nd edn (London: Faber and Faber, 1991), 101. See also Elaine Freedgood, *The Ideas in Things* (Chicago: University of Chicago Press, 2006).
187 Beverly Lemire, 'The Second Hand Trade in England, c. 1600–1850', in *Old Clothes, New Looks: Second Hand Fashion*, eds Alexandra Palmer and Hazel Clark (Oxford: Berg, 2005), 41 (29–48).
188 Dickens, 'Meditations in Monmouth Street', 75.
189 Ibid.
190 Ibid., 76, 78.
191 Ibid., 78.
192 Ibid., 76.
193 Ibid., 75.
194 Ibid.
195 Ibid.
196 'Vagrancy Act 1824', [n.p.].
197 Dickens, '*To* the Earl of Carlisle' (2 January 1849), 467.
198 Dickens, *Haunted Man*, 327–8.
199 Dickens, *Charles Dickens' Book of Memoranda*, 14.
200 See Stone, *Dickens and the Invisible World*, 33–5.
201 Dickens, 'The Uncommercial Traveller' ['Nurse's Stories'], *AYR* 3, no. 72 (8 September 1860): 518 (517–21).
202 Dickens, *Haunted Man*, 362–3.
203 Dickens, '*To* the Earl of Carlisle' (2 January 1849), 467.
204 Boris Arvatov, 'Everyday Life and the Culture of the Thing' (1925), trans. Christina Kiaer, *October* 81 (Summer 1997): 121 (119–28).
205 Dickens, *Haunted Man*, 363.
206 Dickens, *A Christmas Carol*, 83; Dickens, *Chimes*, 107; and Dickens, *Haunted Man*, 326.
207 Dickens, *Haunted Man*, 326.
208 Dickens, *Chimes*, 88.
209 Dickens, *Haunted Man*, 326.
210 Ibid.
211 Ibid.

212 Dickens, 'To the Earl of Carlisle' (2 January 1849), 467.
213 See White, *London in the Nineteenth Century*, 32–3.
214 See Dickens, 'On Duty with Inspector Field', *HW* 3, no. 64 (14 June 1851): 267 (265–70).
215 Dickens, 'To W. C. Macready' (24 May 1851), in *Letters of Charles Dickens*, eds Storey, Tillotson and Nina Burgis, vol. 6, *1850–1852* (Oxford: OUP, 1988), 399 (398–9).
216 Dickens, 'To the Earl of Carlisle' (2 January 1849), 466.
217 Dickens, *Haunted Man*, 326.
218 Ibid., 370.
219 Forster, *Life of Charles Dickens*, 11.
220 Dickens, 'To Dr James Kay-Shuttleworth' (5 October 1848), in *Letters of Charles Dickens*, vol. 5, 418 (418).
221 Dickens, *Haunted Man*, 370.
222 Ibid.
223 Ibid.
224 Stone, 'Dickens' Artistry and *The Haunted Man*', *South Atlantic Quarterly* 61, no. 4 (Autumn 1962): 500 (492–505).
225 Ibid.
226 Ibid., 500.
227 Ibid., 501.
228 Dickens, *Haunted Man*, 331.
229 See Brian Cookson, *Crossing the River: The History of London's Thames River Bridges from Richmond to the Tower* (Edinburgh: Mainstream Publishing, 2006).
230 Dickens, qtd. in Forster, *Life of Charles Dickens*, 30.
231 Ibid.
232 See ibid., 26.
233 Ibid., 8.
234 See Cookson, *Crossing the River*, 271.
235 Dickens, *The Pickwick Papers* (1836–7), ed. James Kinsley (Oxford: OUP, 2008), 107.
236 Ibid.
237 Dickens, *Haunted Man*, 388.
238 Dickens, 'Preface' (December 1843), in *Christmas Carol and Other Christmas Books*, 3 (3).
239 Dickens, qtd. in Forster, *Life of Charles Dickens*, 509.
240 Dickens, *Haunted Man*, 408.
241 Luckhurst, *Science Fiction*, 3.
242 Ibid., 29.
243 Dickens, *Dombey and Son*, 234.
244 Dickens, 'Railway Dreaming', *HW* 13, no. 320 (10 May 1856): 385 (385–8).

245 See Dickens, *Bleak House*, 11.
246 Dickens, *Old Curiosity Shop*, 222.
247 See, for instance, Pip's description of Magwitch: 'Something clicked in his throat, as if he had works in him like a clock, and was going to strike.' Dickens, *Great Expectations* (1860–1), ed. Margaret Cardwell (Oxford: OUP, 2008), 17. This insight owes a debt to Pete Orford, 'Dickens and Science Fiction', *19: Interdisciplinary Studies in the Long Nineteenth Century* 10, *Dickens and Science*, eds Holly Furneaux and Ben Winyard, 2010, http://www.19.bbk.ac.uk/articles/10.16995/ntn.527/ [accessed 21 August 2016].
248 See Dickens, 'No. 1 Branch Line: The Signal-Man', *Mugby Junction, Extra Christmas Number, All the Year Round* 16, no. 400 (22 December 1866): 20–5.
249 Dickens, *Bleak House*, 11.
250 Dickens, *Our Mutual Friend*, 420.
251 See Frank Swinnerton, *The Bookman's London* (1951; repr., London: Baker, 1969), 44–6.
252 Rosemary Jackson, *Fantasy: The Literature of Subversion* (1981; repr., London: Routledge, 1988), 133.
253 See Dickens, *Bleak House*, 450.
254 See Dickens, *Our Mutual Friend*, 74.
255 Clute, 'Dickens, Charles', in *The Encyclopedia of Science Fiction*, 2nd edn, eds Clute and Peter Nicholls (1993; repr., London: Orbit, 1999), 330 (330).
256 Ibid.
257 Catherine Waters, *Commodity Culture in Dickens's* Household Words (Hampshire: Ashgate, 2008), 7.
258 Dickens, 'Preliminary Word', 1.
259 Dickens and Wills, 'Notes for *Household Words*' (*c.* 1849–50), transcribed and published by Philip Collins, *Victorian Periodicals Newsletter*, no. 8 (April 1970): 44 (33–46).
260 Ibid.
261 Ibid., 46.
262 Dickens, '*To* W. H. Wills' (17 November 1853), in *Letters of Charles Dickens*, vol. 7, *1853–1855*, eds Storey, Tillotson, Angus Easson (Oxford: OUP, 1993), 200 (200).
263 This line has many variants across the published editions of *Henry V*.
264 See Dickens, '*To* Michael Faraday' (28 May 1850), *Letters of Charles Dickens*, vol. 6, 106 (105–6).
265 Dickens, '*To* Michael Faraday' (6 June 1850), *Letters of Charles Dickens*, vol. 6, 110 (110).
266 See John Drew, Hazel Mackenzie and Ben Winyard, '*Household Words*, Volume I: March 30 – September 21, 1850', *Dickens Quarterly* 29, no. 1 (March 2012): 63 (50–67).

267 Thomas Stone, 'Chemical Contradictions', *HW* 1, no. 25 (14 September 1850): 591 (591–4).
268 Ibid., 592.
269 See Helen Groth, 'Reading Victorian Illusions: Dickens's "Haunted Man" and Dr. Pepper's "Ghost"', *Victorian Studies* 50, no. 1 (Autumn 2007): 43–65.
270 John Henry Pepper, *True History of the Ghost; And All About Metempsychosis* (1890; repr., Cambridge: CUP, 2012), 12.
271 See Ruskin, 'The Pre-Raphaelite Artists', *The Times*, 30 May 1851, 8 (8).
272 Dickens, 'Old Lamps for New Ones', 266, 265.
273 Ibid., 267.
274 Wells, *Boon, the Wild Asses of the Devil, and the Last Trump* (1915), in *Ann Veronica; And Boon*, vol. 13 of *The Works of H. G. Wells, Atlantic Edition* (London: T. Fisher Unwin, 1925), 450 (391–562).
275 See J. R. Piggott, *Palace of the People: The Crystal Palace at Sydenham 1854–1936* (London: Hurst & Company, 2004).
276 Dickens, letter to W H Wills (10 March 1853), in *Charles Dickens as Editor: Being Letters Written by Him to William Henry Wills His Sub-Editor*, ed. R. C. Lehmann (London: Smith, 1912), 100 (99–102).
277 See George Augustus Sala, *The Life and Adventures of George Augustus Sala, Written by Himself*, vol. 1 (1894; repr., London: Cassell, 1895), 436.
278 Ruskin, '*To* Charles Eliot Norton' (8 July 1870), *Letters of John Ruskin*, vol. 2, 10.
279 Wills and Sala, 'Fairyland in 'Fifty-Four', *HW* 8, no. 193 (3 December 1853): 315 (313–17).
280 Ibid., 314.
281 Ibid., 313.
282 Ibid., 317.
283 Ibid.
284 Ibid.
285 Clute, 'Tim Powers: The Anubis Gates' (1983), in *Horror: 100 Best Books*, eds Stephen Jones and Kim Newman (London: Xanadu, 1988), 193 (193–5).
286 Ibid., 194.
287 Chesterton, *Charles Dickens*, 145.
288 Dickens, Untitled Announcement, *AYR* 2, no. 31 (26 November 1859): 95 (95).
289 Dickens, '*To* Sir Edward Bulwer Lytton' (3 August 1860), in *Letters of Charles Dickens*, vol. 9, *1859–1861*, ed. Storey (Oxford: OUP, 1997), 281 (281).
290 Edward Bulwer-Lytton, qtd. in Percy Fitzgerald, *Memories of Charles Dickens* (Bristol and London: J. W. Arrowsmith, 1913), 215.
291 Ibid.
292 Bulwer-Lytton, 'Sir Edward Bulwer Lytton *to* Charles Dickens' (?27 April 1861), in *Letters of Charles Dickens*, vol. 9, 571 (571).

293 See Leslie Mitchell, *Bulwer Lytton: The Rise and Fall of a Victorian Man of Letters* (London: CUP, 2003).
294 Dickens, '*To* Sir Edward Bulwer Lytton' (12 May 1861), in *Letters of Charles Dickens*, vol. 9, 412 (412–14).
295 Orwell, 'Review of *Jules Verne: A Biography*', 368 and Miéville, 'Introduction' (2005), in Wells, *The First Men in the Moon*, ed. Parrinder (1900–1; repr., London: Penguin, 2005), xix (xiii–xxviii).
296 See Dickens, 'Frauds on the Fairies', *HW* 8, no. 184 (1 October 1853): 97–100.
297 Dickens, '*To* the Earl of Carlisle' (2 January 1849), 466.
298 Dickens, '*To* Sir Edward Bulwer Lytton' (12 May 1861), 413.
299 Ibid.
300 Dickens, qtd. in Fitzgerald, *Memories of Charles Dickens*, 213.
301 Dickens, *Chimes*, 88.
302 Dickens, '*To* Sir Edward Bulwer Lytton' (12 May 1861), 413.
303 See Steven McLean, *The Early Fiction of H. G. Wells: Fantasies of Science* (Hampshire: Palgrave, 2009), 15.
304 Wells, 'To Grant Allen' (*c.* 1895), in *The Correspondence of H. G. Wells*, ed. David C. Smith, vol. 1, *1880–1903* (London: Pickering & Chatto, 1998), 245–6 (245–6).
305 Lytton, 'Letter 397' (17 March 1871), in *The Letters of Sir Edward Bulwer-Lytton to the Editors of Blackwood's Magazine, 1840–1873, in the National Library of Scotland*, ed. Malcolm Orthell Usrey (PhD Diss., Texas Technological College, 1963), 411 (411–12).
306 [Anonymous], 'Might and Magnitude', *AYR* 15, no. 361 (24 March 1866): 255 (255–7). This reference is owed to 'Dickens, Charles', entry updated 2019, *The Encyclopedia of Science Fiction*, 3rd edn online, 2011–present, eds John Clute and Peter Nicholls, http://www.sf-encyclopedia.com/entry/dickens_charles [accessed 13 January 2020].
307 Wells, *Experiment in Autobiography: Discoveries and Conclusions of a Very Ordinary Brain (Since 1866)*, vol. 2 (1934; repr., London: Faber and Faber, 1984), 508.

Chapter 2

1 Anonymous, 'Review of *War of the Worlds*', *Critic* 29 (April 1898): 282 (282).
2 See Theodore S. Hamerow, *The Birth of a New Europe: State and Society in the Nineteenth Century* (London: University of North Carolina Press, 1983), 168.
3 See Frederick Nesta, 'The Myth of the "Triple-Headed Monster": The Economics of the Three-Volume Novel', *Publishing History* 61 (2007): 57 (47–69).
4 See Dickens, 'Address', *Athenaeum*, no. 1008 (20 February 1847): 216 (216).

5 See Laurel Brake, 'The Advantage of Fiction: The Novel and the "Success" of the Victorian Periodical', in *A Return to the Common Reader: Print Culture and the Novel, 1850–1900*, eds Adelene Buckland and Beth Palmer (Surrey: Ashgate, 2011), 21 (9–22).
6 Wells, *Experiment in Autobiography*, vol. 2, 506.
7 See Michael Patrick Hearn, 'Introduction', in *The Annotated Christmas Carol: A Christmas Carol by Charles Dickens*, ed. Hearn (1843; repr., New York: Clarkson N. Potter, 1976), 27 (1–51).
8 See H. Rider Haggard, 'Books Which Have Influenced Me', *British Weekly Extra*, no. 1 (London: British Weekly, 1887), 66–7; Robert Louis Stevenson, 'Some Gentlemen in Fiction', *Scribner's Magazine* 3 (January–June 1888): 764–8 and Wells, 'A General Introduction to the Atlantic Edition', in *The Time Machine; The Wonderful Visit; And Other Stories*, vol. 1 of *The Works of H. G. Wells, Atlantic Edition* (London: T. Fisher Unwin, 1924), xiii (ix–xx).
9 Dickens, 'Frauds on the Fairies', 97.
10 Carey, *The Intellectuals and the Masses: Pride and Prejudice among the Literary Intelligentsia, 1880–1939* (London: Faber and Faber, 1992), vii.
11 [Anonymous], 'Books of the Past Year', *The Court Magazine and La Belle Assemblée* 10, no. 1 (January 1837): 12 (4–14).
12 Julian Hawthorne, 'The Romance of the Impossible', *Lippincott's Monthly Magazine* 46 (September 1890): 412 (412–15).
13 Andrew Lang, 'Realism and Romance', *The Contemporary Review* 52 (July 1887): 683 (683–93).
14 Ibid., 684–5.
15 [Anonymous], 'The Supernatural in Current Literature', *Dundee Courier & Argus*, 7 March 1892, [n.p.].
16 [Anonymous], 'Mr. Oscar Wilde's "Dorian Gray"', *Pall Mall Gazette*, 26 June 1890, 3 (3).
17 Ibid.
18 [Anonymous], 'Recent Novels', *Morning Post*, 3 June 1897, 2 (2).
19 [Anonymous], 'New Books', *Birmingham Daily Post*, 19 January 1886, 7 (7).
20 William Blackwood III, 'The Old Saloon', *Blackwood's Edinburgh Magazine* 141, no. 856 (February 1887): 303 (291–315).
21 MacDonald, 'The Fantastic Imagination', 322.
22 J. R. Hammond, *H. G. Wells and the Modern Novel* (Basingstoke: Macmillan, 1988), 80.
23 Wells, *The Time Machine*, *The New Review* 12, no. 68 (January 1895): 98 (98–112).
24 Wells, *The Time Machine*, *The New Review* 12, no. 69 (February 1895): 219 (207–21) and Wells, *The Time Machine* (1895), ed. Parrinder (London: Penguin, 2005), 35.
25 Wells, *The Time Machine*, *The New Review* 12, no. 71 (April 1895): 462 (453–72) and Wells, *The Time Machine* [Parrinder edn], 68.

26 The serialization reads: 'Consider I have been speculating upon the destinies of our race'.
27 Wells, *The Time Machine*, *New Review* 12, no. 72 (May 1895): 584 (577–88) and Wells, *The Time Machine* [Parrinder edn], 87.
28 Dickens, *Christmas Carol*, 22.
29 See MacDonald, 'Fantastic Imagination', 323.
30 Tolkien, 'On Fairy-Stories', 68.
31 Lewis, 'To Jane Gaskell', 880.
32 Tolkien, 'On Fairy-Stories', 68.
33 'invention, n.', *OED Online*, December 2015, OUP, http://www.oed.com.libproxy.ucl.ac.uk/view/Entry/98969?redirectedFrom=invention [accessed 23 February 2016].
34 This insight owes a debt to private correspondence with Simon Bacon.
35 Wells, *Time Machine* [Parrinder edn], 40.
36 Jameson, *Archaeologies of the Future*, 212.
37 Ibid., 72.
38 Wells, *Time Machine* [Parrinder edn], 41.
39 Ibid., 49.
40 Ibid.
41 Ibid.
42 This discussion owes a debt to Stephen Derry, 'The Time Traveller's Utopian Books and His Reading of the Future', *Foundation* 65 (Fall 1995): 16–23.
43 Lytton, *The Coming Race*, ed. David Seed (1871; repr., Middletown: Wesleyan UP, 2006), 93.
44 Ibid., 31.
45 Wells, *Time Machine* [Parrinder edn], 22.
46 Ibid., 49.
47 Ibid., 32–3.
48 Ibid., 49.
49 Ibid., 62.
50 Wells, 'Preface to the Scientific Romances' (1933), in *H. G. Wells's Literary Criticism*, eds Patrick Parrinder and Robert M. Philmus (Sussex: Harvester, 1980), 244 (240–5).
51 Wells, letter to Henry James (8 July 1915), in *Henry James and H. G. Wells: A Record of Their Friendship, Their Debate on the Art of Fiction, and Their Quarrel*, eds Leon Edel and Gordon N. Ray (London: Rupert Hart-Davis, 1958), 263–4 (263–4).
52 Wells, 'General Introduction to the Atlantic Edition', xi.
53 Dickens, 'Preliminary Word', 1.
54 Wells, *Outline of History*, vol. 1, 10; Wells, *The Undying Fire* (1919), in *The Undying Fire; And Philosophical and Theological Speculations*, vol. 11 of *The Works of H. G. Wells, Atlantic Edition* (London: T. Fisher Unwin, 1925), 80 (1–172) and Wells, *Tono-Bungay* (1908–9), ed. Parrinder (London: Penguin, 2005), 112.

55 Wells, 'To the Editor, *Daily Mail*' (10 October 1906), in *Correspondence of H. G. Wells*, vol. 2, *1904–1918*, 112 (112–15).
56 Arnold Bennett, 'Herbert George Wells and His Work' (1902), in *Arnold Bennett and H. G. Wells: A Record of a Personal and a Literary Friendship*, ed. Harris Wilson (London: Rupert Hart-Davis, 1960), 267 (260–76).
57 Simon J. James, *Maps of Utopia: H. G. Wells, Modernity, and the End of Culture* (Oxford: OUP, 2012), 37.
58 Dickens, 'All the Year Round', 601.
59 Dickens, *Our Mutual Friend*, 267.
60 Wells, 'Preface to Volume I', in *The Time Machine; The Wonderful Visit; And Other Stories*, xxiii (xxi–xxiii).
61 Ibid.
62 Wells, *War of the Worlds* [Parrinder edn], 82.
63 Wells, *The Invisible Man* (1897), ed. Parrinder (London: Penguin, 2005), 37.
64 Wells, *Time Machine* [Parrinder edn], 19.
65 Wells, *War of the Worlds* [Parrinder edn], 164.
66 Wells, 'The Door in the Wall' (1906), in *The Country of the Blind and Other Selected Stories*, ed. Parrinder (2005; repr., London: Penguin, 2007), 381 (365–81).
67 Wells, *Time Machine* [Parrinder edn], 89.
68 Dickens, qtd. in Forster, *Life of Charles Dickens*, 727–8.
69 See [Wells], 'The Immature Fantastic', *Saturday Review of Politics, Literature, Science, and Art* (7 November 1896): 499–500. Wells's articles and reviews for the *Saturday Review* were published anonymously. They have been identified by the invaluable work of Robert M. Philmus in 'H. G. Wells as Literary Critic for the *Saturday Review*', *SFS* 4, no. 2 (July 1977): 166–93.
70 Wells, 'Preface to the Scientific Romances', 241.
71 Wells, 'The Contemporary Novel' (1911), in *A Modern Utopia; And Other Discussions*, vol. 9 of *The Works of H. G. Wells, Atlantic Edition* (London: T. Fisher Unwin, 1925), 359, 358 (355–80).
72 Wells, *The War of the Worlds* [serialization], 'XVII. – The Thunder-Child' and 'XVIII. – London Under the Martians', *Pearson's Magazine* 4, no. 22 (October 1897): 453 (447–56).
73 Ibid.
74 Ibid.
75 Wells, 'Preface to the Scientific Romances', 242.
76 Ibid., 241.
77 Wells, 'To Grant Allen' (c. 1895), 245–6.
78 Dickens, qtd. in Forster, *Life of Charles Dickens*, 378.
79 Wells, 'My Auto-Obituary', *Strand Magazine* 104a (January 1943): 46 (45–7).

80 Ibid.
81 Ibid.
82 This section owes a debt to Pete Orford, 'The Ghosts and the Machine: *A Christmas Carol* and Time Travel', *Academia Edu* https://www.academia.edu/3122878/The_Ghosts_and_the_Machine_A_Christmas_Carol_and_Time_Travel [accessed 9 September 2019].
83 Dickens, *Christmas Carol*, 30, 64.
84 Wells, *Time Machine* [Parrinder edn], 20, 86.
85 Dickens, *Christmas Carol*, 78.
86 Wells, *Time Machine* [Parrinder edn], 88–9.
87 Dickens, *Christmas Carol*, 22.
88 Wells, *Time Machine* [Parrinder edn], 7.
89 Ibid., 11.
90 Wells, *Experiment in Autobiography*, vol. 1, 114.
91 Wells, *Time Machine* [Parrinder edn], 9.
92 Ibid., 44.
93 Ibid., 90.
94 See David Y. Hughes, 'A Queer Notion of Grant Allen's', *SFS* 25, no. 2 (July 1998): 271–84.
95 See Peter Morton, *The Busiest Man in England: Grant Allen and the Writing Trade, 1875–1900* (New York: Palgrave, 2005).
96 Wells, *Time Machine* [Parrinder edn], 44.
97 Ibid.
98 Grant Allen, 'Pallinghurst Barrow' (1892), in *Ivan Greet's Masterpiece* (London: Chatto & Windus, 1893), 67–8 (67–89).
99 Dickens, *Christmas Carol*, 62.
100 Ibid.
101 Michael R. Page, *The Literary Imagination from Erasmus Darwin to H. G. Wells: Science, Evolution, and Ecology* (Farnham: Ashgate, 2012), 162.
102 David L. Pike, *Subterranean Cities: The World beneath Paris and London, 1800–1945* (Ithaca: Cornell UP, 2005), 83.
103 Wells, *Time Machine* [Parrinder edn], 48.
104 Dickens, *Christmas Carol*, 77.
105 Wells, *Time Machine* [Parrinder edn], 78.
106 See Charles Lyell, *Principles of Geology* (1830–1833), selected text from the three-volume 1st edn, ed. James A. Secord (London: Penguin, 1997), 437.
107 See Klaus Mainzer, *Thinking in Complexity: The Complex Dynamics of Matter, Mind, and Mankind* (1994), 3rd edn (London: Springer, 1997), 85.
108 Wells, 'Preface' (1931), in *Time Machine* [Parrinder edn], 95 (93–6).
109 Wells, *Time Machine* [Parrinder edn], 48.

110 Wells, 'What I Believe' (1899), in *When the Sleeper Wakes: A Critical Text of the 1899 New York and London First Edition*, ed. Leon Stover (Jefferson, NC: McFarland & Company, 2000), 385 (384–8).
111 See Leland L. Duncan, *History of the Borough of Lewisham* (1908; repr., London: Blackheath Press, 1973), 150.
112 Wells, *Time Machine* [Parrinder edn], 64.
113 Wills and Sala, 'Fairyland in 'Fifty-Four', 317.
114 Wells, *Time Machine* [Parrinder edn], 64.
115 Ibid.
116 Wills and Sala, 'Fairyland in 'Fifty-Four', 317.
117 Ibid.
118 Wells, *Time Machine* [Parrinder edn], 64–5.
119 Wills and Sala, 'Fairyland in 'Fifty-Four', 317.
120 Wells, *Time Machine* [Parrinder edn], 67.
121 See A. H. Watkins, 'Charles Dickens and H. G. Wells', in *Occasional Papers: Supplement to the H. G. Wells Society*, no. 2 (Middlesex.: The H. G. Wells Society, 1976), 1–3 (1–8).
122 Wells, *Tono-Bungay*, 231.
123 Wells, *The World Set Free: A Story of Mankind* (London: Macmillan, 1914), 68.
124 An earlier version of this section and the following sections was published in shorter altered form in Hadas Elber-Aviram, '"My Own Particular City": H. G. Wells's Fantastical London', *The Wellsian*, no. 38 (2015): 97–117. These sections have been substantially revised for this book. They are included with the kind permission of Simon J. James, who was the editor of the *Wellsian* at the time of the article's publication.
125 See Roy Porter, *London: A Social History* (London: Penguin, 2000), 249.
126 See ibid., 13, 264, 334.
127 Ibid., 250.
128 Ibid.
129 Wells, *Experiment in Autobiography*, vol. 1, 275.
130 Ibid.
131 See White, *London in the Nineteenth Century*, 91.
132 George Lear, letter to Frederick George Kitton (17 December 1886), in Kitton, *Charles Dickens by Pen and Pencil* (London: Sabin, 1890), 131 (131–13).
133 Wells, *War of the Worlds* [Parrinder edn], 82.
134 White, *London in the Nineteenth Century*, 86. See also 'Ealing', in *The London Encyclopaedia,* 3rd edn, eds Christopher Hibbert, Ben Weinreb, Julia Keay and John Keay (1983; repr., London: Macmillan, 2010), 258 (258).
135 'East Ham', in *London Encyclopaedia*, 260 (260).
136 Ibid.

137 See Robert Gray, *A History of London* (1978; repr., London: Hutchinson, 1984), 258–9 and Edward Stanford, 'Stanford's Map of London According to the Local Government Act' (1888), *National Library of Australia*, MAP RM 1942, https://nla.gov.au/nla.obj-231664130/view [accessed 9 September 2019].
138 Wells, 'To Elizabeth Healey' (23 February 1888), in *Correspondence of H. G. Wells*, vol. 1, 82 (81–2). Underlines in original.
139 Hugh McLeod, *Class and Religion in the Late Victorian City* (London: Croom Helm, 1974), 133.
140 See Chris Jeppesen et al., *St Pancras International: 150 Facts for 150 Years* (Gloucestershire: History Press, 2018), 29–32 and Edward Royle, *Radicals, Secularists, and Republicans: Popular Freethought in Britain, 1866-1915* (Manchester: MUP, 1980), 49.
141 See Paul Thompson, *Socialists, Liberals and Labour: The Struggle for London, 1885–1914* (London: Routledge and Kegan Paul, 1967), 18; Richard Flanagan, *'Parish-Fed Bastards': A History of the Politics of the Unemployed in Britain, 1884–1939* (London: Greenwood Press, 1991), 28–9, 247 fn. 24 and Alan Marne McBriar, *Fabian Socialism and English Politics, 1884-1918* (Cambridge: CUP, 1962), 202, fn. 4.
142 Wells, *Invisible Man*, 94.
143 Wells, *Tono-Bungay*, 105.
144 Wells, *Invisible Man*, 103.
145 Ibid., 121.
146 Ibid.
147 Wells, *Tono-Bungay*, 94, 105.
148 Wells, *The Invisible Man*, 120, 121.
149 Wells, 'Preface to the Scientific Romances', 243.
150 James, *Maps of Utopia*, 37.
151 Wells, 'A Story of the Days to Come' (1899), in *Tales of Space and Time* (1899; repr., London: Harper & Brothers, 1900), 232 (165–324).
152 Ibid.
153 Wells, *Experiment in Autobiography*, vol. 1, 275, 276.
154 Ibid., 216.
155 Wells, *A Modern Utopia* (1904–5), eds Parrinder and Gregory Claeys (London: Penguin, 2005), 165.
156 Dickens, *Charles Dickens' Book of Memoranda*, 14.
157 Ibid.
158 Wells, 'The Crystal Egg' (1897), in *Country of the Blind*, 164 (164–81).
159 See White, *London in the Nineteenth Century*, 301.
160 Wells, 'The Crystal Egg', 181.
161 Ibid., 167.
162 Wells, *Kipps: The Story of a Simple Soul* (1905), ed. James (London: Penguin, 2005), 280.

163 Wells, 'The Crystal Egg', 177.
164 Wells, 'A Chat with the Author of *The Time Machine*', 6.
165 Wells, 'The Crystal Egg', 178.
166 Ibid.
167 See White, *London in the Nineteenth Century*, 26.
168 Wells, *War of the Worlds* [Parrinder edn], 161.
169 Ibid., 162.
170 Ibid., 161–2.
171 Ibid., 163, 167.
172 Ibid., 163.
173 Ibid., 167.
174 Ibid., 165.
175 Tom Gibbons, 'H. G. Wells's Fire Sermon: *The War of the Worlds* and the Book of Revelation', *Science Fiction: A Review of Speculative Literature* 6, no. 1 (1984): 12 (5–14).
176 Frank McConnell, *The Science Fiction of H. G. Wells* (Oxford: OUP, 1981), 139.
177 Wells, *War of the Worlds* [Parrinder edn], 73.
178 Ibid., 75.
179 Wells, *War of the Worlds* [serialization], 'XIV. In London' and 'XV. – What Had Happened in Surrey', *Pearson's Magazine* 4, no. 20 (August 1897): 228 (221–32) and Wells, *The War of the Worlds* (London: William Heinemann, 1898), 133.
180 Wells, *The War of the Worlds* (1897), in *The Invisible Man; The War of the Worlds; A Dream of Armageddon*, vol. 3 of *The Works of H. G. Wells, Atlantic Edition* (London: T. Fisher Unwin, 1924), 318 (207–451).
181 Wells, *War of the Worlds* [Parrinder edn], 80.
182 Ibid., 166.
183 Ibid.
184 Ibid., 77.
185 Ibid., 105.
186 Ibid., 170.
187 Ibid., 82.
188 Ibid., 169.
189 Ibid.
190 Ibid., 170.
191 See 'Stanford's map of London according to the Local Government Act'.
192 An extreme example is Stover, *The Prophetic Soul: A Reading of H. G. Wells's Things to Come* (London: McFarland, 1987). More nuanced claims to this effect may be found in Carey, *The Intellectuals and the Masses*, 118–34, 135–51.
193 Wells, *War of the Worlds* [Parrinder edn], 152–3.
194 Ibid., 170.
195 Ibid.
196 ibid.

197 Ibid.
198 White, *London in the Nineteenth Century*, 98.
199 See David Welsh, *Underground Writing: The London Tube from George Gissing to Virginia Woolf* (Liverpool: LUP, 2010), 113, 121.
200 See Sally Mitchell, *Daily Life in Victorian England* (1996), 2nd edn (Westport, CT: Greenwood, 2009), 228–9.
201 Wells, *Experiment in Autobiography*, vol. 1, 30.
202 Ibid.
203 Ibid.
204 Ibid., 199.
205 Ibid., 279.
206 Ibid., 279–80.
207 Wells, *War of the Worlds* [Atlantic edn], 315. c.f. Wells, *War of the Worlds* [serialization], 'XIV. – In London' and 'XV. – What Had Happened in Surrey', *Pearson's Magazine* 4, no. 20 (August 1897): 226 (221–32) and *War of the Worlds* [1898 Heinemann edn], 130. See also Edward Stanford, 'Stanford's Map of Central London' (1897), *National Library of Australia*, MAP RM 1484, https://nla.gov.au/nla.obj-266892784/view [accessed 19 September 2019].
208 Wells, *War of the Worlds* [serialization], 'XXI. – After the Fifteen Days (*continued*)' and 'XXII. – The Epilogue', *Pearson's Magazine* 4, no. 24 (December 1897): 736 (736–45).
209 Wells, *War of the Worlds* [Heinemann edn], 276.
210 John Huntington, *The Logic of Fantasy: H. G. Wells and Science Fiction* (New York: Columbia UP, 1982), 21.
211 Wells, 'The Remarkable Case of Davidson's Eyes' (1895), in *Country of the Blind*, 20 (12–21).
212 Wells, 'Door in the Wall', 366.
213 Wells, 'Remarkable Case of Davidson's Eyes', 21.
214 ibid.
215 Ibid., 16.
216 Ibid., 17.
217 Wells, 'Remarkable Case of Davidson's Eyes', 17.
218 See 'St Pancras', in *London Encyclopaedia*, 803 (803).
219 Wells, 'Remarkable Case of Davidson's Eyes', 17.
220 Ibid., 18.
221 Ibid.
222 Wells, *War of the Worlds* [Parrinder edn], 161.
223 Wells, 'Remarkable Case of Davidson's Eyes', 20.
224 Ibid.
225 This discussion owes a debt to Laura Scuriatti, 'A Tale of Two Cities: H. G. Wells's *The Door in the Wall*, Illustrated by Alvin Langdon Coburn', *Wellsian*, no. 22 (1999): 26–7 (11–28).

226 Wells, 'Door in the Wall', 367.
227 See White, *London in the Nineteenth Century*, 92.
228 See Porter, *London: A Social History*, 260; Charles Booth, *Life and Labour of the People in London, First Series: Poverty* (1891), rev. edn, vol. 2, *Streets and Population Classified* (London: Macmillan, 1902), 28 and 'Charles Booth's London: Poverty Maps and Police Notebooks' (1886–1903), *London School of Economics and Political Science*, https://booth.lse.ac.uk/map/16/-0.2052/51.5095/100/1 [accessed 24 July 2019].
229 Wells, 'Door in the Wall', 373.
230 Ibid., 368.
231 Dickens, 'Preliminary Word', 1.
232 Wells, 'Door in the Wall', 367.
233 Ibid., 369.
234 Ibid., 367.
235 Wells, 'Remarkable Case of Davidson's Eyes', 20.
236 Wells, 'Door in the Wall', 377.
237 Ibid., 373.
238 Ibid.
239 Ibid.
240 Michel de Certeau, *The Practice of Everyday Life*, trans. Steven Rendall (1984; repr., Berkeley: University of California, 1988), 98.
241 Ibid., 102.
242 Wells, 'Door in the Wall', 371.
243 Ibid.
244 Ibid., 372.
245 Ibid., 373.
246 Ibid.
247 Dickens, 'Gone Astray', 553.
248 See ibid., 557.
249 Wells, 'Door in the Wall', 381.
250 Ibid.
251 Wells, 'Fiction about the Future' (1938), in *H. G. Wells's Literary Criticism*, 247 (246–51).
252 Ibid.
253 Ibid.
254 Wells, *Experiment in Autobiography*, vol. 2, 645.
255 Wells, *This Misery of Boots* (1907), in *Anticipations; And Other Papers*, vol. 4 of *The Works of H. G. Wells, Atlantic Edition* (London: T. Fisher Unwin, 1924), 411 (390–414).
256 Ibid., 410.

257 Wells, *When the Sleeper Wakes* (1899), ed. John Sutherland (Ontario: Broadview, 2019), 159.
258 Wells, 'Preface' (1921), in *The Sleeper Awakes and Men Like Gods*, rev. edn of *When the Sleeper Wakes* (London: Odhams, 1921), [8] ([7–9]).
259 Bergonzi, *The Early H. G. Wells: A Study of the Scientific Romances* (Manchester: MUP, 1961), 145.
260 Ibid.
261 Wells, *Modern Utopia*, 238.
262 Wells, *When the Sleeper Wakes* [Sutherland edn], 190–1.
263 Ibid., 191.
264 Ibid., 231.
265 See Wells, *Experiment in Autobiography*, vol. 1, 333–52.
266 See Sutherland, 'A Note on the Text', in *When the Sleeper Wakes* [Sutherland edn], 43 (43–6).
267 See Wells, *Experiment in Autobiography*, vol. 2, 557–85.
268 'Waterloo Station', in *London Encyclopaedia*, 992 (992).
269 Wells, *When the Sleeper Wakes* [Sutherland edn], 152–3.
270 Ibid., 220.
271 Ibid., 221.
272 See Stephen Inwood, *A History of London* (London: Macmillan, 1998), 36.
273 Wells, *Tono-Bungay*, 385.
274 Wells, *Experiment in Autobiography*, vol. 1, 315.
275 Wells, *In the Days of the Comet* (1906), in *In the Days of the Comet; And Seventeen Short Stories*, vol. 10 of *The Works of H. G. Wells, Atlantic Edition* (London: T. Fisher Unwin, 1925), 286 (1–319).
276 Wells, *Tono-Bungay*, 385.
277 James, *Maps of Utopia*, 131.
278 Wells, 'A Dream of Armageddon' (1901), in *Country of the Blind*, 275 (269–95).
279 Ibid.
280 Wells, 'Story of the Days to Come', 268.
281 Wells, *When the Sleeper Wakes* [Sutherland edn], 203.
282 Wells, 'Story of the Days to Come', 323.
283 Wells, *When the Sleeper Wakes* [Sutherland edn], 123.
284 Ibid., 144.
285 Ibid., 204.
286 Carey, *Intellectuals and the Masses*, 147.
287 For a fuller account of this shift and its causes, see Elber-Aviram, 'My Own Particular City'.
288 Wells, *When the Sleeper Wakes* [serialization], *Graphic*, no. 1536 (6 May 1899): 563 (561–3).

289 c.f. Wells, *When the Sleeper Wakes* [Sutherland edn], 258.
290 See [anonymous], 'The 1992 Weekend Conference: The Short Stories of H. G. Wells', *The H. G. Wells Newsletter* 3, no. 3 (Winter 1992): 3 (3–4).
291 Wells, *When the Sleeper Wakes* [Sutherland edn], 259.
292 Wells, *The Sleeper Awakes* [*The Sleeper Awakes and Men Like Gods* 1921 edn], 184.
293 Wells, 'Preface to the New Edition', in *The Sleeper Awakes: A Revised Edition of 'When the Sleeper Wakes'*, rev. edn of *When the Sleeper Wakes* (London: Nelson, 1910), ii (i–ii).
294 Wells, *Outline of History*, vol. 2, 725.
295 See Francis Sheppard, *London: A History* (Oxford: OUP, 1998), 321.
296 Wells, 'Preface to the Scientific Romances', 243.
297 Ibid., 244.
298 Ibid.
299 Wells, *Anticipations* (1901), in *Anticipations; And Other Papers*, 35 (1–282).
300 See Wells, *The Shape of Things to Come* (1933), ed. Parrinder (London: Penguin, 2005), 246.
301 Parrinder, 'Introduction', in *H. G. Wells: The Critical Heritage*, ed. Parrinder (London: Routledge, 1997), 3 (1–31).
302 Orwell, 'Wells, Hitler and the World State', 539.
303 Ibid.
304 Wells, 'Preface' [*The Sleeper Awakes and Men Like Gods* 1921 edn], [8–9].
305 Yevgeny Zamyatin, 'H. G. Wells' (1922), in *A Soviet Heretic: Essays by Yevgeny Zamyatin*, ed. and trans. Mirra Ginsberg (London: Quartet, 1991), 259 (259–90).

Chapter 3

1 Orwell, *Nineteen Eighty-Four*, 103.
2 John Sommerfield, 'Worm's-Eye View', in *The Survivors* (London: John Lehmann, 1947), 29–30 (9–30).
3 See Porter, *London: A Social History*, 417.
4 See 'St Clement Danes', in *London Encyclopaedia*, 753 (752–3).
5 See 'St Martin-in-the-Fields', in *London Encyclopaedia*, 785 (784–5).
6 See Suzanne Bosman, *The National Gallery in Wartime* (London: National Gallery & YUP, 2008), 61 and Nick Cooper, *London Underground at War* (Gloucestershire: Amberley, 2014), 103–4.
7 Orwell, 'London Letter' (17 August 1941), in *A Patriot After All*, 553 (546–53).
8 Orwell, 'London Letter' (29 August 1942), in *All Propaganda Is Lies: 1941–1942*, ed. Davison, vol. 13 of *The Complete Works of George Orwell* (London: Secker & Warburg, 1998), 520 (518–22).

9 Orwell, 'London Letter' (24 July 1944), in *I Have Tried to Tell the Truth*, 303 (300–3).
10 Peake, 'London, 1941' (1941), in *Collected Poems*, 88 (88–9).
11 Peake, 'The Rhyme of the Flying Bomb' [written c. 1947] (1962), in *Collected Poems*, 182 (178–201).
12 Orwell, 'London Letter' (3 January 1941), in *A Patriot After All*, 355 (352–7).
13 Forster, *Life of Charles Dickens*, 11.
14 Wells, 'To Elizabeth Healey', 82.
15 George Woodcock, *The Crystal Spirit: A Study of George Orwell* (1966), 2nd edn (London: Fourth Estate, 1984), 24.
16 Wells, 'To Elizabeth Healey', 82.
17 See Cathy Ross and John Clark, *London: The Illustrated History* (London: Allen Lane, 2008), 267.
18 See John Thompson, *Orwell's London* (London: Fourth Estate, 1984), 51 and Herbert Wright, *London High* (London: Frances Lincoln, 2006), 34–5.
19 See W. J. West, *The Larger Evils: Nineteen Eighty-Four; The Truth Behind the Satire* (Edinburgh: Canongate, 1992), 31.
20 Orwell, *Nineteen Eighty-Four*, 3.
21 Ibid., 5.
22 Ibid.
23 Woodcock, *Crystal Spirit*, 24.
24 Ibid.
25 Orwell, *Nineteen Eighty-Four*, 90.
26 Ibid., 85–6.
27 Woodcock, *Orwell's Message: 1984 and the Present* (Madeira: Harbour, 1984), 24.
28 Orwell, 'Some Thoughts on the Common Toad' (1946), in *Smothered Under Journalism: 1946*, ed. Davison, vol. 18 of *The Complete Works of George Orwell* (London: Secker & Warburg, 1998), 239 (238–41).
29 Ibid.
30 Ibid.
31 Orwell, *Nineteen Eighty-Four*, 229.
32 'decency, n.', *OED Online* (March 2016), OUP, http://www.oed.com.libproxy.ucl.ac.uk/view/Entry/48112?redirectedFrom=Decency [accessed 25 April 2016].
33 Orwell, 'Charles Dickens', 55.
34 Orwell, *The English People* [written 1944] (1947), in *I Have Tried to Tell the Truth*, 205 (109–228).
35 Ibid.
36 Orwell, 'Charles Dickens', 55.
37 Ibid., 37.
38 See Humphry House, *The Dickens World* (1941), 2nd edn (London: OUP, 1960).

39 See letter from Humphry House to George Orwell (3 April 1940), the George Orwell Archive, University College London Special Collections, folio titled 'Letters to Orwell: A–L', Reference Number ORWELL/H/1, leaf 6 (seven leaves altogether).
40 Orwell, 'Charles Dickens', 54.
41 Ibid., 31.
42 My thanks to G. Peter Winnington for referring me to this address and deciphering the better part of it. Its full transcription may be found in Elber-Aviram, 'Dark and Deathless Rabble of Long Shadows', 7.
43 Peake, letter to Nehemiah Asherson (18 July 1951), *PS* 11, no. 4 (April 2010): 32 (32).
44 Peake, *Titus Groan* (1946), in *Illustrated Gormenghast Trilogy*, 5 (1–366).
45 Peake, *Titus Alone*, 764.
46 See Winnington, *Vast Alchemies: The Life and Work of Mervyn Peake* (London & Chester Springs: Peter Owen, 2000), 135.
47 Dickens, *Haunted Man*, 328.
48 Orwell, 'Raffles and Miss Blandish' (1944), in *I Have Tried to Tell the Truth*, 354 (345–58).
49 Orwell, 'Charles Dickens', 55.
50 Orwell, 'Raffles and Miss Blandish', 354.
51 Orwell, 'Charles Dickens', 55.
52 Orwell, 'Raffles and Miss Blandish', 354–5.
53 Ibid., 354.
54 Peake, *Titus Alone*, 755.
55 Peake, *Titus Groan*, 35.
56 Peake, *Titus Alone*, 909.
57 Dickens, *Bleak House*, 290.
58 Peake, Add MS 88931/1/3/7, '"Goremenghast Continued – Book Seven" (Titus Groan chapters 47–57)' [written 1941–2], 44 [paginated erratically], MPA, BL.
59 Dickens, *Bleak House*, 377.
60 Ibid., 280.
61 Ibid., 281.
62 Ibid.
63 Ibid., 284.
64 Peake, *Titus Groan*, 19.
65 Ibid.
66 See Winnington, *Vast Alchemies*, 211.
67 Peake, 'Danse Macabre' [written for Christmas 1954], *Science Fantasy* 21, no. 61 (1963): 47 (46–55).
68 Ibid., 52.
69 Ernest Everon, 'Some Thoughts Anent Dickens and Novel Writing', *The Ladies' Cabinet* (1855): 260 (257–61).

70 Ibid.
71 Smith, *Personal Memoir*, 51–2.
72 F. H. W. Sheppard, 'General Introduction', in *The Parish of St. Anne, Soho*, ed. Sheppard, vols 33–4 of *The Survey of London* (London: Athlone, 1966), 13 (1–19).
73 See Judith R. Walkowitz, *Nights Out: Life in Cosmopolitan London* (New Haven: YUP, 2012), 12.
74 See Winnington, *Vast Alchemies*, 62–3.
75 Ibid., 63.
76 See Ibid., 61.
77 Peake, 'London Fantasy', 4.
78 Ibid.
79 Ibid., 5.
80 Gilmore, *World Away*, 36.
81 Peake, 'London Fantasy', 3.
82 Ibid.
83 Orwell, 'Wells, Hitler and the World State', 539.
84 Ibid.
85 See Tony Judt, *Postwar: A History of Europe Since 1945* (2005; repr., London: Pimlico, 2007), 235.
86 Cyril Connolly, 'Comment', *Horizon* 15, no. 87 (April 1947): 151 (151–4).
87 Orwell, 'Charles Dickens', 44.
88 See Orwell, *Lion and the Unicorn*, 407.
89 Orwell, 'To Frederic Warburg' (30 March 1949), in *Our Job Is to Make Life Worth Living: 1949–1950*, ed. Davison, vol. 20 of *The Complete Works of George Orwell* (London: Secker & Warburg, 1998), 72 (72).
90 Orwell, *Nineteen Eighty-Four*, 197.
91 Smith, *Personal Memoir*, 75.
92 Peake, *Titus Groan*, 11.
93 Moorcock, 'New Worlds: A Personal History', *Foundation* 15 (1 January 1979): 10 (5–18).
94 Ibid.
95 See William R. Nester, *Globalization: A Short History of the Modern World* (New York: Palgrave, 2010), 69.
96 See H. L. Malchow, *Special Relations: The Americanization of Britain?* (Stanford: Stanford UP, 2011), especially 1–47.
97 Orwell, *Lion and the Unicorn*, 408.
98 Orwell, 'Raffles and Miss Blandish', 354.
99 Orwell, *Coming Up for Air* (1939), vol. 7 of *The Complete Works of George Orwell* (1986; repr., London: Secker & Warburg, 1997), 22.
100 Orwell, 'London Letter' (29 August 1942), 520.
101 Ibid.

102 See Brian Stableford, *Scientific Romance in Britain 1890–1950* (London: Fourth Estate, 1985), 151–2, 323–5.
103 Gary Westfahl, *Hugo Gernsback and the Century of Science Fiction* (Jefferson: McFarland, 2007), 151.
104 Ashley, *The History of the Science-Fiction Magazine*, vol. 3, *Gateways to Forever: The Story of the Science-Fiction Magazines from 1970 to 1980* (1976), rev. and exp. edn (Liverpool: LUP, 2007), 69 and Ashley, *The History of the Science Fiction Magazine*, vol. 2, *Transformations: The Story of the Science-Fiction Magazines from 1950 to 1970* (1975), rev. and exp. edn (Liverpool: LUP, 2005), 17.
105 Orwell, 'Personal Notes on Scientifiction' (1945), in *I Belong to the Left*, 221 (221–5).
106 Ibid.
107 Ibid.
108 Orwell, 'Boys' Weeklies' (1940), in *A Patriot After All*, 71 (57–79).
109 Orwell, *English People*, 205 and Orwell, 'Raffles and Miss Blandish', 354.
110 Orwell, *Keep the Aspidistra Flying*, 116.
111 Ibid.
112 Orwell, *Coming Up for Air*, 239.
113 Orwell, 'Some Thoughts on the Common Toad', 239.
114 Peake, *Titus Alone*, 773.
115 Ibid.
116 See Terry Brown, 'Preface 1', in *London High*, 13 (13–6) and Porter, *London: A Social History*, 431.
117 Orwell, *Nineteen Eighty-Four*, 6.
118 See Wright, *London High*, 34.
119 Orwell, *Road to Wigan Pier*, 190.
120 Peake, *Titus Alone*, 765, 757.
121 Peake, *Titus Groan*, 5.
122 Peake, *Titus Alone*, 826.
123 Ibid., 776, 791.
124 Ibid., 827.
125 Ibid.
126 Ibid.
127 Ibid., 829.
128 Ibid., 827.
129 Ibid., 896.
130 Ibid., 762.
131 Ibid., 828–9.
132 Ibid., 791.
133 Peake, Add MS 88931/1/3/27, 'Autograph Manuscript (Titus Alone chapters 12–19)' [written c. 1956], verso of 10 [paginated erratically], MPA, BL.

134 Peake, Add MS 88931/1/3/35, '"Titus Afar" (Titus Alone chapters 89–108)' [written 1957], verso of 81 [paginated erratically], MPA, BL.
135 Peake, *Titus Alone*, 809.
136 Ibid., 791, 760.
137 Ibid., 791, 761.
138 Orwell, *Homage to Catalonia* (1938), vol. 6 of *The Complete Works of George Orwell* (1986; repr., London: Secker & Warburg, 1997), 187.
139 See Kenneth Powell, 'Introduction', in *The City of London: Architectural Tradition & Innovation in the Square Mile*, ed. Nicholas Kenyon (2011; repr., London: Thames & Hudson, 2012), 21, 25 (11–25) and White, *London in the Twentieth Century: A City and Its People* (London: Penguin, 2001), 78–81.
140 See Orwell, 'The True Pattern of H. G. Wells', *Manchester Evening News*, 14 August 1946, 2 (2).
141 See Mark R. Hillegas, *The Future as Nightmare: H. G. Wells and the Anti-Utopians* (New York: OUP, 1967), 130–1.
142 Orwell, 'To Fredric Warburg' (31 May 1947), in *It Is What I Think: 1947–1948*, ed. Davison, vol. 19 of *The Complete Works of George Orwell* (London: Secker & Warburg, 1998), 149 (149–50).
143 Orwell, 'Statement on *Nineteen Eighty-Four*' (July 1949), in *Our Job Is to Make Life Worth Living*, 134 (134–6).
144 See Orwell, 'Wells, Hitler and the World State', 538.
145 Orwell, *Nineteen Eighty-Four*, 260.
146 Ibid., 222.
147 Ibid., 258.
148 Peake, *Titus Alone*, 814.
149 Ibid., 808.
150 Ibid., 893.
151 Elizabeth Bowen, 'Mysterious Kôr' (1944), in *Collected Stories of Elizabeth Bowen*, ed. Angus Wilson (London: Jonathan Cape, 1980), 728 (728–40).
152 Ibid.
153 Orwell, 'London Letter' (3 January 1941), 356.
154 Ibid.
155 See Michael Shelden, *Orwell* (London: Heinemann, 1991), 403.
156 Smith, *Personal Memoir*, 91.
157 Wells, 'Preface' [*The Sleeper Awakes and Men Like Gods* 1921 edn], [8].
158 Wells, *When the Sleeper Wakes* [Sutherland edn], 80.
159 Orwell, *Nineteen Eighty-Four*, 22–3.
160 Wells, *Modern Utopia*, 164.
161 Orwell, 'London Letter' (24 July 1944), 303.
162 Tanya Gardiner-Scott, *Mervyn Peake: The Evolution of a Dark Romantic* (New York: Peter Lang, 1989), 217.

163 Peake, 'Alice and Tenniel and Me: A Talk by Mervyn Peake' (1954), *MPR* 6 (Spring 1978): 24 (20–4).
164 Peake, 'London Fantasy', 3.
165 Ibid., 4.
166 Ibid., 6.
167 Ibid., 7.
168 See Cooper, *London Underground at War*, 39–102.
169 Peake, 'Alice and Tenniel and Me', 24.
170 Orwell, *Nineteen Eighty-Four*, 5.
171 Wyndham Lewis, 'Climax and Change', in *The Writer and the Absolute* (London: Methuen, 1952), 192 (189–93).
172 Dickens, *Chimes*, 88.
173 Orwell, *Nineteen Eighty-Four*, 103.
174 Ibid., 100.
175 Ibid., 30.
176 Ibid., 152.
177 Orwell, *Nineteen Eighty-Four: The Facsimile of the Extant Manuscript*, ed. Davison (London: Secker & Warburg, 1984), 83.
178 Lawrence Phillips, 'Sex, Violence and Concrete: The Post-war Dystopian Vision of London in *Nineteen Eighty-Four*', *Critical Survey* 20, no. 1 (2008): 71 (69–79).
179 Ibid., 72.
180 Orwell, *Nineteen Eighty-Four*, 162.
181 Ibid., 102.
182 Ibid., 120, 119, 120.
183 Ibid., 120.
184 Ibid., 102.
185 Ibid., 121.
186 Ibid., 103.
187 Ibid., 102–3.
188 Wells, *When the Sleeper Wakes* [Sutherland edn], 191.
189 Orwell, *Nineteen Eighty-Four*, 120.
190 Ibid., 100.
191 Henri Lefebvre, *Critique of Everyday Life* (1947), 2nd edn (1958), vol. I, trans. John Moore (1991; repr., London: Verso, 2008), 130.
192 Ibid., 131.
193 Ibid., 119, 248.
194 Orwell, *Nineteen Eighty-Four*, 123.
195 Ibid., 120.
196 Winston's flat is no exception. See Carl Freedman, *The Incomplete Projects: Marxism, Modernity, and the Politics of Culture* (Middletown: Wesleyan UP, 2002), 167.

197 Orwell, *Nineteen Eighty-Four: Extant Manuscript*, 89.
198 Orwell, *Nineteen Eighty-Four*, 133.
199 Ibid., 119.
200 Ibid.
201 Orwell, *Keep the Aspidistra Flying*, 116.
202 Orwell, *Nineteen Eighty-Four*, 133.
203 Ibid., 134.
204 Ibid.
205 Peake, 'London Fantasy', 5.
206 Ibid.
207 Ibid.
208 Peake, *Titus Alone*, 760.
209 Ibid., 761.
210 Gilmore, *World Away*, 15.
211 Ibid., 16, 17.
212 See Maslen, 2nd note to 31, *Collected Poems*, 234.
213 Moorcock, 'Titus Groan: An Untitled Introduction to the Folio Society Edition' (1992), in *Into the Media Web: Selected Short Non-Fiction, 1956–2006*, ed. John Davey (Manchester: Savoy, 2010), 636 (628–37).
214 Peake, *Titus Alone*, 761.
215 Ibid.
216 Ibid., 762.
217 Ibid., 848.
218 Ibid., 850.
219 Ibid., 848.
220 Peake, Add MS 88931/1/3/28, '"A Castle and Sixpence: Book Two" (Titus Alone chapters 28–31)' [written c. 1956–62], 15 [paginated erratically], MPA, BL. Strikethrough in original.
221 Orwell, 'Charles Dickens', 54.
222 Orwell, *Nineteen Eighty-Four*, 247.
223 Ibid.
224 Peake, *Titus Alone*, 851.
225 Ibid.
226 Ibid., 912.
227 Ibid., 943.
228 Orwell, 'Charles Dickens', 41 and Orwell, 'The Re-discovery of Europe' (1942), in *All Propaganda Is Lies,* 211 (209–17).
229 Peake, *Gormenghast* (1950), in *Illustrated Gormenghast Trilogy*, 747 (367–747).
230 Peake, *Titus Alone*, 920.
231 Ibid., 830.
232 Ibid., 770.

233 Orwell, 'To Fredric Warburg' (31 May 1947), 149.
234 Orwell, *Nineteen Eighty-Four*, 43.
235 Ibid., 49.
236 Ibid., 78.
237 Ibid., 84.
238 Ibid.
239 Ibid., 277.
240 Ibid.
241 Ibid.
242 Orwell, 'Personal Notes on Scientifiction', 221.
243 Orwell, 'Riding Down from Bangor' (1946), in *Smothered Under Journalism*, 496 (493–7).
244 Orwell, 'Boys' Weeklies', 69.
245 See John Rodden, 'The Spectre of Der Große Bruder: George Orwell's Reputation in West Germany', *The German Quarterly* 60, no. 4 (Autumn 1987): 530–47 and Philip Thody, *Europe Since 1945* (London: Routledge, 2000), 112–6.
246 Orwell, 'Orwell's Statement on *Nineteen Eighty-Four*', 135.
247 Orwell, 'Boys' Weeklies', 71.
248 Ibid., 70.
249 Ibid., 71.
250 Orwell, 'Raffles and Miss Blandish', 354.
251 See 'To Fredric Warburg' (22 October 1948), in *It Is What I Think*, 457 (456–7).
252 Orwell, *Nineteen Eighty-Four*, 227.
253 Ibid., 179.
254 Ibid., 291.
255 Orwell, 'Just Junk – But Who Could Resist It?' (1946), in *Smothered Under Journalism*, 18 (17–9).
256 Ibid.
257 Dickens, *Old Curiosity Shop*, 19–20.
258 Ibid., 10 and Orwell, *Nineteen Eighty-Four*, 98.
259 Dickens, *Old Curiosity Shop*, 10.
260 Orwell, *Nineteen Eighty-Four*, 98.
261 Ibid., 103.
262 Ibid., 100.
263 See 'Appendix: The Principles of Newspeak', ibid., 325 (312–26).
264 Ibid., 269.
265 Dickens, *Old Curiosity Shop*, 239.
266 Orwell, *Nineteen Eighty-Four*, 97.
267 Ibid., 233–4.
268 Ibid., 233.

269 Ibid.
270 Ibid., 8 and Wells, 'Crystal Egg', 164.
271 Orwell, 'To Julian Symons' (10 May 1948), in *It Is What I Think*, 336 (335–6).
272 Orwell, *Nineteen Eighty-Four*, 154.
273 Wells, 'Crystal Egg', 181.
274 Orwell, *Nineteen Eighty-Four*, 154.
275 Orwell, *Coming Up for Air*, 210.
276 Orwell, *Nineteen Eighty-Four*, 154.
277 Wells, 'A Chat with the Author of *The Time Machine*', 6.
278 Wood's account of Peake's reactions to *The Fellowship of the Ring* specifies that 'the first volume ... had just been published'. Wood, 'A Pupil Remembers', 25.
279 Peake, qtd. in ibid.
280 According to Wood, Peake discussed 'how *Titus III* was progressing' shortly before his 'trenchant comment . . . about *The Lord of the Rings*' (Ibid.). These conversations took place 'towards the end of the Summer Term 1955' (ibid., 23).
281 See Peake, Add MS 88931/1/3/32, '"Titus Groan the Third" (Titus Alone chapters 64–68)' [written 1957], 4, recto to verso [paginated erratically], MPA, BL.
282 Peake, *Titus Alone*, 857.
283 Tolkien, *The Fellowship of the Ring* (1954; repr., London: HarperCollins, 2008), 161.
284 See Peake, Add MS 88931/1/3/32, 4 [paginated erratically], MPA, BL.
285 Tolkien, *Fellowship of the Ring*, 156.
286 See ibid., 159.
287 See ibid., 38 and Tolkien, *The Return of the King* (1955; repr., London: HarperCollins, 2008), 1265.
288 Peake, *Titus Alone*, 873.
289 Ibid., 873–4.
290 Ibid., 874.
291 Ibid., 770.
292 Ibid., 826.
293 Ibid., 853.
294 Peake, letter to Smith (24 October 1943), qtd. in Smith, *Personal Memoir*, 103 (102–5).
295 Lewis, 'To Mervyn Peake' (10 February 1958), in *Collected Letters*, vol. 3, 919 (918–9).
296 Weybright & Talley Publishers, advertising blurb, qtd. in Lucille G. Crane, 'The Gormenghast Trilogy', *Best Sellers: The Semi-Monthly Book Review* 27, no. 1 (1967): 305 (305–6).
297 Dick Adler, 'A Long and Very Sad Groan', *Chicago Tribune*, 7 January 1968, K4 (K4).
298 Smith, *Personal Memoir*, 110.

299 Peake, *Titus Alone*, 929.
300 Orwell, *Nineteen Eighty-Four*, 274.
301 Ibid., 275. c.f. *When the Sleeper Wakes* [Sutherland edn], 199–205.
302 Ibid.
303 Orwell, 'Review of *The Iron Heel* by Jack London; *The Sleeper Wakes* by H. G. Wells; *Brave New World* by Aldous Huxley; *The Secret of the League* by Ernest Bramah' (1940), in *A Patriot After All*, 211 (210–5).
304 Ibid.
305 Ibid.
306 Orwell, *Nineteen Eighty-Four*, 265.
307 c.f. Wells, *The Island of Doctor Moreau* (1896), ed. Parrinder (London: Penguin, 2005), 57–64 and 85–96 and Orwell, *Animal Farm: A Fairy Story* (1945), vol. 8 of *The Complete Works of George Orwell* (1987; repr., London: Secker & Warburg, 1998), 15, 21–2, 89–90.
308 Orwell, *Nineteen Eighty-Four*, 267.
309 Leo Strauss, 'Restatement on Xenophon's *Hiero*' (1954), in *What Is Political Philosophy?; And Other Studies* (1959; repr., Westport: Greenwood, 1973), 96 (95–133) and Strauss, 'Review of Simon R. Yves *Philosophy of Democratic Government*' (1952), in *What Is Political Philosophy?*, 310 (306–11).
310 Orwell, 'Wells, Hitler and the World State', 540.
311 Ibid., 538, 540.
312 Ibid., 539.
313 Ibid.
314 Ibid.
315 Wells, 'Preface to the New Edition' [*The Sleeper Awakes* 1910 edn], ii.
316 Orwell, *Nineteen Eighty-Four*, 280.
317 Peake, *Titus Alone*, 855.
318 Ibid., 867.
319 Orwell, 'The Re-discovery of Europe', 214.
320 Peake, *Titus Alone*, 943.
321 Peake, qtd. in Gilmore, *World Away*, 59.
322 Peake to Maeve (21 June 1945), qtd. in Malcolm Yorke, *Mervyn Peake: My Eyes Mint Gold, a Life* (London: Murray, 2000), 152 (152).
323 Ibid.
324 Peake, 'The Consumptive. Belsen 1945' (1945), in *Collected Poems*, 133 (133–4).
325 John Watney, *Mervyn Peake* (London: Joseph, 1976), 127.
326 Peake, *Titus Alone*, 862, 937.
327 Ibid., 866.
328 Ibid., 843.
329 Ibid., 844.

330 Ibid., 851.
331 Peake, *Titus Alone*, 918.
332 Peake, Add MS 88931/1/3/35, verso of 62 [paginated erratically], MPA, BL.
333 Ibid.
334 Peake, Add MS 88931/1/3/27, verso of 8, MPA, BL.
335 Ibid. Previously published in Gardiner-Scott, *Mervyn Peake*, 176.
336 See Pierre François, '*Titus Alone*, or the Spirit of Carnival "After the Catastrophe"', *PS* 6, no. 3 (October 1999): 16 (4–20) and Lauren R. Moss, *Postmodern Existentialism in Mervyn Peake's Titus Books* (Florida: Raton, Universal Publishers, 2009).
337 Peake, *Titus Alone*, 932.
338 See Don DeLillo, *White Noise* (London: Pan, 1985), especially 242–81.
339 Peake, *Titus Alone*, 912.

Chapter 4

1 See W. H. Auden, 'The Hero Is a Hobbit', *The New York Times*, 31 October 1954, BR37 and Douglass Parker, 'Hwaet, We Holbytla', *The Hudson Review* 9, no. 4 (Winter 1956): 598.
2 See Humphrey Carpenter, *J.R.R. Tolkien: A Biography* (1977), rev. edn (Boston: Mifflin, 2000), 292–309.
3 See Brian Rosebury, *Tolkien: A Cultural Phenomenon* (Basingstoke: Macmillan, 2003), 142 and 'Susan' [*nom de plume*], 'Wacky World of Tolkien Catching on with Youth', *The Los Angeles Times*, 31 August 1966, D4.
4 See 'Vera Chapman', in *A Reader's Guide to Fantasy*, eds Baird Searles, Michael Franklin and Beth Meacham (New York: Avon, 1982), 27 (27).
5 Andy Beckett, *When the Lights Went Out: Britain in the Seventies* (London: Faber and Faber, 2009), 214.
6 See Bruce A. Beatie, 'The Tolkien Phenomenon: 1945–1968', *Journal of Popular Culture* 3, no. 4 (Spring 1970): 689–703.
7 See Moorcock, 'Literature of Acceptance'.
8 See Harrison, 'By Tennyson Out of Disney'.
9 See Harrison, 'Literature of Comfort'.
10 Moorcock, *Epic Pooh*, [5].
11 Ibid., [4].
12 Ibid., [5].
13 Ibid.
14 Moorcock, 'The Michael Moorcock Column: The Dodgem Arrangement' [written 1968], *Speculation* 2, no. 11, issue 23 (July/August 1969): 28 (27–32).

15 For an essay collection on the overlooked sophistication of *The Lord of the Rings*, see Robert Eagleton (ed.), *Reading the Lord of the Rings: New Writings on Tolkien's Classic* (London: Continuum, 2005).
16 Moorcock, 'A New Literature for the Space Age', *NW* 48, no. 142 (May–June 1964): 3 (2–3).
17 Thomas M. Disch, 'The Lessons of the Future', *NW*, no. 173 (July 1967): 2 (2–3).
18 Moorcock, 'Literature of Acceptance', 61.
19 Moorcock, 'New Literature for the Space Age', 3.
20 Wells, *The Discovery of the Future* (1902), in *Anticipations; And Other Papers*, 357 (357–89).
21 Ibid.
22 Ibid.
23 Ibid.
24 Ibid., 358.
25 Wells, *The History of Mr Polly* (1910), ed. James (London: Penguin, 2005), 159.
26 Disch, 'Lessons of the Future', 2.
27 Ibid.
28 Ibid.
29 Moorcock, 'A Place of Perpetual Rehearsal and Audition' (1990), in *London Peculiar and Other Nonfiction*, eds Moorcock and Allan Kausch (California: PM, 2012), 31 (30–3).
30 Dickens, 'Preliminary Word', 1.
31 Disch, 'Lessons of the Future', 2.
32 Dickens, 'Preliminary Word', 1.
33 Disch, 'Lessons of the Future', 2.
34 Ibid., 3.
35 Ibid., 2.
36 Ibid., 3.
37 Dickens, 'Preliminary Word', 1.
38 Disch, 'Lessons of the Future', 3.
39 Ibid.
40 Moorcock, 'Literature of Acceptance', 60.
41 Moorcock explicitly asserted that 'the so-called "new wave"' was 'never a term we used ourselves'. Moorcock, 'A Constant Curiosity' [n.d.], in *London Peculiar*, 145 (141–6). On the American usage of the term to describe the *New Worlds* coterie, see DAW [*nom de plume*], 'New Wave SF', in *England Swings SF: Stories of Speculative Fiction*, ed. Judith Merril (New York: Doubleday, 1968), [n.p.].
42 Moorcock and Paul Walker [interviewer, interview conducted in 1972], 'Michael Moorcock', in Walker, *Speaking of Science Fiction: The Paul Walker Interviews* (Jersey City, NJ: Luna, 1978), 224 (213–28).
43 Moorcock, 'New Worlds: A Personal History', 6.

44 Harrison, 'Literature of Comfort', 169–70.
45 See Harrison, 'Literature of Comfort'.
46 See Moorcock, *Epic Pooh*.
47 Moorcock, 'A Literature of Acceptance', 60.
48 Ibid.
49 Harrison, 'Literature of Comfort', 169.
50 Ibid., 172.
51 Ibid.
52 See the front cover of *NW*, no. 189 (April 1969) and *NWQ* 1 (1971), 53 and 166.
53 Moorcock, 'Editorial', *NW* 49, no. 155 (October 1965): 2 (2–3).
54 Moorcock, 'Place of Perpetual Rehearsal and Audition', 31.
55 Ibid., 32.
56 Moorcock, 'London Peculiar' (2009), in *London Peculiar*, 42 (42–7).
57 Moorcock, 'Place of Perpetual Rehearsal and Audition', 32.
58 Moorcock, 'New Worlds: A Personal History', 5–6.
59 Moorcock, 'Literature of Acceptance', 60 and Moorcock, 'Introduction to This Edition' (1993), in *The New Nature of the Catastrophe*, rev. edn of *The Nature of the Catastrophe* (1971), eds Moorcock and Langdon Jones (London: Millennium, 1993), vi (v–vii).
60 Moorcock, *The Condition of Muzak: A Jerry Cornelius Novel* (London: Allison & Busby, 1977), 211.
61 Moorcock, 'New Worlds – Jerry Cornelius' (1972), in Moorcock, *Sojan* (Manchester: Savoy, 1977), 150 (144–55).
62 Ibid.
63 Moorcock, 'The Dreaming City', *SF* 16, no. 47 (1961): 3 (2–32).
64 Moorcock, *The Final Programme* (1968), first British edn (London: Allison & Busby, 1969), 67. All references to *Final Programme*, save for those sections published in *New Worlds* or intended for publication thereof, are to this edition.
65 Moorcock, 'Introduction to The Michael Moorcock Collection', in *The Cornelius Quartet* (1968–77), rev. one-volume edn, *Michael Moorcock Collection*, ed. John Davey (London: Gollancz, 2013), xv (xiii–xviii).
66 Moorcock, 'Introduction' (2007), in *Elric: To Rescue Tanelorn* (New York: Ballantine, 2008), xviii (xv–xxi).
67 Moorcock and Colin Greenland [interviewer], *Death Is No Obstacle* (Manchester: Savoy, 1992), 29. [interviewer, interview conducted in 1990].
68 See Moorcock, 'Michael Moorcock', 227.
69 Merril, qtd. in Rob Latham, 'A Young Man's Journey to Ladbroke Grove: M. John Harrison and the Evolution of the New Wave in Britain', in *M. John Harrison: Critical Essays*, eds Rhys Williams and Mark Bould (Canterbury: Gylphi, 2019), fn. 2, 37 (21–42).
70 Moorcock, 'Tom Disch Tribute' (2008), in *London Peculiar*, 139 (139–40).

71 Moorcock, *Final Programme*, 113.
72 Moorcock, 'Michael Moorcock: 1939–' (1987), in *Into the Media Web*, 27, 26 (17–43).
73 Moorcock, 'Introduction to *The Michael Moorcock Collection*', xiii.
74 Moorcock [writing as 'Jim Colvin'], 'The Portobello Road' (1966), in *Into the Media Web*, 493 (493–9).
75 White, *London in the Twentieth Century*, 339.
76 Ibid.
77 See ibid., xxvii, 387.
78 Ibid., 349.
79 See Steve Humphries and John Taylor, *The Making of Modern London, 1945–1985* (London: London Weekend Television, 1986), 37.
80 See Shawn Levy, *Ready, Steady, Go: Swinging London and the Invention of Cool* (2002; repr., London: Fourth Estate, 2003); Fiona A. Montgomery, *Women's Rights: Struggles and Feminism in Britain c. 1770–1970* (Manchester: MUP, 2006), 229–58; and David A. J. Richards, *The Rise of Gay Rights and the Fall of the British Empire* (Cambridge: CUP, 2013), 140–207.
81 Moorcock, 'Michael Moorcock: 1939–', 28.
82 Moorcock, *Final Programme*, 115.
83 Ibid.
84 Disch, 'Lessons of the Future', 2.
85 Moorcock, *Final Programme*, 67.
86 Ibid.
87 Ibid., 74.
88 Ibid., 115.
89 Ibid., 75.
90 Ibid., 76.
91 Ibid., 67.
92 Moorcock, 'Editorial: The New Prism', *NW* 49, no. 158 (January 1966): 4 (2–4, 48).
93 Moorcock, *Death Is No Obstacle*, 87.
94 Moorcock, *Final Programme*, 168.
95 Ibid., 115.
96 Moorcock, 'Phase 1', intended for publication in *New Worlds*, published in Moorcock, *Elric*, 198 (181–231).
97 Moorcock, 'Further Information', *NW* 49, no. 157 (December 1965): 55 (49–67).
98 Moorcock, 'Phase 1', 209. The *New Worlds* extract condenses this description.
99 Moorcock, *Final Programme*, 75.
100 Ibid., 77.
101 Ibid., 130.
102 Ibid.

103 Ibid., 130–1.
104 Moorcock, 'Michael Moorcock: 1939–', 29.
105 Ibid.
106 Moorcock, 'Literature of Acceptance', 60.
107 See Moorcock, 'Michael Moorcock: 1939–', 29.
108 Peter Kropotkin, *Mutual Aid: A Factor of Evolution* (1902; repr., London: Freedom Press, 1987), 72.
109 Moorcock, 'Preliminary Data', *NW* 49, no. 153 (August 1965): 111 (98–113).
110 Moorcock, 'Phase 1', 182.
111 Moorcock, 'Preliminary Data', 111.
112 Ibid., 110.
113 Moorcock, *Final Programme*, 167.
114 Moorcock, 'Preliminary Data', 110.
115 Ibid., 109.
116 Ibid., 111.
117 Moorcock, 'Michael Moorcock: 1939–', 31.
118 Moorcock, 'Introduction to This Edition', *New Nature of the Catastrophe*, vii.
119 Ibid.
120 Latham, 'The New Wave', in *A Companion to Science Fiction*, ed. David Seed (Oxford: Blackwell, 2005), 207.
121 [Jones], 'Lead In', *NW*, no. 191 (June 1969): 2 (2–3).
122 Ibid.
123 Moorcock, 'Introduction to This Edition', *New Nature of the Catastrophe*, vii.
124 Moorcock, 'New Worlds: A Personal History', 16.
125 [Jones], 'Lead In', 2.
126 Clute, 'The Repossession of Jerry Cornelius' (1977), in *Cornelius Quartet*, 3 (1–9).
127 Disch, 'Lessons of the Future', 2.
128 Clute, 'Repossession of Jerry Cornelius', 3.
129 Moorcock and Richard Glyn Jones, 'The Rise of the Musician-Assassin', *NW*, no. 213 (Summer 1978): 3 (3–4). I am indebted to Tom Dillon for calling my attention to this piece and generously supplying me with a copy of it.
130 See Moorcock, *Final Programme*, 118.
131 Moorcock, 'The Delhi Division', *NW*, no. 185, 27 (23–7).
132 See Moorcock, 'The Tank Trapeze', *NW*, no. 186 (January 1969): 10 (front cover and 5–10).
133 See Sallis, 'Jeremiad', *NW*, no. 187, 15 (6–15).
134 Moorcock, *Death Is No Obstacle*, 87.
135 See [anonymous], *Derry & Toms Famous Roof Gardens* (Norwich: Jarrold & Sons, 1966), [2].

136 Moorcock, *A Cure for Cancer*, part 1, *NW*, no. 188 (March 1969): 5 (4–20).
137 See ibid. and *Derry & Toms Famous Roof Gardens*, inside of front cover, [n.p.].
138 Ibid.
139 Ibid. c.f. *Derry & Toms Famous Roof Gardens*, inner side of back cover, [n.p.]. The brochure reads 'St. Pauls'.
140 Ibid.
141 See Moorcock, 'Introduction to *The Michael Moorcock Collection*', xviii.
142 Moorcock, 'London Peculiar', 45.
143 Ibid.
144 Ibid.
145 Moorcock, 'Building the New Jerusalem' (1988), in *London Peculiar*, 36 (34–8).
146 Ruth Glass, 'Introduction: Aspects of Change' (1963), in *London: Aspects of Change*, eds Centre for Urban Studies (London: Macgibbon and Kee, 1964), xviii (xiii–xlii).
147 Ibid., xix.
148 Moorcock, 'London Peculiar', 46.
149 Moorcock, *A Cure for Cancer*, part 1, 6.
150 Ibid.
151 Ibid., 7.
152 Ibid.
153 See Alwyn W. Turner, *Crisis? What Crisis? Britain in the 1970s* (London: Aurum, 2008), 29.
154 This description of Jerry owes a debt to Greenland, *Entropy Exhibition: Michael Moorcock and the British 'New Wave' in Science Fiction* (London: Routledge & Kegan Paul, 1983), 141.
155 See Moorcock, 'Delhi Division', 24.
156 Moorcock, *A Cure for Cancer*, part 1, 6.
157 Ibid.
158 See Edward Pilkington, *Beyond the Mother Country: West Indians and the Notting Hill White Riots* (London: I. B. Tauris, 1988).
159 Moorcock, *A Cure for Cancer*, part 2, *NW*, no. 189, 47 (37–57).
160 Moorcock, *A Cure for Cancer*, part 1, 13.
161 Moorcock, *A Cure for Cancer*, part 2, 53.
162 Ibid., 43.
163 Moorcock, 'Introduction to *Expletives Deleted* by Angela Carter' (2006), in *London Peculiar*, 150 (147–52).
164 Moorcock, *A Cure for Cancer*, part 2, 45.
165 Ibid., 47.
166 Ibid., 56.
167 Ibid., 57.
168 Ibid., 49.

169 Moorcock, *Death Is No Obstacle*, 89.
170 Moorcock, 'Literature of Acceptance', 59.
171 David L. Anderson, *The Vietnam War* (Hampshire: Palgrave, 2005), 46.
172 Moorcock, *Death Is No Obstacle*, 90.
173 Moorcock, 'A Million Betrayals' (2006), in *London Peculiar*, 205 (202–7).
174 Moorcock, *Cure for Cancer*, part 1, 8.
175 Ibid.
176 Moorcock, *Death Is No Obstacle*, 90.
177 Moorcock, *A Cure for Cancer*, part 3, *NW*, no. 190 (May 1969): 38 (24–41).
178 Ibid.
179 The second instalment of *Cure for Cancer* specifies that the plague ravaging Europe is the 'bubonic plague' (37).
180 Moorcock, *Cure for Cancer*, part 3, 38.
181 Moorcock, 'A Child's Christmas in the Blitz' (2011), in *London Peculiar*, 13 (5–24).
182 Ibid., 17.
183 Ibid., 15.
184 Moorcock, *Final Programme*, 7.
185 Moorcock, *Condition of Muzak*, 206.
186 Moorcock [as 'Maurice Lescoq'], 'Prologue [Commencement]', in *The English Assassin: A Romance of Entropy* (London: Allison & Busby, 1972), 1. On 'Maurice Lescoq' as a *nom de plume* of Michael Moorcock, see Mark Scroggins, *Michael Moorcock: Fiction, Fantasy and the World's Pain* (Jefferson, NC: McFarland, 2016), 48.
187 Ibid.
188 Moorcock, *Death Is No Obstacle*, 88.
189 Moorcock, *Cure for Cancer*, part 1, 5 and Moorcock, 'A Child's Christmas in the Blitz', 15.
190 Moorcock, *Cure for Cancer*, part 3, 41.
191 Moorcock, *Cure for Cancer*, part 2, 53.
192 Moorcock, *Cure for Cancer*, part 3, 26.
193 Ibid., 36.
194 Moorcock, *Cure for Cancer*, part 2, 41.
195 Moorcock, *Condition of Muzak*, 80.
196 Ibid.
197 Moorcock, *A Cure for Cancer: A Jerry Cornelius Novel* (1969), rev. edn ([London]: Fontana, 1979), 198.
198 The phrase 'anarchic individualism' is taken from Greenland's description of Jerry in *Cure for Cancer*. Greenland, *Entropy Exhibition*, 147.
199 Ray Desmond, *The History of the Royal Botanic Gardens; Kew* (1995), 2nd edn (Kew: Kew Publishing, 2007), 283. See [anonymous], 'The Heath Garden', in [anonymous], *The Royal Botanic Gardens; Kew: Illustrated Guide* (London: Her Majesty's Stationery Office, 1961), 32–3.

200 Moorcock, *A Cure for Cancer*, part 3, 30.
201 Ibid.
202 See 'The Pagoda', in *The Royal Botanic Gardens; Kew*, 5.
203 Moorcock, *A Cure for Cancer*, part 3, 31.
204 See Desmond, *History of the Royal Botanic Gardens*, 49.
205 See ibid.
206 Moorcock, *A Cure for Cancer*, part 3, 30.
207 Ibid.
208 Ibid.
209 In an instance of life imitating art, the eighty wooden dragons have since been restored to Kew's Pagoda, rendering Moorcock's depiction closer to reality than he originally intended.
210 Moorcock, *A Cure for Cancer*, part 4, *NW*, no. 191, 5 (4–17).
211 Ibid., 17.
212 Ibid., 11.
213 Ibid., 17.
214 Ibid.
215 Moorcock and Hester Lacey [interviewer], 'The Inventory: Michael Moorcock', *Financial Times*, 22 July 2016, https://www.ft.com/content/5a30f15e-4e03-11e6-8172-e39ecd3b86fc [accessed 25 January 2020].
216 See 'Holland House and Park', *London Encyclopaedia*, 407 (406–8).
217 See Martin Walker, *The National Front* (Glasgow: Fontana, 1977), 33–4.
218 Moorcock, *Cure for Cancer*, part 4, 17.
219 Ibid.
220 Ibid.
221 Ibid.
222 Ibid.
223 Ibid.
224 Ibid.
225 Ibid.
226 See Peter Hennessy, *Having It so Good: Britain in the Fifties* (London: Allen Lane, 2006), 498.
227 Moorcock, 'Dark Continents, Dying Planets' (2005), in *London Peculiar*, 216 (214–17).
228 See Moorcock, *Condition of Muzak*, 73–4, 83–4. To further complicate matters, a later section of *Condition of Muzak* returns to the idea that Jerry is black-skinned after all (101–2).
229 As discussed earlier in this chapter, Jerry becomes a hermaphrodite at the end of *Final Programme*. His gender and sexuality continue to be in flux. See Moorcock, *Condition of Muzak*, 68 and Maxim Jakubowski, 'Lines of White on a Sullen Sea',

NW, no. 194, 26 (25–7). For a discussion of gender and sexuality in the Cornelius stories, see Tom Dillon, '"Jerry Was Oscillating Badly": Gender and Sexuality in *New Worlds* Magazine', *SFS* 45, no. 1 (March 2018): 161–76.

230 See Moorcock, *Condition of Muzak*, 50 and Moorcock, 'The Dodgem Arrangement', 30.
231 See Moorcock, *English Assassin*, 250–1 and Moorcock, *Condition of Muzak*, 146, 217.
232 Moorcock, *Death Is No Obstacle*, 54.
233 Given that Moorcock completed *Cure for Cancer* by 1967 and considering Moorcock's and Harrison's close working relationship on *New Worlds*, it seems likely though not certain that Harrison would have read *Cure for Cancer* before or during his composition of 'Ash Circus'.
234 Moorcock, *Cure for Cancer*, part 2, 38.
235 Harrison, 'The Ash Circus', *NW*, no. 189, 17 (17–23).
236 See Moorcock, *Cure for Cancer*, part 2, 40.
237 Harrison, 'Ash Circus', 18.
238 Ibid.
239 Ibid.
240 Ibid., 19.
241 Ibid.
242 Ibid.
243 Ibid., 23.
244 Moorcock, *Cure for Cancer*, part 2, 49.
245 'Miss Brunner' is mentioned in Sallis's 'Jeremiad' (12).
246 Harrison, 'Ash Circus', 23.
247 See Sigfried Giedion, *Space, Time and Architecture: The Growth of a New Tradition* (1941), 5th edn (Cambridge, MA: Harvard UP, 1967), 734–9.
248 Harrison, 'The Nash Circuit', *NW*, no. 193 (August 1969): 20 (12–23).
249 Harrison, 'Preface: The Other Side of Some Inexplicable Disaster', in *M. John Harrison*, 1 (1–10). The year of Harrison's move to London is taken from the biographical blurb in Harrison, 'M. John Harrison: No Escape' [interview], *Locus* 51, no. 6, issue 515 (December 2003): 7 (7, 69–70).
250 Ibid., 2.
251 Harrison, qtd. in 'Harrison, Michael John', in vols 53–56 of *Contemporary Authors: Bio-Biographical Guide to Current Authors and Their Works*, ed. Clare D. Kinsman (Detroit: Gale, 1975), 272 (272).
252 Harrison, 'Preface', 2.
253 Harrison, qtd. in 'Harrison, Michael John', 272.
254 Ibid.
255 Harrison, 'Nash Circuit', 19.

256 Ibid.
257 Ibid. c.f. Moorcock, *Cure for Cancer*, part 1, 11.
258 Ibid.
259 Ibid., 21.
260 Harrison, qtd. in 'Harrison, Michael John', 272.
261 Harrison, 'Preface', 2.
262 Harrison, 'Nash Circuit', 14.
263 See Harrison and Richard Glyn Jones [artist], *The Adventures of Jerry Cornelius: The English Assassin*, International Times 1, no. 64, 22.
264 Harrison, 'Nash Circuit', 20.
265 See Pamela Pilbeam, *Madame Tussaud and the History of Waxworks* (London: Bloomsbury, 2003), 202–3.
266 Harrison, 'Nash Circuit', 20.
267 Ibid.
268 Ibid.
269 Ibid.
270 Harrison [as Joyce Churchill], 'The Angle of Attack', *NW*, no. 185, 60 (58–60).
271 Harrison, 'Nash Circuit', 20.
272 Ibid. Ellipsis in original.
273 Jean Baudrillard, *Simulacra and Simulation*, trans. Sheila Faria Glaser (1981; repr., Ann Arbor, MI: University of Michigan, 2006), 99–100.
274 Uta Kornmeier, 'Almost Alive: The Spectacle of Verisimilitude in Madame Tussaud's Waxworks', in *Ephemeral Bodies: Wax Sculpture and the Human Figure*, ed. Roberta Panzanelli (California: Getty, 2008), 73 (67–81).
275 See Walter Benjamin, 'The Work of Art in the Age of Mechanical Reproduction' (1935), in *Illuminations*, ed. Hannah Arendt, trans. Harry Zorn (1968; repr., London: Bodley Head, 2015), 211–44.
276 Harrison, 'Nash Circuit', 21.
277 Ibid., 22.
278 Ibid., 21.
279 Ibid., 22.
280 Ibid., 23.
281 Ibid., 22.
282 Ibid., 21.
283 Harrison, 'The Flesh Circle', in *The Nature of the Catastrophe*, eds Moorcock and Jones (London: Hutchinson, 1971), 155 (149–64).
284 Ibid., 160.
285 Ibid.
286 Ibid.
287 See Harrison, 'Preface', 2.

288 Harrison, 'Flesh Circle', 160.
289 Ibid.
290 Ibid., 161.
291 Ibid.
292 Ibid.
293 Ibid., 164. See also 'Ash Circus', 17.
294 Moorcock, *English Assassin*, 73–4.
295 Ibid., 40.
296 Ibid.
297 Ibid., 230.
298 Ibid., 111.
299 Ibid., 72.
300 Ibid.
301 Moorcock, *Cure for Cancer*, part 1, 20.
302 Moorcock, *English Assassin*, 72.
303 Ibid.
304 Ibid., 88.
305 Moorcock's 'The Dodgem Arrangement' is the exception.
306 See Michael Elliott, 'London: Nothing to Lose but Its Chains; A Survey', *The Economist* 298, no. 7427 (4 January 1986): 6 (1–18).
307 See ibid.
308 See Jan O'Malley, *The Politics of Community Action: A Decade of Struggle in Notting Hill* (Nottingham: Spokesman, 1977), 18.
309 See Dominic Sandbrook, *Seasons in the Sun: The Battle for Britain, 1974–1979* (London: Allen Lane, 2012), 569–95.
310 See Chris Hamnett, *Unequal City: London in the Global Arena* (London: Routledge, 2003), 2, 135–8.
311 See John Davis, 'From GLC to GLA: London Politics from Then to Now', in *London from Punk to Blair*, eds Joe Kerr and Andrew Gibson (London: Reaktion, 2003), 110 (109–15).
312 Geoffrey Evans, *Kensington* (London: Hamish Hamilton, 1975), 161.
313 Moorcock, *Condition of Muzak*, 25.
314 See Evans, *Kensington*, 160.
315 See 'Monastery of the Poor Clares Colettines, Westbourne Park Road', in *Northern Kensington*, vol. 37 of *The Survey of London*, ed. F. H. W. Sheppard (London: Athlone, 1973), 247 (247).
316 Moorcock, *Condition of Muzak*, 204.
317 Ibid., 211.
318 Moorcock, *Death Is No Obstacle*, 107.
319 See Porter, *London: A Social History*, 421 and Hamnett, *Unequal City*, 2, 5.

320 See Robert Hewison, *The Heritage Industry: Britain in a Climate of Decline* (London: Methuen, 1987), 37–47, 131–46.
321 Moorcock, 'London Peculiar', 43.
322 Ibid.
323 Moorcock, 'Heart and Soul of the City' (1990), in *London Peculiar*, 27 (26–9).
324 Moorcock, 'London Peculiar', 42.
325 Ibid., 46.
326 Ibid., 47.
327 Moorcock, 'Norton Goes to the Seaside' (2004), in *London Peculiar*, 298 (298–300).
328 Moorcock, 'Diary: 26th October 2007', in *London Peculiar*, 74 (73–5).
329 Harrison, 'Preface', 3.
330 Ibid.
331 Fiona Rule, *London's Docklands: A History of the Lost Quarter* (Surrey: Ian Allan, 2009), 270.
332 Moorcock, 'Child's Christmas in the Blitz', 19.
333 Ibid.
334 Moorcock, 'Heart and Soul of the City', 29.
335 Harrison and Cheryl Morgan [interviewer], 'Interview: M. John Harrison', *Strange Horizons*, 9 June 2003, http://strangehorizons.com/non-fiction/articles/interview-m-john-harrison/ [accessed 27 December 2019].
336 Ibid.
337 Ibid. and Harrison, 'south london, 1991', posted 21 October 2011, *M John Harrison Blog*, https://ambientehotel.wordpress.com/2011/10/21/south-london-1991/ [accessed 27 December 2019].
338 Moorcock, 'London Peculiar', 46.
339 Ibid., 47.
340 Walter Pater, 'The School of Giorgione' (1877), in *The Renaissance: Studies in Art and Poetry* (1873), 3rd edn (1888; repr., London: Fontana, 1971), 129 (126–44).
341 Moorcock, *Condition of Muzak*, 313.
342 See Louis Marin, *Utopics: Spatial Play*, trans. Robert A. Vollrath (London: Macmillan, 1984), 239–57.
343 Moorcock, *Death Is No Obstacle*, 101.
344 Ibid.
345 Moorcock, 'Preliminary Data', 101.
346 See Moorcock, *Condition of Muzak*, 68.
347 Ibid., 83.
348 Ibid., 58.
349 Ibid., 193.

350 Ibid., 139.
351 Ibid., 141.
352 Ibid., 218.
353 Ibid.
354 Ibid.
355 Ibid.
356 Ibid., 220.
357 Wells, *When the Sleeper Wakes* [Sutherland edn], 60.
358 Moorcock, *Condition of Muzak*, 225.
359 Ibid.
360 Ibid.
361 Ibid.
362 Ibid., 230.
363 Ibid.
364 Ibid., 20.
365 Ibid.
366 Ibid.
367 See Clute, 'Repossession of Jerry Cornelius', 8.
368 Moorcock, *Condition of Muzak*, 22.
369 Paul March-Russell, *Modernism and Science Fiction* (New York: Palgrave, 2015), 142.
370 Moorcock, *Condition of Muzak*, 22.
371 Ibid., 21.
372 Ibid., 25.
373 Ibid., 46.
374 Moorcock, *Cure for Cancer*, part 1, 8.
375 Moorcock, *English Assassin*, 109.
376 Moorcock, *Condition of Muzak*, 52.
377 Moorcock, *Cure for Cancer*, part 4, 11.
378 Moorcock, *Condition of Muzak*, 282.
379 Ibid., 287.
380 Ibid., 257.
381 Ibid.
382 See, for example, Moorcock, *Fabulous Harbours* (London: Millennium, 1995).
383 Moorcock, 'London Peculiar', 47.
384 See 'Harrison, Michael John', 272 and Latham, 'M. John Harrison (1945–)', in *British Fantasy and Science-Fiction Writers Since 1960*, ed. Darren Harris-Fain, vol. 261 of *Dictionary of Literary Biography* (Michigan: Gale, 2002), 236 (227–38).
385 On the autobiographical elements of *Climbers*, see Robert Macfarlane, 'Introduction' (2012), in Harrison, *Climbers* (1989), rev. edn (London: Gollancz, 2013), xiv (xi–xx).

386 Harrison, *Climbers* (London: Gollancz, 1989), 77. All subsequent references to *Climbers* are to this edition.
387 Harrison and Christopher J. Fowler [interviewer, interview conducted 1992], 'A Detective Fiction of the Heart: The First London Interview with M. John Harrison', *Foundation* 58 (Summer 1993): 15 (5–26).
388 Harrison, *Climbers*, 29.
389 Harrison, 'Running Down', *NWQ* 8, 11 (9–42).
390 Ibid.
391 Ibid.
392 Ibid.
393 Ibid.
394 Ibid., 12.
395 Ibid., 13.
396 Harrison, qtd. in Williams and Bould, 'Introduction: Broadly, Harrison', in *M. John Harrison*, 13 (11–19).
397 Harrison, 'The Incalling' (1978), in *Things That Never Happen* (San Francisco: Night Shade Books, 2003), 69 (69–92).
398 Ibid., 71, 70.
399 Ibid., 71.
400 Ibid., 81.
401 See Harrison, 'Gifco' (1992), in *Things That Never Happen*, 259–83 and Harrison, 'The Good Detective', in *You Should Come with Me Now: Stories of Ghosts* ([Manchester]: Comma, 2017), 158–9 (157–64).
402 Harrison, 'The Profession of Science Fiction, 40: The Profession of Fiction', *Foundation* 46 (Autumn 1989): 13 (5–13).
403 Harrison, 'Egnaro' (1980), in *Things That Never Happen*, 125 (105–25).
404 Harrison, 'The Profession of Science Fiction', 12, 13.
405 Harrison dated the story's composition inconsistently as 'February 1966' in his blog post and 'March, 1967' in his afterword to its original publication. See Harrison, 'the first viriconium story', posted 1 February 2014, *The M John Harrison Blog* https://ambientehotel.wordpress.com/2014/02/01/the-first-viriconium-story/ [accessed 1 August 2019] and Harrison, 'Lamia Mutable' (1966/7), in *Again, Dangerous Visions*, ed. Harlan Ellison (London: Millington, 1972), 709 (702–10).
406 Harrison, 'Lamia Mutable', 710.
407 Ibid., 709.
408 Harrison, *The Pastel City* (London: Nel, 1971), 24.
409 Ibid.
410 Harrison and Fowler [interviewer, interview conducted in two parts: the first in 1977, the second in 1980], 'The Last Rebel: An Interview with M. John Harrison', *Foundation* 23 (October 1981): 26 (5–30).
411 Harrison, *In Viriconium* (London: Gollancz, 1982), 35.

412 Harrison's 1980s Viriconium stories and books undermine the world-building established in the 1970s, as discussed in Chapter 5.
413 Harrison, 'Literature of Comfort', 172. c.f. Harrison, 'The Lamia and Lord Cromis', *NWQ* 1, 50–69.
414 Harrison, 'Critical Section: Sweet Analytics', *NWQ* 9 (1975): 212 (208–14). c.f. Harrison, 'Events Witnessed from a City', in *The Machine in Shaft Ten and Other Stories* (St Albans: Panther, 1975), 106–12.
415 Ibid.
416 Ibid.
417 Moorcock, *Mother London* (London: Secker & Warburg, 1988), 391.
418 'A Young Man's Journey to Viriconium/London' is discussed in Chapter 5.
419 Miéville, in Harrison and Bould [interviewer, interview conducted 13 April 2002, with Miéville present], 'Old, Mean and Misanthropic: An Interview with M. John Harrison', in *Parietal Games: Critical Writings by and on M. John Harrison*, eds Bould and Michelle Reid (London: Science Fiction Foundation, 2005), 338 (326–41).
420 Harrison, 'Last Rebel', 29.
421 Harrison, 'Sweet Analytics', 212.

Chapter 5

1 Miéville, 'Long Live the New Weird: Guest Editorial', *Third Alternative* 35 (Summer 2003): 3 (3).
2 Ibid.
3 Robert K. J. Killheffer, 'Fantasy Charts New Realms', *Publishers Weekly: The International News Magazine of Book Publishing and Bookselling* 244, no. 24 (June 1997): 34 (34–6).
4 Stuart Jeffries, 'G2: Space Operas and Far Futures; A Golden Age of British Sci-fi', *The Guardian*, 13 July 2009, 13 (13).
5 Libby Purves, 'The Winter's Tale', *The Times*, 20 December 2010, 12 (12).
6 See Pat Thane, *Divided Kingdom: A History of Britain, 1900 to the Present* (Cambridge: CUP, 2018), 379 and John Campbell, *Margaret Thatcher* (London: Pimlico, 2004).
7 Moorcock, 'The Spencer Inheritance' (1998), in *Jerry Cornelius: His Lives and His Times* (London: Gollancz, 2014), 310 (283–318).
8 Ibid., 297.
9 See Harrison, 'Viriconium Knights' (1981), in *Viriconium Nights* (1984), British edn (London: Gollancz, 1985), 84 (77–97) and Harrison, 'The Luck in the Head' (1984), in *Viriconium Nights*, 19 (11–36).

10 Luckhurst, 'Cultural Governance, New Labour, and the British Science Fiction Boom', special issue on the British Boom, *SFS* 30, no. 3 (2003), 417–35.
11 David Kamp, 'London Swings Again!', *Vanity Fair*, March 1997, 102 (99–144).
12 Stryker Mcguire and Michael Elliott [writers], Katharine Chubbuck, William Underhill, Carla Power and Carol Hall [reporters], 'Why London Rules', *Newsweek*, 4 November 1996, 44 (44–9).
13 Moorcock, 'Introduction to This Edition', *New Nature of the Catastrophe*, vi.
14 See Hamnett, *Unequal City*, 211–22.
15 See 'Breweries', *London Encyclopaedia*, 89 (89–91).
16 See Hamnett, *Unequal City*, 214–17; 'Billingsgate Market (Old)', *London Encyclopaedia*, 69 (69) and 'Battersea Power Station', *London Encyclopaedia*, 48 (48).
17 See Hamnett, *Unequal City*, 223–45 and 'Canary Wharf', *London Encyclopaedia*, 125–6.
18 Wells, *When the Sleeper Wakes* [Sutherland edn], 80.
19 See Hamnett, *Unequal City*, 172–8.
20 Phil Baker, 'Secret City: Psychogeography and the End of London', in *London from Punk to Blair*, 332 (323–33).
21 Luckhurst, 'The Contemporary London Gothic and the Limits of the "Spectral Turn"', 537.
22 Gaiman, 'On Viriconium: Some Notes toward an Introduction' (2005), *Journal*, posted 9 January 2012, http://journal.neilgaiman.com/2012/01/of-introductions-and-viriconium.html [accessed 25 July 2019].
23 See Mendlesohn, *Rhetorics of Fantasy*, 1–58.
24 Wells, 'Door in the Wall', 373, 366.
25 Harrison, 'Author's Introduction' (2003), in *Things That Never Happen*, 12 (11–14).
26 The present discussion owes a debt to Paul Kincaid, 'Kincaid in Short: A Young Man's Journey', *Vector*, no. 267 (Summer 2011): 33–5.
27 Harrison, 'A Young Man's Journey to Viriconium' (1985), in *Viriconium Nights*, 150 (139–58) and 'A Young Man's Journey to London' (2003), in *Things That Never Happen*, 178 (167–85). Subsequent references are to 'A Young Man's Journey to Viriconium', as the two versions are identical in all but the name of the city.
28 Harrison, 'A Young Man's Journey to Viriconium' 140, 153.
29 Ibid., 143.
30 Ibid., 147.
31 Ibid., 139.
32 Ibid., 140, 150.
33 Ibid., 142.
34 Ibid, 146.
35 Ibid., 141.

36 Ibid., 156.
37 Ibid., 157.
38 Harrison, *Climbers*, 211.
39 Ibid.
40 For a fuller discussion of these two scenes, see Ryan Elliott, 'On Versioning', in *M. John Harrison*, 108–10.
41 Harrison, 'A Young Man's Journey to Viriconium', 149 and Harrison, *Climbers*, 20. Variants in *Climbers* read: 'the plate-glass window'.
42 Harrison, 'A Young Man's Journey to Viriconium', 149 and Harrison, *Climbers*, 19. In *Climbers*, 'big plain' and 'or eighteen' are omitted.
43 Harrison and Fowler [interviewer, interview conducted 1985], 'On the Edge: The Last Holmfirth Interview with M. John Harrison', *Foundation* 57 (Spring 1993): 22 (5–26).
44 Ibid., 23.
45 Harrison, 'Author's Introduction', 13–14.
46 Harrison, 'Last Rebel', 10.
47 Miéville, Jeff VanderMeer [interviewer, interview conducted in two parts, the first in 2008, the second in 2012], 'China Miéville and Monsters', *Weird Fiction Review*, posted 20 March 2012, http://weirdfictionreview.com/2012/03/china-mieville-and-monsters-unsatisfy-me-frustrate-me-i-beg-you/ [accessed 4 May 2015].
48 Harrison, '1984 [*sic*] A Young Man's Journey to London', in 'Story Notes' (2003), in *Things That Never Happen*, 438 (435–43).
49 Harrison, 'Profession of Science Fiction', 11.
50 Harrison, qtd. in 'Harrison, Michael John', 272.
51 Harrison, 'Profession of Science Fiction', 11.
52 Ibid., 11–12.
53 Ibid., 11.
54 See Miéville, 'Old, Mean and Misanthropic', 337–8.
55 Miéville, *The Tain*, 293.
56 Ibid., 294.
57 Wells, *War of the Worlds* [Parrinder edn], 164.
58 Miéville, *The Tain*, 229, 230.
59 Ibid.
60 Wells, *War of the Worlds* [Parrinder edn], 165.
61 Miéville, *The Tain*, 229.
62 Wells, *War of the Worlds* [Parrinder edn], 169.
63 Miéville, *The Tain*, 236.
64 Slavoj Žižek, *The Fright of Real Tears: Krzysztof Kieślowski between Theory and Post-Theory* (London: BFI, 2001), 38.
65 Ibid., 35.
66 Wells, *War of the Worlds* [Parrinder edn], 167.

67 Miéville, *The Tain*, 229.
68 Ibid., 231.
69 Ibid., 253.
70 Ibid., 254.
71 Ibid.
72 Wells, *War of the Worlds* [Parrinder edn], 169.
73 Ibid., 7.
74 Miéville, *The Tain*, 290.
75 Andrew M. Butler, 'The Tain and the Tain: China Miéville's Gift of Uncanny London', *CR: The New Centennial Review* 13, no. 2 (Fall 2013): 140 (133–53).
76 Miéville, *The Tain*, 288.
77 Ibid., 299.
78 Ibid., 292.
79 Ibid., 294.
80 Ibid., 292.
81 Ibid.
82 Ibid., 293.
83 Ibid.
84 Ibid., 295.
85 Ibid., 292.
86 Ibid., 293.
87 Ibid., 292.
88 Ibid., 296.
89 Ibid.
90 Ibid., 295.
91 Tolkien, 'On Fairy-Stories', 67.
92 Miéville, *The Tain*, 295.
93 Ibid., 292.
94 Ibid., 295.
95 Gaiman, 'A Speech I Once Gave', [n.p.].
96 Ibid.
97 Ibid.
98 Clute, 'Been Bondage', *Interzone*, no. 126 (December 1997): 54 (52–5).
99 Ibid.
100 Gaiman, 'Neil Gaiman Introduces Neverwhere', [n.p.].
101 Ibid.
102 Ibid.
103 Ibid.
104 Gaiman, 'Neil Gaiman: Of Monsters and Miracles', *Locus* 42, no. 4, issue 459 (April 1999): 4, 66 (4, 66–8).
105 Dickens, qtd. in Forster, *Life of Charles Dickens*, 423.

106 Gaiman, qtd. in 'Well I Never!', *Empire*, 1 October 1996, 136 (136).
107 Ibid.
108 Irvine, 'Urban Fantasy', 201.
109 Ibid., 200.
110 Gaiman, *Neverwhere: Author's Preferred Text*, 9–10. c.f. Gaiman, *Neverwhere*, British edn (London: BBC, 1996), 12; Gaiman, *Neverwhere* (1996), American edn (1997; repr., New York: HarperTorch, 2001), 8–9. Subsequent references are to the *Author's Preferred Text*, which Gaiman considers the 'definitive' version of *Neverwhere*. See Gaiman, 'Introduction to This Text' (2005), *Neverwhere: Author's Preferred Text*, [n.p.].
111 Janin Hadlaw, 'The London Underground Map: Imagining Modern Time and Space', *Design Issues* 19, no. 1 (Winter 2003): 34 (25–35).
112 Janet Vertesi, 'Mind the Gap: The London Underground Map and Users' Representations of Urban Space', *Social Studies of Science* 38, no. 1 (February 2008): 9 (7–33).
113 Gaiman cited Douglas Camfield's *Doctor Who: Web of Fear* (1968) as a direct influence on *Neverwhere*. See Gaiman, 'Foreword by Neil Gaiman: The Nature of the Infection' (2003), in Paul McAuley, *The Eye of the Tyger* (Surrey: Telos, 2003), 9–10 (7–10).
114 Gaiman, *Neverwhere*, 86.
115 Ibid., 45, 18.
116 Ibid., 21.
117 This insight owes a debt to Joseph Cozzi, 'Nevermore: The Influence of Thatcherism on *Neverwhere*', undergraduate paper, submitted November 2018, the University of Notre Dame (USA) in England. Unpublished.
118 Gaiman, *Neverwhere*, 12.
119 Ibid., 23.
120 David Ashford, *London Underground: A Cultural Geography* (Liverpool: LUP, 2013), 169.
121 Gaiman, *Neverwhere*, 142.
122 Ibid.
123 Ibid., 150, 151.
124 Ibid., 162.
125 See J. E. Connor, *London's Disused Underground Stations* (1999), 2nd & enlarged edn (Middlesex: Capital Transport, 2008), 40–3.
126 Gaiman, *Neverwhere*, 162.
127 Ibid., 136.
128 Ibid., 62.
129 See Cyril M. Harris, *What's in a Name?: The Origins of the Names of All Stations in Current Use on the London Underground and Docklands Light Rail with Their Opening Dates* (1977), 4th edn (Harrow: Capital History, 2001).

130 Gaiman, *Neverwhere*, 51.
131 See ibid., 274–5.
132 Ibid., 101.
133 See ibid., 231.
134 Ibid., 132.
135 Ibid., 153.
136 Ibid., 120.
137 Ibid., 137.
138 Ibid., 48.
139 Dickens, *Old Curiosity Shop*, 19.
140 Gaiman, *Neverwhere*, 110–1.
141 Lefebvre, *The Production of Space* (1974), trans. Donald Nicholson-Smith, first English translation (Oxford: Blackwell, 1991), 38.
142 Ibid.
143 Ibid., 16.
144 Ibid.
145 Ibid., 46.
146 See Gaiman, *Neverwhere*, 99.
147 See ibid., 7.
148 See ibid., 273.
149 Ibid., 109.
150 Ibid., 123.
151 Ibid., 124.
152 Ibid., 111.
153 'Harrods', *London Encyclopaedia*, 386 (385–6).
154 See Sean Callery, *Harrods, Knightsbridge: The Story of Society's Favourite Store* (London: Ebury, 1991), 73 and Rupert Neate, 'Harrods Limits Christmas Grotto to £2,000-Plus Spenders', *The Guardian*, 8 November 2019, https://www.theguardian.com/business/2019/nov/08/harrods-restricts-christmas-grotto-to-2000-plus-spenders [accessed 12 January 2020].
155 Gaiman, *Neverwhere*, 15.
156 Ibid.
157 Ibid., 110.
158 Ibid.
159 This insight owes a debt to Holly Prescott, '"Rid Yourself of This Surface Mentality": Re-thinking Urban Space in the Contemporary London Descent Narrative', special issue on *London: Urban Space as Cultural Experience*, ed. Ulrich Kinzel, *LWU: Literatur in Wissenschaft und Unterricht* 43, nos 2/3 (2010): 190, 192 (185–98).
160 Gaiman, *Neverwhere*, 110.

161 Ibid., 110, 116.
162 Ibid., 112, 113.
163 Ibid., 124.
164 Ibid., 110.
165 Ibid., 109.
166 See Gaiman, 'Neil Gaiman Interview', conducted 1996, and 'Audio Commentary with Writer Neil Gaiman', recorded 2003, both in *Neverwhere: The Complete Series*, conceptualized by Gaiman and Lenny Henry, written by Gaiman, directed by Dewi Humphreys (BBC, broadcast September–October 1996), DVD 2007.
167 Gaiman, *Neverwhere*, 372.
168 Tolkien, 'On Fairy-Stories', 79.
169 Gaiman, 'Neil Gaiman Lecture in Full: Reading and Obligation', delivered 14 October 2013, *The Reading Agency*, https://readingagency.org.uk/news/blog/neil-gaiman-lecture-in-full.html [accessed 30 December 2019].
170 Gaiman, 'Neil Gaiman Introduces Neverwhere', [n.p.].
171 Gaiman, qtd. in Alastair Mabbott, 'Fantasies That Stretch into Other Worlds', *The Scotsman*, 4 September 1996, 20 (20).
172 Ibid. and Gaiman, *Neverwhere*, 126.
173 Gaiman, *Neverwhere*, 371.
174 Ibid., 297.
175 Ibid., 141, 142.
176 Ibid., 275.
177 Ibid., 153.
178 Ibid., 52.
179 Ibid., 224.
180 Ibid., 101.
181 Robert Louis Stevenson, 'To Frances Sitwell' (15 September 1874), in *The Letters of Robert Louis Stevenson*, eds Bradford A. Booth and Ernest Mehew, vol. 2, *April 1874–July 1879* (New Haven: YUP, 1994), 53 (52–3).
182 Jane Welsh Carlyle to Jeannie Welsh (23 December 1843), in *Jane Welsh Carlyle: Letters to Her Family*, ed. Leonard Huxley (London: John Murray, 1924), 169 (168–71).
183 Clute, 'Been Bondage', 54.
184 Gaiman, 'A Chat with the Author of the Sandman Series', conducted 7 February 2000, posted 9 February 2000 *CNN – Chat Books*, http://edition.cnn.com/chat/transcripts/2000/2/gaiman/index.html [accessed 29 July 2019].
185 Bould, 'The Dreadful Credibility of Absurd Things: A Tendency in Fantasy Theory', *Historical Materialism* 10, no. 4, 81 (51–88).
186 Miéville, *Perdido Street Station*, [n.p.].
187 Ibid., 194, 688.

188 Ibid., 13 and Harrison, *A Storm of Wings* (London: Sphere Books, 1980), 98.
189 Miéville, 'Messing with Fantasy', *Locus* 48, no. 3, issue 494 (March 2002): 5 (4–5, 75–6).
190 Peake, *Gormenghast*, 495.
191 Peake, *Titus Groan*, 329.
192 Miéville, *Perdido Street Station*, 416.
193 Ibid., 206.
194 Wells, 'Popularising Science', *Nature* 50, no. 1291 (July 1894): 301 (300–1).
195 Miéville, 'Editorial Introduction', 43.
196 Orwell, *Nineteen Eighty-Four*, 37.
197 Miéville, 'Fantasy and Revolution', [n.p.].
198 Tolkien, 'On Fairy-Stories', 68.
199 For an example of Miéville's more level-headed critique of Tolkien, see Miéville and Richard Marshall [interviewer], 'The Road to Perdido: An Interview with China Mieville [sic]', posted 2003, *3am Interview* https://www.3ammagazine.com/litarchives/2003/feb/interview_china_mieville.html [accessed 6 August 2019].
200 Tolkien, 'On Fairy-Stories', 67, 75.
201 Harrison, 'Author's Note', in the American edn of *In Viriconium* (1982), retitled *The Floating Gods* (New York: Timescape, 1983), [n.p.].
202 Ibid.
203 Harrison, *In Viriconium*, 11 and Harrison, 'The Dancer from the Dance' (1985), in *Viriconium Nights*, 101 (99–122).
204 Harrison, 'Lords of Misrule' (1984), in *Viriconium Nights*, 128 (123–35).
205 Harrison, 'Dancer from the Dance', 121.
206 Harrison, 'Luck in the Head', 36.
207 Harrison, 'A Young Man's Journey to London', throughout.
208 Miéville, 'Tolkien – Middle Earth Meets Middle England', *Socialist Review*, no. 259, posted January 2002, http://socialistreview.org.uk/259/tolkien-middle-earth-meets-middle-england [accessed 8 July 2016].
209 Miéville, 'Fantasy and Revolution', [n.p.].
210 Miéville, 'Appropriate Means', [172].
211 Miéville, 'Messing with Fantasy', 5.
212 Ibid.
213 Harrison, 'Sweet Analytics', 212.
214 Miéville, *Perdido Street Station*, 140.
215 Ibid., 20.
216 Jeff VanderMeer, 'Introduction; The New Weird: "It's Alive?"', in *The New Weird*, eds Ann and Jeff VanderMeer (San Francisco: Tachyon, 2008), xvi (ix–xviii).
217 Miéville, *The Scar* (2002; repr., London: Pan, 2003), 38.

218 Ibid., 33.
219 Miéville, *Iron Council* (2004; repr., London: Pan, 2005), 67.
220 Ibid., 70.
221 Ibid., 72.
222 Ibid., 73.
223 Farrell, 'Socialist Surrealism', 284.
224 Joan Gordon has made a similar point with regard to hybridity in Miéville's fantastical fictions, to which this discussion owes a debt. See Gordon, 'Hybridity, Heterotopia, and Mateship in China Miéville's *Perdido Street Station*', special issue on The British SF Boom, *SFS* 30, no. 3, 456–76.
225 Miéville, 'Reveling in Genre', 368.
226 Miéville, 'Editorial Introduction', 42.
227 Ibid., 45.
228 Ibid., 48.
229 Due to the limited compass of this chapter, the following analysis does not discuss the ending of *The Scar*, but the spirit of these remarks pertains equally to the revolution in Armada, which narrowly prevents disaster but hardly promises long-term radical change.
230 Miéville, *Perdido Street Station*, 54.
231 Ibid., 37.
232 Ibid., 867.
233 Ibid., 5, 867.
234 Miéville, *Iron Council*, 224.
235 Ibid.
236 Ibid., 590.
237 Ibid., 224.
238 Ibid., 295.
239 Ibid., 614.
240 Mendlesohn, *Rhetorics of Fantasy*, 113.
241 Miéville and Neil Macdonald [interviewer], 'Monsters, Method, Bas-Lag and Kraken', *Scifilove*, posted 12 May 2010, http://scyfilove.com/2201/china-mieville-exclusive-interview-monsters-method-bas-lag-and-kraken/ [accessed 8 July 2016].
242 See White, *London in the Twentieth Century*, 76 and Graham Pointer, 'The UK's Major Urban Areas', in *Focus on People and Migration* (London: Palgrave, 2005), 47 (45–60).
243 White, *London in the Twentieth Century*, 141.
244 Ibid., 143.
245 Miéville, 'Reveling in Genre', 355.
246 Miéville, *London's Overthrow* (London: Westbourne, 2012), 76.

247 Miéville, *Perdido Street Station*, 617.
248 Miéville, *The Scar*, 594.
249 Miéville and Nick Gevers [interviewer], 'Cities Near, Cities Far: An Interview with China Miéville', [interviewer, interview conducted in November 2002], *Infinity Plus*, posted 2003, http://www.infinityplus.co.uk/nonfiction/intchina2.htm [accessed 5 May 2015].
250 Ibid.
251 Miéville, *King Rat* (1998; repr., London: Pan, 2011), 67.
252 Ibid., 241.
253 Ibid., 273.
254 Ibid. This discussion owes a debt to Bould, 'Mind the Gap: The Impertinent Predicates (and Subjects) of *King Rat* and *Looking for Jake and Other Stories*', special issue on China Miéville, *Extrapolation* 50, no. 2, 307–25.
255 Robert Browning, 'The Piped Piper of Hamelin' (1842), in Browning, *Robert Browning: A Critical Edition of the Major Works*, ed. Adam Roberts (Oxford: OUP, 1997), 125, line 33 (124–32).
256 Miéville, *King Rat*, 163.
257 See Peake, *Titus Alone*, 862, 937.
258 Miéville, *King Rat*, 398.
259 Ibid., 420.
260 Ibid.
261 Miéville, 'Reveling in Genre', 361–2.
262 Miéville, *King Rat*, 258.
263 Miéville, *Perdido Street Station*, 831.
264 Miéville, *King Rat*, 407.
265 Ibid.
266 Ibid.
267 Miéville openly acknowledged *Neverwhere*'s influence on *Un Lun Dun*. See Miéville, 'Acknowledgements', in *Un Lun Dun*, British edn (2007; repr., London: Pan, 2008), [n.p.].
268 Miéville, *Un Lun Dun*, 71.
269 Ibid., 517.
270 Ibid., 509.
271 Ibid., 511.
272 Ibid., 503.
273 Ibid., 514.
274 Ibid., 516.
275 Miéville, *Perdido Street Station*, 5.
276 Paul Kincaid and Niall Harrison (eds), *British Science Fiction and Fantasy: Twenty Years, Two Surveys* (St Albans: BSFA, 2010), 143.
277 Miéville, qtd. in ibid., 149.

278 Ben Aaronovitch, *Broken Homes* (2013; repr., London: Gollancz, 2014), 83.
279 Aaronovitch, *Moon Over Soho* (London: Gollancz, 2011), 235.
280 Aaronovitch, *Whispers Underground* (London: Gollancz, 2012), 389.
281 Aaronovitch, *Lies Sleeping* (London: Gollancz, 2018), 48.
282 Ibid., 104.
283 Aaronovitch, *The Hanging Tree* (London: Gollancz, 2016), 299.
284 Aaronovitch, *Lies Sleeping*, 387.
285 Aaronovitch, *Foxglove Summer* (2014; repr., London: Gollancz, 2015), 8.
286 Aaronovitch, *Lies Sleeping*, 281.
287 Ibid.
288 T. S. Eliot, 'Tradition and the Individual Talent' (1919), in *The Sacred Wood*, rev. edn (1920; repr., London: Faber and Faber, 1997), 41 (39–49).
289 Moorcock, 'Facing the City', 183.
290 Miéville, 'The *Lit* Interview', [n.p.].
291 Adorno, 'Reconciliation Under Duress', 160.
292 Wells, 'Story of the Days to Come', 228.
293 Ibid., 229.
294 Dickens, *Chimes*, 125.
295 Ibid., 124 and Dickens, 'A Christmas Tree', *HW* 2, no. 39 (21 December 1850): 291 (289–95).
296 Dickens, 'New Uncommercial Samples: On an Amateur Beat', *AYR* 1, no. 34 (27 February 1869): 301 (300–3).
297 Ibid., 300.
298 Ibid., 301. See also Dickens, *Bleak House*, 11.
299 Forster, *Life of Charles Dickens*, 11.
300 Dickens, 'New Uncommercial Samples', 301.
301 Wells, *Time Machine* [Parrinder edn], 78.
302 Ibid., 64.
303 Wells, *Experiment in Autobiography*, vol. 2, 570–1.
304 Wells, 'Traffic and Rebuilding' (1911), in *An Englishman Looks at the World: Being a Series of Unrestrained Remarks upon Contemporary Matters* (London: Cassell, 1914), 191 (188–91).
305 Wells, *Tono-Bungay*, 329.
306 Wells, *Anticipations*, 35.
307 Wells, *Experiment in Autobiography*, vol. 1, 30.
308 Wells, *Anticipations*, 35.
309 Ibid., 36.
310 Ibid.
311 Ibid., 56, 35.
312 Peake, 'London Fantasy', 3.

313 Peake, *Titus Alone*, 830.
314 Orwell, 'Wells, Hitler and the World State', 540.
315 Harrison, *Climbers*, 29.
316 Gaiman, qtd. in 'Well I Never!', 136.
317 Ibid.
318 Miéville and Benjamin Eastham [interviewer], 'China Miéville in Conversation with *The White Review*', conducted 15 May 2013, *London Review Bookshop* http://www.londonreviewbookshop.co.uk/events/past/2013/5/china-mieville-in-conversation-with-the-white-review [accessed 4 September 2016].
319 Ibid.
320 Ibid.
321 Miéville, *Kraken* (London: Pan, 2010), 283.
322 Miéville, *Perdido Street Station*, 867.
323 Miéville and Annalee Newitz [interviewer], 'China Miéville Explains Theology, Magic, and Why JJ Abrams Hates You', *io9: We Come from the Future*, posted 8 November 2010, http://io9.com/5605836/china-mieville-explains-theology-magic-and-why-jj-abrams-hates-you [accessed 30 April 2015].
324 Wells, *When the Sleeper Wakes* [Sutherland edn], 191.
325 For Peake on *Bleak House*, see Winnington, *Vast Alchemies*, 283.
326 Peake, Add MS 88931/1/3/9, 'Ideas for Book Two', 2.
327 See Andrew Light, 'Urban Ecological Citizenship' (2003), in *Technology and Values*, ed. Craig Hanks (Sussex: Wiley-Blackwell, 2010), 400 (397–414).

Bibliography

Works cited

Aaronovitch, Ben. *Broken Homes*. 2013. Reprint, London: Gollancz, 2014.
Aaronovitch, Ben. *Foxglove Summer*. 2014. Reprint, London: Gollancz, 2015.
Aaronovitch, Ben. *The Hanging Tree*. London: Gollancz, 2016.
Aaronovitch, Ben. *Lies Sleeping*. London: Gollancz, 2018.
Aaronovitch, Ben. *Moon Over Soho*. London: Gollancz, 2011.
Aaronovitch, Ben. *Whispers Underground*. London: Gollancz, 2012.
Ackroyd, Peter. *London: The Biography*. London: Chatto & Windus, 2000.
Adorno, Theodor. 'An Address on Charles Dickens's *The Old Curiosity Shop*'. 1931. Translated by Michael Hollington. *Dickens Quarterly* 6, no. 3 (September 1989): 95–101.
Adorno, Theodor. *Aesthetic Theory*. 1970. Translated by C. Lenhardt. Edited by Gretel Adorno and Rolf Tiedemann. Reprint, London: Routledge and Kegan Paul, 1986.
Adorno, Theodor. 'Reconciliation under Duress'. In *Aesthetics and Politics*, translated by Rodney Livingstone, edited by Ronald Taylor, 151–76. 1977. Reprint, London: Verso, 1992.
Allen, Grant. 'Pallinghurst Barrow'. 1892. In *Ivan Greet's Masterpiece*, 67–89. London: Chatto & Windus, 1893.
Anderson, David L. *The Vietnam War*. Hampshire: Palgrave, 2005.
Armitt, Lucie. *Fantasy Fiction: An Introduction*. London: Continuum, 2005.
Arvatov, Boris. 'Everyday Life and the Culture of the Thing'. Translated by Christina Kiaer. *October* 81 (Summer 1997): 119–28.
Ashford, David. *London Underground: A Cultural Geography*. Liverpool: Liverpool University Press, 2013.
Ashley, Michael. *The History of the Science-Fiction Magazine*. 4 vols. 1974–8. Revised and expanded editions. Liverpool: Liverpool University Press, 2000–16.
Atterbery, Brian. *Strategies of Fantasy*. Indianapolis: Indiana University Press, 1992.
Baudrillard, Jean. *Simulacra and Simulation*. Translated by Sheila Faria Glaser. 1981. Reprint, Ann Arbor: University of Michigan, 2006.
Beaumont, Matthew. *Nightwalking: A Nocturnal History of London, Chaucer to Dickens*. London: Verso, 2015.
Beckett, Andy. *When the Lights Went Out: Britain in the Seventies*. London: Faber and Faber, 2009.

Bennett, Arnold. *Arnold Bennett and H. G. Wells: A Record of a Personal and a Literary Friendship*. With introduction. Edited by Harris Wilson. London: Rupert Hart-Davis, 1960.

Bergonzi, Bernard. *The Early H. G. Wells: A Study of the Scientific Romances*. Manchester: Manchester University Press, 1961.

Blackwood, William III. 'The Old Saloon'. *Blackwood's Edinburgh Magazine* 141, no. 856 (February 1887): 291–315.

'The Books of the Past Year'. *The Court Magazine and La Belle Assemblée* 10, no. 1 (1 January 1837): 4–14.

Bould, Mark. 'The Dreadful Credibility of Absurd Things: A Tendency in Fantasy Theory'. *Historical Materialism* 10, no. 4 (January 2002): 51–88.

Bowen, Elizabeth. 'Mysterious Kôr'. 1944. In *The Collected Stories of Elizabeth Bowen*, edited by Angus Wilson, 728–40. London: Jonathan Cape, 1980.

Browning, Robert. 'The Piped Piper of Hamelin'. 1842. In Browning, *Robert Browning: A Critical Edition of the Major Works*, edited by Adam Roberts, 124–32. Oxford: Oxford University Press, 1997.

Buckwald, Craig. 'Stalking the Figurative Oyster: The Excursive Ideal in *A Christmas Carol*'. *Studies in Short Fiction* 27, no. 1 (Winter 1990): 1–14.

Bulwer-Lytton, Edward. *The Coming Race*. 1871. Reprinted with notes and introduction. Edited by David Seed. Middletown: Wesleyan University Press, 2006.

Bulwer-Lytton, Edward. *The Letters of Sir Edward Bulwer-Lytton to the Editors of Blackwood's Magazine, 1840–1873, in the National Library of Scotland*. Edited by Malcolm Orthell Usrey. PhD dissertation. Texas Technological College, 1963.

Butler, Andrew M. '*The Tain* and the Tain: China Miéville's Gift of Uncanny London'. *CR: The New Centennial Review* 13, no. 2 (Fall 2013): 133–53.

Carey, John. *The Intellectuals and the Masses: Pride and Prejudice Among the Literary Intelligentsia, 1880–1939*. London: Faber and Faber, 1992.

Carey, John. *The Violent Effigy: A Study of Dickens' Imagination*. 1973. 2nd edn. London: Faber and Faber, 1991.

Carlyle, Jane Welsh. *Jane Welsh Carlyle: Letters to Her Family*. Edited by Leonard Huxley. London: John Murray, 1924.

Carlyle, Thomas. 'Sartor Resartus'. *Fraser's Magazine* 10, no. 56 (1834): 77–87.

Certeau, Michel de. *The Practice of Everyday Life*. Translated by Steven Rendall. 1984. Reprint, Berkeley: University of California Press, 1988.

Chesterton, G. K. *Charles Dickens*. 1906. In *Chesterton on Dickens*, edited by Alzina Stone Dale, with notes and introduction, vol. 15 of *The Collected Works of G. K. Chesterton*, 29–209. San Francisco: Ignatius, 1989.

Clayton, Jay. *Charles Dickens in Cyberspace*. Oxford: Oxford University Press, 2003.

Clayton, Jay. 'The Dickens Tape: Affect and Sound Reproduction in *The Chimes*'. In *Dickens and Modernity*, edited by Juliet John, 19–40. Suffolk: English Association, 2012.

Clute, John. 'Been Bondage'. *Interzone*, no. 126 (December 1997): 52–5.

Clute, John and John Grant, eds. *The Encyclopedia of Fantasy*. 1997. Revised online edn. 1999–present. http://sf-encyclopedia.uk/fe.php?id=0&nm=introduction_to_the_online_text [accessed 16 May 2020].

Clute, John and Peter Nicholls, eds. *The Encyclopedia of Science Fiction*. 1993. 2nd edn. London: Orbit, 1999.

Clute, John. 'Tim Powers: The Anubis Gates'. 1983. In *Horror: 100 Best Books*, with introduction, edited by Stephen Jones and Kim Newman, 193–5. London: Xanadu, 1988.

Cobbett, William. 'To Mr. Canning'. 1823. In *The Opinions of William Cobbett*, edited by James Grande, John Stevenson and Richard Thomas, 84. Surrey: Ashgate, 2013.

Cohen, Jane R. *Charles Dickens and His Original Illustrators*. Columbus: Ohio State University Press, 1980.

Connolly, Cyril. 'Comment'. *Horizon* 15, no. 87 (April 1947): 151–4.

Davis, Paul. *The Lives and Times of Ebenezer Scrooge*. London: Yale University Press, 1990.

Debord, Guy. 'Introduction to a Critique of Urban Geography'. 1955. In *Situationist International: Anthology*, edited by and translated by Ken Knabb, 5–8. Berkeley: Bureau of Public Secrets, 1981.

Defoe, Daniel. *A Tour through the Whole Island of Great Britain*. Vol. 1. 1724–6. Revised edn. London: Dent, 1966.

Derry & Toms Famous Roof Gardens. Brochure. Norwich: Jarrold & Sons, 1966. Guildhall Library, shelf number Pam 21247.

Desmond, Ray. *The History of the Royal Botanic Gardens; Kew*. 1995. 2nd edn. Kew: Kew Publishing, 2007.

Dickens, Charles. 'All the Year Round'. *Household Words* 19, no. 479 (28 May 1859): 601.

Dickens, Charles. *Bleak House*. 1852–3. Edited by Stephen Gill. Reprinted with notes and introduction. Oxford: Oxford University Press, 1998.

Dickens, Charles. *Charles Dickens' Book of Memoranda: A Photographic and Typographic Facsimile of the Notebook Begun in January 1855*. Transcribed and annotated by Fred Kaplan. New York: New York Public Library, 1981.

Dickens, Charles. *Charles Dickens as Editor: Being Letters Written by Him to William Henry Wills His Sub-Editor*. Edited by R. C. Lehmann. London: Smith, Elder & Co., 1912.

Dickens, Charles. *A Christmas Carol: A Facsimile of the Original Manuscript*. Written 1843. London: Cassell, 1897.

Dickens, Charles. *A Christmas Carol and Other Christmas Books*. 1843–1848. With notes and introduction. Edited by Robert Douglas-Fairhurst. Oxford: Oxford University Press, 2006.

Dickens, Charles. 'A Christmas Tree'. *Household Words* 2, no. 39 (21 December 1850): 289–95.

Dickens, Charles. *Dombey and Son*. 1846–8. Reprinted with notes and introduction. Edited by Alan Horsman. Oxford: Oxford University Press, 2001.

Dickens, Charles. 'Frauds on the Fairies'. *Household Words* 8, no. 184 (1 October 1853): 97–100.
Dickens, Charles. 'Gone Astray'. *Household Words* 7, no. 177 (13 August 1853): 553–7.
Dickens, Charles. *Great Expectations*. 1860–1. Reprinted with notes and introduction. Edited by Margaret Cardwell. Oxford: Oxford University Press, 2008.
Dickens, Charles. *The Letters of Charles Dickens*. 12 vols. Edited by Madeline House, Graham Storey, K. J. Fielding, Kathleen Tillotson, Nina Burgis, and Angus Easson. Oxford: Oxford University Press, 1965–2002.
Dickens, Charles. *The Life of Our Lord*. Written 1849. In *American Notes; Pictures from Italy; A Child's History of England; The Life of Our Lord*, vol. 1 of *The Nonesuch Dickens*, edited by Arthur Waugh, Hugh Walpole, Walter Dexter and Thomas Hatton, 855–91. Bloomsbury: Nonesuch, 1938.
Dickens, Charles. *Little Dorrit*. 1855–7. Reprinted with notes and introduction. Edited by Harvey Peter Sucksmith. Oxford: Oxford University Press, 2008.
Dickens, Charles. *Martin Chuzzlewit*. 1843–4. Reprinted with notes and introduction. Edited by Margaret Cardwell. Oxford: Oxford University Press, 2009.
Dickens, Charles. 'New Uncommerical Samples: On an Amateur Beat'. *All the Year Round* 1, no. 34 (27 February 1869): 300–3.
Dickens, Charles and W. H. Wills. 'Notes for Household Words'. Transcribed and published by Philip Collins. *Victorian Periodicals Newsletter*, no. 8 (April 1970): 33–46.
Dickens, Charles. *The Old Curiosity Shop*. 1840–1. Reprinted with notes and introduction. Edited by Elizabeth M. Brennan. Oxford: Oxford University Press, 1997.
Dickens, Charles. 'Old Lamps for New Ones'. *Household Words* 1, no. 12 (15 June 1850): 265–7.
Dickens, Charles. 'On Duty with Inspector Field'. *Household Words* 3, no. 64 (14 June 1851): 265–70.
Dickens, Charles. *Our Mutual Friend*. 1864–5. Reprinted with notes and introduction. Edited by Michael Cotsell. Oxford: Oxford University Press, 2008.
Dickens, Charles. *The Pickwick Papers*. 1836–7. Reprinted with notes and introduction. Edited by James Kinsley. Oxford: Oxford University Press, 2008.
Dickens, Charles. 'A Preliminary Word'. *Household Words* 1, no. 1 (30 March 1850): 1–2.
Dickens, Charles. 'Railway Dreaming'. *Household Words* 13, no. 320 (10 May 1856): 385–8.
Dickens, Charles. *Sketches by Boz: Illustrative of Every-Day Life and Every-Day People*. 1833–6. Reprinted with introduction. Edited by Thea Holme. Oxford: Oxford University Press, 1997.
Dickens, Charles. 'The Uncommercial Traveller' ['Nurse's Stories']. *All the Year Round* 3, no. 72 (8 September 1860): 517–21.
Dickens, Charles. Untitled Announcement. *All the Year Round* 2, no. 31 (26 November 1859): 95.

Dickens, Charles. 'Where We Stopped Growing'. *Household Words* 6, no. 145 (1 January 1853): 361–3.

Disch, Thomas M. 'The Lessons of the Future'. *New Worlds*, no. 173 (July 1967): 2–3.

Duncan, Ian. *Modern Romance and Transformations of the Novel: The Gothic, Scott, Dickens*. Cambridge: Cambridge University Press, 1992.

Eliot, T. S. 'Tradition and the Individual Talent'. 1919. In Eliot, *The Sacred Wood*, revised edn 1920, 39–49. Reprint, London: Faber and Faber, 1997.

Evans, Geoffrey. *Kensington*. London: Hamish Hamilton, 1975.

Everon, Ernest. 'Some Thoughts Anent Dickens and Novel Writing'. *The Ladies' Cabinet* (May 1855): 257–62.

Farrell, Henry. 'Socialist Surrealism: China Miéville's New Crobuzon Novels'. In *New Boundaries in Political Science Fiction*, edited by Donald Hassler and Clyde Wilcox, 272–9. Columbia, SC: University of South Carolina Press, 2008.

Fitzgerald, Percy. *Memories of Charles Dickens*. Bristol and London: J. W. Arrowsmith, 1913.

Forster, John. *The Life of Charles Dickens*. 1871–3. Edited by J. W. T. Ley. One-volume memorial edn. London: Cecil Palmer, 1928.

Gaiman, Neil. 'A Chat with the Author of the Sandman Series'. Conducted 7 February 2000. Posted 9 February 2000. CNN – *Chat Books*. http://edition.cnn.com/chat/tr anscripts/2000/2/gaiman/index.html [accessed 29 July 2019].

Gaiman, Neil. 'Chat with Neil Gaiman'. Conducted 22 October 1998. *Event Horizon*. http://www.astralgia.com/sfzine/chats/transcripts/102298.html [accessed 10 August 2019].

Gaiman, Neil. 'Neil Gaiman Lecture in Full: Reading and Obligation'. Delivered 14 October 2013. The Reading Agency, https://readingagency.org.uk/news/blog/n eil-gaiman-lecture-in-full.html [accessed 30 December 2019].

Gaiman, Neil. 'Neil Gaiman: Of Monsters and Miracles'. *Locus* 42, no. 4, issue 459 (April 1999): 4, 66–8.

Gaiman, Neil. *Neverwhere: Author's Preferred Text*. 1996. Revised edn. London: Headline, 2005.

Gaiman, Neil. 'On Viriconium: Some Notes Toward an Introduction'. 2005. *Journal*. Posted 9 January 2012, http://journal.neilgaiman.com/2012/01/of-introductions-and-viriconium.html [accessed 25 July 2019].

Gaiman, Neil. 'A Speech I Once Gave: On Lewis, Tolkien and Chesterton'. Delivered 2004. *Journal*. Posted 2012, http://journal.neilgaiman.com/2012/01/speech-i-onc e-gave-on-lewis-tolkien-and.html [accessed 26 December 2019].

Gaiman, Neil and Jayme Blaschke [interviewer]. 'Voices of Vision: Neil Gaiman'. Conducted 2002. In *Conversations with Neil Gaiman*, edited by Joseph Michael Sommers, 102–13. Jackson: University Press of Mississippi, 2018.

Gardiner-Scott, Tanya. *Mervyn Peake: The Evolution of a Dark Romantic*. New York: Peter Lang, 1989.

Gibbons, Tom. 'H. G. Wells's Fire Sermon: *The War of the Worlds* and the Book of Revelation'. *Science Fiction: A Review of Speculative Literature* 6, no. 1 (1984): 5–14.

Gifford, James. *A Modernist Fantasy: Modernism, Anarchism, & the Radical Fantastic*. Victoria, Canada: ELS, 2018.

Gilmore, Maeve. *A World Away: A Memoir of Mervyn Peake*. London: Gollancz, 1970.

Gissing, George. 'Oliver Twist'. 1899. In *Essays, Introductions and Reviews*, vol. 1 of *Collected Works of George Gissing on Charles Dickens*, edited by Pierre Coustillas, 87–95. Surrey: Grayswood, 2004.

Glass, Ruth. 'Introduction: Aspects of Change'. 1963. In *London: Aspects of Change*, edited by Centre for Urban Studies, xiii–xlii. London: Macgibbon and Kee, 1964.

Godwin, George and John Britton. *The Churches of London: A History and Description of the Ecclesiastical Edifices of the Metropolis*. London: C. Tilt, 1838.

Gomel, Elana. *Narrative Space and Time: Representing Impossible Topologies in Literature*. New York: Routledge, 2014.

Greenland, Colin. *Entropy Exhibition: Michael Moorcock and the British 'New Wave' in Science Fiction*. London: Routledge & Kegan Paul, 1983.

Greer, Germaine. 'Books of the Century: Germaine Greer on Our Readers' Poll'. *W: The Waterstone's Magazine* 8 (Winter/Spring 1997): 2–9.

Hadlaw, Janin. 'The London Underground Map: Imagining Modern Time and Space'. *Design Issues* 19, no. 1 (Winter 2003): 25–35.

Hammond, J. R. *H. G. Wells and the Modern Novel*. Basingstoke: Pan Macmillan, 1988.

Hardy, Barbara. *Dickens and Creativity*. London: Continuum, 2008.

Harrison, M. John [as Joyce Churchill]. 'The Angle of Attack'. *New Worlds*, no. 185 (December 1968): 58–60.

Harrison, M. John. 'The Ash Circus'. *New Worlds*, no. 189 (April 1969): 17–23.

Harrison, M. John. 'Author's Note'. In American edn of *In Viriconium*, 1982, retitled *The Floating Gods*, n.p. New York: Timescape, 1983.

Harrison, M. John. 'By Tennyson Out of Disney'. *New Worlds Quarterly* 2 (1971): 181–5.

Harrison, M. John. *Climbers*. London: Gollancz, 1989.

Harrison, M. John. 'Critical Section: Sweet Analytics'. *New Worlds Quarterly* 9 (1975): 208–14.

Harrison, M. John and Christopher Fowler [interviewer, interview conducted 1992]. 'A Detective Fiction of the Heart: The First London Interview with M. John Harrison'. *Foundation* 58 (Summer 1993): 5–26.

Harrison, M. John. 'The First Viriconium Story'. Posted 1 February 2014. *The M John Harrison Blog*. https://ambientehotel.wordpress.com/2014/02/01/the-first-viriconium-story/ [accessed 1 August 2019].

Harrison, M. John. 'The Flesh Circle'. In *The Nature of the Catastrophe*, edited by Michael Moorcock and Langdon Jones, 149–64. London: Hutchinson, 1971.

Harrison, M. John. 'Harrison, Michael John'. In vols 53–56 of *Contemporary Authors: Bio-Biographical Guide to Current Authors and Their Works*, edited by Clare D. Kinsman, 272. Detroit: Gale, 1975.

Harrison, M. John. *In Viriconium*. London: Gollancz, 1982.
Harrison, M. John and Cheryl Morgan [interviewer]. 'Interview: M. John Harrison'. *Strange Horizons*, 9 June 2003, http://strangehorizons.com/non-fiction/articles/interview-m-john-harrison/ [accessed 27 December 2019].
Harrison, M. John. 'Lamia Mutable'. Written 1966/7. In *Again, Dangerous Visions*, edited by Harlan Ellison, 702–10. London: Millington, 1972.
Harrison, M. John and Christopher Fowler [interviewer, interview conducted in two parts: the first in 1977, the second in 1980]. 'The Last Rebel: An Interview with M. John Harrison'. *Foundation* 23 (October 1981): 5–30.
Harrison, M. John. 'A Literature of Comfort'. *New Worlds Quarterly* 1 (1971): 166–72.
Harrison, M. John. 'The Nash Circuit'. *New Worlds*, no. 193 (August 1969): 12–23.
Harrison, M. John and Christopher Fowler [interviewer, interview conducted 1985]. 'On the Edge: The Last Holmfirth Interview with M. John Harrison'. *Foundation* 57 (Spring 1993): 5–26.
Harrison, M. John. *Parietal Games: Critical Writings by and on M. John Harrison*. Edited by Mark Bould and Michelle Reid. London: Science Fiction Foundation, 2005.
Harrison, M. John. *The Pastel City*. London: Nel, 1971.
Harrison, M. John. 'The Profession of Science Fiction, 40: The Profession of Fiction'. *Foundation* 46 (Autumn 1989): 5–13.
Harrison, M. John. 'Running Down'. *New Worlds Quarterly* 8 (1975): 9–42.
Harrison, M. John. 'south london, 1991'. Posted 21 October 2011. *M John Harrison Blog*. https://ambientehotel.wordpress.com/2011/10/21/south-london-1991/ [accessed 27 December 2019].
Harrison, M. John. *A Storm of Wings*. London: Sphere Books, 1980.
Harrison, M. John. *Things That Never Happen*. San Francisco: Night Shade Books, 2003.
Harrison, M. John. *Viriconium Nights*. 1984. British edn. London: Gollancz, 1985.
Hawes, Donald. *Charles Dickens*. London: Continuum, 2007.
Hawthorne, Julian. 'The Romance of the Impossible'. *Lippincott's Monthly Magazine* 46 (September 1890): 412–15.
Hibbert, Christopher, Ben Weinreb, Julia Keay and John Keay, eds. *The London Encyclopaedia*. 3rd edn. London: Pan Macmillan, 2010.
Hood, Thomas. 'Master Humphrey's Clock'. *Athenaeum* (7 November 1840): 887–8.
Hopkins, R. Thurston. *H. G. Wells: Personality, Character, Topography*. London: Cecil Palmer, 1922.
Huntington, John. *The Logic of Fantasy: H. G. Wells and Science Fiction*. New York: Columbia University Press, 1982.
Jackson, Rosemary. *Fantasy: The Literature of Subversion*. 1981. Reprint, London: Routledge, 1988.
James, Simon J. *Maps of Utopia: H. G. Wells, Modernity, and the End of Culture*. Oxford: Oxford University Press, 2012.
Jameson, Fredric. *Archaeologies of the Future: The Desire Called Utopia and Other Science Fictions*. 2005. Reprint, London: Verso, 2007.

John, Juliet. *Dickens's Villains: Melodrama, Character, Popular Culture*. Oxford: Oxford University Press, 2001.

Johnson, Edgar. *Charles Dickens: His Tragedy and Triumph*. Vol. 1. London: Gollancz, 1953.

Jones, Langdon. 'Lead In'. *New Worlds*, no. 191 (June 1969): 2-3.

Kamp, David. 'London Swings Again!'. *Vanity Fair* (March 1997): 99-144.

Kerr, Joe and Andrew Gibson, eds. *London from Punk to Blair*. London: Reaktion Books, 2012.

Killheffer, Robert K. J. 'Fantasy Charts New Realms'. *Publishers Weekly: The International News Magazine of Book Publishing and Bookselling* 244, no. 24 (June 1997): 34-6.

Kincaid, Paul and Niall Harrison, eds. *British Science Fiction and Fantasy: Twenty Years, Two Surveys*. St Albans: BSFA, 2010.

Kitton, George. *Charles Dickens by Pen and Pencil*. London: Sabin, 1890.

Kornmeier, Uta. 'Almost Alive: The Spectacle of Verisimilitude in Madame Tussaud's Waxworks'. In *Ephemeral Bodies: Wax Sculpture and the Human Figure*, edited by Roberta Panzanelli, 67-81. California: Getty, 2008.

Kropotkin, Peter. *Mutual Aid: A Factor of Evolution*. 1902. Reprint, London: Freedom Press, 1987.

Lang, Andrew. 'Realism and Romance'. *The Contemporary Review* 52 (July 1887): 683-93.

Latham, Rob. 'The New Wave'. In *A Companion to Science Fiction*, edited by David Seed, 202-16. Oxford: Blackwell, 2005.

Lefebvre, Henri. *Critique of Everyday Life*. vol. 1. 1947. 2nd edn 1958. Translated by John Moore. Reprinted with notes and introduction. 1991. Reprint, London: Verso, 2008.

Lefebvre, Henri. *The Production of Space*. 1974. Translated by Donald Nicholson-Smith. First English translation. Oxford: Blackwell, 1991.

Lemire, Beverly. 'The Second Hand Trade in England, c. 1600-1850'. In *Old Clothes, New Looks: Second Hand Fashion*, edited by Alexandra Palmer and Hazel Clark, 29-48. Oxford: Berg, 2005.

Lewes, G. H. 'Dickens in Relation to Criticism'. *Fortnightly Review* 11 (February 1872): 141-54.

Lewis, C. S. *The Collected Letters of C. S. Lewis*. With notes and introductions. Edited by Walter Hooper. 3 vols. London: HarperCollins, 2004-6.

Lewis, C. S. *The Chronicles of Narnia*. 1950-6. Reprint, London: HarperCollins, 2004.

Lewis, C. S. 'Is Theology Poetry?'. 1952. In *C. S. Lewis: Essay Collection and Other Short Pieces*, edited by Lesley Walmsley, 10-21. London: HarperCollins, 2000.

Lewis, Wyndham. 'Climax and Change'. In *The Writer and the Absolute*, 189-93. London: Methuen, 1952.

Luckhurst, Roger. 'The Contemporary London Gothic and the Limits of the "Spectral Turn"'. *Textual Practice* 16, no. 3 (2002): 527-46.

Luckhurst, Roger. 'Cultural Governance, New Labour, and the British Science Fiction Boom'. Special issue on the British Boom, edited by Istvan Csicsery-Ronay, Jr., *Science Fiction Studies* 30, no. 3 (November 2003): 417–35.

Luckhurst, Roger. *Science Fiction*. Cambridge: Polity, 2005.

MacDonald, George. 'A Journey Rejourneyed'. Two Parts. *The Argosy: A Magazine of Tales, Travels, Essays, and Poems* 1, nos 1–2 (December 1865–January 1866): 53–63, 127–33.

MacDonald, George. *The Marquis of Lossie*. 1877. Reprint, London: Cassell, 1927.

MacDonald, George. *The Princess and the Goblin and Other Fairy Tales*. Edited by Shelley King and John Pierce. Toronto: Broadview, 2014.

March-Russell, Paul. *Modernism and Science Fiction*. New York: Palgrave, 2015.

Masson, David. *British Novelists and Their Styles: Being a Critical Sketch of the History of British Prose Fiction*. Cambridge: Macmillan, 1859.

McConnell, Frank. *The Science Fiction of H. G. Wells*. Oxford: Oxford University Press, 1981.

Mcguire, Stryker and Michael Elliott [writers], Katharine Chubbuck, William Underhill, Carla Power and Carol Hall [reporters]. 'Why London Rules'. *Newsweek* (4 November 1996): 44–9.

McKenzie, Peter. 'Memories of Mervyn: A Review of John Watney's Biography with Reminiscences and Other Contributions'. *Mervyn Peake Review* 4 (Spring 1977): 17–26.

McLeod, Hugh. *Class and Religion in the Late Victorian City*. London: Croom Helm, 1974.

Mendlesohn, Farah and Edward James, eds. *The Cambridge Companion to Fantasy Literature*. Cambridge: Cambridge University Press, 2012.

Mendlesohn, Farah and Edward James. *Rhetorics of Fantasy*. Middletown: Wesleyan University Press, 2008.

Mendlesohn, Farah and Edward James. *A Short History of Fantasy*. London: Middlesex University Press, 2009.

Miéville, China and Mark Bould [interviewer]. 'Appropriate Means: An Interview with China Miéville'. *New Politics* 9, no. 3 (Summer 2003): 169[–176].

Miéville, China. 'Author Q&A'. Posted 2010. Random House. http://www.randomhouse.com/rhpg//rc/library/display.pperl?isbn=9780345497529&view=qa [accessed 10 August 2019].

Miéville, China and Benjamin Eastham [interviewer]. 'China Miéville in Conversation with *The White Review*'. Conducted 15 May 2013. *London Review Bookshop*. http://www.londonreviewbookshop.co.uk/events/past/2013/5/china-mieville-in-conversation-with-the-white-review [accessed 4 September 2016].

Miéville, China and Annalee Newitz [interviewer]. 'China Miéville Explains Theology, Magic, and Why JJ Abrams Hates You'. *io9: We Come from the Future*. Posted 8 November 2010. http://io9.com/5605836/china-mieville-explains-theology-magic-and-why-jj-abrams-hates-you [accessed 30 April 2015].

Miéville, China and Jeff VanderMeer [interviewer, interview conducted in two parts, the first in 2008, the second in 2012]. 'China Miéville and Monsters'. *Weird Fiction Review*. Posted 20 March 2012. http://weirdfictionreview.com/2012/03/china-mieville-and-monsters-unsatisfy-me-frustrate-me-i-beg-you/ [accessed 4 May 2015].

Miéville, China and Nick Gevers [interviewer, interview conducted in November 2002]. 'Cities Near, Cities Far: An Interview with China Miéville'. *Infinity Plus*. Posted 2003, http://www.infinityplus.co.uk/nonfiction/intchina2.htm [accessed 5 May 2015].

Miéville, China. 'Editorial Introduction'. *Historical Materialism* 10, no. 4 (January 2002): 39–49.

Miéville, China and John Newsinger [interviewer]. 'Fantasy and Revolution: An Interview with China Miéville'. *International Socialism Journal*, no. 88, Autumn 2000, http://pubs.socialistreviewindex.org.uk/isj88/newsinger.htm [accessed 2 May 2015].

Miéville, China. 'Introduction'. In H. G. Wells, *The First Men in the Moon*, 1900–1, reprinted with notes and introduction, edited by Patrick Parrinder, xiii–xxviii. London: Penguin, 2005.

Miéville, China. *Iron Council*. 2004. Reprint, London: Pan Books, 2005.

Miéville, China. *King Rat*. 1998. Reprint, London: Pan Books, 2011.

Miéville, China. *Kraken*. London: Pan Books, 2010.

Miéville, China. *London's Overthrow*. London: The Westbourne Press, 2012.

Miéville, China. 'Long Live the New Weird: Guest Editorial'. *The Third Alternative* 35 (Summer 2003): 3.

Miéville, China. 'Messing with Fantasy'. *Locus* 48, no. 3, issue 494 (March 2002): 4–5, 75–6.

Miéville, China and Neil Macdonald [interviewer]. 'Monsters, Method, Bas-Lag and Kraken'. *Scifilove*. Posted 12 May 2010. http://scyfilove.com/2201/china-mieville-exclusive-interview-monsters-method-bas-lag-and-kraken/ [accessed 8 July 2016].

Miéville, China. *Perdido Street Station*. London: Pan Books, 2000.

Miéville, China and Joan Gordon [interviewer]. 'Reveling in Genre: An Interview with China Miéville'. Special issue on the British Boom, edited by Istvan Csicsery-Ronay, Jr., *Science Fiction Studies* 30, no. 3 (November 2003): 355–73.

Miéville, China. *The Scar*. 2002. Reprint, London: Pan Books, 2003.

Miéville, China. *The Tain*. In *Looking for Jake and Other Stories*, 2005, 225–300. Reprint, London: Pan Books, 2011.

Miéville, China. 'Tolkien – Middle Earth Meets Middle England'. *Socialist Review*, no. 259, posted January 2002, http://socialistreview.org.uk/259/tolkien-middle-earth-meets-middle-england [accessed 8 July 2016].

Miéville, China. *Un Lun Dun*. British edn 2007. Reprint, London: Pan Books, 2008.

'Might and Magnitude'. *All the Year Round* 15, no. 361 (24 March 1866): 255–7.

Miller, J. Hillis. 'The Fiction of Realism: *Sketches by Boz, Oliver Twist*, and Cruikshank's Illustrations'. In *Dickens Centennial Essays*, edited by Ada Nisbet and Blake Nevius, 287–318. Berkeley: University of California Press, 1971.

Moir, George. 'Modern Romance and Novel'. c. 1830–42. In *Victorian Criticism of the Novel*, edited by Edwin M. Eigner and George J. Worth, 39–57. Cambridge: Cambridge University Press, 1985.
Moorcock, Michael. *The Condition of Muzak: A Jerry Cornelius Novel*. London: Allison & Busby, 1977.
Moorcock, Michael. *The Cornelius Quartet*. 1968–77. Revised one-volume edn. *Michael Moorcock Collection*. With introduction. Edited by John Davey. London: Gollancz, 2013.
Moorcock, Michael. *A Cure for Cancer*. Serialization. *New Worlds*, nos 188–91 (March–June 1969): 4–20, 37–57, 24–41, 4–17.
Moorcock, Michael. *A Cure for Cancer: A Jerry Cornelius Novel*. 1969. Revised edn. London: Fontana, 1979.
Moorcock, Michael and Colin Greenland [interviewer, interview conducted in 1990]. *Death Is No Obstacle*. Manchester: Savoy, 1992.
Moorcock, Michael. 'The Delhi Division'. *New Worlds*, no. 185 (December 1968): 23–7.
Moorcock, Michael. 'The Dreaming City'. *Science Fantasy* 16, no. 47 (1961): 2–32.
Moorcock, Michael. 'Editorial'. *New Worlds* 49, no. 155 (October 1965): 2–3.
Moorcock, Michael. 'Editorial: The New Prism'. *New Worlds* 49, no. 158 (January 1966): 2–4, 48.
Moorcock, Michael. *Elric: To Rescue Tanelorn*. New York: Ballantine, 2008.
Moorcock, Michael. *The English Assassin: A Romance of Entropy*. London: Allison & Busby, 1972.
Moorcock, Michael. *Epic Pooh*. Dagenham: British Fantasy Society, 1978.
Moorcock, Michael. 'An Excellence of Peake'. *Peake Studies* 6, no. 4 (April 2000): 7–13.
Moorcock, Michael. *The Final Programme*. 1968. First British edn. London: Allison & Busby, 1969.
Moorcock, Michael. 'Further Information'. *New Worlds* 49, no. 157 (December 1965): 49–67.
Moorcock, Michael. *Into the Media Web: Selected Short Non-Fiction, 1956–2006*. Edited by John Davey. Manchester: Savoy, 2010.
Moorcock, Michael [writing as 'James Colvin']. 'A Literature of Acceptance'. *New Worlds*, no. 178 (December 1967/January 1968): 59–61.
Moorcock, Michael. 'Mervyn Peake—An Obituary'. *New Worlds*, no. 187 (February 1969): 57–8.
Moorcock, Michael and Paul Walker [interviewer, interview conducted in 1972]. 'Michael Moorcock'. In *Speaking of Science Fiction: The Paul Walker Interviews*, 213–28. New Jersey: Luna, 1978.
Moorcock, Michael. 'The Michael Moorcock Column: The Dodgem Arrangement'. Written 1968. *Speculation* 2, no. 11, issue 23 (July/August 1969): 27–32.
Moorcock, Michael. *Mother London*. London: Secker & Warburg, 1988.
Moorcock, Michael. 'A New Literature for the Space Age'. *New Worlds* 48, no. 142 (May–June 1964): 2–3.

Moorcock, Michael. 'New Worlds—Jerry Cornelius'. 1972. In *Sojan*, 144–55. Manchester: Savoy, 1977.
Moorcock, Michael. 'New Worlds: A Personal History'. *Foundation* 15 (1 January 1979): 5–18.
Moorcock, Michael. 'Preliminary Data'. *New Worlds* 49, no. 153 (August 1965): 98–113.
Moorcock, Michael and Richard Glyn Jones [artist]. 'The Rise of the Musician-Assassin'. *New Worlds*, no. 213 (Summer 1978): 3–4.
Moorcock, Michael. 'The Spencer Inheritance'. 1998. In *Jerry Cornelius: His Lives and His Times*, 283–318. London: Gollancz, 2014.
Moorcock, Michael. 'Starship Stormtroopers'. *Anarchist Review* 1, no. 4 (1978): 40–4.
Moorcock, Michael. *Wizardry & Wild Romance: A Study of Epic Fantasy*. 1987. Revised edn. Austin: MonkeyBrain, 2004.
Moorcock, Michael and Allan Kausch, eds. *London Peculiar and Other Nonfiction*. Oakland, CA: PM, 2012.
Moorcock, Michael and Charles Platt. 'Barbarella and the Anxious Frenchman'. *New Worlds*, no. 179 (February 1968): 13–23.
Moorcock, Michael and Langdon Jones, eds. *The New Nature of the Catastrophe*. Revised edn of *The Nature of the Catastrophe*, 1971. London: Millennium, 1993.
'Mr. H. G. Wells on Socialism'. *Science Schools Journal* 18 (February 1889): 152–5.
Naipaul, V. S. *The Enigma of Arrival*. London: Penguin, 1987.
Orwell, George. *The Complete Works of George Orwell*. With notes and introductions. Vols 1–9 1986–7. Edited by Peter Davison. 20 vols. Vols 1–9 reprint, London: Secker & Warburg, 1997–8.
Orwell, George. *Nineteen Eighty-Four: The Facsimile of the Extant Manuscript*. Edited by Peter Davison. London: Secker & Warburg, 1984.
Ostry, Elaine. *Social Dreaming: Dickens and the Fairy Tale*. London: Routledge, 2002.
Page, Michael R. *The Literary Imagination from Erasmus Darwin to H. G. Wells: Science, Evolution, and Ecology*. Farnham: Ashgate, 2012.
Parrinder, Patrick. 'The Age of Fantasy'. 1982. In Parrinder, *The Failure of Theory: Essays on Criticism and Contemporary Fiction*, 109–14. Sussex: Harvester, 1987.
Parrinder, Patrick, ed. *H. G. Wells: The Critical Heritage*. London: Routledge, 1997.
Pater, Walter. 'The School of Giorgione'. 1877. In *The Renaissance: Studies in Art and Poetry*, 1873, 3rd edn 1888, 126–44. Reprint, London: Fontana, 1971.
Peake, Mervyn. 'Alice and Tenniel and Me: A Talk by Mervyn Peake'. 1954. *Mervyn Peake Review* 6 (Spring 1978): 20–4.
Peake, Mervyn. 'Book Illustration, a Radio Talk'. 1947. *Mervyn Peake Review* 9 (Autumn 1979): 14–22.
Peake, Mervyn. 'Danse Macabre'. Written for Christmas 1954. *Science Fantasy* 21, no. 61 (1963): 46–55.
Peake, Mervyn. *Drawings by Mervyn Peake*. London: Grey Walls, 1949.
Peake, Mervyn. *The Illustrated Gormenghast Trilogy*. 1946–59. One-volume edn. *Titus Alone* revised edn 1970. Reprinted with introduction. 1992. London: Vintage, 2011.

Peake, Mervyn. Letter to Nehemiah Asherson. 18 July 1951. *Peake Studies* 11, no. 4 (April 2010): 32.
Peake, Mervyn. 'London Fantasy'. 1949. *Peake Studies* 9, no. 4 (April 2006): 3–7.
Peake, Mervyn. *Mervyn Peake: Collected Poems*. With notes and introduction. Edited by R. W. Maslen. Manchester: Carcanet, 2008.
Pepper, John Henry. *True History of the Ghost; And All About Metempsychosis*. 1890. Reprint, Cambridge: Cambridge University Press, 2012.
Phillips, Lawrence. 'Sex, Violence and Concrete: The Post-War Dystopian Vision of London in *Nineteen Eighty-Four*'. *Critical Survey* 20, no. 1 (2008): 69–79.
Pike, David L. *Subterranean Cities: The World Beneath Paris and London, 1800–1945*. Ithaca: Cornell University Press, 2005.
Porter, Roy. *London: A Social History*. London: Penguin, 2000.
Prickett, Stephen. *Victorian Fantasy*. Sussex: Harvester, 1979.
'Review of *War of the Worlds*'. *Critic* 29 (April 1898): 282.
Roberts, Adam. *The History of Science Fiction*. 2006. 2nd edn. London: Palgrave, 2016.
Rule, Fiona. *London's Docklands: A History of the Lost Quarter*. Surrey: Ian Allan, 2009.
Rushdie, Salman. 'Influence'. In *Step Across This Line: Collected Non-Fiction, 1992–2002*, 69–76. London: Jonathan Cape, 2002.
Ruskin, John. *The Works of John Ruskin*. Library edn. Edited by E. T. Cook and Alexander Wedderburn. 39 vols. London: George Allen, 1903–12.
Sala, George Augustus. *The Life and Adventures of George Augustus Sala, Written by Himself*. Vol. 1. 1894. London: Cassell, 1895.
Sala, George Augustus, and W. H. Wills. 'Fairyland in 'Fifty-Four'. *Household Words* 8, no. 193 (3 December 1853): 313–17.
Sallis, James. 'Jeremiad'. *New Worlds*, no. 187 (February 1969): 6–15.
Sanders, Andrew. *Authors in Context: Charles Dickens*. Oxford: Oxford University Press, 2003.
Sheppard, F. H. W. 'General Introduction'. In *The Parish of St. Anne, Soho*, edited by Sheppard, vols 33–34 of *The Survey of London*, 1–19. London: Athlone, 1966.
Slater, Michael. 'The Christmas Books'. *The Dickensian* 65 (1969): 17–24.
Slater, Michael. 'Introduction'. In *Dickens 1970*, edited by Slater, ix–xiii. London: Chapman & Hall, 1970.
Smith, Gordon. *Mervyn Peake: A Personal Memoir*. London: Gollancz, 1984.
Sommerfield, John. 'Worm's-Eye View'. In *The Survivors*, 9–30. London: John Lehmann, 1947.
Stevenson, Robert Louis. *The Letters of Robert Louis Stevenson*. Edited by Bradford A. Booth and Ernest Mehew. Vol. 2. April *1874–July* 1879. New Haven: Yale University Press, 1994.
Stone, Harry. 'Dickens' Artistry and *The Haunted Man*'. *South Atlantic Quarterly* 61, no. 4 (Autumn 1962): 492–505.
Stone, Harry. *Dickens and the Invisible World*. London: Macmillan, 1979.

Stone, Thomas. 'Chemical Contradictions'. *Household Words* 1, no. 25 (14 September 1850): 591–4.

Strauss, Leo. *What Is Political Philosophy?; And Other Studies*. 1959. Reprint, Westport: Greenwood, 1973.

Suvin, Darko. 'Considering the Sense of "Fantasy" or "Fantastic Fiction": An Effusion'. *Extrapolation* 41, no. 3 (Fall 2000): 210–47.

Tolkien, J. R. R. *The Fellowship of the Ring*. 1954. Reprint, London: HarperCollins, 2008.

Tolkien, J. R. R. 'On Fairy-Stories'. In *Essays Presented to Charles Williams*, edited by C. S. Lewis, 38–89. London: Oxford University Press, 1947.

'Vagrancy Act 1824'. *Official Home of UK Legislation*; National Archives, http://www.legislation.gov.uk/ukpga/Geo4/5/83/section/4 [accessed 3 December 2015].

Vanderbeke, Dirk. 'The Sub-Creation of Sub-London: Neil Gaiman's and China Miéville's Urban Fantasy'. In *From Peterborough to Faëry: The Poetics and Mechanics of Secondary Worlds; Essays in Honour of Dr. Allan G. Turner's 65th Birthday*, edited by Dirk Vanderbeke and Thomas Honegger, 141–65. Zurich and Jena: Walking Tree Publishers, 2014.

VanderMeer, Jeff. 'Introduction; The New Weird: "It's Alive?"'. In *The New Weird*, edited by Ann and Jeff VanderMeer, ix–xviii. San Francisco: Tachyon, 2008.

Vertesi, Janet. 'Mind the Gap: The London Underground Map and Users' Representations of Urban Space'. *Social Studies of Science* 38, no. 1 (February 2008): 7–33.

Vint, Sherryl. 'Introduction: Special Issue on China Miéville'. Special issue on China Miéville, edited by Sherryl Vint, *Extrapolation* 50, no. 2 (2009): 197–9.

Waters, Catherine. *Commodity Culture in Dickens's Household Words*. Hampshire: Ashgate, 2008.

Watney, John. *Mervyn Peake*. London: Joseph, 1976.

Wells, H. G. 'A Chat with the Author of *The Time Machine*'. 1895. Edited by David C. Smith. *The Wellsian*, no. 20 (Winter 1997): 3–9.

Wells, H. G. *The Correspondence of H. G. Wells*. 4 vols. Edited by David C. Smith. London: Pickering & Chatto, 1998.

Wells, H. G. *The Country of the Blind and Other Selected Stories*. With notes and introduction. Edited by Patrick Parrinder. 2005. Reprint, London: Penguin, 2007.

Wells, H. G. *Experiment in Autobiography: Discoveries and Conclusions of a Very Ordinary Brain (Since 1866)*. 2 vols. 1934. Reprint, London: Faber and Faber, 1984.

Wells, H. G. *H. G. Wells's Literary Criticism*. Edited by Patrick Parrinder and Robert M. Philmus. Sussex: Harvester, 1980.

Wells, H. G. *Henry James and H. G. Wells: A Record of Their Friendship, Their Debate on the Art of Fiction, and Their Quarrel*. With introduction. Edited by Leon Edel and Gordon N. Ray. Urbana: University of Illinois, 1958.

Wells, H. G. *The History of Mr Polly*. 1910. Reprinted with notes and introduction. Edited by Simon J. James. London: Penguin, 2005.

Wells, H. G. 'The Immature Fantastic'. *Saturday Review of Politics, Literature, Science, and Art* (7 November 1896): 499–500.

Wells, H. G. *The Invisible Man*. 1897. Reprinted with notes and introduction. Edited by Patrick Parrinder. London: Penguin, 2005.

Wells, H. G. 'Is Life Becoming Happier?'. In *The Way the World Is Going: Guesses & Forecasts of the Years Ahead*, 190–9. London: Benn, 1928.

Wells, H. G. *Kipps: The Story of a Simple Soul*. 1905. Reprinted with notes and introduction. Edited by Simon J. James. London: Penguin, 2005.

Wells, H. G. *A Modern Utopia*. 1904–5. Reprinted with notes and introduction. Edited by Patrick Parrinder and Gregory Claeys. London: Penguin, 2005.

Wells, H. G. 'My Auto-Obituary'. *The Strand Magazine* 104a (January 1943): 45–7.

Wells, H. G. *The Outline of History; Being a Plain History of Life and Mankind*. 1919–20. 4th revision. 2 vols. London: Cassell, 1925.

Wells, H. G. 'Popularising Science'. *Nature* 50, no. 1291 (July 1894): 300–1.

Wells, H. G. *The Sleeper Awakes and Men Like Gods*. Revised edn of *When the Sleeper Wakes*. London: Odhams, 1921.

Wells, H. G. *The Sleeper Awakes: A Revised Edition of 'When the Sleeper Wakes'*. Revised edn of *When the Sleeper Wakes*. London: Thomas Nelson and Sons, 1910.

Wells, H. G. 'A Story of the Days to Come'. 1899. In *Tales of Space and Time*, 165–324. 1899. Reprint, London: Harper & Brothers, 1900.

Wells, H. G. *The Time Machine*. 1895. Reprinted with notes and introduction. Edited by Patrick Parrinder. London: Penguin, 2005.

Wells, H. G. *The Time Machine*. Serialization. *The New Review* 12, nos 68–72 (January–May 1895): 98–112, 207–21, 329–43, 453–72, 577–88.

Wells, H. G. *Tono-Bungay*. 1908–9. Reprinted with notes and introduction. Edited by Patrick Parrinder. London: Penguin, 2005.

Wells, H. G. 'Traffic and Rebuilding'. 1911. In *An Englishman Looks at the World: Being a Series of Unrestrained Remarks upon Contemporary Matters*, 188–91. London: Cassell and Company, 1914.

Wells, H. G. *The War of the Worlds*. 1897. London: William Heinemann, 1898.

Wells, H. G. *The War of the Worlds*. 1897. Reprinted with notes and introduction. Edited by Patrick Parrinder. London: Penguin, 2005.

Wells, H. G. *The War of the Worlds*. Serialization. *Pearson's Magazine* 3, nos 16–18 (April–June 1897): 363–73, 486–96, 598–610 and *Pearson's Magazine* 4, nos 19–24 (July–December 1897): 108–19, 221–32, 329–39, 447–56, 558–68, 736–45.

Wells, H. G. 'What I Believe'. 1899. In *When the Sleeper Wakes: A Critical Text of the 1899 New York and London First Edition*, 1899, reprinted with notes and introduction, edited by Leon Stover, 384–8. North Carolina: McFarland & Company, 2000.

Wells, H. G. *When the Sleeper Wakes*. 1899. Reprinted with notes and introduction. Edited by John Sutherland. Ontario: Broadview, 2019.

Wells, H. G. *When the Sleeper Wakes*. Serialization. *The Graphic*, nos 1519-36 (January-May 1899): 9-11, 41-3, 73-5, 105-7, 137-9, 169-71, 201-3, 233-5, 265-7, 297-9, 329-31, 361-3, 393-5, 433-5, 465-7, 497-9, 529-31, 561-3.

Wells, H. G. *The Works of H. G. Wells, Atlantic Edition*. 28 vols. With prefaces. London: T. Fisher Unwin, 1924-7.

Wells, H. G. *The World Set Free: A Story of Mankind*. London: Macmillan, 1914.

Wells, H. G. *'42 to '44: A Contemporary Memoir Upon Human Behaviour During the Crisis of the World Revolution*. London: Secker & Warburg, 1944.

Welsh, Alexander. 'Time and the City in *The Chimes*'. *The Dickensian* 73 (1977): 8-17.

West, W. J. *The Larger Evils: Nineteen Eighty-Four; The Truth Behind the Satire*. Edinburgh: Canongate, 1992.

Westfahl, Gary. *Hugo Gernsback and the Century of Science Fiction*. Jefferson, NC: McFarland, 2007.

Weybright & Talley Publishers. Advertising blurb. In Lucille G. Crane, 'The Gormenghast Trilogy', *Best Sellers: The Semi-Monthly Book Review* 27, no. 1 (1967): 305-6.

White, Jerry. *London in the Nineteenth Century: A Human Awful Wonder of God*. London: Jonathan Cape, 2007.

White, Jerry. *London in the Twentieth Century: A City and Its People*. London: Penguin, 2001.

Williams, Raymond. *The Country and the City*. London: Chatto & Windus, 1973.

Williams, Rhys and Mark Bould, eds. *M. John Harrison: Critical Essays*. Canterbury: Gylphi, 2019.

Winnington, G. Peter, ed. *Mervyn Peake: The Man and His Art*. London: Peter Owen, 2006.

Wood, John. 'Mervyn Peake: A Pupil Remembers'. *Mervyn Peake Review* 12 (Spring 1981): 15-28.

Woodcock, George. *The Crystal Spirit: A Study of George Orwell*. 1966. 2nd edn. London: Fourth Estate, 1984.

Woodcock, George. *Orwell's Message: 1984 and the Present*. Madeira Park: Harbour, 1984.

Yorke, Malcolm. *Mervyn Peake: My Eyes Mint Gold, a Life*. London: Murray, 2000.

Young, Helen. *Race and Popular Fantasy Literature: Habits of Whiteness*. New York: Routledge, 2016.

Zamyatin, Yevgeny. 'H. G. Wells'. 1922. In *A Soviet Heretic: Essays by Yevgeny Zamyatin*, edited by and translated by Mirra Ginsberg, 259-90. London: Quartet, 1991.

Žižek, Slavoj. *The Fright of Real Tears: Krzysztof Kieślowski between Theory and Post-Theory*. London: British Film Institute, 2001.

Works consulted

Ashley, Michael and Robert A. W. Lowndes. *The Gernsback Days: The Evolution of Modern Science Fiction from 1911-1936*. Holicong: Wildside Press, 2004.

Beatie, Bruce A. 'The Tolkien Phenomenon: 1945–1968'. *Journal of Popular Culture* 3, no. 4 (Spring 1970): 689–703.
Benjamin, Walter. 'The Work of Art in the Age of Mechanical Reproduction'. 1935. In *Illuminations*, 1968, edited by Hannah Arendt, translated by Harry Zorn, 211–44. Reprinted with notes and introduction. London: Bodley Head, 2015.
Booth, Charles. 'Charles Booth's London: Poverty Maps and Police Notebooks'. 1886–1903. London School of Economics and Political Science. https://booth.lse.ac.uk/map/16/-0.2052/51.5095/100/1 [accessed 24 July 2019].
Booth, Charles. *Life and Labour of the People in London, First Series: Poverty*. 1891. Revised edn. Vol. 2. *Streets and Population Classified*. London: Macmillan, 1902.
Borer, Mary Cathcart. *The City of London: A History*. London: Constable, 1977.
Bosman, Suzanne. *The National Gallery in Wartime*. London: National Gallery and Yale University Press, 2008.
Bould, Mark. 'Mind the Gap: The Impertinent Predicates (and Subjects) of *King Rat* and *Looking for Jake and Other Stories*'. Special issue on China Miéville, edited by Vint, *Extrapolation* 50, no. 2 (2009): 307–25.
Bould, Mark. 'What Kind of Monster Are You?: Situating the Boom'. Special issue on the British Boom, edited by Istvan Csicsery-Ronay, Jr., *Science Fiction Studies* 30, no. 3 (November 2003): 394–416.
Brake, Laurel. 'The Advantage of Fiction: The Novel and the "Success" of the Victorian Periodical'. In *A Return to the Common Reader: Print Culture and the Novel, 1850–1900*, edited by Adelene Buckland and Beth Palmer, 9–22. Surrey: Ashgate, 2011.
Butler, Andrew M. 'Thirteen Ways of Looking at the British Boom'. Special issue on the British Boom, edited by Istvan Csicsery-Ronay, Jr., *Science Fiction Studies* 30, no. 3 (November 2003): 374–93.
Callery, Sean. *Harrods, Knightsbridge: The Story of Society's Favourite Store*. London: Ebury, 1991.
Campbell, John. *Margaret Thatcher*. London: Pimlico, 2004.
Carpenter, Humphrey. *J.R.R. Tolkien: A Biography*. 1977. Revised edn. Boston: Mifflin, 2000.
Chadwick, Edwin. *Report on the Sanitary Condition of the Labouring Population of Great Britain*. 1842. Reprint, Edinburgh: Edinburgh University Press, 1965.
Chalklin, Christopher. *The Rise of the English Town, 1650–1850*. Cambridge: Cambridge University Press, 2001.
Clute, John and John Grant, eds. *The Encyclopedia of Fantasy*. 1997. Reprint, New York: St. Martin's Griffin, 1999.
Clute, John and Peter Nicholls, eds. *The Encyclopedia of Science Fiction*. 1993. 3rd edn online. 2011–present. http://www.sf-encyclopedia.com/category/all [accessed 16 May 2020].
Connor, J. E. *London's Disused Underground Stations*. 1999. 2nd and enlarged edn. Middlesex: Capital Transport, 2008.

Cookson, Brian. *Crossing the River: The History of London's Thames River Bridges from Richmond to the Tower*. Edinburgh: Mainstream Publishing, 2006.

Cooper, Nick. *London Underground at War*. Gloucestershire: Amberley, 2014.

Cozzi, Joseph. 'Nevermore: The Influence of Thatcherism on Neverwhere'. Undergraduate paper, submitted November 2018, The University of Notre Dame (USA) in England. Unpublished.

DAW [*nom de plume*]. 'New Wave SF'. In *England Swings SF: Stories of Speculative Fiction*, edited by Judith Merril, n.p. New York: Doubleday, 1968.

DeLillo, Don. *White Noise*. London: Pan Books, 1985.

Derry, Stephen. 'The Time Traveller's Utopian Books and His Reading of the Future'. *Foundation* 65 (Fall 1995): 16–23.

Dickens, Charles. 'Address'. *Athenaeum* no. 1008 (20 February 1847): 216.

Dickens, Charles. 'No. 1 Branch Line: The Signal-Man'. *Mugby Junction, Extra Christmas Number, All the Year Round* 16, no. 400 (22 December 1866): 20–5.

Dillon, Tom. '"Jerry Was Oscillating Badly": Gender and Sexuality in *New Worlds* Magazine'. *Science Fiction Studies* 45, no. 1 (March 2018): 161–76.

Dolzani, Michael. 'Introduction'. 2004. In *Northrop Frye's Notebooks on Romance*, vol. 15 of *Collected Works of Northrop Frye*, edited by Dolzani, xxi–lvii. Toronto: University of Toronto Press, 2004.

Drew, John, Hazel Mackenzie, and Ben Winyard. 'Household Words, Volume I: March 30 – September 21, 1850'. *Dickens Quarterly* 29, no. 1 (March 2012): 50–67.

Duncan, Leland L. *History of the Borough of Lewisham*. 1908. Reprint, London: Blackheath Press, 1973.

Eagleton, Robert, ed. *Reading The Lord of the Rings: New Writings on Tolkien's Classic*. London: Continuum, 2005.

Ekman, Stefan. 'Urban Fantasy: A Literature of the Unseen'. *Journal of the Fantastic in the Arts* 27, no. 3 (2016): 452–69.

Elber-Aviram, Hadas. 'Dark and Deathless Rabble of Long Shadows: Peake, Dickens, Tolkien, and "This Dark Hive Called London"'. *Peake Studies* 14, no. 2 (April 2015): 7–32.

Elber-Aviram, Hadas. '"My Own Particular City": H. G. Wells's Fantastical London'. *The Wellsian*, no. 38 (2015): 97–117.

Elliott, Michael. 'London: Nothing to Lose but Its Chains; A Survey'. *The Economist* 298, no. 7427 (4 January 1986): 1–18.

Flanagan, Richard. *'Parish-fed Bastards': A History of the Politics of the Unemployed in Britain, 1884–1939*. London: Greenwood Press, 1991.

François, Pierre. '*Titus Alone*, or the Spirit of Carnival "After the Catastrophe"'. *Peake Studies* 6, no. 3 (October 1999): 4–20.

Freedgood, Elaine. *The Ideas in Things*. Chicago: University of Chicago Press, 2006.

Freedman, Carl. *The Incomplete Projects: Marxism, Modernity, and the Politics of Culture*. Middletown: Wesleyan University Press, 2002.

Gaiman, Neil. 'Foreword by Neil Gaiman: The Nature of the Infection'. 2003. In Paul McAuley, *The Eye of the Tyger*, 7–10. Surrey: Telos, 2003.

Gaiman, Neil. *Neverwhere*. 1996. American edn 1997. Reprint, New York: HarperTorch, 2001.

Gaiman, Neil. *Neverwhere*. British edn. London: BBC, 1996.

Gaiman, Neil. *Neverwhere: The Complete Series*. Conceptualized by Neil Gaiman and Lenny Henry, written by Neil Gaiman, directed by Dewi Humphreys. BBC, broadcast September–October 1996, DVD 2007.

Giedion, Sigfried. *Space, Time and Architecture: The Growth of a New Tradition*. 1941. 5th edn. Cambridge, MA: Harvard University Press, 1967.

Gordon, Joan. 'Hybridity, Heterotopia, and Mateship in China Miéville's *Perdido Street Station*'. Special issue on the British Boom, edited by Istvan Csicsery-Ronay, Jr., *Science Fiction Studies* 30, no. 3 (November 2003): 456–76.

Gray, Robert. *A History of London*. 1978. Reprint, London: Hutchinson, 1984.

Groth, Helen. 'Reading Victorian Illusions: Dickens's "Haunted Man" and Dr. Pepper's "Ghost"'. *Victorian Studies* 50, no. 1 (Autumn 2007): 43–65.

Haggard, H. Rider. 'Books Which Have Influenced Me'. *British Weekly Extra*, no. 1, 66–7. London: British Weekly, 1887.

Hamerow, Theodore S. *The Birth of a New Europe: State and Society in the Nineteenth Century*. London: University of North Carolina Press, 1983.

Hamnett, Chris. *Unequal City: London in the Global Arena*. London: Routledge, 2003.

Harris, Cyril M. *What's in a Name?: The Origins of the Names of All Stations in Current Use on the London Underground and Docklands Light Rail with Their Opening Dates*. 1977. 4th edn. Harrow: Capital History, 2001.

Harrison, M. John and Richard Glyn Jones [artist]. *The Adventures of Jerry Cornelius: The English Assassin*. *International Times* 1, no. 64, 22.

Harrison, M. John. 'Events Witnessed from a City'. In *The Machine in Shaft Ten and Other Stories*, 106–12. St Albans: Panther, 1975.

Harrison, M. John. 'The Good Detective'. In *You Should Come with Me Now: Stories of Ghosts*, 157–64. Manchester: Comma, 2017.

Harrison, M. John. 'The Lamia and Lord Cromis'. *New Worlds Quarterly* 1 (1971): 50–69.

Harrison, M. John. 'M. John Harrison: No Escape'. Interview. *Locus* 51, no. 6, issue 515 (December 2003): 7, 69–70.

Hearn, Michael Patrick. 'Introduction'. *The Annotated Christmas Carol: A Christmas Carol by Charles Dickens*, reprinted with notes and introduction, edited by Hearn, 1–51. New York: Clarkson N. Potter, 1976.

Hennessy, Peter. *Having It so Good: Britain in the Fifties*. London: Allen Lane, 2006.

Hewison, Robert. *The Heritage Industry: Britain in a Climate of Decline*. London: Methuen, 1987.

Hillegas, Mark R. *The Future as Nightmare: H. G. Wells and the Anti-Utopians*. New York: Oxford University Press, 1967.

House, Humphry. *The Dickens World*. 1941. 2nd edn. London: Oxford University Press, 1960.

Houston, Gail Turley. *Consuming Fictions: Gender, Class, and Hunger in Dickens's Novels*. Carbondale and Edwardsville: Southern Illinois University Press, 1994.
Hughes, David Y. 'A Queer Notion of Grant Allen's'. *Science Fiction Studies* 25, no. 2 (July 1998): 271–84.
Humphries, Steve and John Taylor. *The Making of Modern London, 1945–1985*. London: London Weekend Television, 1986.
Inwood, Stephen. *A History of London*. London: Pan Macmillan, 1998.
Jakubowski, Maxim. 'Lines of White on a Sullen Sea'. *New Worlds*, no. 194 (September–October 1969): 25–7.
Jeppesen, Chris, et al. *St Pancras International: 150 Facts for 150 Years*. Gloucestershire: History Press, 2018.
Judt, Tony. *Postwar: A History of Europe Since 1945*. 2005. Reprint, London: Pimlico, 2007.
Kincaid, Paul. 'Kincaid in Short: A Young Man's Journey'. *Vector: The Critical Journal of the British Science Fiction Association*, no. 267 (Summer 2011): 33–5.
Latham, Rob. 'M. John Harrison (1945–)'. In *British Fantasy and Science-Fiction Writers Since 1960*, edited by Darren Harris-Fain, vol. 261 of *Dictionary of Literary Biography*, 227–38. Michigan: Gale, 2002.
Lawton, Richard. 'Census Data for Urban Areas'. In *Census and Social Structure: An Interpretive Guide to 19th Century Census for England and Wales*, edited by Lawton, 82–145. Abingdon: Frank Cass, 1978.
Levy, Shawn. *Ready, Steady, Go: Swinging London and the Invention of Cool*. 2002. Reprint, London: Fourth Estate, 2003.
Lewes, G. H. 'Literature'. *Leader* 3, no. 142 (11 December 1852): 1189.
Light, Andrew. 'Urban Ecological Citizenship'. 2003. In *Technology and Values*, edited by Craig Hanks, 397–414. Sussex: Wiley-Blackwell, 2010.
Lyell, Charles. *Principles of Geology*. 1830–1833. Selected text from the three-volume 1st edn. With introduction. Edited by James A. Secord. London: Penguin, 1997.
Macfarlane, Robert. 'Introduction'. 2012. In Harrison, *Climbers*, 1989, revised edn, xi–xx. London: Gollancz, 2013.
Mainzer, Klaus. *Thinking in Complexity: The Complex Dynamics of Matter, Mind, and Mankind*. 1994. 3rd edn. London: Springer 1997.
Malchow, H. L. *Special Relations: The Americanization of Britain?*. Stanford: Stanford University Press, 2011.
Marin, Louis. *Utopics: Spatial Play*. Translated by Robert A. Vollrath. London: Macmillan, 1984.
McBriar, Alan Marne. *Fabian Socialism and English Politics, 1884–1918*. Cambridge: Cambridge University Press, 1962.
McLean, Steven. *The Early Fiction of H. G. Wells: Fantasies of Science*. Hampshire: Palgrave, 2009.
Miéville, China and Richard Marshall [interviewer]. 'The Road to Perdido: An Interview with China Mieville [sic]'. Posted 2003. *3am Interview* https://www.3am

magazine.com/litarchives/2003/feb/interview:china_mieville.html [accessed 6 August 2019].

Miller, J. Hillis. 'The Genres of *A Christmas Carol*'. *The Dickensian* 89, no. 3 (Winter 1993): 193–206.

Mitchell, Leslie. *Bulwer Lytton: The Rise and Fall of a Victorian Man of Letters*. London: Cambridge University Press, 2003.

Mitchell, Sally, *Daily Life in Victorian England*. 1996. 2nd edn. Connecticut: Greenwood, 2009.

'Monastery of the Poor Clares Colettines, Westbourne Park Road'. In *Northern Kensington*, vol. 37 of *The Survey of London*, edited by F. H. W. Sheppard, 247. London: Athlone, 1973.

Montgomery, Fiona A. *Women's Rights: Struggles and Feminism in Britain c. 1770–1970*. Manchester: Manchester University Press, 2006.

Moorcock, Michael. *Fabulous Harbours*. London: Millenium, 1995.

Moorcock, Michael. 'The Tank Trapeze'. *New Worlds*, no. 186 (January 1969): front cover and 5–10.

Morton, Peter. *The Busiest Man in England: Grant Allen and the Writing Trade, 1875–1900*. New York: Palgrave, 2005.

Moss, Lauren R. *Postmodern Existentialism in Mervyn Peake's Titus Books*. Florida: Raton, 2009.

Nesta, Frederick. 'The Myth of the "Triple-Headed Monster": The Economics of the Three-Volume Novel'. *Publishing History* 61 (2007): 47–69.

Nester, William R. *Globalization: A Short History of the Modern World*. New York: Palgrave, 2010.

O'Malley, Jan. *The Politics of Community Action: A Decade of Struggle in Notting Hill*. Nottingham: Spokesman, 1977.

Orford, Pete. 'Dickens and Science Fiction: A Study of Artificial Intelligence in *Great Expectations*'. *19: Interdisciplinary Studies in the Long Nineteenth Century* 10, *Dickens and Science*, edited by Holly Furneaux and Ben Winyard, 2010, http://www.19.bbk.ac.uk/articles/10.16995/ntn.527/ [accessed 21 August 2016].

Orford, Pete. 'The Ghosts and the Machine: *A Christmas Carol* and Time Travel'. *Academia Edu*, https://www.academia.edu/3122878/The_Ghosts_and_the_Machine_A_Christmas_Carol_and_Time_Travel [accessed 9 September 2019].

Osborne, Edward. *Cornelius. Osborne's London and Birmingham Railway Guide*. London: Simkin, Marshall & Darton & Clark, 1840.

Parker, Douglass. 'Hwaet, We Holbytla'. *The Hudson Review* 9, no. 4 (Winter 1956): 598.

Peake, Mervyn [artist]. Cover picture. *New Worlds*, no. 189 (April 1969): front cover.

Peake, Mervyn [artist]. Drawings [untitled]. *New Worlds Quarterly* 1 (1971): 53 and 166.

Philmus, Robert M. 'H. G. Wells as Literary Critic for the *Saturday Review*'. *Science Fiction Studies* 4, no. 2 (July 1977): 166–93.

Picard, Liza. *Victorian London: The Life of a City 1840–1870*. 2005. Reprint, London: Phoenix, 2006.

Piggott, J. R. *Palace of the People: The Crystal Palace at Sydenham 1854–1936*. London: Hurst & Company, 2004.

Pilbeam, Pamela. *Madame Tussaud and the History of Waxworks*. London: Bloomsbury, 2003.

Pilkington, Edward. *Beyond the Mother Country: West Indians and the Notting Hill White Riots*. London: I. B. Tauris, 1988.

Pointer, Graham. 'The UK's Major Urban Areas'. In *Focus on People and Migration*, 45–60. London: Palgrave, 2005.

Powell, Kenneth. 'Introduction'. In *The City of London: Architectural Tradition & Innovation in the Square Mile*, 2011, edited by Nicholas Kenyon, 11–25. Reprint, London: Thames & Hudson, 2012.

Prescott, Holly. '"Rid Yourself of This Surface Mentality": Re-thinking Urban Space in the Contemporary London Descent Narrative'. Special issue on London: Urban Space as Cultural Experience, edited by Ulrich Kinzel, *LWU: Literatur in Wissenschaft und Unterricht* 43, nos 2/3 (2010): 185–98.

Rahn, Suzanne. 'The Sources of Ruskin's *Golden River*'. *The Victorian Newsletter*, no. 68 (Fall 1985): 1–9.

Richards, David A. J. *The Rise of Gay Rights and the Fall of the British Empire*. Cambridge: Cambridge University Press, 2013.

Richmond, Vivienne. *Clothing the Poor in Nineteenth-Century England*. Cambridge: Cambridge University Press, 2013.

Rodden, John. 'The Spectre of Der Große Bruder: George Orwell's Reputation in West Germany'. *The German Quarterly* 60, no. 4 (Autumn 1987): 530–47.

Rosebury, Brian. *Tolkien: A Cultural Phenomenon*. Basingstoke: Macmillan, 2003.

Ross, Cathy and John Clark. *London: The Illustrated History*. London: Allen Lane, 2008.

The Royal Botanic Gardens; Kew: Illustrated Guide. London: Her Majesty's Stationery Office, 1961.

Royle, Edward. *Radicals, Secularists, and Republicans: Popular Freethought in Britain, 1866–1915*. Manchester: Manchester University Press, 1980.

Rushdie, Salman. *The Satanic Verses*. London: Penguin, 1988.

Sandbrook, Dominic. *Seasons in the Sun: The Battle for Britain, 1974–1979*. London: Allen Lane, 2012.

Schwarzbach, F. S. *Dickens and the City*. London: Athlone, 1979.

Scroggins, Mark. *Michael Moorcock: Fiction, Fantasy and the World's Pain*. North Carolina: McFarland, 2016.

Scuriatti, Laura. 'A Tale of Two Cities: H. G. Wells's *The Door in the Wall*, illustrated by Alvin Langdon Coburn'. *The Wellsian*, no. 22 (1999): 11–28.

Searles, Baird, Michael Franklin and Beth Meacham, eds. *A Reader's Guide to Fantasy*. New York: Avon, 1982.

Shelden, Michael. *Orwell*. London: Heinemann, 1991.

Sheppard, Francis. *London: A History*. Oxford: Oxford University Press, 1998.

Stableford, Brian. *Scientific Romance in Britain 1890–1950*. London: Fourth Estate, 1985.
Stanford, Edward. 'Stanford's Map of Central London'. 1897. *National Library of Australia*. MAP RM 1484. https://nla.gov.au/nla.obj-266892784/view [accessed 19 September 2019].
Stanford, Edward. 'Stanford's Map of London According to the Local Government Act'. 1888. *National Library of Australia*. MAP RM 1942. https://nla.gov.au/nla.obj-231 664130/view [accessed 9 September 2019].
Stevenson, Robert Louis. 'Some Gentlemen in Fiction'. *Scribner's Magazine* 3 (January–June 1888): 764–8.
Stovall, Tyler Edward. *The Rise of the Paris Red Belt*. Berkeley: University of California Press, 1990.
Stover, Leon. *The Prophetic Soul: A Reading of H. G. Wells's Things to Come*. Jefferson and London: McFarland, 1987.
Swinnerton, Frank. *The Bookman's London*. 1951. Reprint, London: John Baker, 1969.
Taft, Joshua. 'Disenchanted Religion and Secular Enchantment in *A Christmas Carol*'. *Victorian Literature and Culture* 43 (2015): 659–73.
Thane, Pat. *Divided Kingdom: A History of Britain, 1900 to the Present*. Cambridge: Cambridge University Press, 2018.
Thody, Philip. *Europe Since 1945*. London: Routledge, 2000.
Thompson, John. *Orwell's London*. London: Fourth Estate, 1984.
Thompson, Paul. *Socialists, Liberals and Labour: The Struggle for London, 1885–1914*. London: Routledge and Kegan Paul, 1967.
Tolkien, J. R. R. *The Return of the King*. 1955. Reprint, London: HarperCollins, 2008.
Turner, Alwyn W. *Crisis? What Crisis? Britain in the 1970s*. London: Aurum, 2008.
Walker, Martin. *The National Front*. Glasgow: Fontana, 1977.
Walkowitz, Judith R. *Nights Out: Life in Cosmopolitan London*. New Haven: Yale University Press, 2012.
Watkins, A. H. 'Charles Dickens and H. G. Wells'. *Occasional Papers: Supplement to the H. G. Wells Society*, no. 2, 1–8. Middlesex: The H. G. Wells Society, 1976.
Watney, John. 'Introduction'. In *Peake's Progress: Selected Writings and Drawings of Mervyn Peake*, 1978, edited by Maeve Gilmore, 13–33. Reprint, London: British Library, 2011.
Wells, H. G. *The Island of Doctor Moreau*. 1896. Reprinted with notes and introduction. Edited by Patrick Parrinder. London: Penguin, 2005.
Wells, H. G. *The Shape of Things to Come*. 1933. Reprinted with notes and introduction. Edited by Patrick Parrinder. London: Penguin, 2005.
Welsh, David. *Underground Writing: The London Tube from George Gissing to Virginia Woolf*. Liverpool: Liverpool University Press, 2010.
Winnington, G. Peter. *Vast Alchemies: The Life and Work of Mervyn Peake*. London and Chester Springs: Peter Owen, 2000.
Wright, Herbert. *London High*. London: Frances Lincoln, 2006.
'The 1992 Weekend Conference: The Short Stories of H. G. Wells'. *The H. G. Wells Newsletter* 3, no. 3 (Winter 1992): 3–4.

Archives of MSS

The George Orwell Archive. University College London, Special Collections, London, UK.

The H. G. Wells papers, 1845–1946. The Rare Book & Manuscript Library, University of Illinois at Urbana-Champaign, Champaign, Illinois, US.

The Mervyn Peake Archive. The British Library, London, UK.

Index

Aaronovitch, Ben   190-2
Adorno, Theodor   6, 47, 193

Bulwer-Lytton, Edward   58-60
   Coming Race, The   60, 64-6
   Strange Story, A   59-60

Carlyle, Thomas   47, 181
Chesterton, G. K.   3, 7, 8, 14, 58, 98, 174

Dickens, Charles   1, 3, 4-11, 14-19, 21, 23, 24, 27-60, 61-4, 66-9, 71, 72-3, 74, 76, 77, 78, 82, 85, 86, 87-8, 90, 95, 96-101, 103-4, 107, 108, 113, 114, 117, 120-3, 127, 128, 130, 133-5, 136, 144-5, 148, 156-7, 158, 160, 163, 169, 172, 174, 178, 179, 182, 187, 191, 192, 193-4, 195, 196
   Bleak House   4, 7, 10-12, 14-15, 55, 72, 77, 101-2, 115, 196
   Chimes, The   16, 23, 30, 39-45, 51, 55, 57, 60, 113, 193
   Christmas Carol, A   23, 30-8, 39, 40, 44, 49, 51, 54, 64, 68-73, 87, 93, 158, 181
   'Gone Astray'   40-1, 86
   Great Expectations   14, 55, 187
   Haunted Man, The   23, 29, 30, 39, 45, 46, 49-54, 57, 76, 100, 193, 196
   Household Words   56-8, 128, 133-4
   'Meditations in Monmouth Street'   47-9, 101, 178
   'Moor eeffoc' fantasy   6-9, 14, 15, 17-18, 36, 53, 78, 95, 100, 113, 136, 167, 169, 172
   Old Curiosity Shop, The   46-7, 55, 77, 120-2, 178
   Our Mutual Friend   4, 55, 67, 71, 77
   'Preliminary Word, A'   6-7, 56, 133-4

Gaiman, Neil   1, 3, 9, 14-15, 21, 23, 24, 36, 165, 167, 173-82, 183, 186, 190, 195

Neverwhere   14-15, 24, 36, 165, 167, 173-82, 186, 190

Harrison, M. John   1, 8, 9, 12-14, 15, 20, 21, 23, 24, 131, 133, 134-5, 149-53, 156, 157, 161-3, 166, 167-70, 172, 173, 182, 183, 184, 192, 195
   'Ash Circus, The'   149-50, 153
   Climbers   8, 161, 169
   'Flesh Circle, The'   149, 152-3
   'Nash Circuit, The'   149, 150-2, 153, 161
   Viriconium saga, The   8, 161-3, 166, 167-70, 172, 173, 182-3
   'Young Man's Journey to Viriconium/London, A'   8, 163, 167-70, 172, 173, 183

Lefebvre, Henri   114, 117, 178
Lewis, C. S.   2, 17-19, 21, 36, 64, 125, 128, 174, 195
   Narnia Chronicles, The   18-19, 21, 36, 128, 174, 195
London   7-8, 9-10, 11-12, 14, 15, 16, 17, 18-19, 23, 24, 25, 27-8, 29, 30, 31-4, 35, 36, 37-45, 46-9, 51-4, 55, 57-8, 68-9, 70-5, 76-81, 82-6, 87-94, 95-6, 97-8, 103-5, 106-18, 120-3, 133, 136-40, 142-63, 165-81, 188-92, 193-7
   Battersea   11, 116, 166, 180
   British Museum   171, 177
   Camden Town   32, 69, 83, 151, 161, 162
   City of London, The   31-3, 35, 40, 41, 69, 86, 93, 95, 98, 109, 166, 177
   Convent of St Clares, The   155, 158-60
   Crystal Palace, The   16, 57-8, 72-3, 81, 194
   curiosity shops   46-7, 77, 120-3, 178-80
   Derry & Toms Famous Roof Gardens   142-4, 145-6, 147, 154, 155, 159

Greater London Council   137, 160, 165
Hampstead   74–5, 79, 81, 83, 97, 171
Harrods   179–80
Holland Park   137, 142, 145, 147–9, 154, 158, 160
Holland Park Avenue (*see* Holland Park)
Holloway   150–1, 161
Islington   97, 166, 177
Kensington   69, 72, 82, 84–6, 137, 142–3, 145, 155, 171
Kew Gardens   147
Knightsbridge   153, 177, 179
Ladbroke Grove (*see* Notting Hill)
London Bridge   52–4, 90, 156
London County Council   72, 73, 74
London Underground, The   82, 112, 113, 175, 176–8
Madame Tussauds   151–2, 153
Monmouth Street (*see* Seven Dials)
National Gallery (*see* Trafalgar Square)
New Oxford Street (*see* Oxford Street)
Notting Hill   84, 85, 136–8, 142, 143, 144, 145, 147, 149, 154–5, 158–9, 160, 166, 191
Oxford Street   29, 51, 60, 82, 99
Regent's Park   80, 82, 150
St Dunstan in the West   40–2, 44–5, 53, 156
St Martin-in-the-Fields   7, 78–9, 95, 113, 114
St Martin's Lane   7, 53, 78, 136, 169
St Pancras (district)   74–5, 81, 83, 97
St Paul's Cathedral   89–90, 93, 143
Senate House   97, 108
Seven Dials   47–9, 77–8, 101, 103, 122, 193
Soho   11, 104, 111, 151
Trafalgar Square   78, 95, 109, 114, 115, 138
Tufnell Park   150, 151, 162
Villiers Street   139, 140, 157

MacDonald, George   2, 16–17, 21, 28, 62, 63, 64, 192
Miéville, China   1, 3, 8, 9, 15, 20–1, 23, 24, 58, 60, 163, 165, 167, 169, 170–3, 176, 180, 182–90, 191, 192–3, 195–6

Iron Council   184, 185–6, 187–8
King Rat   165, 189–90
Perdido Street Station   1, 4, 20, 182–4, 185, 186–7, 196
Scar, The   184–5, 189
Tain, The   8, 15, 165, 167, 170–3, 176, 180, 186, 190
Un Lun Dun   165, 190
Moorcock, Michael   1, 3, 9, 12, 14, 15, 19, 20, 21, 22, 24, 106, 116, 130, 131–49, 150, 153–61, 162, 163, 166, 167, 173, 183, 192, 195 (*see also* New Worlds magazine)
Condition of Muzak, The   137, 146, 149, 155–61
Cure for Cancer, A   141–9, 150, 154, 155, 157, 158
English Assassin, The   153–5, 157, 159
Final Programme, The   135–41, 144, 146, 150, 151, 154, 157

New Worlds magazine   8, 12, 14, 20, 24, 131–8, 140, 141–3, 145, 149, 150, 162, 167, 195 (*see also* Moorcock, Michael)
Dean, Mal   138–9
Sallis, James   142, 149, 150
New Worlds Quarterly (*see New Worlds* magazine)

Orwell, George   1, 9, 10, 14, 15, 19, 21, 23–4, 33, 60, 78–9, 94, 95–100, 103, 104, 105–17, 118–23, 125, 126–8, 129, 130, 134, 135, 182–3, 191, 192, 194–5, 196
'Common decency'   24, 98, 100, 106, 117, 121, 196
Nineteen Eighty-Four   10, 24, 78–9, 95–6, 97–8, 105–6, 108, 109–15, 117, 118–23, 126–8, 129

Peake, Mervyn   1, 8, 9, 10–12, 13, 14, 15, 19–20, 21, 23–4, 96, 98, 99–105, 106, 107–9, 110–13, 114, 115–18, 123–6, 127, 128–30, 135, 136, 162, 172, 176, 182, 183, 192, 194–5, 196
'Danse Macabre'   101, 103
Gormenghast   118, 125, 182

'London Fantasy'   11, 104–5,
    112–13, 115
Sketches from Bleak House   11–12,
    101–2
Titus Alone   11, 96, 100, 101, 107–9,
    110–13, 116–18, 123–6, 128–30,
    176, 182, 189
Titus Groan   8, 10–11, 99–100, 101,
    103, 114, 125, 182

Rivers of London (series) (*see* Aaronovitch,
    Ben)
Romance   5–7, 9, 10, 11, 18, 23, 30, 36–9,
    47, 50, 52, 56, 58–60, 61–3, 66,
    67–8, 71, 75, 76, 85, 98, 110, 125,
    126, 134, 160, 182, 194, 196
  'Romance of familiar things'   6, 7, 9,
    10, 11, 18, 37, 38, 39, 47, 50, 56, 58,
    67, 85, 98, 134, 160
  scientific romance   9, 23, 30, 58–60,
    61–2, 66, 67–8, 71, 75, 76, 110, 126,
    182, 196
Rural Fantasy tradition   2, 15–19, 20, 21,
    22–3, 24, 27, 28, 30–1, 35–6, 63–4,
    123–4, 125, 126, 128, 131, 132, 135,
    163, 173, 174, 180, 182, 183, 191,
    192, 193, 195, 197
  definition   21–2
  related to Lewis   17–19, 36, 64, 125,
    128, 174, 195
  related to MacDonald   16–17, 28, 63–4
  related to Ruskin   15–16, 17, 23, 28,
    30–1, 35–6
  related to 'Sub-creation'   64
  related to Tolkien   17–18, 19–20, 22,
    23, 36, 64, 123–4, 125, 128, 131,
    163, 180, 191, 192, 195
Ruskin, John   2, 15–16, 17, 19, 21, 23, 28,
    30–1, 33, 34–6, 37, 57, 192
  King of the Golden River, The   23,
    30–1, 33, 34–6, 37

Sala, George Augustus (*see* Wills, W. H.)
Secondary-World fantasy   17–18, 64,
    125–6, 162–3, 167, 172–3, 174, 176,
    180–2, 183–8, 195

Tolkien, J. R. R.   2, 8, 14, 17–18, 19, 20–1,
    22, 23, 24, 36, 64, 123–4, 125, 128,
    131–2, 133, 134, 163, 167, 172, 173,
    180, 183, 184, 191, 192, 195
  Lord of the Rings, The   14, 19, 20, 21,
    22, 24, 36, 123–4, 125, 131–2, 163,
    173, 183, 184, 191

Urban Fantasy tradition   1–2, 4, 5, 6–9,
    10–12, 14–15, 17, 18, 19–20, 21,
    22–5, 27, 28, 29–30, 31–8, 53,
    54, 55, 61–2, 63–4, 68–73, 94, 96,
    97, 99, 105, 114, 120–6, 128, 130,
    132–5, 141–2, 157–8, 162–3, 167,
    168–75, 180–4, 191, 192–7
  definition   1–2, 21–2
  related to Dickens   4, 5, 6–9, 17, 18, 19,
    29–30, 31–8, 53, 54, 55, 99, 193–4
  related to Gaiman   14–15, 21, 167,
    173–5, 180–2, 195
  related to Harrison   14, 20, 162–3,
    168–70, 183
  related to 'invention'   63–4
  related to Miéville   15, 20–1, 167,
    170–3, 182–4, 192–3, 195–6
  related to Moorcock   14, 20, 157–8
    (*see also* related to *New Worlds*
    magazine)
  related to *New Worlds* magazine   12,
    14, 20, 132–5, 141–2, 195
  related to Orwell   10, 19, 96, 97, 105,
    114, 120–3, 128, 194–5
  related to Peake   10–12, 19–20, 96, 97,
    105, 114, 123–6, 128, 194–5
  related to Wells   9–10, 17, 18, 19,
    61–2, 64, 68–73, 94, 194

Wells, H. G.   1, 5, 8, 9–10, 15–19, 21, 23,
    24, 28, 30, 36, 55–60, 61–94, 95, 97,
    105, 107, 109–12, 117, 120, 122–3,
    126–8, 132, 134, 135, 137, 158, 166,
    167–8, 169, 170–3, 176, 182, 187,
    192, 193, 194, 195, 196
  'Crystal Egg, The'   76–9, 95, 120, 122–3
  'Door in the Wall, The'   36, 67, 83–7,
    122, 137, 167–9, 172
  'Dream of Armageddon, A'   88, 90,
    91, 93
  Invisible Man, The   61, 67, 75, 126, 182
  Island of Doctor Moreau, The   61,
    126–7, 182

'Remarkable Case of Davidson's Eyes, The'   83–4, 85, 122–3
Sleeper Awakes, The (see *When the Sleeper Wakes*)
'Story of the Days to Come, A'   88, 90, 193
Time Machine, The   8, 9, 55, 61, 63–6, 67–73, 76, 81, 88, 126, 176, 182

Tono-Bungay   75, 89, 187
War of the Worlds, The   9–10, 61, 67, 68, 74, 76, 79–81, 82–3, 84, 126, 170–3
When the Sleeper Wakes   18, 87–94, 109–11, 114, 126–8, 158, 176, 196
Wills, W. H.   56, 57–8, 72–3
   'Fairyland in 'Fifty-Four'   57–8, 72–3

www.ingramcontent.com/pod-product-compliance
Lightning Source LLC
Chambersburg PA
CBHW072124290426
44111CB00012B/1763